Songs Upon The Rivers

Robert Foxcurran
Michel Bouchard
Sébastien Malette

Songs Upon the Rivers

The Buried History of the French-Speaking
Canadiens and Métis from the Great Lakes
and the Mississippi Across to the Pacific

Baraka
Books

Montréal

© Baraka Books

ISBN 978-1-77186-081-9 pbk; 978-1-77186-092-5 epub; 978-1-77186-093-2 pdf; 978-1-77186-094-9 mobi/pocket

Cover by Folio infographie
Cover Painting: "Voyageurs at Dawn" by Frances Anne Hopkins, 1871 (LAC, 1989-401-3 and C-002773k).
Back Cover Painting: Winter Travelling in Dogsled, Paul Kane, 1852 (ROM, The Honourable George William Allan Collection, 912.1.48).
Map page 116 by Julie Benoît
Book design by Folio infographie

Legal Deposit, 4th quarter 2016

Bibliothèque et Archives nationales du Québec
Library and Archives Canada

Published by Baraka Books of Montreal
6977, rue Lacroix
Montréal, Québec H4E 2V4
Telephone: 514 808-8504
info@barakabooks.com
www.barakabooks.com

Printed and bound in Quebec

We acknowledge the support from the Société de développement des entreprises culturelles (SODEC) and the Government of Quebec tax credit for book publishing administered by SODEC.

Société
de développement
des entreprises
culturelles
Québec

Financé par le gouvernement du Canada
Funded by the Government of Canada | Canadä

Trade Distribution & Returns
Canada and the United States
Independent Publishers Group
1-800-888-4741 (IPG1);
orders@ipgbook.com

Contents

Note to the reader

In this volume, we have sought to be respectful and to use wherever possible the names that various First Nations Communities use to name themselves both present and past. However, as we are relying on historical sources and want to present past narratives unvarnished, this means that terms such as "Indian" will appear instead of "First Nations" in some passages and racist terms such as "squaw," "savage," and "half-breed" will also be included in cited texts. We kept these terms because confronting the prejudices of the past helps us better understand the social forces at play at that time as well as those that continue to shape relations between indigenous populations with larger Euro-American society. Readers will notice the use of the term *Canadien* in italics. It was the self-description of French-speaking inhabitants of the Saint-Lawrence Valley and much of North America since the late seventeenth century. In this context it enables us to distinguish these people and their descendants from people from France or Canadians of British background, who only began describing themselves as Canadians during the first half of the nineteenth century.

Andrew (André) Dominique Pambrun, ca. 1880, unknown photographer.

Foreword

By Sam Pambrun

Like the controversy over whether or not the Vikings discovered America, this book, *Songs Upon The Rivers*, examines an alternative to popular history. Foxcurran, Bouchard and Malette's non-traditional story of those who first settled the West and particularly the Pacific Northwest is a fascinating account of Métis and (French) *Canadiens*, the cultural group central to their narrative. The story is personal to those of us who have Métis roots. I first learned of it while a fifth-grade student at Athena Elementary School. It was easy to be aware of our *Canadien* ancestry in Athena in 1957 because several of my class-mates were Native Americans or mixed-blood children who lived on the nearby Umatilla Indian Reservation and attended the small schools of Athena and Weston, Oregon.

During the late 1880s, the Umatilla Reservation was the depository for a sizeble migration of Métis people from *le Village des Canadiens*, a community that even-tually became known as Frenchtown. *Le Village des Canadiens* was located in the Walla Walla Valley in today's Washington State, approximately twenty-five miles north of the Reservation. It was first settled by Joseph Larocque in 1823. Larocque was an employee of the Montreal-based North West Company who worked at Fort Nez Percés, a fur trade-era post at the confluence of the Walla Walla and Columbia Rivers. The merger of the North West Company with the Hudson's Bay Company between 1821 and 1824 expanded the operations and manpower of the enlarged company down the Columbia River to the Pacific coast.

Larocque "married" Lizette Walla Walla in 1824, built a house with the per-mission of her family, settling amongst them at a location twenty miles up the Walla Walla Valley from Fort Nez Percés. Soon Larocque's Métis friends and family located near them, creating the loosely organized Frenchtown commun-ity, a French-speaking, culturally friendly place of part-time and retired fur trade employees. The community enjoyed the rich loam soil of the Walla Walla Valley and proximity to the mercantile store at Fort Nez Percés. Larocque's peers also married local Indian women, mostly from the Walla Walla and Cayuse Tribes. The book *Songs Upon The Rivers* tells this regional story as well as other sagas of Métis people throughout the Oregon Territory. The pattern was the same wherever beaver pelts were traded.

It took about fifty years to extract *"Les Canadiens"* from the rich farmlands of the Walla Walla Valley. The 1846 U.S.-Canadian Boundary Settlement placed Frenchtown well within United States of America Territory. Where the Frenchtown Métis had been a majority among the few "white" settlers, by the 1860s they found themselves an unwanted minority. The shift from employees of the "Masters of the Land" to aliens in a foreign country was somewhat gradual, as the Hudson's Bay Company influence waned in successive increments. The American government wasn't able to immediately exert its authority over its newly acquired "wilderness."

Fortunately for Frenchtown, the U. S. Congress passed the Slater Bill (1885) and the Dawes Act (1887), devices used by the Métis of the Walla Walla Valley to acquire land, or "Allotments" in the name of their native wives and mothers, on the Umatilla Reservation. The Frenchtown Métis exodus to the Umatilla Reservation was typical but not without pain; similar to experiences documented in *Songs Upon the Rivers* throughout the Pacific Northwest and elsewhere in North America. I first became aware of this exodus while attending public school in Athena, Oregon.

My fifth-grade teacher, Mrs. Florence Gilliland, affectionately known to one and all as "Foghorn Gilliland," required a unit on the Oregon Trail as a part of the state-mandated American history curriculum for all Oregon fifth graders. Her assignment was to talk to our parents, aunts and uncles, grandparents or other relatives to determine who in our family traveled here on the Oregon Trail, and tell their story. Students were to interview, take notes, and research the Great American Westward Migration and prepare a paper and oral presentation on their family's experiences on the Oregon Trail. The assumption was that every family in Athena and Weston could trace their roots back to the Oregon Trail. The questions we were to answer, I later discovered, came from an 1893 log book of the first Umatilla County Pioneer Picnic in Weston, Oregon.

When I told my dad of this assignment I thought he'd gone crazy; he laughed so hard he almost rolled off the sofa. He finally calmed down enough to tell me, with tears in his eyes, that we were the wrong kind of "Pioneers" and did not come to Oregon on the Oregon Trail. He suggested that I talk to Mrs. Gilliland about getting an alternative assignment.

Mrs. Gilliland obviously knew more about my family background than me; she told me to interview my family and prepare a paper and oral presentation on

Allotment Day, Normal Rainville, ca. 1889. 1. Angie McBean; 2. Sarah Clara Bonenfant Duffy [Dauphin] and (3) son William; 4. Selene [Célina] Gagnon; 5. Mary McIntire; 6. Rose Damon; 7. Josephine La Fave [likely Lefebvre]; 8. Catherine Murry; 9. Adaline Gardipee [Gariépy] Lucier; 10. Mrs. Damon; 11. Mrs. Conoyer [Cornoyer née Mary Sophie Belique a variation of Belleque derived from Bélec]; 12. Melvina Rainville Picard; 13. Felecite Dauphin Pambrun; 14. Baby Clarence LaBrach [Labrache likely origin Labrèche]; 15. Maggie La Brach; 16. Marian Parr [Mary Ann (née Gendron) Parr]; 17. La Rose Bonifer [Bonenfant]; 18. Mary Jane Bushman [Beauchemin]; 19. Mrs Louis Bergevin & daughter [Rose Virginia Picard Bergevin and daughter Minnie]; 20. Carrie La Fave; 21. Sophie Gagnon; 22. Willie Cameron; 23. Eliza Cameron; 24. Jane Woodward Wilson; 25. Charley Wilson; 26. Mary St. Dennis [St-Denis]; 27. Hattie Pambrun; 28. Cora Woodward; 29. Rose Pambrun; 30. Alfred La Brach; 31. Willie Pambrun [son of Felicite Dauphin Pambrun (13) and brother to Hattie (27) and Rose (29)]; 32. Henry La Brach; 33. Agnes La Fave; 34. Julie Martin.

This photo was taken when husbands and fathers went out with the Indian Agent to select "allotments"—tribal lands withdrawn from the Umatilla Confederated Tribes Reservation and granted to individual members following the 1885 Slater Act and the 1887 Dawes Act. Lands then deemed "surplus" by the United States government were later sold to settlers, leaving the Confederated Tribes of the Umatilla Reservation a checkerboard of tribal land and private property. Included in the first wave of allotments were Métis descendants granted allotment lands based on their kinship ties with the Cayuse, Umatilla or Walla Walla nations (or in the case of individuals, such as Andrew Dominique Pambrun, service rendered to these nations).*

* The photo belonged to Normal Rainville, a relative of Melvina in the photo. Normal is said to have gotten his name after his mother was asked "how was your confinement [pregnancy]?" and she answered "normal." The Rainville house built on the allotment land remains a twisted pile of metal and foundation stones in a wheat field on Rainville road.

the route and story of how my family came to Oregon. This was my first venture into the history of the Métis people who first explored, worked, and settled on the Columbia Plateau.

Here's how I did my Métis research. At our family's Thanksgiving gathering, I asked Mrs. G's questions, using a narrow window of opportunity between dessert and the noisy naps that ensued. My aunts and uncles reacted the same as my father, with howling laughter and tears of mirth. They chattered all at once while I was poised with my pencil and notebook. Finally, some order prevailed and I learned my ancestors were not American, got nowhere near the Oregon Trail, and came here prior to the American overland emigrants. Further, I learned my great-great-grandfather arrived in the Oregon Territory in 1824 as an employee of the "foreign company" that traded horses and furs with the Indians. I asked if this didn't make me a "Pioneer," too. Again, I had to wait until the laughter subsided.

I also learned that I was part Indian. Being Indian or part Indian in the 1950s community of Athena was not an advantage. No one had ever heard of Métis. Mixed bloods were called half breeds, were mostly dirt poor and considered scary, alcoholic, uneducated people to be avoided. The neighboring town of Weston had a little more tolerance for Indian people but not much more. Only within the last twenty years has there been any substantial progress in multicultural relations within the communities bordering the Umatilla Reservation.

Since that fateful Thanksgiving Day I've asked many, many questions about my family background and studied fur trade and early regional history. I've followed the trails my ancestors traveled and tracked them across the continent, from York Factory on Hudson's Bay to Fort George at Astoria. I've visited the sites of the fur trade posts and other locales where they resided and tried to imagine the landscape they would have gazed upon while having breakfast 190 years ago. Tamastlikt Cultural Institute of the Confederated Tribes of the Umatilla Reservation has a motto: "We're Still Here; We've Always Been Here; We Will Always Be Here." I feel the same way.

The Pambrun family is not unique to this region; all one has to do is drive around in the Walla Walla Valley or on the Umatilla Reservation and check out the back roads with French names to understand the impact of *Canadiens* in the area. Pierre-Chrysologue Pambrun was the first of our family to come to Oregon. He came from Vaudreuil, Quebec, by way of a dozen Hudson's Bay Company posts. He arrived at Fort Nez Percés in 1831, just in time to participate in America's Manifest Destiny. Pierre and his spouse of Métis origins, Catherine "Kitty" Umfreville, extended their hospitality to such American dignitaries as Jason and Daniel Lee, Nathaniel Wyeth, Marcus and Narcissa Whitman, and Captain Benjamin Bonneville as they made their way to the Promised Land.

Pierre and Kitty had eight children, who eventually scattered all over North America. Their eldest son, Andrew Dominique (1821-1895), was educated at Red River Academy (Winnipeg) and returned to the Northwest to work for the Hudson's Bay Company, interpret a major Indian Treaty, scout for the U.S. Army, and farm in the rich Walla Walla Valley. His history is typical of the *Canadiens* on the Umatilla Reservation today.

Songs Upon The Rivers includes specifics of Métis life in the Walla Walla Valley and on the Umatilla Reservation that surprised me. The authors found and recorded minute details of Métis presence, character, and humor that I've observed in my family and other Reservation families. That these character "flaws" seem to be common among Métis is comforting information. The story they tell of the *Canadien* experience in the Pacific Northwest, to my knowledge, has never been told in such detail and with such accuracy.

Sam Pambrun is a past president of the Frenchtown Historic Foundation, a private, non-profit organization established in 1993 for the purpose of commemorating le Village des Canadiens in the Walla Walla Valley. Frenchtown acquired fifty-seven acres of land in 2009, including the sites of the Saint Rose of Lima Catholic Mission and the Frenchtown Cemetery. The Foundation built roads and trails, parking, signs and interpretive panels, and a picnic shelter on a twenty-seven-acre parcel and gifted the other thirty acres to the Confederated Tribes of the Umatilla Indian Reservation, their first foothold in the Walla Walla Valley since 1855. The architects of this endeavor have been thirteen dedicated volunteer board members and past presidents Russell and Claro Bergevin and Dan Clark. A sample of the descendant families who still live in the Frenchtown vicinity includes: the Allard, Beauchamp, Bushman [Beauchemin], Bergevin, Bonifer [Bonenfant], Brisbois, Duffy [Dauphin], Farrow [Farron], Forest [Forêt], Gagnon, LaCourse, LaFave, Larocque, McBean, McKay, Morisette, Pambrun, Picard, Rainville, and Raymond families. We thank you Rob, Michel, and Sébastien for your efforts to tell our story.

Andrew Dominique Pambrun and younger brother Alexandre Pambrun at Spring Hollow Creek, on the Umatilla Indian Reservation, Oregon, ca. 1880. Andrew (André) Dominique Pambrun (left) was born in 1821 at Cumberland House on the Saskatchewan River. He did some schooling at Red River, where he also taught, rushed to California for gold, and then worked for the Hudson's Bay Company in the Oregon territory starting 1851. He spoke, read and wrote French, English and Latin, was conversant in most Sahapatain and Salish dialects and Chinook Jargon, and was a sought-after interpreter. Alexandre Pambrun (right) was born in New Caledonia, BC, in 1829. He followed the California Gold Rush before settling in the Oregon Territory in 1850, where he worked for the Hudson's Bay Company. In his life, he was a freighter, a miner and a carpenter throughout the Pacific Northwest and Western Canada. He built the house in the picture for his older brother in about 1878.

Introduction

Nations are created through the burial of inconvenient history. Such is the case with the Canadian and American nation-states, whose national narratives both selectively remember and forget their respective histories, as such narratives must do. One telling example is the American battle cry, "Remember the River Raisin!" heard after the Battle of Frenchtown, named for another settlement located on the frontier in southeast Michigan. This forgotten battle during the War of 1812 has all but passed from memory, while the 1836 Battle of the Alamo is remembered—though fewer Americans were killed at the Alamo. In fact, the Alamo war cry itself was borrowed from the River Raisin call to arms. Alas, forgetting is never incidental. Both battles featured archetypically heroic Americans (both frontier militia from Kentucky and Tennessee, as chance would have it) massacred by vicious and "savage" enemies. The Alamo tale continues to be glorified in Hollywood and song, while the River Raisin remains consigned to the realm of trivia. However, to "Remember the River Raisin" is also to remember the French of Frenchtown and could lead to the uncomfortable realization that the Americans were not the first to venture westwards. Such remembrances would also underscore the fact that United States' Manifest Destiny was not guaranteed in the early decades of the Republic's existence. In order to push westwards, it was necessary to forge alliances with the descendants of the first French settlers who were astute transcultural traders and tireless travelers crisscrossing the continent. To "Remember the River Raisin" is thus to acknowledge that the western United States was built upon the foundation of the older French Empire and the *Canadien* and *Créole* and *Métis* descendants of the colonial French who remained as continental vanguards. This would put into question the whole framework of American history, one that is remembered, or to be more precise, misremembered.

The Battle of Raisin River, also known as the Battle of Frenchtown, was fought on January 22, 1813. The British and allied Indians defeated the American forces that were seeking to retake Detroit. Hundreds of American soldiers were killed, and hundreds more taken prisoner. After the battle, the Native American allies of the British killed dozens of wounded American prisoners. This incident came to be called the Raisin River Massacre.

The historical amnesia surrounding the Battle of Raisin River and the War of 1812 is a telling indicator of the forgotten history of the United States and that of the French-speaking populations that had shaped the destiny of the United States and Canada. From the Great Lakes and Illinois Country to the Pacific, the French *Canadiens* and Créoles would be the first to explore and settle the lands that would become Canada and the United States, forging alliances and kin ties with the indigenous nations that inhabited these lands. Their knowledge and skills would be co-opted by the later "explorers" who "discovered" and "mapped" the terrain. To remember the Battle of Frenchtown would require remembering that the Americans had not been the first settlers and that their success had required alliances with the descendants of the French.

Then there was that victorious battle fought two years later, just south of another French town, one that helped heal the wound and erase the painful memories of battles lost at too many former French frontier settlements such as the River Raisin, Châteauguay, Détroit, Isle-aux-Noix, and Michilimackinac. This one stunning victory, of course, was the Battle of New Orleans. Here, too, the victory was remembered in song. However, it has become a tale of the hero-ics of one of the American generals and his late-arriving countrymen from Tennessee and Kentucky who were thrown into the breach in the final days of the campaign. The local French-speaking Louisiana militia has been written out of the national story. If mentioned at all, the Louisiana militia's contribution and commitment are minimalized, reduced to the exotic by highlighting only the Lafitte brothers and their pirates. Otherwise, it just wouldn't seem to fit properly (Albright, 1991).

To "Remember the Alamo" obliged Americans to remember the Mexicans, if only briefly, before the role of the descendants of those very same Mexicans in Texas was diminished (at least until recently). On the other hand, the history of the French settlers and their role in the making of the United States has been so thoroughly buried that it goes totally unnoticed. Thus, the essence of the American nation is to have forgotten the very act of forgetting, even when con-fronted with those phantom traces of a French presence left behind in the topography.

Generations of historians would conveniently ignore the Gallic names on the terrain mapped by men such as Meriwether Lewis and William Clark, while omitting from their historical accounts the men the "explorers" relied upon to ensure that they could successfully traverse the continent, men such as Toussaint Charbonneau, François Labiche, Jean-Baptiste Lepage, Pierre Cruzatte, and Georges Drouillard. While Georges Drouillard was their principal scout, trans-

The Voyageurs, Arthur Heming, 1915. Arthur Heming (1870-1940) was a prominent Canadian artist whose work featured northern scenes and landscapes. This "chronicler of the North" brought Canadian motifs to the world and particularly the voyageurs. This scene that would have been central to the lives of the engagés (employees): the few minutes dedicated every hour to *faire une pipe* or literally "make a pipe." They would keep track of distance based on the number of pipes required to cover the watery expanse.

lator, and hunter, Sacagawea's husband, Toussaint, in particular, has been ridiculed as part of the general propensity to grossly overstate Sacagawea's role in the expedition (Vaugeois, 2007). Furthermore, Lewis and Clark were serenaded by the French folk songs with accompaniment by Pierre Cruzatte and his fiddle, which were central to the voyageur repertoire, as their French songs have resonated along the rivers of the continent for generations. Cruzatte provided a major component of the entertainment and "ice-breaker" package deployed when visiting Indian villages along the way. In addition to the five men and one child (Jean-Baptiste Charbonneau) comprisng the *Canadien* and Métis contingent accompanying Lewis and Clark all the way to the Pacific, two other often forgotten sets of their countrymen were involved as the expedition ascended the Missouri River to the Mandan villages and their winter encampment. There were the dozen *Canadien* boatmen who pulled the keelboat up the river and then returned the following spring to St. Louis with the journals and specimens of the expedition's first year. On the way up, one of these engagés, named La Liberté, had also been designated to be the translator for the Oto tribe, while another, named François Rivet, added to Cruzatte's fiddle music in entertaining the Mandans by dancing upside down on his hands. Then there were also those multi-lingual *Canadien* traders they encountered on the way up who were either already embedded in one of the nations, or heading back down after another winter with one of them. For the critical translation and general intelligence services in estab-lishing peaceful relations with the tribes living along the River, Lewis and Clark relied upon the likes of Régis Loisel, Pierre Dorion (both father and son), Joseph Gravelines, René Jusseaume, François Larocque, and Pierre-Antoine Tabeau (Ronda, 1984). Within several years of the expedition's return in 1806, such par-ticipants as Pierre Dorion, Jr. and François Rivet, who had not gone all the way to the Pacific on the initial round, crossed the Rockies, permanently relocating to the Columbia Basin where numerous descendants live today.

To some readers, these translation, guide, and transportation services might sound like trivial functions, but they were not. Two points should be remem-bered. First, the American Captains were totally dependent upon this other eth-nic group, one that had supposedly been confined to the Lower St. Lawrence Valley after 1763, and hence relegated to the margins of North American history. Second, this was the first communication by representatives of the U.S. Government with the inhabitants of the middle and upper Missouri following the famous 1803 Louisiana purchase. It is one thing to sign an agreement with a European government, but quite another for a small band of men to show up in the middle of the continent to let the locals know that the rules had now changed. They would henceforth be governed by a new Great Father, one who insisted that they desist from fighting, raiding, and retaliating, while announcing his inten-tion to impose a new regime for trading. Artful diplomacy would have to precede governance. Translators and guides mattered, as well as those ensuring the trans-portation of expeditions.

It is the descendants of the French settlers who ensured that men such as Lewis and Clark successfully crossed the continent, and returned. All the while, they recorded the French names of the locales that had already been topographically baptized by generations of French-speakers. Though Lewis and Clark never downplayed the role of the men in their expedition who had served as guides and translators in the lands they mapped, editors and historians have written out of their accounts the contributions of the *Canadien*, Créole, and Métis mem-bers of the Lewis and Clark expedition.

Their omission and their burial of this past not only mis-represents history, it also mutes what is in many ways a very admirable moment in history. The des-cendants of the French in the Americas forged a new identity, one that was not

Un canadien en raquette allant à la guerre sur la neige, Claude–Charles Bacqueville de La Potherie, 1722.. After visiting New France in 1749 Swedish-Finnish botanist Pehr Kalm wrote: "Though many nations imitate the French customs, yet I observed, on the contrary, that the French in Canada, in many respects, follow the customs of the Indians, with whom they converse every day. They make use of the tobacco-pipes, shoes, garters, and girdles of the Indians. They follow the Indian way of making war with exactness; they mix the same things with tobacco; they make use of Indian bark-boats, and row them in the Indian way; they wrap square pieces of cloth round their feet instead of stockings; and have adopted many other Indian fashions." (Pinkerton, 1812, p. 682.)

dependent on the state. The French came to be *Canadien;* this was the term that the French settlers born in New France called themselves in their new lands, and did not reject their mixed Euro-Indigenous heritage. These *Canadien* pioneers learned indigenous languages, while maintaining their own, and could successfully navigate between cultures. They practiced syncretism, or the fusion of different beliefs and practices, before syncretism became the norm, adopting what was beneficial from their Native American neighbours, while proudly maintaining their culture and heritage. While Anglo-Americans came to embrace ideals of racial "purity," the *Canadien* would see nationality as a cultural choice, a conscious decision to become and remain *Canadien.* In the end, while the *Canadiens* were busy opening up the American West, when they weren't looking, British North America swiped their name, and the Americans systematically took over their homes and those of their Indian kin, then took away their identity, and effectively removed them from the story.

In his *1493: Uncovering the New World Columbus Created,* Charles Mann (2011, p. xix) borrows from the Cuban folklorist Fernando Ortiz Fernández the term "transculturation" to describe a process whereby one group of people embraces culture from another and transforms it, wherein they "make it their own by adapting, stripping, and twisting it to fit their needs and situation." Mann notes that what is borrowed can include a song, food, or even an ideal. Though Mann does not specifically address the French legacy in North America, the process of *métissage* is certainly a form of transculturation. The French settlers, as they became *Canadien* and later Métis—mixing both in terms of kinship and culture—adopted those features of Native American life that were essential to their survival. However, it was more than material culture, to borrow Mann's term: they were also seeking an ideal, freedom. This freedom was pushing the first French settlers to leave the French forts, take indigenous wives and become whenever possible free traders. This was a defining feature that began long before the British conquest of New France and lasted well into the nineteenth century. Their dreams of freedom were also inextricably tied to the creation of a global economic system that followed Christopher Columbus' (Cristóbal Colón's) first Atlantic crossing.

These descendants of the French in North America would work to achieve the dreams that had pushed the monarchs of Europe to finance trading expeditions around Africa to Asia and across the Atlantic. By the early 1800s, the fur trade companies had crossed the continent and tied European capital, North American labor, and Chinese markets into one world system. It is necessary to rethink our assumptions of history. As Mann (2011, p. xviii) writes: "In some respects this image of the past—as a cosmopolitan place, driven by ecology and economics—is startling to people who, like me, were brought up on accounts of heroic navigators, brilliant inventors, and empires acquired by dint of technological and institutional superiority."

Rather than seeing the *Canadien*, Créole, and Métis as backwater bumpkins, it is necessary to evaluate them as important actors in the global trade. Men such as the immigrant grandson of French Huguenot refugees who had fled to Germany for purposes of religious freedom, known by his anglicized name of John-Jacob Astor, made his initial fortune in the fur trade thanks to partnerships he had with the French-speaking elites of the American West. He then used the capital from the fur trade to buy up much of Manhattan, as the Astors would become the city's and the nation's wealthiest family.

It is necessary to analyze the history of the continental French-speakers in terms of both local and global history to truly appreciate their contribution to the rise of the American and Canadian nation-states. Whether it was the Battle of Frenchtown (1813) in the Detroit area, or the other Battle of Frenchtown (1856) in the Oregon Country decades later, the descendants of the original French settlers were central actors to the economic, political, and social history of the continent, even if their contribution has been largely relegated to the footnotes of history.

After Hull surrendered Detroit in August 1812, a Canadian militia, the Essex County Militia unit under the command of Ebenezer Reynolds was deployed southward to a forward position, setting up camp at Frenchtown. As Essex County was located across the Detroit River and had been settled by the French *Canadien*, the overwhelming majority of the volunteers in the Essex Militia were men such as Pierre Beauchamp, Jean-Baptiste Bertrand, and François Campeau. A new American unit of Kentucky recruits advancing northward under an elderly veteran of the War of Independence, General James Winchester, responded to messengers from Frenchtown pleading for rescue. Orders from the British commander to the militia unit were to confiscate the livestock and considerable provisions stored in the barns of the residents, then burn down the entire settlement. The Kentuckians, reinforced by a hundred local residents of Frenchtown, attacked on January 18, 1813, driving a force of sixty-three largely French-Canadian militiamen and two hundred Potawatomi Indians back, north of the River Raisin. The Americans won the first Battle of Frenchtown, or River Raisin. Four days later, however, a reinforced detachment of around 600 British regulars and militiamen with 800 Indian allies under Proctor's command carried off a surprise counterattack. This was only a surprise because Winchester had laughed off multiple warnings by local *Canadiens* of a large British force approaching from the north. The Essex militia, composed primarily of *Canadiens*, immediately out-flanked the U.S. Seventh Infantry on the right. Orders from Winchester to retreat turned into a rout. These were followed by Winchester's capture and subsequent orders to the entire force to surrender, even though his left flank had successfully repulsed three successive British assaults.

Of the combined force of 934 men, thirty-three escaped. A total of 495 Americans were taken prisoner by Proctor's troops, while 406 were killed, missing, or taken prisoner by the Indians. The day following the second Battle of Frenchtown on January 23, 1813, sixty to sixty-five wounded American soldiers left behind in Frenchtown were massacred by Indian allies of the British. Many of those who escaped through the woods were Frenchtown residents, joining General William Harrison's force. Harrison, a future president of the United States, thought so much of these troops, that sometime later he was quoted as saying that the River Raisin men were "the best troops in the World" (Hutchison & Hutchison, 2004, pp. 19-28).

The Raisin River is perhaps a troubling case for the national American narrative as it underscores how the frontier lands that existed before they were divided between nation-states were inhabited not only by Indians but also by the descendants of the first French settlers of New France, their Native American wives, and their Métis children. The Battle of Raisin River was fought in the shadows of a "Frenchtown" and the "French" inhabitants of the region would be instrumental in the war as allies, while others would fight alongside British forces. To accurately "Remember the River Raisin," then, would be to recall an era where the Anglo-Americans were not yet dominant, one where it was necessary to call upon the earlier settlers to help keep the British forces at bay. The War of 1812 was also problematic as it had no clear victor, though it did ensure American control over the territories of the Old Northwest and shaped later American policy that would push the indigenous Native Americans out of their ancestral lands, while marginalizing their allies and kin, the French-speaking *Canadiens* and Métis. Nonetheless, this history of forgetting would be repeated at every stage of the American expansion. The *Canadiens* and Métis descendants would be instrumental as guides and allies in the push westwards, but they would be first derided then later shunned by history.

A telling case is the derogatory accounts of Washington Irving from the nineteenth century. Irving was writing a second-hand account of history, but given that he was chronicling contemporary history, he could not completely omit the *Canadiens*. Instead, he mocks them, describes them as wholly inferior to the Anglo-Americans, as his goal was to write an American national narrative that presents the Anglo-Americans as brave warriors trekking westwards. To do this, he had to establish a duality, one that sets into moral opposition the American and the *Canadien*. In *The Adventures of Captain Bonneville* (1837), he contrasts the "Mountaineers" and affirms that they are a different class from the *Canadien* voyageur, saying of the former that a man who "bestrides a horse must be essentially different from a man who cowers in a canoe. We find them, accordingly, hardy, lithe, vigorous, and active" (Irving, 1850, p. 14).

Irving then drives the point home (Irving, 1850, p. 18):

> And here we would remark a great difference, in point of character and quality, between two classes of trappers, "American" and the "French," as they are called in contradistinction. The latter is meant to designate the French creole of Canada or Louisiana; the former the trapper of the old American stock, from Kentucky, Tennessee, and others of the Western States. The French trapper is represented as a lighter softer, more self-indulgent kind of man. He must have his Indian wife, his lodge, and his petty conveniences. He is gay and thoughtless, takes little heed of landmarks, depends upon his leaders and companions to think for the common weal, and, if left to himself, is easily perplexed and lost.

Thus Irving opposes the self-indulgent "French" trapper to the solid American of "old stock" who stands on his own, notices every landmark and can retrace his routes across the continent. Though Irving (1850, p. 18) uses the term "French creole of Canada and Louisiana," he nonetheless continues by using the term

Winter Travelling in Dogsled, Paul Kane, 1852. The canoe was the primary means of travel in summer. In winter dog sleds were used. This was risky. Traveling to a new post from Fort Kilmaurs, Pierre Chrysologue Pambrun's dog team broke through the ice as they crossed a lake. The voyageurs wasted nothing and dogs were also a source of meat. The team feasted on the dog that evening before setting on their way the next morning (Tassé 1887: 308). In Kane's painting, the sash (*ceinture fléchée*) is prominent as well as the *capot* or hooded cloak and the flower motif decorating the sleds, flowers being the defining style of Métis beadwork.

"Canadian," which would refer to the French-speaking *Canadien*, and even speci-fies the "creole and Canadian," suggesting that he understood that these were in effect distinct populations, with the Canadian being creole, but the creole not being necessarily Canadian. Logically, the "creole" he is referring to is the French creole of Upper Louisiana that he referred to a few sentences earlier.

He concludes his comparison by affirming that one American equals three Canadians "in point of sagacity, aptness at resources, self-dependence, and fear-lessness of spirit" (Irving, 1850, p. 18). Thus, Irving, who was certainly fully aware that the [French-]Canadians were much more numerous than the American

"Mountaineer," is seemingly trying to compensate for the much fewer numbers of American trappers by presenting them as qualitatively superior. In spite of his biases and desire to write an American national narrative whereby the heroic protagonists are the Americans of old stock, he nonetheless sees a need to mention the *Canadien*, albeit to berate them. Later historians would often not even mention the French Créole or *Canadien*. Our goal is to provide a better, less biased account of the French, Créole, *Canadien* and Métis based on the primary sources.

Astor, Irving and the *Canadiens*

New lines were being drawn on maps back East, which resulted in the French-Canadian West falling out of British North American and Canadian national history. To ensure that they would not be written back into American history, matters had to be settled on another front. Washington Irving, knowing his Anglo-American audience, found an effective manner by which to qualitatively discount the role of the *Canadiens* and their Creole and Metis kin in the history of the American West. Diminishing them on the qualitative axis required similar treatment as to their quantitative presence. He had already handled that issue fairly effectively in the book he had published a year earlier, *Astoria* (Irving, 1836).

While Astor's ship-borne party had set sail from New York harbor for the mouth of the Columbia with its predominantly *Canadien* contingent, the overland party made its way up to northern Michigan, to recruit more *Canadiens* at Michilimackinac, the straits where Lake Michigan empties into Lake Huron. Here a complex of Indian villages of the Chippewa and other nations had existed for centuries. The French had established their own trading center there in the 1660s, a century and a half earlier. In 1810, the trading post was located on modern-day Mackinac Island, Michigan, across from the older mainland establishments at the Village of Mackinaw City and neighboring St. Ignace, with Gros Cap just to the west. The larger Bois Blanc Island with its modern-day town of Pointe aux Pins is several miles off to the southeast of Mackinac Island.

Washington Irving (1886b, p. 102), after using his literary license to characterize the *Canadien* Nor'westers found there, continues by insisting that at the time he was writing in the 1830s, the *Canadiens* and Métis were no longer present in the region. He states: "The fur companies no longer assemble there; the navigation of the lakes is carried on by steam boats and shipping, and the race of traders, and trappers, and voyageurs, and Indian dandies, have vapoured out of their brief hour and disappeared."

This well-written and convincing prose is simply not true. Both the U.S. census of 1830 and the well-documented trip of Alexis de Tocqueville in 1831 tell quite a different tale as to the demographic weight of the *Canadiens* and Métis who remained. Irving felt the need to once again return to the level of catchy

Indians Completing a Portage, William Armstrong, 1873. The portage, that came to refer both to the act and location of carrying loads overland, was grueling for the voyageurs as they hauled packs, often over steep hills, to avoid rapids and waterfalls. Each voyageur was expected to carry two ninety-pound bales of furs or supplies on his back, in effect carrying more than his own weight over rough territory.

cliché characterizations to downplay the people who continued to live in Michigan, denying their very existence. Then, he berates their ancestors with his description of the *Canadien* "dandies" and how being both childlike and overly feminine, they had to be enlisted by calling upon their vanity. Irving (1886b, p. 104) describes one alleged tactic in recruiting the engagés:

> Among the recruits who had enlisted he distributed feathers and ostrich plumes. These they put in their hats, and thus figured about Mackinaw, assuming airs of vast importance, as "voyageurs in a new company that was to eclipse the North-west." The effect was complete. A French Canadian is too vain and mercurial a being to withstand the finery and ostentation of the feather.

Irving (1886b, p. 105) nonetheless highlights the nature of the culture and the identity of these men living in Michigan. They had their fiddles, he describes the "snatches of old French songs," and he stresses that they are Canadian French.

To Washington Irving's (1850, 1886b) use of anecdotes to make them look like fools or worse in the late 1830s, we can add Don Berry's 1961 classic, *A Majority of Scoundrels: An Informal History of the Rocky Mountain Fur Company*. In the first section of his first chapter, Berry (1961, p. 7) sets the tone of the story with the following qualifiers for describing both the Voyageurs and the rivermen in St. Louis. He describes the Voyageurs as "canoemen, those of the flashing paddles and endless song, the red feather in the hat, the braggadocio and strut" (Berry, 1961, pp. 6-7). Turning to the men working in St. Louis, he specifies that "the rivermen were still French, but a slightly different breed."

Though Washington Irving belittles, insults, and ridicules the *Canadiens* and Métis, comparing them to mules, when he even admits they were present, he grudgingly recognizes their skills as voyageurs.

Berry then describes how they were able to muscle fully loaded boats and navigate one of the most treacherous rivers of the world. He adds that they "shared with the *frères du nord* [northern brothers] their roistering gaiety and coxcombry, their ruffling and strutting" (Berry, 1961), but specifies that they also have the same "reputation for absolute and unequivocal cowardice." Clearly the Voyageurs he describes are only a step above mules, but useful for purposes of river transport.

The language chosen by the historians to describe the men is telling. Though they are described as quite masculine in many ways—they muscled loaded keelboats—the description also in many ways feminizes the French portraying them as being somewhat vain, conceited dandies. This is not coincidental for American authors tend to portray the French as being somewhat less masculine, less noble, than their Anglo-American counterparts. Nonetheless, the French are mentioned briefly, if only to be disparaged, before being disposed of by later generations of historians. Contemporary historians rarely even say as much.

Then there was yet another "The Adventures of …" book written in the 1870s on the banks of the Connecticut River that featured a nefarious "half-breed." The author reminisces on his childhood along the Mississippi River, one that introduced many of us to the most suspect and dangerous creature of the American West, the half-breed. This was Mark Twain's (1892) *The Adventures of Tom Sawyer*. That "murderin' half-breed" was Injun Joe (Twain, 1892, p. 107). To help the reader along in understanding this character, Twain (1892, pp. 220, 124) referred to him in such terms as the "half-breed devil," and to highlight his moral fabric the author adds, "and plainly this miscreant had sold himself to Satan." Injun Joe was animated by one goal: revenge. He clarified this point by explaining to one wavering partner in crime, "The Injun blood ain't in me for nothing" (Twain, 1892, p. 108).

It was heartening 135 years later to see that in one showing of the TV Western series entitled "Lonesome Dove," an effort was made to include and represent a

Half-breeds Running Buffalo, Paul Kane, ca. 1849–1856. Bison came to be central to the fur economy. The bison would be hunted, the meat dried, pounded into powder and mixed with melted fat, and occasionally berries, with the cooled mixture packed in rawhide bags for storage. This high-energy food could be easily kept for years in caches and was central to the voyageur diet as it provided a compact food that could easily be carried in canoes and would provide easy sustenance at times when food was scarce.

variety of ethnic groups as part of a 'typical' scene in the American southwest. The past was portrayed in order to reflect the contemporary American audience, and all of the characters portrayed were good guys in a story about the 'way back when.' The storyline still needed one antagonist, though, and a particularly sinister, brutal one, incapable of human compassion. Interestingly, they found one who would offend virtually no one, ethnically, politically, or otherwise. He was just called the Half-Breed. Perhaps this represents 'progress of sorts' in matters of storytelling and entertainment, but it does not necessarily challenge the narrative of American history.

In the twenty-first century, we would think that a more nuanced treatment of these actors might be in order. Their history must be exhumed if we are truly to understand the history of the two nation-states, Canada and the United States, and how the French, *Canadiens,* and Métis were among the catalysts that contributed to the rise of the United States; yet they have been actively forgotten, their leading role eclipsed by somewhat minor characters such as Jim Bridger and Kit Carson, who have consequently been memorialized in American songs.

In the chapters that follow, the buried history of the French *Canadien*, Créole and Métis who inhabited the lands of the continent before borders were mapped is excavated and reconstituted. By rereading old works and effectively extracting what historiographers have invariably omitted, we propose a new historical narrative with an alternative model for the emergence of a Métis national identity, one that seeks to place the Métis in a continental framework. We trace the expansion of the United States westward and demonstrate how at each stage of their expansion they encountered French-speaking inhabitants in the northern borderlands who kept their language, while adopting many elements of the culture and ethos of their Native American kin and neighbors under the rubric they called *Canadien*, an ethnonational identity. This national identity was from the beginning the outcome of a *métissage,* the product of a mixing of populations and cultures. From Philadelphia to the Pacific, American "pioneers" would encounter the *Canadien* in their borderlands, and would then marginalize and displace them before conveniently forgetting they had ever been there. In the final chapter we explore some of the consequences of this history being buried and forgotten on both sides of the United States-Canada border.

Forgotten histories are not merely academic matters. They have consequences for extant communities. In the United States, communities are seeking to define themselves even though their histories have been buried, and their legitimacy thus denied. In Canada, Métis communities must challenge the state to affirm their status as Métis, with judges required to assume the role of historians trying to sort through buried Canadian history. On both sides of the border, a much larger history must be pieced together to tell a story that is closer to the past underlying both countries.

CHAPTER 1

Writing History, Burying the Past

Nestled in the National Statuary Hall in Washington, D.C., are a hundred statues honoring and commemorating two representatives from each state's history. Gazing upon the statues representing Washington and Oregon, visitors might mistakenly believe that Quebec had colonized these Pacific Northwestern states, as three of the four individuals were born there. The "Father of Oregon," John McLoughlin—baptized Jean-Baptiste by his French-speaking mother—was born in Rivière-du-Loup and became the Chief Factor for the Hudson's Bay Company in the Pacific Northwest operating out of Fort Vancouver on the Columbia River. The second person representing Oregon is a Methodist missionary, Jason Lee, who was born in Stanstead, Quebec. Washington State's statues feature Congregationalist missionary Marcus Whitman and, providing something of a balance to the display's overall gender, religion, and ethnicity, Mother Joseph.

Born Esther Pariseau in Saint-Elzéar, Quebec, Mother Joseph of the Sacred Heart was among the first women architects of the nineteenth century and is considered a leading figure in the history of the State of Washington, just as Jean-Baptiste (John) McLoughlin, is for Oregon. Both have monuments to them in the Natonal Statuary Hall Collection in Washington, D.C.

These statues are a testament to the role that French-speaking *Canadiens* played in the settling of the region. However, for the observant visitor, there is something else hidden behind the carefully selected statues, something not on proud display, but rather inferred. These statues hint at a deeper, richer history: that of the Métis and French-*Canadien* families who settled in the shadows of the forts and along the fertile valleys of the Pacific Northwest. Their story has been largely overlooked in the later histories. Indeed, those histories written by the descendants of Anglo-American settlers who came to the region in later decades relegated these original founding families to footnotes, to cursory references,

Mother Joseph. Born Esther Pariseau in Saint-Elzéar, Québec. Mother Joseph of the Sacred Heart was among of the first women architects of the nineteenth century and is considered a leading figures in the history of the State of Washington, just as Jean-Baptiste (John) McLoughlin, is for Oregon. Both have monuments to them in the Natonal Statuary Hall Collection in Washington, D.C. She led the first contingent of five nuns of the Sisters of Providence to Vancouver, Washington in 1857, subsequently founding a regional network of hospitals, schools and orphanages.

or isolated markers and monuments scattered across Washington and Oregon like seemingly random dots on a map. By examining the roles of the far-ranging Voyageurs in the process of creating a hybrid culture in the region, as well as identifying the unique hallmarks and self-identity of that culture, we begin to connect the disparate dots. What's more, we will be better equipped to understand the parallels of this formative cultural footprint as it relates to the historical happenings elsewhere in North America. We will start to see beyond the stony faces of carefully chosen icons in the National Statuary Hall and peer into the forgotten historical and cultural context of why those leaders of the *Canadien* and Métis community are being so honored.

This history's neglect stems in part from the fact that, somehow along the way, the western lands settled by the French-Canadians, who called themselves *Canadiens*, mostly ended up in the U.S. and not Canada. Their West, before anybody tripped over the 49th parallel, stretched from the modern states of Michigan and Illinois, through Missouri, Wisconsin, and Minnesota, along the Missouri on out to Montana, Oregon, and Washington. The French-speaking *Canadiens* and Métis traveled and explored the territory, formed alliances with local indigenous peoples, and served as guides and translators for the English and American explorers and settlers to follow. More than a quarter of the original

Carte de l'Amérique Septentrionale, Jacques-Nicolas Bellin, 1743. At its peak, the French territories stretched far to the West and the North. What is too easily overlooked, however, are the communities and settlements that emerged prior to the Conquest of Acadia and New France by the British and how the inhabitants of this territory remained spread over a continent, shaping the history of the states (Canada and the United States) that would emerge.

Lewis and Clark expedition, including chief interpreter Georges Drouillard, were of French and Métis descent. Most of them were recruited from the French settlements of Illinois, with a large number possessed of a mixed heritage with French-speaking fathers and Native American mothers. Georges Drouillard's own mother was, in fact, Shawnee (Chaouanon).

These French-speaking people established settlements across the western territories they helped to explore and map. However, things changed as the English and Americans rose to colonial preeminence and as territories were ceded by treaty in 1763, 1783, 1794, 1814, 1818, 1842, and 1846. Every time competing colonial powers drew a new line, most of the French *Canadiens* and their Métis offspring were left behind; south or west of these arbitrary demarcation lines, territories they had shared with Native Americans soon became inundated with a new sort of settler.

The anthropologist Eric Wolf, in *Europe and the People Without History*, describes how history is written by the victors. Nowhere is this more evident than in the schoolbook versions of the history of the United States. He writes, "the ever-changing boundaries of the United States and the repeated involvements of the polity in internal and external wars, declared and undeclared, are telescoped together by the teleological understanding that thirteen colonies clinging to the eastern rim of the continent would, in less than a century, plant the American flag on the shores of the Pacific" (Wolf, 1982, pp. 5-6). The French-speaking *Canadiens* and Métis are left out of such grand narratives, rendered without histories. In truth, their histories do exist, but are relegated to the local and the parochial. Wolf presents an alternative to traditional historiography, one whereby "both the people who claim history as their own and the people to whom history has been denied emerge as participants in the same historical trajectory" (1982, p. 23). This book thus seeks to chronicle the participation of the French-speaking and Métis populations in a history that does not end with the fur trade, but rather that reveals their crucial role in the greater historical context.

Writing History

To make the West "American," it was necessary to forget the descendants of French colonists that were already there. Generations of French, later *Canadien*, *Créole*, and Métis, had crisscrossed the continent, forged close ties with the continent's indigenous nations, founded settlements and cities, and had sometimes assisted or resisted Americans as they ventured westward. Their history, a discordant note in the harmony that had to be English and Anglo-Saxon and usuallly Protestant, was replaced by the exploits of Anglo-American "mountain men" and heroes whose tales provided much more sonorous tones. Successive waves of French-speaking traders and settlers would be replaced by the Bridgers, Meekers, and Smiths. The French speakers of the Pacific Northwest were simply the last of a noble genealogy of forgotten "Frenchmen," as America's Manifest Destiny sought to ensure its continental reach as well as the hegemony of the dominant language, culture, and ethnic group: the white, Anglo-Saxon—or at very least Anglo-Conformist—American.

Richard Flores provides an insightful illustration as to how history is made and the past remembered. In *Remembering the Alamo: Memory, Modernity, and the Master Symbol* (2010), Flores explores the making of cultural memory and its links to official historical discourse. Cultural memory involves those media that are not specifically identified as "history," but invariably do shape the larger narrative, including those of historians. According to Flores (2010, p. xv): "cul-

Boat Encampment, Paul Kane ca. 1849–1856. The Métis, but also the French-speaking Iroquois, played a pivotal role in pushing the fur trade over the mountains. Iroquois such as Pierre dit Tête-Jaune mapped the Yellowhead Pass, while Thomas the Iroquois guided David Thompson over the Athabasca Pass as they crossed to continental divide to reach the headwaters of the Columbia and follow its waters down to the Pacific.

tural memory refers to those aspects of memory that exist outside of official historical discourse, yet are 'entangled' with them." These aspects of memory include what is learned in schools, but also what is learned from comic books or graphic novels, movies, popular novels, museums, and countless other forms of discursive practice that shape how individuals "remember" the past. In the case of the Alamo, Flores examines how memories are tied not only to the shaping of the understanding of the past, but also to an understanding of the contemporary relationship between "Anglos" and "Mexicans."

The past is not just remembered: "The Alamo did not emerge full blown as a site of public history but is the cumulative effect of multiple representations that have etched its compelling story into the reservoir of American cultural memory" (Flores, 2010, p. xv). The same is true of the history of the American West. The past that is remembered was shaped by nineteenth-century newspaper articles, five-and-dime novels, songs, movies, and a history informed by literature and the need for heroic figures. We submit that the narrative of contemporary historians is still shaped by the larger cultural memory as a number of themes continue to propagate themselves in the history books telling the story of the American West. The line between historiography and memory is blurred at best, non-existent at worst, when it comes to recounting the history of the French in the West and particularly in the Oregon Country and Pacific Northwest.

Flores highlights that "remembering" requires "forgetting," as Sturken (1997) suggests. The essential element that Flores rightfully identifies is the active nature of forgetting. It is necessary to actively erase what must be forgotten in order to ensure that the correct memories are brought to the fore. Flores (2010, p. xv) writes, "[…] forgetting is not a passive experience; like remembering, it is an active process that involves erasure. Memory, in being selective, actively forgets or 'silences the past,' as Michel-Rolph Trouillot (1995) writes." This is seen in the case of the cultural memory surrounding the Whitman "massacre" (See Chapter 7). In the 1880s, a series of pieces were published in the principal Oregon newspaper where the authors came out with all quills slashing, lashing out against a woman who had dared to challenge popular memory, questioning the actions of Marcus and Narcissa Prentiss Whitman. These Protestant missionaries, killed by a a small group of enraged Cayuse neighbors, were martyrs to the nation.

Here, we see the active nature of forgetting whereby those who dare to seek to publicly remember the less-than-illustrious moments of the past that challenge popular myths are castigated. Or, as Trouillot (1995, p. 2) would have it, this is an example of the past as a narrative of "that which is said to have happened," as opposed to the past as sociohistorical process or what actually happened.

Trouillot (1995, p. 2) notes, "Human beings participate in history both as actors and narrators." We would add that not all narrations are recorded, as Wolf (1982) remarks, and not all narrations are remembered. In the case of the Pacific Northwest, few recall French served as the *lingua franca* of the territory for close to two generations, and that the first settlers were largely French-speaking *Canadien*, Métis, Iroquois (or peoples from the Haudenosaunee Confederation) and even a few descendants of Huron-Wendat, Abenaki, and other first nations from what was known as *Le Canada* that existed for two centuries before the modern Canadian state was formed in 1867. This is certainly what Trouillot (1995, p. 3) would qualify as the semantic ambiguity of the vernacular use of the word history, as there is the "irreducible distinction and yet an irreducible overlap between what happened and that which is said to have happened."

"History" has to be probed to better understand how narratives are subtly phrased in order to leave erroneous impressions on the reader, though the intent is not truly known. An example of this is the tendency to present lists that inverse

The fighting trapper: or, Kit Carson to the rescue, 1874. Kit Carson was relatively a minor figure on the Frémont expedition who, thanks to mythmakers, became a household name in the United States, almost as if he was the leader. Frémont wrote much more about others on the expedition, above all the *Canadiens*, and particularly Basil Lajeuenesse. Yet the five and dime novels invariably made the heroes of the West Anglo-American, usually Protestant and blond, thus excluding the *Canadiens* and Métis.

the numeric importance of cohorts in the past. The French-*Canadiens*, for example, will be listed last after Americans or the British as being "mountain men," even though they were the largest contingent.

Likewise, when the Pacific Northwest trade on both sides of the 49th parallel is discussed, the Scottish contribution is invariably highlighted, while the role of the French—*Canadien*, Métis, Iroquois, and others—is largely ignored, rarely named, and at best left as a faceless mass not considered worthy of historical recollection. The lists enumerated thus reinforce an image of the past whereby Anglo-Americans dominate both the past and the present, even though they were a minority in the past among both the "mountain men" and the earlier settlers of the Pacific Northwest who had been closely tied to the fur economy.

Much of history is mythic. Flores (2010, p. xv) provides a good working definition: "Myths, and cultural memories more generally, are not stratospheric tales but deeply grounded narratives through which communities express their heartfelt convictions." History thus is based on the expectation that historiography will be based on fact not fiction, but the mythic element of history is created through selective glorification of past events or addition of narrative elements that were clearly fabricated. If no single American survived the Alamo, how do we know that William Barret Travis drew a line in the sand, asked those willing to fight to the death to cross it, and not one man there did not cross the line (Trouillot, 1995, p. 10)? It was a good story, and Texas historians and authors of Texas history books chose not to question this unprovable fact, having long ago concurred that "it doesn't really matter whether it is true or not" (Trouillot, 1995, p. 10).

Fictional elements are thus kept in official historiography as they buttress the narrative. This is seen elsewhere, notably in the works of Bernard De Voto, which skirt the line between history and fiction. Not only is narrative built by mixing both fact and fiction, as Trouillot (1995, p. 19) notes, historiography in the United States "produced its own silences on African-American slavery" as a case in point, and we argue that American historiography continues to produce silences on the role of those who spoke French—both *Canadiens* and Indigenous peoples—in the settling of the American West, and in particular, the Pacific Northwest.

The Mythic West

The myth-making began before the West was integrated into the United States. A unifying thread cutting across the history of the West is that it was wild, lacking in civilization, and in desperate need of American civilization. As the West was a fearsome place, it was necessary to find heroes capable of taming the wild frontier; only historical individuals depicted as strong-armed demigods, preferably cut of Anglo-Saxon wool, could pave the way for western settlement (Etulain, 1996, p. xix). The development of new technologies to produce cheap pulp paper led to the staggering rise of five-and-dime novels that frequently depicted such cultural icons as Billy the Kid, Calamity Jane, Wild Bill Hickok, and Kit Carson. These novels were sold to a voracious readership in the eastern United States, who bought hundreds of thousands of these novels, and who largely believed the overly dramatic and romanticized depictions they contained (Etulain, 1996, pp. xix-xxi).

Along with these popular publications, newspaper accounts and later popular movies would create the mythical west, cultivating a "cult of masculinity" (Etulain, 1996, p. xxii). This, however, was not only tied to journalists, authors, and historians, but also military men. Quite often, the *Canadien* voyageur is depicted by various historical accounts in terms that would best be described as feminine, thus creating what we would argue are stereotypes of voyageurs as being less masculine than their Anglo-American contemporaries.

Janet LeCompte (1997) clearly demonstrates just how French the American West really was, and how this fact contrasts with the mythic West sold by both writers and historians. She notes: "the ratio of 'Frenchman' to Americans in the fur trade of the United States was not one to four but four to one." This ratio is based on the research conducted by Hiram Martin Chittenden, who spent six years scanning fur trade papers and estimated that at least four-fifths of the approximately five thousand men in the American fur trade were of French-Canadian (*Canadien*) or Mississippi Valley Métis or Créole background.

This work was corroborated by William R. Swagerty, who examined the 1830 American Fur Company contracts and noted how the French surnames exceeded by far the Anglo-Saxon surnames at all levels: as voyageurs, laborers, and even the bourgeois, the managers (LeCompte, 1997, p. 11). Those who spoke French were important at every level of the American fur trade, even among the ranks of the company owners. Yet, historical accounts largely exclude them. "Despite the numerical preponderance of the French in the West, myths and romantic stereotypes of trappers have persuaded well-known historians that mountain men were American frontiersman" (LeCompte, 1997, p. 12). Leading American historians such as Frederick Merk (*History of the Westward Movement*), William H. Goetzmann (*Exploration and Empire*), and Bernard DeVoto (*Across the Wide Missouri*) simply assumed that the fur trade was conducted almost exclusively by Anglo-Americans (LeCompte, 1997, p. 12). This is a perfect case of history being written to chronicle what is said to have happened as opposed to what really happened.

Bernard De Voto certainly lionized a handful of "mountain men," but he also chronicled how some Anglo-Americans came to be seen as the driving force among these same "mountain men." De Voto writes, "It was chance that gave Bridger a greater celebrity than Fitzpatrick; he came to be eyes and brains for the Army at a time when newspapermen were coming west and could give national expression to local reputation, whereas Tom's culminating services were to departments of the government which had not yet hired press agents" (De Voto, 1975, p. 227).

As for Kit Carson, De Voto also credits the media for his fame: "he happened to work for a man who had genius for publicity, a wife with an equal genius for it, and a father-in-law who had the same genius and a national broadcasting booth as well" (De Voto, 1975, p. 228). The man in question was John Charles Frémont, whose account includes scant mention of both Bridger and Carson—though clearly Carson was a much more congenial personality to the eastern-American

Canoe Manned by Voyageurs Passing a Waterfall, Frances Anne Hopkins, 1869. "The ratio of 'Frenchmen' to Americans in the fur trade of the United States was not one to four but four to one," wrote Janet LeCompte (1997). Frances Anne Hopkins painted this based on her experience. Married to Hudson's Bay Company official in 1858, she traveled the major trade routes and was the woman in the voyageur canoes she painted. Her paintings provided a detailed visual account of the men, their apparel, and their lives.

media than the French who constituted the main personalities of Frémont's expedition and official account (Frémont, 1845). De Voto still mythologizes the men in question: "These three—and it is sagacious not to rank or even differentiate them—are the mountain man as master craftsman, partisan, explorer, conqueror, and maker and bequeather of the West. They are important historically because they were the best of a trade group, small and shortlived, who had a maker's part in extending the national boundaries and the national consciousness to continental completion" (De Voto, 1975, pp. 227-228). In this way, De Voto helps to establish the narrative that will continue on to contemporary historians.

A small number of American mountain men are invariably presented as being representative of the epoch. This has often been perpetuated in modern histories at the state level. Charles LeWarne (1986, p. 71), for example, writes: "Some mountain men, like Jim Bridger, Jedediah Smith, Kit Carson, and Joe Meek, became famous. As they traveled and trapped and hunted, they came to know the woods, mountains, rivers, and valleys intimately. They crossed mountain passes and ridges, followed streams, and roamed through valleys to places no white men had seen before." LeWarne does not ask, in his otherwise superb history of the state of Washington, why these particular men became famous; and in presenting the mountain men, he downplays the importance of the French, be they *Canadien* or Métis. When describing the rendezvous that brought together trappers and traders at a preselected locale to trade and socialize, he lists "mountain men, company representatives, old-time French-Canadian trappers, traders from rival companies, and Indians bringing teepees" (LeWarne, 1986, p. 70).

By placing the French-Canadian after the mountain men, it leaves the impression that they were less numerous, and stating that they are "old-time" suggests that they were somehow less advanced than their American peers. Though LeWarne does not state it overtly, he leaves the overall impression that the French *Canadiens* were secondary to the trade, while in reality they constituted the bulk of the mountain men.

At times, the authors of the romantic biographies of these American mountain men must acknowledge the existence of the *Canadien* in the American West. Shannon Garst (1952, pp. 15-16), in her book *Jim Bridger: Greatest of the Mountain Men*, does acknowledge that the Main Street in St. Louis when Bridger was an adolescent was actually called "La Rue Principale," [Main Street] and she does mention that it was the *Canadien* voyageur that had fueled Bridger's desire to become a mountain man: "There were Mexicans in bright-colored serapes, American army officers in uniform, Negro slaves, sullen, blanketed Indians who had taken on the vices of the white men and none of the virtues. Most exciting of all were the *voyageurs* (French Canadian boatmen) and trappers who came out of the wilderness with the aura of adventure clinging to them. Those were the ones Jim stared at, wondered about, and envied."

However, such overt admissions of the large numbers of *Canadien* voyageurs in the American West actually became rarer to nonexistent in contemporary historiography. Even De Voto (1975, p. 225) describes in detail the embellished life of Lucien Fontenelle, a man described as being from New Orleans who, allegedly, "was of noble French blood, some say of royal blood, and there had been a mysterious romance in his earlier life." De Voto (1975, p. 225) interestingly notes that the story and history of men such as Fontenelle were too easily overlooked: "Fontenelle is worth a biography but no one has written it yet."

Likewise, Gene Caeser (1961, p. 27) in his book *King of the Mountain Men: The Life of Jim Bridger* mentions the French and their role in the fur trade, referring to the "old feudal-lord traders of St. Louis, Chouteau and Pratte and Berthold and Brazzeau, popularly known as the French Fur Company." Though depicted as "feudal," which is to say not as modern and progressive as the Americans, they are at least mentioned. The same is true of the voyageurs that he cites as holding a near-monopoly on the "wilderness rivers," and Caesar (1961, pp. 104-105) does mention that one of Bridger's partners was *Canadien*: "The third was Jean-Baptiste Gervais, a typical French trapper and trader, cheerful and patient, contrasting as strongly with his partners as *voyageurs* had contrasted with brawling keelboatmen before steam came to the Missouri." He nonetheless conforms to the narrative norm, depicting the *Canadien* as cheerful, patient (i.e., not independent and challenging authority), somewhat childish. But, at least they were mentioned, and a bit of their story was told, which is more than can be said of many contemporary historical accounts of the American West.

Over time, the role of the American mountain men is amplified in the mythmaking. While Carson played a modest role in Frémont's expeditions, later generations of novelists enhanced his importance. By the 1940s, Frank Beals, in his novel and history entitled *Kit Carson*, a text clearly intended for school children, had promoted Carson to the effective leader of the Frémont expeditions. In this account, which includes a smidgen of history and a large dollop of legend, Frémont is described as having asked the ship's captain on the Missouri whether he had heard of Carson. Beals then provides this fictional reply: "'Heard of him? Who has not heard of him? He has roamed over this western country for years. He knows every foot of it. He has been in more tight places and had more narrow escapes than any other man out here. And Indians? Why, he is never happy unless he is in a fight with them,' answered the captain" (Beals, 1943, pp. 78-79). A few pages later, Beals (1943, p. 82) affirms that "Kit led the party by the shortest route to Fort Laramie," and the illustration that accompanies the text shows Carson front and center. In reality, it was the *Canadien* guides and interpreters who played a much more central role in Frémont's expeditions; however, by the twentieth century Carson had eclipsed even Frémont as the most important figure in the expedition.

A contemporary historian, Richard White, also lists the Anglo-Americans, then the French-Canadians and the Iroquois as the mountain men. He adds a very national component to his account, describing the mountain men as part of an American vanguard:

> These shaggy adventurers who hunted beaver in the mountains formed an odd wedge for American commercial expansion. The mountain men, as they came to be called, first moved up the Missouri River, creating a complex series of links with the Indian peoples they encountered. They entered the West as harbingers of an American imperialism that would deliver the West to the United States, but most of them probably never thought of themselves as either imperialists or capitalists. (R. White, 1991a, p. 46)

Ironically, the mountain men are presented as carriers of American imperialism, when most would have defined themselves as *Canadien*. The master narrative remains unchanged, and the continuity from De Voto to White is evinced in mythic elements maintained in historiography, adding to the heroic story of the American West.

Along somewhat similar lines, Richard White (1991b) succumbs to an outlook inadvertently tinged with Manifest Destiny when he wraps up an otherwise magnificent work by treating The Middle Ground full of *Canadien* and Métis actors as limited in time and place. The Middle Ground as defined by White ends in 1815 and is confined to the American Midwest, instead of an on-going process of a dynamic frontier zone, one shifting outward in line with national expansion and demographic displacement.

The same is also true in modern historical accounts of the Pacific Northwest, as here, too, the French speakers are minimized and their role pushed to the background. The primary college text book in use over the last two decades for the history of the Pacific Northwest, authored by the eminent regional historian, Professor Carlos Arnaldo Schwantes (1989), identifies Canadians as one of the largest immigrant groups, as did Sid White and S.E. Solberg (1989) in their *Peoples of Washington*. However, whereas White and Solberg provide specifics as to locations, numbers, and occupations, Schwantes, unlike the other national/ethnic groups he mentioned, offered not a word on *Canadiens* or Métis. He does, however, provide background on the earliest contingents of ethnic minority groups that were barely present at the time, but have since become more numerous and visible since World War II. LeWarne, for his part, (1986, p. 67) does write: "Besides the British and Americans, there were French Canadians and members of several Indian groups. Hawaiians, called Kanakans, were brought in to do manual labor; they lived in a village of their own. A Hawaiian (Owyhee) church was built inside the stockade with a Kanaka chaplain." Once again, the French *Canadiens* are listed much lower than the British and Americans, even though they would have been by far the most numerous demographic contingent in the period under discussion, after that of the Native Americans. In LeWarne's narrative, the French speakers play a minor role. Even in describing other regions of the United States, he minimizes the importance of the French-Canadians: "The heart of North America remained blank on maps. Its edges had been touched by Spanish explorers in the Southwest, by French-Canadian trappers following streams out from the Great Lakes, and by other fur traders venturing up the Missouri River" (LeWarne, 1986, p. 56). French Canadians only "touched" the region, despite the fact that they had founded its principal city, St. Louis. Thus, across the United States, both popular history and academic historiography share a common narrative whereby the French *Canadiens* and Métis are mentioned, but invariably

Simon Plamondon, born April 1, 1800, Saint-François du Lac, Québec. Enthralled by the fur trade life, Simon traveled to the Mississippi, then the Missouri, before crossing the Rockies and heading to Fort George (Astoria) in 1816 where he worked as a trapper. By all accounts, Simon had Abenaki ancestry. After the Cowlitz captured him, he ingratiated himself to them, and married Chief Scanewa's daughter, Thas-e-muth (Veronica). Simon Plamondon guided Commodore Charles Wilkes in his overland journey and played an important role in the early Oregon and Washington history. His descendants are prominent in the contemporary Cowlitz Tribe.

demoted to a minor, inconsequential role in the history. Our goal is to provide an account closer to the history that actually happened, as Trouillot put it.

The contribution of the French *Canadiens* occasionally breaks through the established walls of American historiography. Robert Ficken and Charles LeWarne (1988, pp. 20-21), in their centennial history of the state of Washington, did identify Simon Plamondon as the likely first settler: "The land north of the Columbia was settled slowly at first. Simon Plamondon, the French-Canadian who established the Hudson's Bay Company farm on the Cowlitz Prairie, built his own home there in the late 1820s, becoming apparently the first permanent white settler above the Columbia." The use of the word "apparently," however, casts doubt on the statement, allowing the reader the option of believing that Plamondon was not truly the first settler. Furthermore, no further mention is made in the rest of the book of the *Canadiens* or the Métis. Hopefully, more information on the role of the French in the history of the Pacific Northwest will eventually reach the general textbooks used in schools and colleges. Resistance from popular cultural memory that has pushed the French-speaking peoples out of the historical narrative could however mean that historiography will continue to downplay their contribution.

Considerable research examining the origins of the Métis identity has been published. One controversial point is whether any Métis identities existed outside the confines of the Red River Valley. An offshoot is whether "Métis" should be capitalized when referring to the mixed-ancestry populations found elsewhere in North America, notably the Great Lakes region, but also beyond. This historical research, though appreciated, ignores a crucial element: the older *Canadien* identity has been oddly left out of most discussions of the origins of the Métis or the ethnogenesis—in some instances, the term *Canadien* is dropped into the discussion with little explanation provided as to the origins of *Canadien* in relation to Métis identity (Dickason, 1985; Edmunds, 1985; Murphy, 2012; Peterson, 1985; Spry, 1985).

When Jacqueline Peterson (1985, p. 54) discusses the early settlement of Detroit, for example, she writes: "whereas the narrow, ribbon farm lots of Canadiens and métis were scattered along the east side of the river north as far as Lake St. Clair," suggesting that the Canadian and the Métis were separate and distinct populations. She does not discuss the likelihood that the Métis were part and parcel of the larger *Canadien* community.

The historical evidence clearly suggests that one could be both a *Canadien* (prior to the word being captured by a nation-building state) and a Métis. This arguably carries not only a reference to the mixed Euro-Indigenous heritage of a particular person, but also denotes the specific cultural heritage as a "country-born" *Canadien*, part of this collective yet trans-territorial "plus" identity as a Métis that was readily recognized both by outsiders and insiders under terms such as "Bois-Brulé," Michif, or Métis.

In short, just as someone in Canada today can have multiple and sometimes overriding collective identities, there is no reason to assume the *Canadien* and Métis identity ought to be conceived as mutually exclusive. By the same token, as discussed in Chapter 9, there is no reason to restrict the possibility that the Métis peoples developed an ethnic identity outside the classical perimeters of modern sociology, which often asks for some contained geographical boundaries—or worse, to make such a development contingent upon nationalist narratives akin to their modern European counterparts in order to "prove" the existence of a "collective consciousness."

In their multiple trajectories, both the *Canadien* and Métis collective identity didn't restrict themselves to meticulous geographical boundaries (mostly due to the nature of the voyageur culture that pre-shaped both identities in significant respect), nor to a single and closed kinship group, as both *Canadien* and Métis identity have allowed in their composition various entries from different

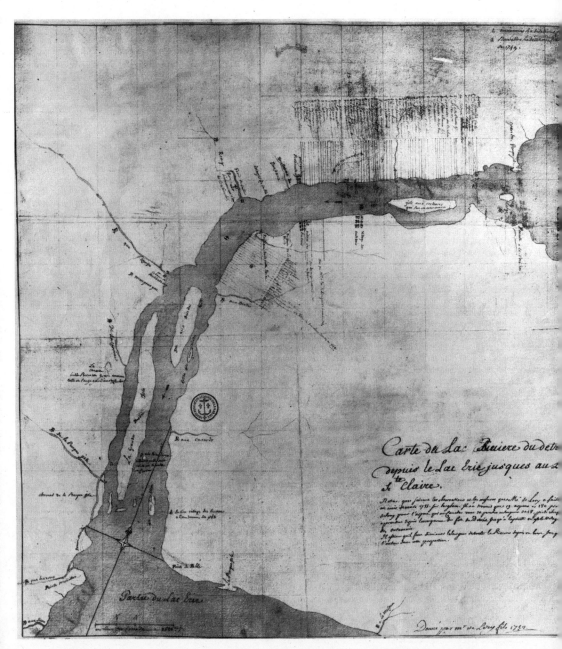

Carte de La Rivière du Détroit depuis le Lac Érie jusques au Lac Ste Claire, Joseph Gaspard Chaussegros de Léry, 1752. Maps like this 1752 map of the Detroit area can be found for communities across the continent, bearing witness to the presence of *Canadiens* and Métis settlers well before the Anglo-Americans moved west. They built their homes close together along both sides of the river and farmed long strips of land behind their cabins. Only a small portion of the land fronted the river, which facilitated transportation.

indigenous groups without dissolution. Rather, as evidence shows, the cultural binders for trans-territorial and truly multicultural identities such as the early *Canadien*-Métis were elements that could readily travel and adapt to shifting conditions over an immense and diverse landscape. A shared language (significantly French), shared spiritual beliefs and rituals (significantly impregnated with Catholicism), and a conciliatory position towards elements of indigenization, taken together, gave a cultural and collectivist substance to the conjugation of "*Canadien*" and "Métis."

An intriguing case analyzed in detail by Suzanne Sommerville is that of Marie-Anne Magnan dite Lespérance. Marie-Anne was the illegitimate daughter of Jean Magnan dit Lespérance. Her father returned to Saint-Lawrence Valley with his daughter, and her existence was recorded in the Catholic Church baptismal records when she was two-and-a-half years old. Her mother is listed as simply a female Sioux, and the location of her birth is not recorded. Years later, after her father's death, she was arrested and charged with theft. In the court records of February 16, 1730, she self-identified as *Canadienne* (Sommerville, 2004). Clearly, having a Native American mother did not disqualify her from being *Canadienne*.

We also have the case of Louis Riel, who used concomitantly the identifications of "*Canadien*," "*Français*," and "*Métis*" in one single term, "*Canadien-Français métis*," even when he referred to the People of his "new Nation."[1]

Finally, we have the interesting case of Marie Rose Delorme Smith, who never identified as "Métis" in the homogeneous way such identity is sometimes portrayed today, although she was clearly a member of what is now deemed by some as the heart of the "Métis Historic Nation" (MacKinnon, 2012). While Peterson and others are correct in affirming that being of mixed ancestry does not make one necessarily "Métis" (an affirmation of identity which is linked to collective dimension), being "Métis" or "Half-Breed" or even from "mixed-indigenous ancestry" did not disqualify an individual from being *Canadien* in its earlier acceptations. Moreover, the emergence of the Métis ethnic group in North America cannot be reduced to a single form of political manifestation, which must necessarily express itself in what we would need to recognize as a classic form of nationalist narrative bound to a single geographical point of origin (i.e., Red River Settlement).

Peterson does indirectly acknowledge that those of mixed heritage eventually became *Canadien*, stating how, "In later years, old settlers of French Indian ancestry would have the opportunity to present themselves as French Canadian creoles" (Peterson, 2012, p. 40). Peterson, however, continues to use the term "creole," and we would argue that those of mixed Euro-Indigenous heritage became *Canadien*-Métis, and long before those "later years" of which Peterson writes.

The term Créole is also used in places where the French speakers never identi-fied themselves as Créole. Russell David Edmunds (1985, pp. 187-188) affirms that the close association between the French and the Native Americans in the Old Northwest had created a new people, and they "dominated both the French creole and Indian communities." Later he refers to the "creole French" and cites William Keating, who is quoted as referring to inhabitants of Fort Wayne as "chiefly of Canadian origin, all more or less imbued with Indian blood" (Edmunds, 1985, p. 189). Keating thus affirms that the "métis" considered themselves *Canadien*, highlighting significant identity overlaps between the *Canadien* and Métis popu-lation in the Old Northwest (See Chapter 2).

Lucy Murphy (2012) also writes of the Créole identity of the Old Northwest, yet pays scant attention to the *Canadien* identity even though she notes how, "In Illinois, a 1797 census divided the adult males into four categories: '*français, creole, canadien, américain.*' Historian Carl Ekberg found that some people of mixed ancestry were certainly included in the category of *creole*" (Murphy, 2012, p. 234). This latter statement may be true but definite evidence exists showing that people of mixed heritage were included under the *Canadien* identity. Moreover, examples of the term *Canadien* being applied to the French speakers abound in the Great Lakes region as well as the Illinois Country and the "Middle West," as William Keating also affirmed. The most remarkable is the case of the man described by Alexis de Tocqueville (1865, p. 244) as *Canadien* who, when asked, specifies that he is a *bois-brûlé*, the son of a *Canadien* and a Native American woman, referring then to a "singular race of métis" inhabiting the borderlands of Canada and part of the United States. Tocqueville, however, was just happy to be able to speak in his language, French, with this man who was by all appearances "Indian," yet not.

Peterson also provides a potentially confusing expression by referring to "French Canadian creoles." She writes: "the creole and mixed-descent popula-tion was soon outnumbered, as had been the case a generation earlier with the old French Canadian creole towns of the Illinois Country" (Peterson, 2012, p. 34). Here, the use of French Canadian and creole together is confusing, as *Canadien* and Créole are seen as distinct populations, and the French descendants of the Illinois Country—including the mixed-descent populations—would have pre-dominantly defined themselves as *Canadien*.

Perhaps even more problematic is how Peterson contrasts the alleged assimi-lation of the mixed French-indigenous population (the Métis) by waves of American settlers to argue that a true "Métis" ethnic group did not emerge that was in any way comparable to the one crystalized by the two "Rebellions" (or two cases of resistance) led by Louis Riel. Yet the outcome in both the Great Lakes areas and the Pacific Northwest was very similar to that of Riel. This included the flooding of newcomers, the dispersal of Métis descendants, the destruction of the ways of life by which their identity was consolidated, as well as their quasi-cultural extinction and very recent cultural revitalization.

The distinction between the *Canadien* and the *Créole* is further exemplified by the work of John (Jean) Charles Frémont (1845, p. 9), who refers to "Creole and Canadian voyageurs" as two distinct populations. Frémont clearly distinguishes the two populations, and as a French-speaking son of a French émigré,* he would certainly have understood the subtle nuances of identity expressed in the French language. It thus appears that the historical formation of a number of identities in North America has been overlooked—identities that grew out of the fractured French colonial period. Understanding the emergence of these older national identities is necessary in order to better understand the significance of the Métis identity that would arise out of the older identities, often in concomitant and non-exclusivist ways.

Three primary national identities emerged from the French colonization of North America. In the Maritimes the *Acadien* identity, described as the first case of métissage, gave rise to a distinct group-identity (Karahasan, 2006, Macleod 2013). Settlers who cleared the sea marshes to establish fields and villages forged the *Acadien* identity. The *Canadiens* living in the colony of New France called the *Acadiens* "*défricheurs d'eau,*" given that that they occupied lands wrested from the sea using their dykes, known to them as *aboiteaux*, to clear the ocean and plant crops and raise stock. These *aboiteaux* were also used as roads connecting *Acadien* settlers. As the *Acadiens* occupied a liminal zone and did not drive out the indigenous Mi'kmaq in order to occupy their territories, they maintained peaceful and cordial relations with the Mi'kmaq and Malecite nations. The capital of Acadie was Port-Royal, located near what is now Annapolis, Nova Scotia. The *Acadien* identity survived deportation, and even in Quebec, where they were surrounded by fellow French speakers, the *Acadien* identity was maintained for over a century, extending even into Kansas and Alberta where, in the Comeau family, it lasted well into the twentieth century (M. Bouchard, 2008; Karahasan, 2006; MacLeod, 2013).

Interestingly, Acadians of mixed-heritage were identified with the ethnonym "métis" and described as forming "distinct" communities from both the Europeans and Micmac by Francois-Edmé Rameau de Saint-Père in 1890 (Jean, 2011). The same can be said of "Acadian-métis" communities identified as forming distinct peoples in a series of newspaper articles in *L'Étendard, Le Canadien,*

---

* An alternate account of Charles Frémont's origins claims that John Charles Frémont's father was Louis-René Frémont who allegedly left Lower Canada for the French colony of Saint-Domingue and was imprisoned by the British. Having escaped, he makes his way to Virginia and settles in the American South as a refugee, going by the name of Charles Frémon to avoid detection (Rolle, 1999, p. 3).

La Minerve, La Justice and *The Morning Chronicle* on February 18 and 19, 1886 that describe the riots of Paspébiac, on the southern shores of the Gaspésie region of Quebec.

The *Canadien* identity becomes somewhat more convoluted than its *Acadien* counterpart, as the name was later usurped by the modern nation state of Canada—a state that appropriated many of the symbols of the French-speaking *Canadien* (maple leaf, national anthem, beaver, etc.). Gilles Gougeon (1993), interviewing one of the leading experts on the history of New France, Robert Lahaise, summarizes the emergence of the *Canadien* identity in seeking to answer how the inhabitants of the territory came to see themselves as *Canadien,* sometimes pronounced and written as *Canayen.* Though the territory is known as New France, it was actually referred to as "Nouvelle-France dite Canada," and in the earliest accounts from New France the St. Lawrence River was also called the "rivière du Canada" (Arsenault, 2004, p. 25; Gougeon, 1993, p. 17).

Adding to the confusion is the fact that in the early years of New France, the term *Canadien* was often used to designate the indigenous peoples or indigenized settlers inhabiting the Saint-Lawrence Valley. The term *Canadien,* used to signify those individuals of French ancestry born and living in Canada (New France), emerged under governance of Frontenac between 1672 and 1682 (his first term as governor of New France). However, in this period, the terms *Canadien* and Créole were both used by the Baron de Lahontan, a friend of Frontenac (Gougeon, 1993, p. 19). Later, even the Baron de Lahontan would come to use *Canadien* exclusively; in his 1703 publication, he provides the following definition: "*Canadiens, sont des naturels de Canada nez de père et de mère François. On appelle ceux des Isles de l'Amérique Méridionale Créoles*" (de Lom d'Arce de Lahontan, 1703, p. 270). [Canadiens are native to Canada born of a French mother and father. We call those born in the southern islands of America Créoles.]

By the end of the seventeenth century, *Canadien* would be the sole ethnonym designating the new nation that would stretch from the city of Quebec to the deep forests that stretched across the Great Lakes and into the Ohio and Illinois Country. It is important to note also that *Canadien* and *Acadien* were two distinct identities.

The term *Canadien* would become hegemonic precisely when the French were consolidating their positions in the Great Lakes region, and thus the *Canadien* ethnonym would implant itself in the *Pays d'en Haut* and would maintain itself well into the twentieth century. A reading of the work of Pierre François Xavier de Charlevoix, a Jesuit professor, reveals more than three dozen cases of the word *Canadien* being used in the third volume alone of his history of New France. Charlevoix traveled to New France in 1720 and later published a three-volume account of the colony. His account affirms that the *Canadiens* were located far into the upper country, *le Pays d'en Haut*. He writes, as a case in point, "*Pendant qu'on y travailloit, le Chevalier de Tonti arriva avec environ vint Canadiens établis chez les Illinois,*" [While we were at work there, the Knight of Tonti arrived with some twenty Canadiens settled among the Illinois.] (de Charlevoix, 1744b, p. 385).

These *Canadiens* would form the nuclei of communities across the Great Lakes region and the Illinois Country. Charlevoix also reveals that the term Créole was not used in the colony by the eighteenth century to name the *habitants* or inhabitants of the country. He writes, "*Les Canadiens, c'est-à-dire, les Créoles du Canada, respirent en naissant un air de liberté, qui les rend fort agréables dans le commerce de la vie, & nulle part ailleurs on ne parle plus purement notre Langue. On ne remarque même ici aucun accent*" (de Charlevoix, 1744c, p. 79). [The Canadiens, that is to say the Créoles of Canada, breathe at birth an air of freedom which renders them quite pleasant in both business and life, and nowhere else do we speak more purely our language. We do not notice here any accent.] This passage subtly underscores how the French in Europe understood Créole to mean their compatriots born overseas: Charlevoix specifies that the term *Canadien* applies to the Créoles of Canada for his readership in France, not that the term Créole is used in New France. Charlevoix also explains that the *Canadiens* are different from the French in France, as they are born breathing in the "air of liberty." The *Canadiens* thus were seen by the French administrators as being of a different character, free-spirited. The Count of Bougainville even remarked, "*Il semble que nous soyons de nations différentes, et même ennemies*" (Gougeon, 1993, p. 23). [It seems as if we are from different nations and even enemies] Thus, in the early decades of the eighteenth century, the *Canadiens* were seen as a different "nation" from the French, and they would be therefore a different "nation" from both the *Acadiens* and the Créoles of lower Louisiana.

The modern history of what became Louisiana effectively began when the *Canadien* identity was already taking shape, since Louisiana began to be settled when the *Canadien* identity was already becoming entrenched in New France. The French history of Louisiana begins when René Robert Cavelier de la Salle travels from New France to the headwaters of the Mississippi and down to the delta, claiming the territory for France and naming it *Louisiane* in honor of the reigning French monarch. In 1699, Pierre LeMoyne d'Iberville—who was born in New France—left France and sailed to the Gulf of Mexico, where he located once again the mouth of the Mississippi and founded the first capital of Louisiana, Biloxi, just east of the delta. With the sea route mapped, settling the territory would begin in earnest. In the decades that followed, settlers would be sent to the new colony from France and Germany, and slaves would be brought to Louisiana to work in the newly established plantations.

Monument to La Salle, Indianola, Texas, Overlooking The Gulf of Mexico. René Robert Cavelier de la Salle canoed down the Mississippi to the delta and claimed the entire region that he called La Louisiane for France. His final voyage to find the mouth of the Mississippi after crossing the Atlantic ended in tragedy.

The term Créole is now largely associated with the descendants of the African slaves in American popular culture—either those brought directly to Louisiana, or having arrived from other French colonies (mainly Haiti, or Saint Domingue)—yet the term Créole in the eighteenth and nineteenth century identified those descendants of French settlers who were the elite of Louisiana society, both during the French regime and during the Spanish rule that followed. The "Cajuns," from "*Acadiens*," may have gripped popular American imagination in more recent decades, but in fact the Créoles were the dominant French-speaking community in lower Louisiana well into the twentieth century. As George Cable suggests (1885, p. 42), "Neither Spanish nor American domination has taken from the Creoles their French vernacular. This, also, is part of their title; and, *in fine*, there seems to be no more serviceable definition of the Creoles of Louisiana than this: that they are the French-speaking, native portion of the ruling class." The French settlers of Louisiana, unlike the *Canadien*, adopted a term Créole that was current in France at the time the colony was being settled. *Canadiens* and Créoles would meet in Saint-Louis in the last third of the eighteenth century

Understanding the origins of these three national identities—*Canadien*, *Acadien*, and Créole—is essential to understanding the intertwined emergence of the more Métis national identity. Whereas Sleeper-Smith (2001) posits that the children of the French men and indigenous women of the Great Lakes did not have a nationality, but rather an identity founded on kinship, we submit that these children often had a nationality, and that nationality was *Canadien*. As Charlevoix observed, men calling themselves *Canadien* were living in the Illinois Country; indeed, a number of other authors continually bring up the *Canadien* designation to describe the populations living in the Great Lakes region as well as the Illinois Country. The children of *Canadiens* in the Illinois Country were also identified as "Métis" (Houghton, 1918). Thus, the children of mixed heritage could be integrated into two communities with many overlapping circles of penetration: they could join their mother's community, or establish themselves in the shadows of the French forts and missions—even abandoned ones—and adopt the language and ethnonym of their *Canadien*-Métis fathers.

These two possibilities are not mutually exclusive, as the reality of these peoples was often more complex and fluid than we have come to believe. All three populations examined here had varying degrees of *métissage*, as the men quite often took wives from the Native American nations. This was certainly the case in *Acadie*, for example, where a cleric, Pierre-Antoine-Simon Maillard, had written in 1753, "that he did not expect more than fifty years would elapse before the French colonists were so mixed with the Micmacs and the Malecites that it would be impossible to distinguish them" (Dickason, 1985, p. 24).

Over the generations, though, this history of mixing would largely be forgotten—even buried—by contemporary political voices aiming at limiting "Métis identity" to some Western-based communities in order to circumscribe the privileges linked with its recent constitutional recognition in Canada since 1982.

Emergence of a *Canadien* and Métis National Identity

The expansion of the British and later Americans was blocked by the French colonial forces that prevented the English colonies from expanding to the north and west. Before reaching the Mississippi, and beyond it the Pacific, they would have to dislodge the French as a military power in the Americas. This was done over a century with the conquest of Acadia in 1710, the Expulsions of the Acadians that began in 1755, the conquest of New France (Quebec City in 1759 and Montreal in 1760), followed by the Treaty of Paris in 1763, and the final sale of Louisiana in 1803 to the United States.

Though the French military and colonial regime was definitively extinguished by 1803, the descendants of the first French colonists remained. In New France, alternatively called Canada by the French, the inhabitants referred to themselves

homme Acadien.

Homme Acadien, Jacques Grasset de Saint-Sauveur, ca. 1788-1796. The history of French and First Nations in North America features various layers of métissage (mixing) both in terms of culture and parentage. The *Acadiens*, for example, featured numerous marriages bringing together the French and their Mi'kmaq neighbors. Thus, most *Acadiens* would have native ancestry. Although all *Acadiens* do not identify themselves as Métis, some do, either as *"Acadien métis"* or simply *"Métis."*

as *Canadien*, a term already in use by the seventeenth century and that has persisted into the twenty-first century. However, the *Canadiens* were made into a minority and came to be labeled as French-Canadians following several dramatic political changes. These included the forced 1840 Act of Union following the 1838 Rebellions that abolished Upper and Lower Canada, followed by the 1848 political reorganization of the united Province of Canada with responsible government granted to the legislative assembly, and then, finally, with the creation of the Dominion of Canada in 1867 that included the Province of Quebec as one component within the federation. This new identification developed as the

English, Scots and others gradually came to identify themselves as Canadian in the second half of the nineteenth century.

In the Maritimes, the French settlers and their descendants had come to call themselves *Acadien*, whereas in Louisiana the French speakers called themselves the Créoles of Louisiana. This latter term was used by both the original French settlers of Louisiana—those who came to Louisiana directly from France, as opposed to the Acadians who progressively re-settled the southwestern region over several decades, coming to be known as the "Cadiens" or Cajuns—and the French and Créole-speaking descendants of African slaves brought to North America from their colonies in the Caribbean. The boundaries were nonetheless quite malleable and there was a great deal of mixing occurring in Louisiana.

Most of the descendants of the first French settlers remained in the Americas. The French were already using the term Métis (and the variant Métif) to refer to those with mixed-heritage—European and indigenous—by the end of the seventeenth century. It was first used when speaking of the mestizo of Latin America and later would be used to speak of those with French and indigenous mixed heritage. An older variation of Métis was Métif, a term that will also be used by Gabriel Franchère in the 1810s to describe a man of mixed heritage to the West of the Rocky Mountains, in what is now Washington State. Though the 1820 publication uses the word Métif, the handwritten original manuscript as scanned by Aubin (Aubin & Franchère, 2002) used "mitif," suggesting that this was not a term imposed by Franchère, but rather one that was already in use in the Pacific Northwest. We will therefore include the term "Métis" to refer to all those communities of mixed-heritage both to the East and West of the Rockies, and to the North and South of the 49th parallel.

Unlike Acadia, women from France, be they the *filles du roi* in New France or the *filles à la cassette* in Louisiana, were sent to *Canadien* and Créole communities in an effort to ensure that most *Canadiens* in the core of both colonies would be to a lesser extent the product of the unions of French and Native American women. Although ample evidence of Métis or "Bois-Brulés" can be found in both Lower Canada and Upper-Canada, in the more distant territories of the *Pays d'en Haut*, Upper Louisiana, and the Red River there would be much more mixing and intermarriage, giving rise to groups like the *Canadien-Métis*.

Due to specific circumstances in the Canadian Prairies, some individuals and communities eventually came to identify themselves collectively as part of a "Métis Nation" apart from the Canadian identity, in a context in which the latter came to be increasingly associated with the Canadian nation-building project permitting various encroachments on the lands of the mixed-blood populations out West. This is an important segment of the history of the Métis Peoples of

North America, yet the ideological decision to reserve the capitalized "Métis" only for the descendants of mixed-ancestry of the Red River Valley or the Canadian Prairies is unfounded. This decision is based on the reductive interpretation of what could constitute the emergence of an ethnic identity. The distinction between "M" and "m" Métis to denote the difference between what would be the descendants of a people endowed by a "Collective Consciousness" versus what would be the descendants of lower form or immature "metis" communities, here reduced to the accidental and unaware status of being "merely-mixed," is unacceptable. (See Chapter 9)

The *Canadien* and Métis Settlements of the Pacific Northwest

The North West Company recruited the first settlers for the Pacific Northwest from its Canadian Prairie outposts and from Montreal. Reinforcements followed from the Red River district (Assiniboia), where the Hudson's Bay Company had developed a flourishing agricultural colony in the 1820s. This region was developing as a center of Métis culture in the Northwest, but it was also building upon the older French presence in the Illinois and the Great Lakes regions, dating back to the previous century. Though the development of the Métis can be traced to the establishment of fur trading posts in the Red River Valley and farther east and north in Rupert's Land, it is also tied to the history of the French forts and settlements that dotted the territories to the south of the Great Lakes and down the adjacent rivers to the Mississippi.

With the early colonization of New France, French settlers had fanned out across the continent. Many of these original soldiers and settlers remained in France's former colonies after the conquest of New France and the later sale of Louisiana. One such French settlement was located at a strategic mid-point in the continent, a linking settlement created at the turn of the seventeenth and eighteenth centuries in what is now southern Illinois. French settlements were located along the bottomlands of the Mississippi between the Cahokia and Kaskaskia rivers. This enclave deep in the interior of the continent soon grew to over half a dozen villages and several thousand settlers. The cluster of villages centered on the military and political authority vested in the commandant located at Fort de Chartres (now partially reconstructed), near the town of Prairie du Rocher, and extended as far east as Vincennes, Indiana.

The year before the lowering of the French Bourbon flag at Fort de Chartres in 1765, a new town would be founded just upriver on the opposite shore by a Louisiana Créole family, the Laclède-Chouteau clan. This settlement, named Saint-Louis, would quickly fill the subsequent void, becoming the commercial and political center for the region. Lewis and Clark recruited a number of crew members from this French enclave prior to embarking on their journey westward.

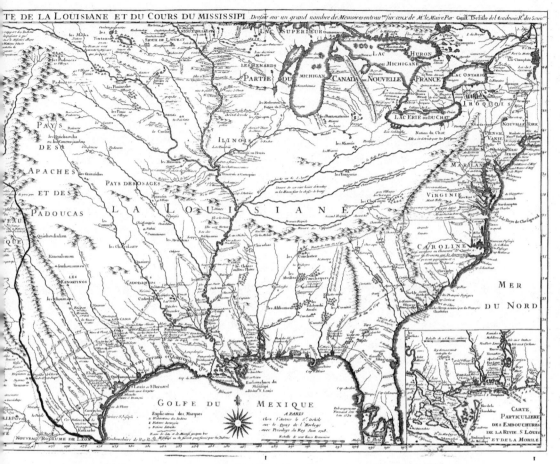

Carte de la Louisiane et du cours du Mississippi [map of North America], Guillaume de l'Isle, Paris, 1718. The Mississippi was the river that connected the St. Lawrence and the Great Lakes to the Gulf of Mexico. It cuts through the continent and provided a channel to move goods down to Lower Louisiana. In 1673 Louis Joliet accompanied by Father Jacques Marquette sailed down the Mississippi, but did not reach the Gulf of Mexico, turning back when they reached the Arkansas River. In 1682, René-Robert Cavelier de La Salle went down the Illinois to the Mississippi and named the new territory "Louysiane," which later became Louisiane and then Louisiana in honor Louis XIV. By establishing themselves in this territory, the French effectively encircled the thirteen English colonies on Atlantic seaboard and split the Spanish colony of New Spain. Note that inset of map provides details showing the two older Gulf coast French settlements of Biloxi and Mobile, plus the portage site between Lake Pontchartrain and the Mississippi where construction of New Orleans had just begun in 1718.

French settlers tended more often to take indigenous wives, and some of their children and descendants came to coalesce into autonomous communities in the upper Great Lakes and upper Mississippi regions. They founded villages and towns such as la Baie Verte (Green Bay), Michilimackinac, Prairie du Chien, Juneautown (later Milwaukee), Chicago, and St. Paul in the late 1700s and early 1800s. Some stayed behind in these growing settlements, needing to adapt to the waves of Americans that migrated to their territories and who had little tolerance for French-speaking "half-breeds" and their "Indian" ways. Others withdrew into the local swamp country along the rivers of southwestern Michigan and north-western Indiana, or continued to retreat further inland across the Mississippi and then Missouri. Still others followed a more northerly route into upper Michigan or the remote lake country of northern Minnesota and onto the Red River Valley. Ultimately, many ended up out on the plains beyond, somewhere between the 40th and 60th parallels.

As the beaver trade collapsed, the buffalo herds of the northern plains beckoned, drawing many of the French and indigenous mixed-blood populations westward to the Red River. Out there, a Métis culture and people emerged, organized around the buffalo hunt and relying upon the Red River carts adopted from the French-European culture that were used to transport goods across the plains. While more permanent settlements tended to shift laterally northward up the Red and Assiniboine Rivers in the early 1800s, Métis settlements could be found on the Pembina across North Dakota, along the upper Missouri River, and eventually central Montana. Somewhat later in the century, following a sequence of civil and military struggles with the new authorities of the Canadian Federation, other Red River bands began to permanently relocate during the 1870s and 1880s in a northwesterly direction, up the two branches of the Saskatchewan River.

One of the first names given to this population was the French term *Bois-Brûlé*, signifying charred or burnt wood. It is hypothesized that this term was a translation of the Chippewa appellation for them, *Wisahkotewan Niniwak* (Dusenberry, 1985, p. 120; Karahasan, 2006, p. 192). Linguistically, as long as the fur trade was going strong, the French language remained the *lingua franca* of the voyageurs and the Métis, though in certain regions a new bilingual mixed language emerged that was a fusion of French words, notably nouns, and Cree verbs. This new language is now known as "Michif," but the historical record indicates that it was not the main language spoken by most Métis, who continued instead to speak predominantly French, as well as one or more indigenous languages, well into the twentieth century.

The border—the 49th parallel—set in the 1818 Treaty cut across the territories inhabited by the Métis, running right through the heart of their community in

FRENCH HALF-BREED.

French Half-Breed, Frederic Remington, ca. 1892. The various names included *Bois-Brulé*, Métis, Mitif, "half-breed," and more but the phenomenon was the same: they were the children and descendants French trappers and voyageurs who traveled across the continent, took wives from among the native nations, and often settled along the rivers.

Pembina. For decades, the 49th parallel was ignored, as Métis traveled from the Red River to St. Paul and back. The Métis relied on the fur trade and worked to serve the needs of the competing companies. They were independent traders who sold pemmican—dried and crushed bison meat mixed with fat and berries—a staple of the fur trade that could easily be stored for months and which fed the voyageurs who paddled the waterways of the northwest transporting furs and trade goods across the continent. Pemmican and buffalo hides were sold to the North West Company and Hudson's Bay Company posts in the Red River, as well as in the later settlement of St. Paul to the south located on the upper Mississippi.

The Métis did come into conflict at times with the indigenous peoples in the territory: The Sioux, and later further west, the Blackfeet and Crow, who guarded their territories and would often fight to block the Métis from encroaching. As the American settlement continued to advance, however, the Métis and the Native Americans would both be forced to retreat further westward, until there was no place to go.

Though the main concentration of French-speaking people was in the St. Lawrence Valley, strings of French communities remained in the Great Lakes region and down the Ohio and Mississippi Valleys. With the continued need for skilled paddlers for the fur trade, competing trading companies seeking furs would recruit people who spoke French, including the *Canadiens* of the St. Lawrence Valley and the French-speaking Catholic Iroquois of Quebec, to serve as laborers in the fur trade. These men (as women did not join the convoys of men paddling out to the distant territories) would spend decades working for the companies, retiring in the shadows of their fur trading forts. They took local wives, and their children forged new identities—the best-known being that of the *Bois-Brûlé*, or the Métis. By early in the 1800s, the *Canadiens*, the Métis, and the French-speaking Catholic Iroquois had crossed the mountains and reached the Pacific coast.

The Iroquois Freemen

The Iroquois initially penetrated the region around 1808 under contract with the Montreal-based North West Company. Along with the Métis of the Great Lakes and Red River regions, these Iroquois were among the original freemen, or free agents, of the business. They quickly established their own base of operations in the Northern Rockies. Personal alliances of friendship and marriage with the Têtes-Plates (Flatheads), Kootenai, and the Nez Percé were key to maintaining their independence *vis-à-vis* the fur company monopolies, be they British or American-chartered. Their close relations with the interior tribes of the Northwest can be contrasted with the conflict-riddled early relationships with the tribes west of the Cascades, conflicts that sometimes degenerated into bloodshed—as occurred with the tribes of the Cowlitz and Umpqua Country. Despite a bad start near the coast, however, the situation improved over time.

In short order, the Iroquois spread from the Northern Rockies throughout the Pacific Northwest. They left behind many descendants among the interior tribes of the Pacific Northwest, especially among those that became the Confederated Salish and Kootenai Tribes of the Flathead Reservation. The territories of these confederated tribes covered what are now northwestern Montana, northern Idaho, and parts of Washington State and British Columbia. Indirectly, through their close relations with the Flathead and Nez Percé, the Iroquois familiarized these Northwest populations with the tenets of Christianity. This influence was greatly reinforced during the winter of 1829-30 by two young men who had returned to their tribes after attending the Anglican school at Red River for four years. The two were sons of prominent chiefs of the Spokane and Kootenay tribes. Re-named for Hudson's Bay Company Board members, they went by Spokan Garry and Kootenay Pelly. Lecturing and preaching to their own people, as well as gatherings including Nez Percé, Cœur d'Alene, Pend d'Oreille and Flatheads, the two immediately stirred up a high level of interest in Christianity throughout the tribes of the upper Columbia [Josephy, 1965, 84-90 and Ruby & Brown, 1981, 69-70].

In his book *The Adventures of Captain Bonneville*, Washington Irving introduced his readership to the presence of a band of Iroquois whose winter quarters were located on the Racine Amère (Bitter Root) River in what would now be Montana. Irving (1857, p. 107) notes, "They were of the remnants of a party of Iroquois hunters, that came from Canada into these mountain regions many years previously, in the employ of the Hudson's Bay Company." This party would have been led by an Iroquois by the name of "le grand Pierre" (the tall Pierre) Tevanitagon, who was later killed in a battle with the Blackfeet and after whom the valley of Pierre's Hole was named. Eugène Laveille, in his biography of Father De Smet, traces the migration of the Iroquois to a band of Catholic Iroquois who left Caughnawaga Mission (now Kahnawake) near Montreal between the years 1812 and 1820; this band would have traveled across the Mississippi Valley before settling in the territory of the Flatheads (Laveille, 1915, pp. 98-99).

Not only did these Iroquois also often speak French, they were at times strong proselytizers for the Catholic Church in their own right. One of the Iroquois, Ignace La Mousse—anglicized as Ignatius and referred to as Old Ignatius—had been baptized and married by the Jesuits, and often spoke to the Flatheads of his faith and beliefs, sharing with them his Catholic prayers. Laveille (1915, p. 99) writes that, "Beneath his native ruggedness and rare intelligence, the soul of an apostle lay hidden in Old Ignatius." His courage and loyalty acquired for him an influence, as well as the marriage ties, that united the Iroquois newcomers with the Flatheads. The conclusion of his discourse, according to Laveille (1915, p. 99) was always the same appeal: "send for a Black Robe to instruct them and show them the way to heaven."

Old Ignatius also reached out to the Pend d'Oreille and Nez Percé, neighboring peoples on friendly terms with the Flatheads (Tetes Plates), sharing with them the tenets of the Catholic faith. The names given to many of the indigenous nations of the Pacific Northwest were French, as the first outsiders to re-name them were the French-speaking voyageurs. Some were eventually translated into English, but many French names remained.

On several occasions during the 1830s delegations composed of a variable mix of Nez Percé, Flatheads, and Iroquois headed down the Missouri to St. Louis, a settlement that had been established in the eighteenth century by the Chouteaus, a family of French traders from New Orleans. The first delegation was Nez Percé, descending to St. Louis in 1831 with a returning caravan led by Lucien Fontenelle and Andrew Drips of the American Fur Company. Four of the Nez Percé made it all the way to St. Louis where they met with Bishop Rosati and William Clark, (still Superintendant of Indian Affairs), while Fontenelle acted as their guardian and sponsor. Three of the Nez Percé fell ill in St. Louis, with only one making it back to his people the following year, after returning up river with Fontenelle on an American Fur Company steamboat, the Yellowstone, then overland in Fontenelle's pack train (Josephy, 1965, 96-99).

Old Ignatius was himself killed along with his Flathead and Nez Percé companions by a Sioux war party as the third delegation made its way down the Platte River. On one of these expeditions, the party encountered protestant Methodists. The Methodists however, continued on to the Oregon Territory. Even following the tragic third failed expedition, a fourth delegation was organized that included two Iroquois, the Young Ignatius, and Peter Gaucher, who "had some knowledge of French," and left once again in direction for St. Louis (Laveille, 1915, p. 102). It is only after this fourth expedition that their request would be granted, and Father Pierre-Jean De Smet would travel westwards to the Rocky Mountains to serve as missionary and priest to the Iroquois, Flatheads, and other peoples of the Northwest. By then the Nez Percé had received a Protestant missionary group.

Not merely of religious import to the region's history, the Iroquois were aggressive trappers and consummate traders; though it is not always obvious, the Iroquois left their names on the maps and in the histories of the American West. As previously mentioned, the valley frequented by *Le grand* Pierre Tevanitagon in the 1820s became Pierre's Hole. Located just west of the Grand Tetons, it became a major battle site and later the locale of an important fur trade rendezvous. Another Iroquois hunter named John Grey, whose original name was Ignace Hatchioraquasha, co-founded Kansas City with François Chouteau and James McGee, permitting them to later profit from the migration along the Oregon Trail. Other Iroquois would be central to the history of the West, yet are easily overlooked in later histories. One such Iroquois pathfinder, a man known simply as Baptiste, figures prominently in the genealogy of one of the founding families of the Pacific Northwest and Montana. In his book, *Scottish Highlanders Indian Peoples: Thirty Generations of a Montana Family*, James Hunter describes Baptiste as a mixed-blood "freeman" who had made his way into the Columbia Country in the wake of the Nor'westers. Part Mohawk, Baptiste was a veteran of the War of 1812 who had fought with the British and had regaled his daughter, Catherine McDonald, with his stories of the war (Hunter, 1996, p. 105). Catherine in turn entertained her children with her account of the major trapping expedition that she and her father participated in, following the Colorado River down to the Gulf of California. Hunter (1996, p. 113) notes that "Baptiste […] would have pronounced his daughter's name in the French fashion because—like most all the other mixed blood freemen who followed the Nor'westers and the Bay Company across the Rockies—he was French speaking."

Also, as French was the only language shared by Catherine and her husband, Angus McDonald, this was the language of their household—the language spoken by *their* children (according to John Hunter in a personal communication to John Jackson). As the accounts of Baptiste's life as well as that of Old Ignatius illustrate, the French language was still in the 1830s a continental *lingua franca*, spoken from the Pacific, across the mountains, all the way to the Mississippi, down to Louisiana, and up north to the Great Lakes and across most of what is now Canada.

The Contested Northwest or the Northwest Contested?

All the leading colonial powers including Spain, Russia, Great Britain, and the U.S. explored the Pacific Northwest. After the War of 1812, the Treaty of 1818 drew the western border between British and American territories—the two primary powers in North America—at the 49th parallel to the Continental Divide of the Rocky Mountains. They settled on a joint control and occupancy of the Oregon Country to the West of the Continental Divide. The British had already asserted their presence in the region in the course of the War of 1812 with the Montreal-based North West Company, followed by the Hudson's Bay Company, establishing a number of forts along the Columbia River. Though the Hudson's Bay Company was British-owned, the nineteenth-century workers west of the divide spoke mainly French. A large segment of the employees of the fur trading companies of the Pacific Northwest also spoke French, including the short-lived, New York-based Pacific Fur Company, founded in 1810 and sold in 1813 to the North West Company. The North West Company later merged with its rival, the Hudson's Bay Company, and after the merger between 1821 and 1824 the London-based Hudson's Bay Company would dominate the business.

The fate of the region, however, was eventually to be decided by the opening of the Oregon Trail from the Missouri River to the Oregon Country. The first American settlers arrived by wagon train in 1841, leading to the migration of thousands of settlers from the Eastern United States to the Oregon Country over the following decade. In 1846, Great Britain and the United States agreed that Britain would cede its claims to the lands south of the 49th parallel to the west of the Continental Divide; in turn, the United States would abandon all claims to the lands north of the 49th parallel. A large percentage of the French-Canadian and increasingly Métis employees of the Hudson's Bay Company would remain in the Oregon Country, a territory that would become the states of Oregon and Washington, along with western Montana. Having spent the greater part of their adult lives in the American Northwest, they now called this home.

The largest single French-Canadian settlement, scattered above the falls in Oregon's Willamette Valley, was called French Prairie. One of its component villages, Champoeg, was destroyed in a flood in the 1860s, but others—St. Paul, St. Louis, Butteville, and Gervais—are still there. Champoeg is now part of a state park and historic site of the same name. Their stories have been well researched and incorporated into mainstream Oregon state history. This has not been the case for their brethren north of the Columbia in Washington State and western Montana. In western Washington Territory, the oldest French-Canadian settlement—and the region's first Catholic Church, St. François Xavier—were both located at Cowlitz Prairie, just north of modern-day Toledo. Most of the subsequent settlements, however, were within the Columbia River basin on the far side of the Cascade Mountains.

In spite of the challenges facing the Métis in the Red River, recruiting settlers to leave the Red River Valley to relocate to the Oregon Country in the early 1840s proved challenging. Given the uncertain status of the Oregon territories, settlers were unwilling to enter into long-term leases on property. Nonetheless, twenty-three families, mostly Métis, were assembled by Assiniboia Governor Duncan Finlayson in June 1841 and left the Red River settlement on a three-month over-land trek to Fort Vancouver. After a short stay at the post, John McLoughlin directed fourteen English-speaking Métis families to lands at Fort Nisqually, and the remaining families, composed of French-*Canadiens* and Métis, to Cowlitz Farms (Foxcurran, 2012, pp. 22-26).

Complaints over conditions of settlement were immediately voiced: houses were not completed, and farm implements were in short supply. The greater problem hindering colonial development, however, was the lure of life across the Columbia River in the fertile Willamette Valley—a place where Euro-American settlement had been prospering for over a decade and where the prevailing expectations were that rights to patented land would be guaranteed. The families that had been settled under lease arrangements on the rocky soil around Fort Nisqually had drifted south of the Columbia by late 1843. The more favorable conditions at Cowlitz Landing, on the other hand, caused that colony to expand to sixty-four people by the same date. These thirteen French-*Canadien* families at Cowlitz Farms constituted the first European-American settlement in what is now Washington, founded on a principally agricultural base.

The presence of French-speaking people is recorded in the "Frenchtowns" that remain in what was the historic Washington Territory. These include the Frenchtown of Western Montana, an outer suburb of Missoula, and the

Frenchtown that is marked solely by an historic site on the outskirts of Walla Walla in southeastern Washington State. Each of these Frenchtowns served as a refuge in the interior for settlers who had found themselves in the way of "progress" in the Willamette Valley and areas closer to the coast. The destiny of each settlement was closely entangled with those of nearby reservations of the Umatilla and the Flathead. The Frenchtown of Washington State also served as the site of an important battle pitting local native populations against the encroaching American colonial powers. Each of these Frenchtowns was subsequently eclipsed in turn by its Anglo-American twin city upstream—Walla Walla and Missoula (Foxcurran, 2012, pp. 22-26).

Background to these Frenchtowns and the founding families that shaped the history of the American West and Pacific Northwest will be the subject of future works. Connecting the dots increasingly reveals patterns worthy of note. However, these roadside attractions are generally treated as local anecdotes and not as part of a broader regional or continental phenomenon. As Wolf (1982, p. 23) explains, it is necessary to "delineate the general processes at work in mercantile and capitalist development, while at the same time following their effects on the micro-populations studied by ethnohistorians and anthropologists."

It became increasingly apparent that this entailed much more than producing a history of a few families like the Chouteau, Robidoux, or the St. Vrain families, who had left their names behind as founders of towns in California, Colorado, Kansas, Missouri, Montana, and North Dakota. Nor is it solely a case of providing accounts of individuals such as the poor, bushwhacked Jacques Laramie in Wyoming, whose name and legacy is tied to a river, a mountain range, a fort, a treaty, a university, and a town. It is not the simple question of recording relevant toponyms around the Northwest, such as the names of many of the tributaries of the Columbia-Snake river system, and the names of towns such as the Dalles and Boise—or topographical terms like coulee, butte, plateau, or prairies that could not be found in an English dictionary two centuries ago yet figure prominently in the maps of the United States.

Rather, the goal is to understand the larger historical forces that shaped the history of the French-speaking people of American West and the Pacific Northwest in order to record their contribution to the history of the region and the continent. This includes the economic forces that shaped the fur trade, the expansion of the Hudson's Bay Company, which founded the first permanent agricultural and manufacturing settlements, the company's eventual withdrawal from the Oregon Country, and the demographic forces that shaped the early history of the state.

Even though the seminal economic role of the Hudson's Bay Company in Washington state history is generally recognized, the demographics associated with its operations are typically ignored, or at best relegated to a marginally relevant footnote. Generally true of histories encompassing the larger American West, this is especially the case for the state of Washington, where most of the HBC facilities and personnel west of the Rockies were initially located. While the HBC slowly expanded northward, the large majority of the thousand or so former employees and family members identified in the first Catholic Church census remained in the Pacific Northwest, relocating initially to the south of the Columbia River.

Starting around 1830, as previously mentioned, they began settling around Champoeg and St. Paul, along the Willamette River, in an area that came to be called French Prairie. These settlers accounted for roughly sixty percent of the original Astorian, North West Company, and HBC employees that had permanently relocated to the Pacific Northwest over four decades. Still others settled in the Washington Territory, while a small number of employees followed the HBC and James Douglas north to Vancouver Island and up the Fraser River Valley, into central British Columbia and along the Pacific Coast of Canada (Foxcurran, 2012, pp. 22-26).

The original settlers served to shape the demography of the Washington frontier. Immigrants from Canada and Great Britain combined constituted the largest single group of Euro-American settlers in Washington Territory until the 1880s. Migrants from Canada continued to move into Washington during the first half of the twentieth century and constituted the state's largest foreign-born population (Sid White & Solberg, 1989, p. 17).

The *Canadiens* that went west and settled to the south of the 49th parallel often fall out of Canadian history, yet are never truly written into American national history. Local histories often do acknowledge the importance of the Canadian migration—notably accounts such as James Davis' (2000) *Frontier Illinois* and Mark Wyman's (1998) *The Wisconsin Frontier*, which examine the history of the French settlement of these territories in some depth. In Washington State, however, the topic of Canadian migration and settlement, whether English, French, or Métis, is largely ignored, and it is necessary to present some background information.

The Fur Trade and the Pacific Northwest

At the same time the Lewis and Clark Expedition was heading back over the Rocky Mountains in 1806, the North West Company based in Montreal was sending its parties into the interior of the Pacific Northwest to establish permanent outposts. Simon Fraser took the lead in the upper Fraser River basin, followed by David Thompson and his team in the upper and middle Columbia basin. The North West Company workforce—a mix of Iroquois and various other indigenous groups, Métis, French *Canadiens*, and Highland Scots—fanned out across the interior northwest over the next several years. In 1811, the Americans,

Fort Vancouver, Washington Territory, Gustav Sohon, 1854. John McLoughlin (baptized Jean-Baptiste, in Rivière-du-Loup, Quebec) was chief factor of Fort Vancouver established in 1825 following the merger of the North West Company and the Hudson's Bay Company. He oversaw a multilingual and multicultural mix of employees. French was the principal language used at the fort.

under the direction of John Jacob Astor in New York, returned to the mouth of the Columbia River to establish a foothold for Astor's Pacific Fur Company. This new Pacific outpost was intended to expand upon the existing coastal trade in sea otter furs for export to China on ships based out of Boston and other American seaports. Sailing out of New York, the mixed crew was predominantly *Canadien* and Scot, along with a number of Kanakas, the indigenous people of Hawaii, who were picked up during a resupply stop in what was then known as the Sandwich Islands (Hawaii).

With the outbreak of the War of 1812 and the subsequent expected arrival of the British navy in Astoria, the partners in Astoria sold the Pacific Fur Company two years later to the North West Company. The new owners as of 1813 retained much of the workforce in place. Little changed for the employees, as many were former employees of the North West Company. The flag as well changed—temporarily—for a few decades until the region became incorporated into the United States in the 1840s. Pacific Northwest fur trading consolidated even further following a merger of the North West Company with its bitter rival, the London-based Hudson's Bay Company.

As was the case with the previous acquisition, a large portion of the local work force was retained, with many of those who were not re-hired invariably remaining in the region. Many of the former employees had been either adopted by or married into local tribes, gaining through kinship access to hunting grounds and trading networks. Some began operating increasingly as members of these tribes while engaging in the fur trade as independents, or *gens libres* (freemen). Furthermore, several of the factors had previously worked for the North West Company farther east, including Nor'westers such as John McLoughlin and Peter Skeen Ogden.

The HBC's Fort Vancouver and its Cosmopolitan Village

Fort Vancouver was established in 1825 with the Columbia Department's reorganization following the merger of the North West Company and the Hudson's Bay Company. The merger had occurred in London in 1821, but it took until the fall of 1824 for the new management to arrive on site and begin the realignment of facilities and manpower. Orders to replace Spokane House by the construction of a much larger Fort Colville complex located directly on the Columbia River were initiated on the way down to the coastal Fort George headquarters inherited from the North West Company. This company, as previously mentioned, had in turn acquired Fort George from Astor's Pacific Fur Company in 1813 during a state of war between the two colonial empires. Along the same lines as the seminal Spokane House, the cramped Fort George would be reduced to a port and piloting facility, while a more spacious setting would be located upriver for the new headquarters. Space was needed to establish more self-sufficient operations that could also serve as a base for directly exporting a more diverse set of products to Alaska, California (a state of the newly independent First Mexican Empire from 1821 until the American invasion of 1846), Hawaii, and places beyond.

The new Hudson's Bay Company Governor, George Simpson, chose a site that North West Company employees had come to call Jolie Prairie, which covered the slopes extending gradually up from Point Bellevue on the Columbia. The new post would bear the name of the most prominent explorer of the region, the Royal Navy's Captain Vancouver. Vancouver had mapped the Pacific Northwest shoreline in detail between 1792 and 1794, while wintering in Maui. Well-tanned crew members including Puget, Whidbey, and numerous others left their names on local maps alongside those of prominent Royal Navy Admirals of the day such as Rainier and Hood. Vancouver's men had also been the first Europeans to explore up the Columbia, having attained a point just above the new fort. The name Fort Vancouver was a bit of a misnomer, as it was in fact not much of a fort. It did, however, develop quickly into a diversified farming, manufacturing, ranching, and trading plantation whose operations stretched for many miles along the north side of the Columbia River, near its confluence with the Willamette. Operations included a major sawmill, workshop for coopers, a blacksmith shop, apple orchards, extensive fields of grain, dairy farming, plus cattle and sheep herds soon numbering in the hundreds, then thousands—with everything being produced destined either for local use or for external trade.

Governor Simpson brought with him the former North West Company wintering partner and doctor from Rivière-du-Loup, Quebec, whose name was John McLoughlin, though he had been baptized Jean-Baptiste. His father was Irish Catholic, and his mother, Angélique, was a very devout Catholic mother who considered herself French-Canadian and raised her children accordingly. She was estranged from her father, Malcolm Fraser, who was a Presbyterian Scot. Malcolm had served as a junior officer with Highlanders at the Battle of the Plains of Abraham in 1759, and had returned as one of the officers involved in the successful defense of Quebec City when the American Revolutionary Army attacked it in 1775. Immediately after the Conquest, Malcolm was awarded the seigneury of Mount Murray, located just over a hundred kilometers down the north shore of the St. Lawrence, across from Rivière-du-Loup. Angélique was born there around 1760, followed by three younger brothers named Alexander, Joseph, and Simon. Alexander Fraser later became a partner in the North West Company, and Dr. Simon Fraser became an officer in the British Army. Both of these uncles, along with the maternal grandfather, were to play prominent roles in the education and the early career of bilingual Jean-Baptiste McLoughlin, and his younger Brother, Dr. David McLoughlin, who would practice his profession in Paris.

As Chief Factor at Fort Vancouver, McLoughlin oversaw a multicultural and multilingual mix of employees who had worked for the Hudson's Bay Company or the North West Company—or both. As David Lavender writes, the French language was the principal language at the Fort, along with the Chinook trade jargon, a pidgin that was used for trade and commerce across the Oregon Territory up into what is now central British Columbia. The employees had a tendency to segregate themselves within the Fort, with the French *Canadiens* and Métis (half-breeds) in one area, the Hawaiians in another location, and the English-speakers in an entirely separate place. Most of the women living at the Fort were wives from neighboring indigenous peoples, notably the Chinook, with some from Salish and Sahaptian-speaking tribes. New hires might later come in from England, Scotland, and even a few from Ireland, but the core of staffing would remain former Nor'westers. Moreover, the French speakers would remain the largest contingent of employees in the forts.

Episcopal clergyman, geographer, and geologist Charles Grenfell Nicolay (1846, p. 173) visited Fort Vancouver in 1843, providing another, more detailed description of the village and surrounding operations: "Beyond the fort are large granaries and storehouses; and before it, on the bank of the river, is the village in which the servants of the company reside; in all, the residents may be seven hundred. In the village is a hospital." Nicolay continues his description with an account of a magnificent farm of more than 3,000 acres, with sawmills cutting hundreds of thousands of board feet per year. From this outpost the Company not only shipped goods back to Great Britain, but also engaged in active trade with the Sandwich Islands (Hawaii), California, and the Russian settlements. Nicolay (1846, p. 174) describes how the guns and palisades of the Fort had been taken down, making way for a thriving commercial and agricultural center.

For nearly two decades, from the late 1820s to the late 1840s, the Fort Vancouver plantation and its village constituted the largest metropolitan center along the Pacific coast of what are now the U.S. and Canada. Nicolay (1846, p. 174) provides a telling account of the inhabitants of Fort Vancouver:

> The Company's servants are principally Scotch and Canadians, but there is also a great number of half-breeds, children of the Company's servants and Indian women. These are generally a well-featured race, ingenious, athletic, and remarkably good horsemen; the men make excellent trappers, and the women, who frequently marry officers of the Company, make clever, faithful, and attentive wives; they are ingenious needlewomen, and good managers. They frequently attend their husbands in their trading excursions, in which they are most useful; they retain some peculiarities of their Indian ancestors, among which is the not infrequent use of the moccasin, though usually it is made of ornamented cloth, instead of deerskin.

The Canadians that Nicolay refers to in this passage would be *Canadiens*, the French-speaking voyageurs. Nicolay (1846, pp. 80-81) also describes in detail the "joyous chorus of their boat-songs, as their canoes or batteaux [sic] dance madly over the foam of the torrent, to the inexperienced eye threatening immediate destruction, and which, indeed, even their skill and courage cannot always prevent."

A final account highlighting the cultural diversity and the stratification that existed in Fort Vancouver is that of English-Canadian painter Paul Kane, a man who traveled across the continent with voyageurs, visiting the Pacific Northwest later in the 1840s. Kane (1859, p. 171) details the multicultural and multilingual nature of Fort Vancouver in an account of his arrival in 1846:

> FORT VANCOUVER, the Indian name of which is Katchutequa, or "the Plain," is the largest post in the Hudson's Bay Company's dominions, and has usually two chief

factors, with eight or ten clerks and 200 voyageurs, residing there. Our society was also enlivened by the addition of the officers of Her Majesty's ship of war the "Modeste," which had been on this station for two years, and lay in the river opposite the establishment. The buildings are enclosed by strong pickets about sixteen feet high, with bastions for cannon at the corners. The men, with their Indian wives, live in log huts near the margin of the river, forming a little village — quite a Babel of languages, as the inhabitants are a mixture of English, French, Iroquois, Sandwich Islanders, Crees and Chinooks.

Kane's description differs from that of Nicolay's from a few years earlier in that he specifies that the palisades and bastions were still standing. Kane (1859, p. 172) does stress the "immense herds of domesticated horned cattle" that the Fort now owns, imported by Dr. McLoughlin from California, as well as the rich farms eight miles inland that produce "more grain than the fort consumes" with surpluses being shipped to the Sandwich Islands (Hawaii) and the Russian dominions. It is clear from all accounts, then, that Fort Vancouver was emerging as a thriving and growing center—a center in which the use of French was dominant

HBC's Fort Colville at Kettle Falls

The second largest establishment of the Hudson's Bay Company west of the Rockies was Fort Colville, a trading post in the northeast corner of what is now Washington State. As Fort Vancouver supplanted the cramped Fort George (Astoria) near the mouth of the Columbia River, Fort Colville replaced Spokane House, which had been set up in 1810 by the North West Company's David Thompson, Jacko Finlay, and Finan McDonald a year before Astor's crew established a post at the mouth of the Columbia. During the first of Governor Simpson's three visits to the Columbia District following the HBC-NWC merger, he chose a site for the new Fort Colville directly on the Columbia near a major indigenous village and trade center at Kettle Falls. The village was located just below the falls, with the HBC complex just above them. Kettle Falls is a later translation of the French name the *Canadiens* gave the falls, *les Chutes des Chaudières*, describing the cavities or cauldrons naturally occurring below them. Kettle Falls had been a major portage and gathering point of Native Americans on the Columbia for millennia, and thus was an ideal location to establish a fur trading post.

Along with the surrounding farmland, the Fort Colville complex included a store, a blacksmith, a windmill, and a boatyard. The fort came to dominate the inland fur trade in the northwest, second in importance only to Fort Vancouver. The surrounding fertile soil supplied nearly all of the Hudson's Bay Company food supplies in the upper Columbia River region. The windmill helped provide flour to the post and to the surrounding villages and settlers, while the boathouse built small river craft that would transport supplies up the Columbia or for portage over the Rocky Mountains. The HBC's Fort Colville establishment remained operational until 1871. The two smaller downstream outposts lying between it and Fort Vancouver along the Columbia were Forts Okanogan and Walla Walla. Each of these outposts were located at the confluence of a tributary river of the same name, though Fort Walla Walla also went intermittently by the name of Fort Nez Percé.

HBC and Indigenous Relations in the Pacific Northwest

The economic forces and the need for the Hudson's Bay Company to maintain peaceful relations with the neighboring indigenous peoples shaped early relations with them. In his biography of Isaac Stevens, Kent Richards (1993) points out that under the stewardship of the Hudson's Bay Company it was agreed that the indigenous peoples should receive fair treatment from the Company. Employees of the company such as McLoughlin took indigenous or Métisse wives, thus entering into kinship alliances with local populations and bringing the two groups closer together over time. The relationship between the Company and the Native Americans upon whom it depended was founded upon policies that required that the Company treat their trading partners consistently.

During his long tenure in the Northwest, John McLoughlin became a larger-than-life figure, respected by settlers and Native Americans alike; he ruled with a firm hand, but he did not interfere much with the indigenous way of life (Richards, 1993, p. 192). The close and mutually beneficial relations of the early contact period are evident in the evolution of an existing pidgin, the Chinook Jargon, which would be used by European traders and their indigenous trading partners across the Pacific Northwest.

The Chinook Jargon (or Chinuk Wawa)

Though French was the *lingua franca* among the newcomers of European and mixed-heritage backgrounds, the complete linguistic picture among the new arrivals is much more complex. With an increasingly indigenous and mixed work force, along with an admixture of French-speaking Iroquois from back east and Kanakas from the Hawaiian Islands, the polyglot Hudson's Bay Company and its predecessors in the Pacific Northwest operated linguistically at three different levels. English served as the written language and was used primarily among the officers (many of whom also knew Gaelic), while the spoken language of almost all of the employees—and their children—was French, the language also spoken by the officers when they addressed their men or in conversing with their own Métisse wives and children. The pidgin known as the Chinook Jargon in English, or the Chinuk Wawa by its native speakers, was spoken with local indigenous groups, with native wives originating from local tribes, and initially with children of mixed heritage. It is perhaps important to point out that individual employees were usually comfortable with one or more indigenous languages, depending upon previous postings, as well as the native language of wives and in-laws.

An example of bilingualism further inland would be the *Canadien* accompanying the Jesuit Father Pierre-Jean de Smet, who spoke enough Sioux to serve as translator, cultural guide, and interpreter, and thus defuse a potentially hostile situation and ensure that the Sioux warriors would accept the Catholic priest (P.-J. de Smet, 1875, p. 68). Consequently, this core community—actually a network of communities numbering roughly one thousand people by the early 1840s in the Pacific Northwest —was usually at least bilingual, while many were polyglots speaking three or four languages. The Chinook Jargon, a pidgin language, originally bridged multiple Native and European tongues, providing a mode of communication that served for an initial period, until people became sufficiently conversant in two or more languages during an interim period. Later generations would become unilingual English speakers.

The Chinook Jargon represents one of the most unique aspects of the Pacific Northwest's history, and (like so many other aspects) straddles the 49th parallel. Unlike similar trade pidgins that developed along our eastern shores in the early contact period, including the Basque-Algonquinian in use with the cod fisheries off Newfoundland and Acadia, Delaware Jargon in the mid-Atlantic region, and the one called Mobilian in heavy use along the gulf states of the future United States in the late sixteenth and seventeenth century, the Chinook Jargon survived and remained in wide-spread use into the early twentieth century.

The populous *Canadien* and Métis settlements at Fort Vancouver and in the Willamette Valley served as crucibles where the mature pidgin formed, as George Lang (2008) has shown. Historians Robie Reid (1942) and Frederick Howay (1943) reported that the Astorians and North West Company found a mixed dialect still heavily reliant on the earlier Nootka Jargon. Over time, however, Chinook and French words supplanted many of the original Nuu-chah-nulth words (Mackie, 1997, p. 296). French was the working language of the British fur trade, even on the Pacific coast. "'Speaking the Canadian French as fluently as I do English,' Londoner George Roberts recalled, 'when I came to this country little more than French was heard'" (Mackie, 1997, p. 296). The French traveler, Eugène Duflot de Mofras, who traversed the region in 1841-1842 claimed that Chinook included "innumerable" French expressions. "Many natives," he wrote, "especially the children, can understand our language [French] without difficulty" (Mackie, 1997, p. 296).

French as Lingua Franca

We submit that the French language served as a continental *lingua franca* from the St. Lawrence across the Old Northwest and the Great Plains, up the Missouri and the Canadian prairies, all the way to the Pacific coast. In subsequent chapters, it will be shown how French was pervasive in the early history of the American and Canadian West and that the language, though submerged by later waves of migration, managed to survive in the Pacific Northwest well into the twentieth century. For a while, French ate away at the Chinook Jargon, making the pidgin increasingly "Frenchified."

George Lang (1991, p. 52) points out the bias of contemporary researchers who too often study the history of the fur trade but neglect its crucial linguistic underpinnings. His observations more than twenty-five years ago ring true today:

> It is as if native and white cultures fell into contact and conflict without the mediation of language; as if the language in which most official fur trade records survive and in which we now write its history was the language in which it occurred; as if, in fact, language learning, in particular that of the indigenous ones which were the Voyageur's stock-in-trade, were not an essential component of the 'many tender ties' that bound him, his family, and the trade together. (Lang, 1991, p. 52)

Lang's central point is that there was no true continental trade pidgin in the fur trade; rather, it was voyageur French that served as the main medium of communication across the continent during the fur trade, both to the north and south of the 49th parallel. Many mid-nineteenth century visitors to the American West were astonished to hear Native Americans address them in French, which was the language used as the Americans pushed west. Indeed, many *Canadiens* served as boatmen and interpreters, thus ensuring the success of the Lewis and Clark Expedition. Lang (1991, p. 53) writes: "as long as the socioeconomic conditions of the fur trade prevailed, Voyageur French was the operative mediative language on the ground in northern North America." It will be shown that this was equally valid in the Pacific Northwest.

In recent years, however, greater emphasis has been placed on Michif, a veritable bilingual mixed language composed of largely French nouns and Cree verbs. Peter Bakker (1989, 1997, 2003), a Dutch linguist, has written extensively on Michif, emphasizing how the language spoken by the Métis differs from other French dialects, while focusing on this language, one that is largely a mixture of French and Cree.

There is a great deal of confusion surrounding the term Michif. This appellation is applied to the fused French-Cree bilingual mixed language, and is used by some, not all, to refer to the French language spoken by Métis, with the term Michif certainly having derived from the Métis pronunciation of the older term Métif and signifying the descendants of the French-speaking voyageurs and their indigenous wives. The European language spoken by the majority of the histor-ical Métis would have been at its core French, with archaisms and some phonetic particularities that distinguish it from other forms of French on the continent. Naturally, this language would feature a number of indigenous loan words, but it would still be French.

An example of one such variety of Métis *Canadien* French is provided by the French Oblate priest, Adrien-Gabriel Morice, who describes a language that is composed of French words, but whose syntax was influenced by indigenous lan-guages. He gives this example as to how he would have to speak to the Métis to be understood in northern British Columbia: "*L'bon Dieu son garçon quand çà i devient la même chose comme nous autres, le Yâble c'lui-là quasiment tout le monde son bourgeois. Y en a il est faraud, y en a il est fou, puis quasiment tous i fait pas bon ene aut'sorte. Rien que que'ques-uns il est comme i faut: c'lui-là il est dans la Judée, l'bon Dieu ses gens son pays*" (Adrien G. Morice, 1897, p. 157). [Morice provides the standard French rendition: "*Quand le Fils de Dieu se fit homme, le démon était maître de presque tout le monde. Beaucoup étaient orgueilleux, beaucoup étaient adonnés à la luxure et Presque tous se livraient à d'autres désordres. Quelques-uns seulement étaient justes, et ceux-là se trouvaient en Judée, le pays du peuple de Dieu.*" This translates as: "When the Son of God became man, the Devil was master of almost everyone. Many were proud, many were engaged in lechery, and almost all delivered themselves to other disorders. Only a few were just, and those ones were in Judea, the land of God's people."]

The example that Morice provides is quite typical of the French language spoken by the Métis, and not the Michif bilingual mixed language. There are no indigenous loan words in the example provided by Morice, and the verbs are French, but it does have grammatical elements common to Métis speakers that have been recorded elsewhere. The use of a particular form of possessive, for example, highlighted in Morice's passage—*L'bon Dieu son garçon* instead of *le garçon du bon Dieu* and *l'bon Dieu ses gens son pays* instead of *le pays des gens (du peuple) du bon Dieu*—was also noted in the spoken language of other Métis to the East of the Rocky Mountains. This particular form of possessive was cer-tainly due to the influence of the Cree or other indigenous languages (Papen, 1984, p. 129).

This language, the language of the Métif that was still by and large French, was pushed aside politically in the recent past in favor of the mixed language of Michif, which has been consecrated as "the language of the Métis people of Canada and the United States" by Wikipedia—going from one form of language spoken by some Métis, a language that would have been marginal to the Métis communities even in the nineteenth century, to the language supposedly spoken by *all* Métis.

Though northern British Columbia is distant from the lower Columbia, it was nonetheless part of the same cultural network during the fur trade. Men and goods would move up and down the Columbia and Fraser Rivers, and noteworthy HBC workers such as Pierre-Chrysologue Pambrun worked in the district of New Caledonia (now northern British Columbia) before relocating to his ultimate residence in what is now southeastern Washington. Thus, if the Métis of the periphery of the larger cultural and trade zone spoke French, then clearly the Métis of the core areas of the fur trade would certainly have spoken that language as well, and would likely have spoken a more standard voyageur French given the greater numbers that had settled in the Columbia basin. The historical and linguistic evidence has forced linguists to acknowledge that the mixed language Michif, a fusion primarily composed of southern Plains Cree and French, was only spoken by a minority of the continental Métis. In his latest publication, Peter Bakker (2012, p. 172) concurs: "It [Michif] has probably always been a minority language among Métis. Some were predominantly or exclusively French speakers, whereas others were speakers of Saultaux, Swampy Cree, or Plains Cree."

The mixed language certainly arose among those buffalo hunters who wintered with indigenous kin, whereas the Métis farmers were predominantly French-speaking (Bakker, 2012, p. 173). As such, even in the Red River Valley and surrounding territories where we find speakers of the mixed language, Michif speakers are still a minority as compared to those Métis who spoke either French or a Métis dialect of French. Even those who spoke the mixed language would certainly have been bilingual in both Cree and French, and this bilingualism (and multilingualism with the growing importance of English) would have been maintained well into the twentieth century.

The linguistic and historic evidence demonstrates that the *Canadien* voyageurs, often depicted disparagingly by the English as somewhat uncouth—or, as one documentary describes them, the "truck drivers" of the fur trade—were skilled linguists adept at living in a multilingual environment (Lang, 1991, p. 52). These voyageurs could speak a number of languages and would willingly spend extended periods living in indigenous villages, invariably taking local women as wives. The *Canadiens* who elected to be voyageurs perhaps chose the life as it offered greater freedoms than were possible in either France or the settlements of New France (Canada). However, as Lang notes, the voyageur never did abandon his language or develop a true pidgin/creole, as even the mixed language of Michif was and is marginal (Lang, 1991). The voyageur can instead be characterized by "virtuoso bilingualism" (Lang, 1991, p. 61), whereby he prospered in a multilingual environment in which his skills in navigating the linguistic landscape as well as the physical terrain ensured his success. Lang (1991, p. 61) also points out, however, that the voyageur also "prepared his own demise" when the multilingual terrain was incorporated into states that pushed unilingual agendas while divesting the indigenous peoples of their lands. This is evident in the history of the Pacific Northwest on both sides of the border, where the voyageurs would establish a foothold in the region, then later serve as cultural translators and mediators between the American or British-Canadian government agents and indigenous peoples; once Anglo-American or British-Canadian hegemony was fully imposed, the voyageurs would be shunted aside, their language, descendants, and stories simply written out of history.

From Fort to Settlement

Five years into his tenure as Chief Factor at a rapidly growing Fort Vancouver, John McLoughlin began to back away from implementing an interim HBC requirement affecting retiring employees. The policy called for the return of all employees to the places where they had been hired once they had completed their employment contracts. For most *Canadiens* this would be Montreal. Hudson's Bay Company policy originally sought to prohibit the settlement of retired employees around its extensive farmlands surrounding Fort Vancouver, though the policy continued in the immediate vicinity of Fort Vancouver until the late 1840s.

McLoughlin began to relax the policy for outlying locations by the late 1820s. Most of those who wanted to settle in the region following the completion of their contracts chose to cross the Columbia River and paddle up the Willamette. Later, others went to one of the approved settlement areas to the north of the Columbia River or farther inland. Then, with the cession of territories south of the 49th parallel to the United States, the Hudson's Bay Company no longer had the power or authority to enforce its policies. Retired employees came to settle the lands surrounding Fort Vancouver and other outposts, making land claims that fall under U.S. law which involved, among other things, making a documented statement of their intention to become citizens.

With the arrival of the U.S. Army in 1849 and the Donation Land Law of the following year, the rights of French *Canadien* and Métis settlers in and around the newly Americanized town obtained under the Provisional Government became firmly cemented. However, the Donation Land Law also prompted settlers from other regions of United States to migrate there. Also known as the Oregon Land Law, it allowed Americans and "American half-breeds" over the age of eighteen who had resided in the territory prior to 1850 to claim any 320 acres of unsurveyed lands and receive title for those lands if they resided and cultivated those lands for four consecutive years. At that time, few of these "American Half-Breeds," as they were referred to in the legislation, were actually American citizens or spoke much English. However, they could comply simply by formally declaring their intention to become Americans. Hawaiians who had worked for the Hudson's

Bay Company could not stake a claim. Blacks who began arriving in small numbers later with the other Americans were also thereby formally excluded from land claims, at least initially. However, this exclusion of blacks was ignored north of the Columbia. Single women were also excluded, as only a married man could claim an additional 320 acres on his wife's behalf. The rules were then adjusted for settlement going forward. Any "White American" male over the age of twenty-one who arrived between December 1, 1850, and December 1, 1853, could claim 160 acres, and an additional 160 acres if they were married. The timeline was later extended to 1855. Men of indigenous-white mixed race, after December 1850, were technically excluded, which could provide opportunities for white American claim-jumpers.

An examination of the Munnick's Catholic Church Records of the Pacific Northwest for the Fort Vancouver area in the 1850s reflects the waning influence of the Hudson's Bay Company as the new settlers moved in to claim their homesteads. Records of baptisms, weddings, burials, and conversions all show a shrinking HBC presence. However, the passing of the act required that the indigenous peoples who had inhabited their traditional territories be relocated and their rights to the land extinguished. The 1850s witnessed the beginning of forced relocation of the indigenous nations to reserves. Conflicts erupted between the original inhabitants of the territory and the new settlers claiming their lands in the Oregon Country, conflicts—and even open warfare—that will be examined in another work.

With the American Army stationed on a nearby ridge, the Hudson's Bay Company Fort Vancouver remained as a trading and agricultural establishment, but quickly began its inexorable decline. In 1849, the Board of Management that replaced the retired McLoughlin relocated the HBC headquarters to Fort Victoria, a territory that remained under British tenure. Through the 1850s, the HBC trading post continued to do good business, but with ever fewer dedicated employees in place. The HBC's Fort Vancouver operation was left to run down in the course of the decade, and was finally shut down in 1860.

Fort Colville would thrive for decades, being one of the last of the HBC establishments to be abandoned in Washington State in 1871. The fort persisted some twenty-five years after a treaty extended the 49th parallel beyond the Rockies to the Pacific, giving the United States sovereignty over the territory. The 1846 treaty had left Fort Colville forty miles south of the new border. According to Barman and Watson (1999), during the intervening forty-six years, some 250 employees of the HBC had cycled through the fort, and many had stayed in the area after their contracts had finished.

The site of the HBC trading post has since disappeared. Abandoned in 1871, the remaining buildings burned down in a fire in 1910, and the building of the

Grand Coulee Dam in 1941 flooded the falls and the remains of Fort Colville. Today, only an engraved stone marker commemorates the HBC establishment located next to St. Paul's Catholic Church, dating from 1847, on the hill just to the southwest of the former HBC post, whose ashes are now scattered below the waters of Lake Roosevelt. As the sole remaining structure from the Canadian period, the St. Paul Mission church represents an impressive structure in the traditional French Canadian "post and sill" style of squared logs built up within a frame. Bordered by its cemetery a few hundred yards to the north towards the lake, St. Paul's is one of the oldest buildings in Washington State.

Conversations in and around the town of Kettle Falls indicate a general awareness of families still in the area descending from the former HBC employees, classifying themselves as "white" or "Indian," according to the ongoing mix over the intervening generations, along with personal and social identification preferences. Moreover, the local phone book shows a number of French-Canadian names. Such traces of a *Canadien* and Métis past are explored below, including the pressures that forced the Métis and some French *Canadiens* to either be classified as "white" or as "Indians" to be relocated to reserves.

Relocation and War

The relatively peaceful cohabitation that marked the Hudson's Bay Company era of the Pacific Northwest's history would be overturned with the sudden arrival north of the Columbia of several thousand Americans in the early 1850s. These newcomers proceeded to develop and sub-partition the land that would become Washington territory, designating some 14,000 Native American residents for removal to reserves. The politics of tolerance were replaced with new racial politics that sought to divide the "civilized" from the "savage"—a savage that included the hybridized populations such as the French *Canadien* who had adopted Native American ways of life, or their racially mixed Métis descendants who were now viewed with suspicion. The racial politics of the second half of the nineteenth century would call into question the status of the French *Canadien* and Métis in what would become the State of Washington. The goal of the new Anglo-American settlers was to prepare the Oregon and later Washington territories for statehood and further integration into the federal system. To do this, it was deemed necessary to relocate the indigenous peoples, the Native Americans who already inhabited the territory. However, there was some ambiguity as to what to do with the French *Canadien* and Métis who were perceived as too close in culture to the "savage" Native Americans, yet had elements of "civilized" culture as defined in nineteenth-century racial discourse. This would raise political debates in a decade marked by warfare, beginning with the 1847 Whitman massacre in Walla Walla, during which several Native American nations rose up against the encroaching settlers and fought against their relocation to reserves on relatively small, marginal territories.

In 1853, the northern and eastern territories of the Oregon Country were divided and reorganized into the Territory of Washington, a territory that soon included what is now Washington State, northern Idaho, and western Montana. Whereas Oregon would become a state in 1859, just prior to the outbreak of the Civil War, Washington only gained statehood in 1889. One challenge the territorial administrators faced was the questionable demographics of the state: many of the inhabitants were born in British territories and in many cases were French-speaking Catholics or Métis. The year 1845 saw the first handful of Americans turning north at Fort Vancouver to venture into the hinterlands in the direction of Puget Sound. Official 1850 census figures reported that only 87 of the 192 adult Clark County residents were born in the United States. For Lewis County, which covered both the Cowlitz corridor and Puget Sound, the ratio of American nativity, while slightly higher, was still 157 out of 313 adults. Northern Oregon remained, to a considerable extent in practical terms, British territory. Such issues were prominent in the early politics of the territory. The priority item on the agenda of the first meeting of the Washington territorial legislature in 1854 called for the immediate resolution of the question of voting rights for the Métis and French *Canadiens*. Some legislators argued that most of the *Canadiens* were pioneers who helped open up the country and who paid taxes. Other citizens, however, petitioned for the denial of voting privileges to anyone who could not read or write English (which would exclude most *Canadiens* and Métis). After a heated debate, the legislature granted the vote to "half-breeds" who election judges determined had adopted the habits of civilization, a compromise that allowed *Canadien* farmers to vote but excluded the *Canadiens* living among indigenous groups (Pioneer and Democrat, 1854, p. 1).

As the Hudson's Bay Company withdrew from the Washington Territory, other institutions would rise in prominence in its place, such as the Catholic Church (see Chapter 7). The Church mediated the incorporation of the French-speaking communities and indigenous peoples into new political structures—first territorial, then state—in both Oregon, Idaho, western Montana, and Washington. This mediation, however, could not preempt the conflicts and wars that would follow in the 1840s and 1850s. The French-speaking settlers of the region were very often literally caught in the crossfire. Their story, rarely told, deserves attention.

Fort Pierre on the Missouri, ca 1833, Karl Bodmer. Pierre Chouteau founded this fort as a trading post in 1832. It was the lynchpin of the fur trade and central to the affairs of the Western Department of the American Fur Trade Company owned by John Jacob Astor. Located at the midpoint between Saint Louis and the northern fur trading territories of Montana and North Dakota, if was an important transit point and meeting place for traders and indigenous nations. Visitors to Fort Pierre included Prince Maximilian as well as Jean-Jacques (John James) Audubon. In 1855, Fort Pierre was bought by the United States Army and served as a military base before being abandoned.

CHAPTER 2

The French Empire and the First Métis of the Old Northwest

A river always runs through the story of a Métis settlement. Their fathers and grandfathers having worked their way out paddling across the continent, the Métis would settle on the outskirts of the forts of the fur trading companies. Using alliances of marriage, which gained access to indigenous hunting grounds, they would typically keep a garden and sell any furs that came their way to current or former employers. Likewise, they provided access to trade goods for their local, Native American in-laws. Take a river valley around which a Native American band or tribe rotated its seasonal hunting-fishing-gathering cycles, add to it a nearby Euro-American fur trading post, and you invariably have a new sum: a Métis community, a Métis, or as often called in English, a Half-Breed community.

These communities might initially be located alongside a trading post, but over time they would drift upriver, or relocate over the hill, so as to not encroach upon the expanding ranching and farming prerogatives of their former employer. Much the same as with military families today, when these men reached the age of thirty or forty, family lives and careers increasingly conflicted. The employees of the fur trade were continually being relocated from one wintering site to another, sometimes in different corners of the continent. The grinding work that would see the men spending full days in their canoes from spring's thaw to winter's freeze wore down the men prematurely. Early retirement was the norm, and like the pattern farther east, the local trading company diversified into a broader range of products and services. In sustaining the labor force, the company would rely less on hiring 'back east' and shift increasingly to hiring the young Métis men of the second and third generations. To this mix of voyageur fathers and indigenous mothers in the Pacific Northwest was also added the Iroquois and Abenaki freemen, with a growing dependence on indigenous Hawaiian laborers in the course of the 1840s, and newcomers from the British Isles (Barman & Watson, 2006). The hiring of the latter two groups increased over time as the *Canadiens* and Métis either retired or shifted toward the role of independent contractors and freemen. Thus, it was along the shores of the Columbia and its tributaries that Métis communities and settlements would put down roots. Indeed, thousands of their descendants still reside there to this day.

These early Métis communities were also shaped by the blossoming network of French-speaking Catholic missionaries sent out from Quebec, supplemented by people hailing from the French-speaking countries of Europe—Belgium, France, and Switzerland—as well as those who were products of French-language Catholic educational institutions in Italy and the Netherlands. Additionally, the U.S. Army showed up in 1849 to ensure American hegemony over the old aboriginal and fur trading territories from the Pacific Northwest to south of the 49th parallel, policing the territory and consolidating the dwindling "Indian" population onto ever smaller and more tightly besieged reservations.

For some Métis, these reservations served as a final refuge. Still others struggled to integrate into the new Anglo-American communities of settlers suddenly pouring in over the Oregon Trail. This history was merely the final phase of a sequence of similar developments that rolled across the northern borderlands of what was becoming the United States—the final stage of an American expansion that had started with the settling of the colonies on the shores of the Atlantic and pushed its way westward to the Pacific. This movement westward was nonetheless influenced by the legacy of an earlier Empire: the French, who had explored and claimed much of the continent, and whose sons had scoured the continent as traders or employees of the fur trade all the way to the Pacific, making these distant territories their homes.

A Different Sort of Colonial Empire

The French Empire in North America differed from other major European empires that colonized the mainland in that it did not rely heavily on settlers from the mother country. Admittedly, the French-held islands in the Caribbean were more akin to the European status quo, as the French islands were remarkable only for the brutal efficiency of their plantations. In the territories of North America claimed by France, however, colonists were purposely restricted to the lower reaches of the two great river systems providing access to the interior. As a nation fighting to re-establish and maintain its position as Europe's preeminent power during most of the seventeenth and eighteenth centuries, France discouraged emigration, as it did any large peripheral claim on financial resources. Frenchmen and the nation's wealth were needed at home. France's North American empire—a frugally founded empire with few colonists—would instead be based in great part on a system of alliances with the continent's indigenous peoples, not their subjugation. This resulted in a more restricted yet diffuse approach to empire building, and perpetuated a highly diluted authority *vis-à-vis* the indigenous peoples.

New France's relatively small number of settlers made it necessary for the French to forge alliances with local indigenous populations, both to wage war against other imperial forces (the Dutch in New Netherlands, for example, and the British in New England) and to secure a stake in the trade of goods that served as an income source from these northern holdings. The French colonies of New France (Canada) and Acadia would never be as profitable as the British colonies on the Atlantic coast, or those of France in the Caribbean or the cod fisheries off the coast of Newfoundland. The Virginia colony had developed a strain of tobacco that served as a rich source of outbound trade—in no small part due to the new addiction to smoking in England and other European states. In the northern colonies, fishing and whaling provided a valuable source of income, as did the African slave trade.

The need for land and slaves made alliance with the indigenous peoples unnecessary. They were thus being pushed off their lands to make space for tobacco or other crops. At the end of the seventeenth century, the southern English colonies took another tack as indentured white servants began to be replaced by imported black slaves, while Native North Americans were increasingly being sold into bondage and placed on slave ships in Charleston harbor and elsewhere, headed for the West Indies. This effectively removed many eastern North American Indians from their lands, preventing their escape into the forests to reunite with other indigenous nations.

The model of settlement in the southeastern British colonies began to resemble that of the Spanish and Portuguese colonies further south, while the French colonies in the Caribbean gave rise to an aristocratic class reliant on slave labor to harvest tobacco, sugar, and eventually cotton. In a minor variation, on the mainland, the Spanish and Portuguese farms, ranches, and missions tended to rely heavily on virtually enslaved "peons" of local extraction.

In the northern territories, France needed the indigenous peoples to ensure the survival of the French holdings, as well as to provide furs for trade—with furs representing the sole on-shore commodity deemed profitable, given the discovery of gold or other lucre in these regions lay in the distant future. The alliances with the aboriginal groups were based on a set of diplomatic, commercial, and military relations, the terms of which were not all that unfavorable to the original inhabitants. Over time these relations were increasingly reinforced through intermarriage.

In return for a limited and very theoretical subordination to the King through his Governor, referred to as Onontio by the indigenous peoples of the Great Lakes region, and granting the right to trade and trap on terms favorable to the French, it was actually the indigenous people themselves who received what little tribute was exacted from either party. Wealth flowed from the Imperial authorities to the aboriginal communities; as such, the wealth generated by empire and commerce was redistributed.

Consequently, a different sort of commonwealth developed. The French colonists settled on lands that, for reasons still not fully known, had been abandoned by their earlier inhabitants, notably the St. Lawrence Valley, whose peoples Jacques Cartier had encountered in the sixteenth century. It is reported that they were gone by the time Samuel de Champlain returned six decades later at the start of the seventeenth century. In Acadia, the French settlers used dykes (*aboiteaux* as they were called by the Acadiens) to push back the ocean's high tides and create fields out of salty seaside marshes.

In both cases, the first French settlers did not displace indigenous allies to establish their fields; the relatively small numbers of colonists enabled the French to maintain settlers without having to displace indigenous peoples. Because of this, the French population grew slowly, while the number of British colonists grew exponentially. The French court never viewed the French colonies as a source of wealth, but rather as a drain on the King's treasuries. Eventually, save for two islands (St. Pierre and Miquelon, later kept to ensure French fishing rights to Atlantic cod), the northern French colonies were easily divested, as these lands were considered, as dubbed by Voltaire, no more than a "few acres of snow."

It is worth noting that from the beginning, in North America, the French approached their colony with a different vision, and this was evident in the vision of the very first Governor of New France, Samuel de Champlain. In his seminal biography of Champlain, David Hackett Fischer (2009) hones in on this difference and its roots. Champlain's first encounter with indigenous nations marked the beginning of a distinct pattern of colonization quite unlike any other in the long history of European colonial relations in the Americas. He writes:

> This war-weary soldier had a dream of humanity and peace in a world of cruelty and violence. He envisioned a new world as a place where peoples of different cultures could live together in amity and concord. This became his grand design for North America. (Fischer, 2009, p. 7)

This spirit of openness and tolerance is quite at odds with the era's reigning ethos where too often the goal was to either enslave or exterminate the indigenous populations.

In hindsight, there were only two real surprises: first, the length of time it took to dislodge the French governmental authorities, which was a direct result of the strong alliances forged with indigenous nations; second, the significance of the actual role the residual French colonists—be they *Canadiens*, Créoles, or Métis,

The Founder of Quebec, the Ancient Capital of Canada

Samuel de Champlain, etching by E. Ronjat, on left. "Samuel de Champlain," portrait by Théophile Hamel, on right. Champlain left an indelible mark on North America as the founder of Quebec and the driving force in the creation of a permanent French settlement in North America that would thrive because of his vision of trade and alliances with the indigenous nations. No painting, engraving or drawing based on the true image of Samuel de Champlain exists. The iconic images of Champlain that have been used to represent him for generations, are in fact of Michel Particelli d'Emery who was immortalized in an engraving by Balthazar Moncornet in 1654. In the 1850s, Moncornet's engraving was forged and the subject in the painting rebaptized as Samuel de Champlain.

either secular or religious—would play in the development of the Western part of the U.S. and Canada. Two characteristics of the French Empire, however, bore a resemblance to the respective empires of Portugal and Spain. With France being a Catholic nation, it comes as no surprise that Catholic missionaries played a major role in coordinating the work of empire with the representatives of the state. Also, though not on the scale of the other two empires further south, over time a significant part of the mixed heritage population would claim parentage from both indigenous peoples and European settlers. The offspring were referred to as *mestizo* in Spanish, or *métis* and its earlier alternative variation *métif* in French. In Portuguese the word is pronounced virtually the same as in Spanish, but spelled *mestiço*, with the cedilla on the 'c' to giving it the softer 's' or 'z' sound. Though obviously this mixing of the races also occurred in British colonies of North America, it would represent a smaller percentage of the overall population compared to the three Catholic empires.

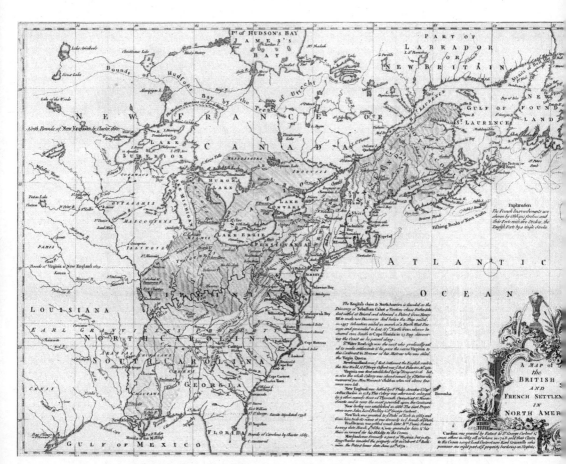

A Map of the British and French Settlements in North America, 1755. Already in 1755 the mapmakers were recording the tensions bringing the French and English closer to war. This map highlights the British "just claims" and the "encroachments" of the French underscoring the tensions that would lead to war. The map was published a year after fighting began in North America with the Jumonville Affair and one year before the official outbreak of the Seven Years' War, a war that would end with the Conquest of New France. The year that the map was published was also the year that British forces would deport the Acadians from their homes in the Maritimes.

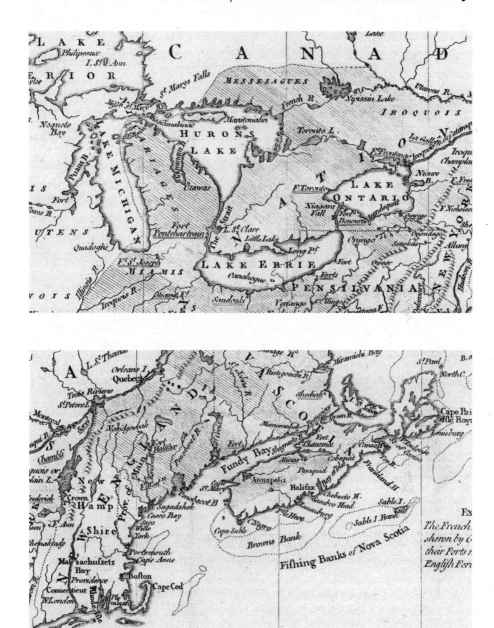

This *Pax Gallica*, of course, did not include peace with all indigenous peoples. From the beginning, in 1608, Samuel de Champlain stepped into a world of inter-nation warfare. He found himself participating directly in military operations. First it was an alignment with the Algonquins, and then the Hurons, allied at that juncture against the dominant Iroquois. This soon expanded to include other victims of Iroquois raids, such as the Ottawa, Potawatomi, Illinois, and Ojibwa (or Chippewa). Later on and farther west, there were periodic episodes of retalia-tion against former allies who had turned on and massacred Frenchmen. This retribution was most notably directed at the Natchez on the lower Mississippi, the Fox tribe in the Midwest, and intermittently with certain bands of Sioux. In the north, the core alliance was built around the smaller, weaker nations that had felt the wrath of the Iroquois; forming a confederation of sorts, these groups were receptive to the intervention and support of an outsider. A similar dynamic would develop later in the Columbia Plateau in the early nineteenth century, where a loose alliance of tribes strove to offset the dominance of the well-armed Blackfeet on the neighboring Plains.

The settling near the mouths of the river systems that drained the central and eastern regions of the continent began slowly during the latter years of the reign of the Henri IV (1589-1610), the founder of France's Bourbon dynasty and France's only Protestant King. Growth of the French colonies continued under his son, Louis XIII, who was raised a Catholic, but achieved its highest level of immigra-tion during the period from 1665-1672 under Henri's grandson, Louis XIV, his principal minister, Colbert, and the Intendant of Canada, Jean Talon. During the seventeenth century, settlement of this French immigrant population was limited to the north along the shores of the St. Lawrence, in addition to Acadia or the Souriquoi Country on the east coast (now Nova Scotia). The term "Souriquoi" still in use in Acadian-Métis contemporary communities is mentioned by Antoine-François Prévost (1777, p. 28). This came to be known as the *Pays d'en Bas*, or low country, juxtaposed as it was to the vast interior of the continent, which constituted the *Pays d'en Haut*, or the upper country.

The Catholic Iroquois of the St. Lawrence

During the French Regime another group vital to the fur trade established itself in the St. Lawrence Valley: the Catholic Iroquois. As the French forged alliances, they also provided refuge to those indigenous peoples fleeing from the Iroquois Confederation based out of what is now upstate New York, and their New England militia allies. These refugee bands of formerly large nations comprised initially the Huron–Wendat, and several bands of Abenaki. Many were survivors seeking protection from the Iroquois, whether in Canada or in the shadow of the French Forts of the Great Lakes. Later, in addition to the Huron and Abenaki, many

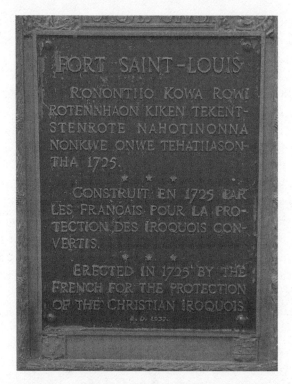

Fort Saint-Louis was built in what is now Kahnawake in 1725 to protect the Iroquois who converted to Catholicism. The chapel was built in 1720 and parts of it still stand. Iroquois freemen played an important role in the fur trade across the continent to the Pacific Northwest.

Iroquois who had converted to the Catholic faith also moved to the St. Lawrence Valley, where they were promised land and refuge. After a peace treaty had been concluded with the Iroquois in 1667, the Jesuits sent missionaries to the Iroquois and succeeded in converting a considerable number.

In the 1670s, the first families relocated to the St. Lawrence Valley. In 1680, a *seigneurie* to be managed by the Jesuits was established to provide lands for the Catholic Iroquois. Claude-Charles Le Roy dit Bacqueville de la Potherie, who resided in New France until his departure in 1701, notes that there were close to one thousand Iroquois settled in Sault du Saint-Louis on the southern shore of the Saint Lawrence across from the Island of Montreal—now Kahnawake—including Iroquois from the five nations of the Iroquois Confederation (de Bacqueville, 1753, p. 360). However, Claude-Charles de Bacqueville (1753, p. 363) oddly enough notes that, *"Ils chantent la grande Messe et disent leurs prieres en la langue Algonkine, pour éviter une jalousie qui auroit pu naître entre les cinq Nations."* [They sing the High Mass and say their prayers in the Algonquin language in order to avoid any jealousy that could arise between the five Nations.] This was

observed in spite of the fact that the Iroquois and the Algonquin had been enemies even before Samuel de Champlain arrived. Perhaps if nothing else, this
strange note may indicate some amount of intermarriage.

Given that the contemporary community of Kahnawake defines itself as
proudly Mohawk, English-speaking, with significant numbers abandoning the
Catholic Faith in recent decades, it is perhaps difficult to imagine that the
Iroquois at the end of the 1700s would have spoken French as their second language and would have been fiercely Catholic. Enmity grew over the decades
largely due to the encroachment of the *Canadien* settlers who would be granted
title to the lands promised to the Iroquois in collusion with the Catholic Church.
That and the growing hegemony of the English language which came to be the
language of political and economic power encouraged the Iroquois to integrate
into an English-speaking world which also led them to turn their backs on the
French language. Nevertheless, the Iroquois recruited by the North West
Company to travel west were both Catholic and fluent in both French and their
native language. This was likewise true of the band of Catholic Iroquois freemen
who would settle in western Canada and the Pacific Northwest.

Le Pays d'en Haut

An extensive network of small military forts, trading posts, and missions were
set up along the waterways in the *Pays d'en Haut*, those lands west of the
St. Lawrence in the Great Lakes region and beyond. They were often located near
indigenous groups' villages as well as at strategic locations such as the narrows
where Lakes Superior and Michigan empty into Lake Huron, and where the latter passes into Lake Erie, and from there into Lake Ontario via the falls at
Niagara. Other outposts linked up with the Mississippi either via the Chicago
and Illinois Rivers, with the Kankakee and Wabash Rivers via the St. Joseph
River; and Green Bay via the Fox and Wisconsin Rivers. The regional command
post for these lake outposts was originally Michilimackinaw, located at the narrows between Lakes Michigan and Huron during the late 1600s.

During a consolidation phase, it was replaced temporarily early in the century
by a budding new enclave founded at the next narrows down the lake system by
Antoine de la Mothe, sieur de Cadillac. This eventually included a contingent of
permanent settlers and was named Détroit, meaning *the narrows* in French. After
1715, Michilimackinac would re-emerge as the dominant military outpost and
trading center in the Great Lakes region, while a more diversified economy
developed around Detroit.

In *The Middle Ground*, Richard White (1991b, p. 84) provides a synopsis of the
workings of the alliance system that upheld the French Empire in North America
at the dawn of the eighteenth century:

The alliance was centered on Quebec, the home of Onontio, and it was formulated in the language of kinship to which both the French and the Algonquians attached great significance. Leaders of both the French and the Algonquians negotiated according to ritual forms which placed the French Governor, Onontio, in the position of father to the Indians, of which the Ottawas were his eldest sons. The French were quite at home with such patriarchal formulations and attached quite specific meanings to them. For them all authority was patriarchal, from God the Father, to the king (the father of his people), to the father in his home. Fathers commanded; sons obeyed. The Ottawa understood the relationship differently. A father was kind, generous, and protecting. A child owed a father respect, but a father could not compel obedience. In establishing a middle ground, one took such congruence as one could find and sorted out their meanings later.

Within the alliance, these ritual forms for father and son thus had a built-in ambiguity that would influence the course of negotiations that followed the founding of Detroit.

The specific negotiations White refers to are those following an outbreak of violence in 1706 around the newly established fort at Detroit. This involved the five nations that Onontio had convinced to relocate to the new outpost after the end of the Iroquois Wars following La grande paix de Montreal (the Great Settlement of Montreal) in 1701. These negotiations included three Ottawa nations—Sinagos, Kiskakons, and Sables—plus the Miamis and the Huron-Petuns. Each nation had their own village in the surrounding area outside the walls of the French fort.

In the wake of France's retrenchment of its network of the outposts at the turn of the century, incessant quarrels, feuds, and warfare broke out among the nations. Onontio's ability to effectively mediate and arbitrate to preserve the alliance among the gathered indigenous peoples had been seriously compromised. As a result, this period of anarchy and trauma ushered in the development of a new consensus in the *Pays d'en Haut*. Richard White (1991b, p. 149) provides specific examples:

> The Potawatomis of Saint Joseph responded to the turmoil that followed the crisis of 1706 at Detroit by asking for a return of licensed traders, a garrison, and a French commander. By 1712 the Peorias recalled the days of Tonti and Fort Saint Louis as a golden age of peace and plenty and contrasted it with the violence and deprivation of their present condition. The Weas, too, asked for French officers and missionaries.

In seeking to escape the burdens of village politics, the French found that refusing to mediate quarrels often meant deeper entanglement in them over time. The tactics of "ignore and avoid" failed to work for very long—such were the burdens of empire, especially one based on tribute being distributed to the "subjected" nations, not gathered in. There was no easy out to the necessity of gift giving and tribute paid out to the allies.

Substantial resources were required despite efforts to run the empire "on the cheap and easy" without a major military—and financial—commitment, and at the same time refusal to send over a significant number of colonists. Adding to the difficulty were the British, who constantly lay in wait on the sidelines, seeking opportunities to undermine the alliance system by stripping France of its indigenous allies in the *Pays d'en Haut*. One Onontio, Governor Beauharnois, would struggle to make this case to Louis XV and his advisors in Versailles. Richard White (1991b, p. 177) describes those efforts:

> Unable to isolate Indians, the French had to mediate between them to keep them from the British by other methods. As Beauharnois argued in attempting to prevent the Crown from breaking promises he had made to the Weas and their neighbors: "The stratagems resorted to by the English to attract our Savages, compel me to use great circumspection toward them, and to Content them as much as I can." They "were kept in check solely by careful management, and ... would seize the first pretext to break the word they have given me were I to fail to keep mine."

The careful management Beauharnois spoke of became institutionalized into a system of alliance chiefs, medals, gifts, and mediation. Less a militant extension of French power than a forum for maintaining peace, the alliance blended Algonquian rituals, the kinship connections between villagers, and French goods into a potent force. The chiefs, French and Algonquian, were the human center of this alliance; from them radiated the network of ties that bound Onontio to his children.

France's need to redistribute wealth in the interest of establishing and maintaining an alliance in eighteenth-century North America would be very similar to that of the U.S. on the far side of the Atlantic two and a half centuries later, during the early years of NATO. This position cannot be sustained without a significant commitment of largesse to maintain the loyalty of allies, each with its own calculation of self-interest. To lubricate the process, the U.S. would be required to sprinkle gold dust by redistributing technology and jobs in negotiating each and every joint project to which their allies signed up during NATO's critical first 15 years (Foxcurran, 1986).

The Métis Become Established in the Old Northwest – Through 1715

Historians from Francis Parkman (1983) to Guy Frégeault (1944) and W. J. Eccles (1983) have artfully related the tale of the establishment of the Métis in the Old Northwest, which included much of what the French called the *Pays d'en Haut*, and is comprised of the contemporary states of Ohio, Indiana, Illinois, Wisconsin, Michigan, and much of Minnesota. Most recently, and directly relevant to the subject at hand, Gilles Havard (2003) produced the magnum opus, *Empire et métissages: Indiens et Français dans le pays d'en Haut 1660-1715*. Havard's *Empire et métissages* covers the first half-century of development of a hybrid, or mixed-blood, population in the area of "la Nouvelle France" referred to as the *Pays d'en Haut*. He describes the actors—nations, families, individuals, missionaries, military officers, fur traders, *coureurs de bois*, and government administrators—as well as the sequence of events contributing to the development of this new ethnic group and society on the outer perimeter of a stunted empire.

On its periphery—which incidentally accounted for most of its claimed territorial jurisdiction—this empire was based on the norms of the indigenous peoples' world wherein the cohesion of an alliance with individual nations was reinforced by the liberal generosity of the senior chieftain, Onontio, who was the appointed Governor of the French King. The Europeans could profit from the fur trade, but wealth redistribution was the price to be paid to the local indigenous allies, who received tribute from the self-styled overlord; they paid nothing, instead agreeing to provide military service when summoned by Onontio, somewhat along feudal lines. Mutual accommodation was the rule, though time and numbers would be working to shift the balance of power against the indigenous peoples over the long term. This empire was peculiar inasmuch as it remained in the stage of a military-diplomatic alliance supported by mutually beneficial commerce for an extended time period. Many empires start out in this manner, but far fewer retain such a balance of forces for so long.

Mutual acculturation would have an impact, though most members of this hybrid society, according to Havard, would remain fundamentally "Indian" through absorption into their mothers' nations. Such a loose term, however, lacks a single and all-encompassing meaning. Initially, the majority of the fathers, after a number of years, would return from the *Pays d'en Haut* to the *Pays d'en Bas* along the lower St. Lawrence, or to France. Southern Illinois and southeastern Michigan around Detroit were the principal exceptions, with the French establishing settlements there. In these areas, settler families—be they of European or mixed heritage—held together over the generations within their growing European and Christian enclaves, while generally maintaining peaceful relations with their indigenous neighbours. Due to its northern clime, Michilimackinac in northern Michigan never developed a base of settlers practicing agriculture; instead, Michilimackinac continued to be a major commercial center, with a significant Métis population that remained tied to an odd mix of trade and subsistence well into the nineteenth century.

Living outside the more settled regions, where the power of the French Governor was limited, these *coureurs de bois* were often characterized by the authorities—both spiritual and secular—disparagingly, as *hors-la-loi* (outlaws),

---

* The term *coureurs de bois* is used in France whereas in Quebec and French Canada the common term is *coureur des bois*. Both are used in this book.

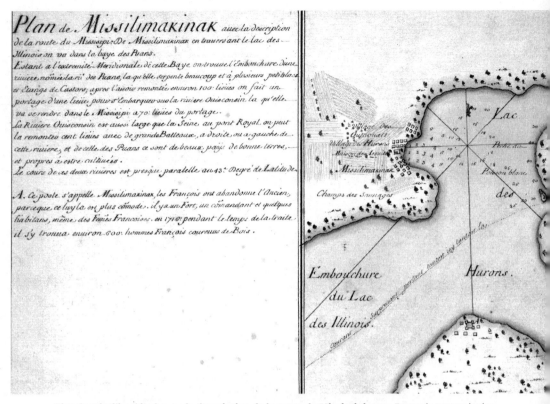

Plan de Missilimakinak avec la description de la route du Mississipi, 1717. Fur trade centers had to be established at halfway points to facilitate the movement of trade goods to the interior and furs to sea ports. Under the French, Fort Michilimackinac became a hub. The *hivernants* (winterers) would bring the furs there, while the *mangeurs de lard* would bring trade goods from the St. Lawrence Valley and return before the waters froze. A distinction began to emerge between the men who stayed in the *Pays d'en haut* (the upper territories), who were much closer to the indigenous peoples, and the Canadiens who lived along the Saint Lawrence. The former referred somewhat derogatively to the men coming in as the *mangeurs de lard* who ate the salted lard that they packed with them made from the pork being raised in the farms of the St. Lawrence Valley.

libertins (debauched vagabonds), or bandits. Further west in the Rockies and beyond, they later came to be called *les gens libres,* or freemen, where they tended to operate as independent contractors *vis-à-vis* the larger consolidated fur trading companies. Havard estimates that in the 1650s some 300 men annually would leave the French colonies to become *coureurs de bois.* By the 1680s, their numbers grew to between 500 and 800 annually, after which time their numbers began to drop. By the end of the 1820s, Peterson (1985, p. 63) and Havard (2003, pp. 77, 327 and 669) estimate that the Métis descendants of these men numbered between 10,000 and 15,000, having since settled to the south and west of Lakes Superior and Huron.

A qualifier provided by Susan Sleeper-Smith (2001) in her *Indian Women and French Men: Rethinking cultural encounter in the Western Great Lakes* is useful at this point. First, she reminds us that "The use of *Metis* [to describe mixed-ancestry] is rare in seventeenth and eighteenth century manuscript sources." Then, in the next two sentences, she makes an important distinction related to the size of the local community:

> At many smaller posts, such as Fort St. Joseph in Michigan and Ouiatenon in Indiana identity was defined by kin rather than ethnicity or nationality. In the colonial world of the pays d'en haut, a distinctive Metis population evolved at the larger fur trade communities, such as Michilimackinac and Green Bay. (Sleeper-Smith, 2001, p. 8)

The primary documents, however, suggest a somewhat different interpretation. The concept of *métissage* is, in our opinion, incorporated in the ethnonym *Canadien*, and it was the broader *Canadien* nation that would come to be seen as distinct from their French brethren.

One of the earliest examples of the use of the term Métis is found in an early eighteenth-century handwritten manuscript credited to Gédéon de Catalogne, now preserved in Quebec's National Archives. De Catalogne arrived in New France in 1683 and took part in a number of military expeditions, staying on until his death in 1729. Though best known for his maps of New France and Acadia, he is also credited with authoring the text that is now known by the title *Recueil de ce qui s'est passé au Canada, au sujet de la guerre tant des Anglais que des Iroquois, depuis l'année 1682* (Thorpe, 1969). Here we find the following passage illustrating how a *Canadien* could also be Métis:

> *Quelques années aprez, le nommé Dubeau, Canadien, un des plus forts du païs, métis, fils d'un François et d'une huronne, qui avoit esté gardé de Monsieur de Frontenac, estant allé aux Outaouacs, estant à la chasse, y fut pris par les Iroquois qui le lièrent et comme il sçavoit parler leur langue il s'entretenoit avec eulx et s'attira un peu leur confiance et n'estoit plus sy serré.* (Poore, 1883, p. 607)

> A few years later, the one named Dubeau, Canadien, one of the strongest in the country, métis, son of a Frenchman and a Huron woman, who had been kept by Mister de Frontenac, having gone to the Ottawa, while hunting, was captured by the Iroquois who bound bound him and as he knew how to speak their language, he talked with them, gained their confidence and wasn't bound as tight.

In this passage, Dubeau is identified first as *Canadien*. A number of traits are then used to describe him: he is the strongest of the country, he is "métis"; the son of a Frenchman and a Huron woman. He is *Canadien*, though openly acknowledged as métis, though in the original manuscript is "mitit,"[*] and he is

---

[*] To best understand this passage, it is necessary to compare three existing versions of the handwritten document. The first was first published in 1871 in Quebec and is seen as the least

fluent in the language of the Iroquois. This passage identifies how children of mixed marriages can and do become *Canadien*, arguably a national identity.

It is often suggested that Métis identity has been generally assimilated into one or another national community, French or Indian. In the seventeenth and eighteenth centuries, evidence indicates that the children of mixed unions were sometimes integrated into their mother's communities, effectively becoming a full member of their mother's nation, or incorporated into their father's world, usually living in the proximity of a French fort and becoming *Canadien*. This binary theory risks melding together two distinct national identities already evolving in parallel fashion, namely that of the *Candiens* and the French (or other European newcomers).

Such binary reduction misses the third option of a continuum between the early indigenized-*Canadien* and Métis identity, expressed then in non-mutually excluding terms. (Interestingly, the earliest French sources from New France without exception refer to the Native Americans using the term nation. Though they may be labeled savage and barbarian, they are still defined and described in national terms, like the French.) In the Red River Valley in later generations, French-Canadians, Métis, and *Canadien* identities came to be increasingly wedged apart. Being Métis, however, was not initially antithetical to being *Canadien* in its early acceptation. The writings of General Collot (1826) clearly demonstrate this at the end of the 1700s. Only in the nineteenth century in the Red River Valley, as pressure mounted on the *Canadiens* living in the St. Lawrence Valley to renounce their *métissage* and assert their racial equivalence to the British occupiers (Delâge, 2011), would the *Canadien*-Métis suffering from the encroachment of incoming waves of new settlers come to see themselves as a nation distinct from

---

accurate and opens by stating that the manuscript is rife with spelling errors and much is unintelligible (de Catalogne, 1871). This version, according to Le Blant (1948, p. 154) was based on a second-hand copy of the original. In this version, the comma between country and Métis is omitted in the passage cited, thus having Dubeau being the strongest man of a Métis country. The second version, the one cited above, was included in a collection of texts and manuscripts that had been collected by the Archives of the Province of Quebec and was certainly based on a rereading and transcription of the original. Though much closer to the original, it still contains various errors as Le Blant (1948, p. 156) highlights. The third published version is the one that is credited as most accurate, published integrally by Robert Le Blant in his volume examining the history of New France (de Catalogne, 1948). The main difference between the Le Blant version and the second version is that he observes that the word used was "mitit" that he notes in his footnotes was "Métis" (Le Blant, 1948, p. 250) . Given that de Catalogne spelled phonetically and his manuscript is marked by its spelling errors, the options are that the word would have rhymed with "petit" with the final "t" of "mitit" being silent, or quite possibly he meant to write "mitif" which would correspond to Gabriel Franchère's spelling of the word close to a century later. Whichever might be the case, it is clear that he is using the word as it was used in the colony in the eighteenth century, making it a local term, not one imposed by an outsider.

Canadian Habitant in Winter, Frances Anne Hopkins, ca. 1858. Though the historical memory has been forgotten, accounts and paintings from the era demonstrate that the *Canadien* living in the Saint Lawrence Valley had adopted many of the cultural features often associated with the Métis: they wore moccasins, leggings, the "*capot*" (hooded cloak) tied with a brightly colored sash (*ceinture fléchée*) and tuque in the winter was as much a feature of the *Canadien* farming the lands of the Saint Lawrence as that of the *Canadien* and Métis of the fur trade.

the new nascent French Canadian nation. However, in American settings such as St. Louis, due to the distinctiveness of American nation-building, those of mixed heritage would not have felt it necessary to abandon the use of the term *Canadien*. This is true even if French texts were using the term Métis to describe people of mixed heritage, and even if priests such as De Smet were in turn referring to individuals as Métis based on their mixed heritage. A case in point is the French translation of Zebulon M. Pike's (1812, p. 368) voyage to New Mexico where the French translation refers to "*le caractère bienfaisant des Métis et des Créoles*" which parallels Pike's (1889, p. 238) own words in which he wrote in English "the hospitality and goodness of the Creoles and Mestis."

France Clamps Down on the *Coureurs de Bois*

In 1685, Louis XIV appointed a new governor of New France, Jacques-René de Brisay, Marquis de Denonville, with express orders to contain the growing numbers of *coureurs de bois*. Pierre-François-Xavier de Charlevoix (1744a, p. 532-533), in his history of New France, affirms that, "*M. de Dénonville revient ensuite aux Coureurs de Bois, dont il dit que le nombre est 'tel, qu'il dépeuple le Pays des meilleurs Hommes, les rend indociles, indisciplinables, débauchés, & que leurs Enfans sont élevés comme des Sauvages.'*" [Mister de Dénonville returned to the Coureurs de bois, whose numbers he said were such that they were emptying the country of its best men, rendering them unruly, not disciplinable, debauched and that their children were raised like Savages.]

As France was actively encouraging the demographic growth of its colony of Canada at that time, the drain of men to the *Pays d'en Haut* ran counter to the goals of the French Crown. Here there is a clear reference to the children that the *coureurs de bois* were siring: not only were the men becoming undisciplined and debauched, but also their children were being raised "as Savages."

In 1679, along similar lines, the French King had already instructed an earlier Governor of New France, Frontenac, that the "*vagabonds*" or "*coureurs de bois*" were not to be tolerated—that there should be no excuses, as these men were seen as ruining and emptying the country of its inhabitants as well as annihilating commerce. The Church was also notably critical of the trade in the *L'Eau-de-vie*, or alcohol, that was perceived to cause much hardship and interfere in the salvation of the peoples they sought to convert (de Charlevoix, 1744c, pp. 112, 302). In order to try to restrain the out-migration of *Canadiens* to the *Pays d'en Haut* as *coureurs de bois*, the French authorities instituted a system of *congés de traite*, or trade licenses, that attempted to limit both the number of traders and voyageurs that could leave New France.

As one might expect in such matters, the policies of the French Crown did not stop the expansion of the French outposts. Deftly playing upon the desire of the King and Church to limit the number of *coureurs de bois*, Antoine de La Mothe-Cadillac proposed the creation of an outpost at Détroit to better control trade and to promote the conversion and assimilation of the indigenous peoples. In a thesis addressed to the Count of Maurepas and approved by the French Crown, La Mothe-Cadillac argued that his plan would not only be profitable for all, including the inhabitants of Canada, but would also ensure that the indigenous peoples would be both converted and would all speak French within a decade. In his words, "*il fera civiliser et humaniser les Sauvages, en sorte que la pluspart ne parleront que la langue françoise en dix ans, que, par ce moyen, de païens ils deviendront enfans de l'Eglise et par conséquent bons sujets du Roy*" (Margry, 1887, p. 139). [He will civilize and humanize the Savages, so that most will speak only the French langauge in ten years and by this means the pagans will become children of the Church and consequently good subjects of the King.]

La Mothe-Cadillac argued that the *coureur de bois* would be tied to the new fort, as France's indigenous allies would come to the fort to trade. The goal was to ensure that neither the fur trade nor *libertinage* (free relations with indigenous women) would entice the men to strike out on their own. To combat these temptations, he proposed that the men be locked in the fort at night. Encouraged to live in houses close to the fort and to plant crops, the surrounding peoples would be "humanized" as well as (or in the process of being) converted to Catholicism and taught French. In this utopian vision that La Mothe proposes, even the challenge of finding wives would be addressed; French-speaking, Catholic, indigenous women, he explains, would naturally prefer marrying a mediocre Frenchman to the best of their own nation:

> *Et lorsqu'il y aura des Sauvagesses qui parleront bon françois, et qui seront instruites de nostre foy, s'il y a des soldats ou d'autres François qui veuillent les espouser, il y faut donner les mains, et si le Roy vouloit faire quelque gratification en faveur de ces mariages, ce seroit encore mieux et cela engageroit ces pauvres filles à se convertir plus facilement. Il est certain qu'il n'y a point de Sauvagesse, je ne sçaîs par quelle inclination, qui n'aime mieux se marier à un médiocre François qu'au plus considérable de sa nation, et tous les Sauvages se font honneur de ces sortes d'alliances, si bien que les enfans, qui en proviendroient, ne parleroient plus que françois, et auroient de l'aversion pour la langue sauvage, comme l'expérience le fait voir tous les jours dans le Canada.* (Margry, 1887, p. 146)

> [And when the Savage women will speak French well, and will be taught in our faith, if there are soldiers or other Frenchman who want to marry them, we must give them their hands [in marriage] and if the King wants to provide some gratification in favor of these marriages, that will be even better and this will encourage these poor girls to convert much more readily. It is certain that there is no Savage woman, for whatever inclination, who would not prefer to marry a mediocre Frenchman than the most exemplary man of their nation, and all the Savages are honored by such unions, so much so that all the children who are produced by such unions will only speak French and will have an aversion for the savage language as experience demonstrates daily in Canada.]

Antoine de La Mothe-Cadillac's grandiose plan would not be fully realized, but in 1700, he was granted permission to go to the "straits," *détroit*, running between Lakes Huron and Erie, and establish Fort Pontchartrain du Détroit. This endeavor would solidify the French presence in the *Pays d'en Haut* and push the *Canadiens* deeper into the continent. From there, they would expand down the Mississippi to the Missouri, and eventually push across the continent all the way to the Rocky Mountains.

Canadien: Une Nouvelle Nation

By the end of the seventeenth century, the *Canadiens*, the descendants of the French who had settled in the colony of Canada, were considered by the French soldiers and clerics passing through the colony to be a separate people with their own form of national character. Claude-Charles Le Roi de Bacqueville, a French nobleman and officer who had been stationed in New France at the end of the seventeenth century, describes the *Canadien* as he would the Iroquois or any other indigenous nations that he encountered in the Americas. According to him, the *Canadien* men, not the women, are seen as particularly distinct from their French cousins. In fact, Le Roi lauds the women as being less savage than expected: "*Quoique les Canadiennes soient en quelque façon d'un Nouveau Monde, leurs manieres ne sont pas si bisarres ni si sauvages qu'on se l'imagineroit. Au contraire ce sexe y est aussi poli qu'en aucun lieu du Royaume*" (de Bacqueville, 1753, p. 366). [Though the *Canadiennes* [*Canadien* women] are in some way from a New World their manners are neither as bizarre or as savage as one would imagine them. On the contrary, this sex is as polite as any locale in the Kingdom.]

He does, however, highlight the tensions that existed between the citizens of Quebec City and Montreal, as well as the differences in terms of personality. The women of Quebec, it would seem, did not like the manners of the women of Montreal. The latter were perceived as freer, but also—by Le Roi's account—of good faith, very wise, and very judicious. He describes the men as having good qualities: the *Canadiens* like war, are brave, have at least some disposition to learn the Arts, and are capable of learning easily what they are taught; however, they are also a bit vain, presumptuous, they like material goods, and tend to be spend-thrifts (de Bacqueville, 1753, pp. 366-367).

The lure of economic opportunity drove the *Canadiens* up the rivers and deep into the forests and plains of North America to seek out trade. Le Roi de Bacqueville writes that the *Canadien* would go out as fur traders and spend quickly what was earned. However, he tempers his reproach by stating how the fur trade is what allowed the *Canadien* to survive. He writes, "*Quand je blâme le Canadien d'avoir trop d'attache au bien il est un peu excusable, car le païs de Canada n'est pas riche, chacun en cherche selon son industrie, & sans le commerce du Castor la plus grande partie ne pourroit vivre du revenu de ses terres*" (de Bacqueville, 1753, p. 367). [When I blame the *Canadien* for being too tied to material goods, it is a bit excusable as the country of Canada is not rich and each much seek according to their work and without the beaver [fur] trade [as] the majority could not live from the [sole] revenue of their [farm] lands.]

Though the *Canadien* was never depicted as an exceptional farmer and tireless *paysan*, he did excel in his tireless treks through the wilderness. Le Roi de Bacqueville (1753, p. 148) describes in complimentary terms how an expedition

French River Rapids, Paul Kane, ca. 1849–1856. Étienne Brulé, perhaps the first true *coureurs des bois* or "runners of the woods," navigated the French River, or the Rivière des Français, that flows into Georgian Bay on Lake Huron in 1610 and served as an interpreter for Samuel de Champlain five years later having learned the Huron language. Champlain journeyed down the river, as did Pierre-Esprit Radisson and thousands of others. Radisson traveled to England, aggrieved that his furs had been seized as he did not have a permit to trade in the upper countries (*Pays d'en haut*). This led to the establishment of the Hudson's Bay Company in London based on the information he provided of a northern salty sea, Hudson's Bay. The French river linking Lake Nipissing and Lake Huron was a major fur trade artery connecting the Great Lakes and points West to the Saint Lawrence.

had left Montreal in March and had sustained the exhausting pace until June 20, and that, "*il falloit être Canadien pour suporter les incommoditez d'une si longue traverse.*" [One had to be *Canadien* in order to tolerate the inconveniences of such a long journey.]

Over the two decades preceding the re-establishment of the fort at Michilimackinac in the early eighteenth century, French colonial policy under-went a wild swing involving a consolidation that greatly reduced the presence of the French government and military in the *Pays d'en Haut*. France, like Britain later, was already having trouble controlling their settlers, and many of the younger men were voting with their feet. Earlier in the seventeenth century, a large percentage of the indentured servants working in Canada had returned to France after the expiry of their three-year contracts. Later in the century, with a larger permanent population established in the St. Lawrence Valley, the problem the colonial administrators faced was no longer the out-migration east back across the Atlantic to France. It was now the migration of the settlement's young men west into the vast interior of the continent, seeking both profit and greater freedom. Like the Indian men with whom they traded, and into whose families they married, tilling the soil was not a favored option for most who chose to migrate permanently to the *Pays d'en Haut*.

The incessant warfare that raged in Europe and characterized Louis XIV's reign not only weakened France, but indirectly reinforced the British colonies with an infusion of French migrants. The third of these wars, The War of the League of Augsburg (1688-1697), ended with the Treaty of Ryswick. During this war, Louis XIV's and General Louvois's high-handed behavior effectively united all of the Protestant nations and principalities of northern Europe against France. The war started after some 200,000 of France's Calvinist Huguenots, were forced to flee the country following the Revocation of the Edict of Nantes in October 1685 and the severe repression that followed. The French word "refugee" entered the English lexicon at the time due to the scale of the tragedy.

This conflict quickly crippled the nation, both economically and militarily, as the outrage spread. It is estimated that France's navy alone lost half of its officer corps to the navies of The Netherlands and Great Britain during the six peak years of flight, from 1685-1691. The Army's officer corps suffered a high defection rate as well. Their names would pepper the ranks of the officer corps of these two nations for many generations to come. This would also include the armies of Prussia, and ultimately those of a united Germany and the United States.

Preoccupied by war on the continent, France had lacked the resources necessary to encourage greater colonization in its North American colonies earlier under Louis XIII and his principal minister, the Cardinal de Richelieu, let alone effectively police these distant lands. Moreover, when Protestant colonization in its North American colonies was forbidden in 1627, it meant that the French who would leave France in large numbers would settle either in one of the nations of Protestant Europe, or eventually their overseas colonies.

Louis XIV's subsequent attempts to regulate human behavior and the most fundamental aspects of life among his subjects soon extended to North America. These Protestant refugees were still forbidden to relocate to France's mainland colonies which meant that the thousands who came to North American over the following decades ended up in the consolidated British (and formerly Dutch) colonies. The French Protestants who did settle in New France (Samuel de

Champlain was likely a Protestant by birth, and Gédéon de Cologne, who had definitely been a Protestant) had no choice but to be very discreet or convert to Catholicism in order to be allowed to stay in the colony and move up in social rank.

Sons of settlers in New France were deserting their parents' farming communities, beckoned as unlicensed fur traders by the freedom and adventure of the *Pays d'en Haut*. The War of the League of Augsburg and the short peace that followed the Treaty of Ryswick in 1697, had a major impact on France's colonial policy in North America. To enforce the commercial licensing system and minimize expenses, the Governor made the drastic decision in the 1690s to shut down the vast system of military and trading posts that had been painfully built up over a half-century across the territory of the Great Lakes and the Ohio Valley. The little that remained was consolidated in two new settlements: one at Detroit and the other in Kaskaskia on the Mississippi River in the *Pays des Illinois*, known later in English as the Illinois Country.

In *Madame Montour et son temps*, Simone Vincens (1979) explains one of the unintended consequences of this policy decision. In 1699, only forty-six *coureurs de bois* trickled back to the St. Lawrence Valley, even though hundreds had been residing in Michilimackinac. The men who remained behind took Native American wives, raised families, and thus fathered Métis lineages that would come to the fore in the nineteenth century (Vincens, 1979, p. 152).

The French government reversed course, but only after the War of Spanish Succession in 1713. Before dying two years later, Louis XIV obtained international recognition for keeping his grandson on the Spanish throne, while the Acadians and their Mi'kmaq relations were traded away to the British by the Treaty of Utrecht in 1713.

For a generation, however, a black market had flourished as free traders plied distant territory for furs. The descendants of these *coureurs de bois* jelled into the nucleus of Métis communities that would eventually stretch north and west, reaching all the way to the Pacific. Farther north, the French Canadian-Métis and Half-Breeds would come to see themselves as a new nation distinct from the nation-building project deployed by Ottawa to assert an ever-Westerly British-North-American and then Canadian statehood, here clashing with the Métis' claim to aboriginal title "due to the Indian blood running through their veins" (Riel, 1985, p. 279). The descendants of the French "country-born" in the American territories, however, including those with mixed indigenous ancestry, often continued to call themselves *Canadien*, when not reverting to their matrilinial tribal identity.

The keeping of a *Canadien* identity, even with the recognition of Métis ancestry, is not necessarily a contradiction, as the Americans and even the continental

French had viewed the *Canadien* as having been "half Savage." Pierre Pouchot (1781, p. xxxiv), in describing the last war pitting the French against the British in North America, notes that the French did not distinguish their own colonists from the "Savages." He writes how, *"On supposoit même en France à un Canadien une figure extraordinaire, & des mœurs encore plus étranges. Dans la Nouvelle-Angleterre, quoique voisins du Canada, on regardoit encore dans la derniere guerre, les habitants de cette contrée comme des demi Sauvages, parce qu'on y étoit persuadé que les François prenoient des femmes parmi les Sauvages."* [They believed even in France that the *Canadien* was such an extraordinary figure with even stranger mores. In New England, even though they are neighbors, they looked upon them even in the last war, the inhabitants of this country [the *Canadiens*] as half Savages because they were convinced that the French took wives among the Savages.]

The Americans would have seen the *Canadien* as 'half Savage,' as they were believed to have taken wives among the Native Americans. Even the French would have seen their *Canadien* kin as having strange customs that were closer to the indigenous peoples of North America than to recognizable French customs. Considerable efforts were deployed later to erase from the newly formed "*Canadien*" identity associated with the project of its statehood any memory of past mixed heritage, denying that there had been any significant Métissage; however, for the distant *Canadien* of the Old Northwest pushing westwards, the *Canadien* could remain "half Savage" with little need to affirm a Métis identity, as the American Other already presumed the *Canadien* to be a distinct and often "mixed" people.

Jack Kérouac was very aware of this *Canadien* past and the mixing. In his writings, he constantly referred to the combined French and Native heritage and what he described in Visions of Gerard as the place "the French came when they came to the New World, the hardness of the Indians they must have embrothered to be able to settle and have them as conspirators in the rebellion against contrarious potent churly England." He was obviously aware also of their common fate at the hands of the Anglo-Americans, and particularly Amherst, during and after the "French and Indian War." Describing his experience at a New York City College he attended on a football scholarship, he wrote in The Vanity of Duluoz, "we all had to sit in the auditorium and be led in the singing of 'Onward Christian Soldiers' by English Professor Christopher Smart, followed by 'Lord Jeffrey Amherst' which was a song no more appropriate for me to sing (as descendant of French and Indian) than it was for the Jewish kids to sing 'Onward Christian Soldiers.'"

The Catholic Church had strongly supported the government's crack-down on both the Huguenots and the *coureurs de bois*. The Huguenots were considered heretics posing a fundamental threat to Christianity, while the *coureurs de bois* were considered to be debauched souls having left behind their Catholicism and corrupted the indigenous peoples instead of leading them to Christianity. The decision to close distant outposts in 1696 and to consolidate the French presence in two forts was also tied to attempts to curtail the illegal trade and the illicit relations maintained by the *coureurs de bois* with the natives.

Nonetheless, in the interior of North America, the genesis and growth of an independent hybrid population continued unabated. Jacqueline Peterson (1985, p. 42) points out that French officials, both clerical and secular, were surprised to find that the abandoned posts served as the nuclei for these emerging communities: "Instead, as the missionaries discovered, Indian villages located adjacent to former trading stations were sheltering Canadian outlaws, some of whom, by 1702, had taken Indian wives."

Though French policy did not officially allow these relations, the commanders of the forts often turned a blind eye to the connections that were formed between the French and the neighboring native villages. The lone remaining Jesuit missionary, Étienne de Carheil, accused a succession of "unchaste commandants," notably Antoine de La Mothe-Cadillac, of encouraging the men to leave the barracks to establish separate houses for themselves with their native consorts (Peterson, 1985, pp. 42-43). At St. Ignace (French Fort Buade), French *coureurs de bois* were living in the Huron and Ottawa villages despite the 1702 recall.

By the 1700s, illegal traders were also settling in the Illinois Country—first around Peoria and then the more distant villages of Kaskaskia and Cahokia on the Mississippi River. In 1715, acting Governor Ramezay and Intendant of Canada Michel Begon reported that "about 100 coureurs escaped to Cahokia where they joined forty-seven others who had previously settled there" (Peterson, 1985, p. 43). They continued by declaring the "retreat for the lawless men both of this colony and of Louisiana" and that the wives of these men were by and large Kaskaskias and Peorias (Peterson, 1985, p. 43).

As the French forces once again expanded outwards after 1714, new outposts would be created, which in turn would further encourage the development of mixed French and indigenous settlements. These outposts included Fort Miamis (now Fort Wayne) in northern Indiana (1715); Fort St. Joseph in southwestern Michigan (1715) near the town of Niles; and Fort St. François at La Baye, or Green Bay (1717). More forts would be established in a dozen other points, stretching all the way from Lake Superior to Lake Winnipeg and beyond (Peterson, 1985, p. 45). The sites chosen invariably allowed some cultivation, as they were located in warmer micro-climates close to large bodies of water. In all these places, "self-contained metis communities were to develop in the eighteenth century"

(Peterson, 1985, p. 45). Across the continent, many of these communities would remain primarily French-speaking, quite often until well into the twentieth century.

Susan Sleeper-Smith (2001, p. 42) explains how the earlier policy shift at the end of the seventeenth century had proven over the longer term to be another decisive step in the process of developing a more autonomous, bi-cultural group of traders in the *Pays d'en Haut*:

> Despite Indian protests, the trade ban went into effect. The 1696 edict transformed legal traders into illegal traders. Those who remained in the west sought the protection of Native communities, thus furthering their dependence on Indian people. During the nineteen years of the ban, traders and Indians became increasingly interdependent. The coureur de bois who found refuge in his wife's household accommodated to, and even assimilated into, a world structured by Native American custom and tradition.

Sleeper-Smith (2001, p. 42) argues that the French men were transformed into "Indian husbands, fathers, and brothers," but this is perhaps an oversimplification of the social relations being established, an underestimation of the power of an existing—yet inherently relational—national consciousness among them. She submits that kinship "was more flexible than nationality, ethnicity, or race in constructing identity," yet the evidence suggests otherwise. A century later, the descendants of these unions would still proudly affirm their ties to France, continued to speak the French language, while simultaneously valuing elements of their indigenous identities, and most importantly defining themselves as *Canadien*.

The "flexibility" that characterizes early *Canadien* identifications below the 49th parallel and elsewhere cannot simply be explained through an insistence on kinship over what could be interpreted as a lack of "national identity" or even a lack of "collective consciousness." Instead, such *Canadien* identities, we submit, were not yet prisoners of the modern "Canadian" nation-building narrative. The degree of flexibility characterizing early *Canadien* identifications that accommodated the co-existence of indigenous and non-indigenous national identities in non-mutually excluding terms appears more visible at a distance from the conflictual zone associated with the "Canadian" nation-building project. This project produced monological and homogenizing demands for a single nationalist narrative that had to expunge or subordinate any other vectors of collective identification that could defy the absolute assertion of sovereignty, be they indigenous, Acadian, French-Canadian, or otherwise.

While it is true that some men and women, as well as some of their children and descendants, were integrated into pre-existing indigenous nations through kinship networks, many *also* became *Canadien*, carrying this new collective and often strongly indigenized identification as "country-born" or "French-Indian," often beyond the geographical scope by which we now ascribe and limit modern Canadian identity. They would play an important role in opening the more distant West in the nineteenth century as *engagés* and free traders.

The *Canadien* of the Old Northwest: 1715-1765

After a dozen years or so, in the final days of the War of Spanish Succession, the French began to reinforce their presence in the forts of the *Pays d'en Haut*. The isolated outposts at Detroit and Kaskaskia were reinforced, and Michilimackinac was re-established as a central trading and military post. Here, in Michilimackinac, the French would establish a pattern that would be repeated by the later trading companies, notably the North West Company, whereby a central fort would serve as a midpoint for trade. At these forts, crews wintering in the *Pays d'en Haut* and those wintering in the *Pays d'en Bas* could exchange furs for trade goods and provisions at a summer rendez-vous point, then each return home before the snow and ice set in.

In 1716, Louis de la Porte Sieur de Louvigny had left Quebec with a force of 425 men plus farmers, carpenters, and an armorer, destined for the straits of Michilimackinac. The decision to reoccupy this strategic military site was accompanied by the reopening of the licensed trade and the extension of amnesty to all the illegal *coureurs de bois* who could return to the St. Lawrence. Few went home, and the *coureurs de bois* continued their illicit trade. In fact, their numbers multiplied as license holders inflated the number of canoes allowed, sneaking unknown hundreds of anonymous men into the field. Some of these men trafficked in places where no licenses had been granted, but by and large they tended to congregate about the cordon of wilderness posts garrisoned after 1714.

Although the garrison at the straits of Michilimackinac was the largest in the region during the French regime, with its commandant outranking all his counterparts, after the initial deployment, the military force rarely numbered more than thirty-five men. Greater numbers would have served little purpose. They were not occupying a hostile population. The garrisons at other posts were considerably smaller and after 1742 these men were generally employees of commandant-traders who had leased or licensed the rights to engross the profits of a given area. At Michilimackinac, as elsewhere, the garrison engaged in little military activity; instead, it "served primarily to protect traders" and the free flow of goods and furs across the straits (Peterson, 1985, p. 46).

With a limited military presence, Michilimackinac was first and foremost a thriving center of trade. In the summer, merchants or their representatives traveled to the fort of Michilimackinac to supervise trade and oversee the unpacking of trade goods and the packing of pelts that would then be shipped to Montreal, while thousands of visiting indigenous peoples would congregate around the fort to trade. The *bourgeois,* or traders who had wintered in distant places, would in turn travel with their voyageurs to the Michilimackinac post to receive their wages before returning to Montreal or going back to the distant lands where they would spend the winter trading for furs. As the summer ebbed and the rivers began to freeze, the population of the fort would dwindle, leaving the soldiers garrisoned there with their consorts as well as a variety of servants and slaves (generally of indigenous, but also of African origin, especially further south in Illinois Country). The inhabitants of the fort also included the retired voyageurs and traders (Peterson, 1985, pp. 46-47).

The descriptions that remain of the settlement during the French regime uncannily parallel the description of Fort William (located in what is now Thunder Bay, Ontario) by Gabriel Franchère (1820) decades later. Though the merchants and the elite of the fur trade would be replaced by newcomers from the British Isles after the British conquest of New France, the underlying structure of the fur trade with its reliance on voyageurs and bourgeois wintering in far away lands would remain. In both settings, voyageurs would settle on the outskirts of forts with their wives and children, giving rise to unofficial Métis communities.

While establishing a network of forts and trading outposts, the French also succeeded in finding the mouth of the Mississippi River. Hernando de Soto was the first European to see the great river, reaching it on May 8, 1541, and crossing it upstream from east to west. In the following century, French explorers began to map the river, starting from the northern territory of Canada. Departing from St. Ignace in 1673, Louis Joliet, accompanied by the Jesuit Father Marquette and five voyageurs, paddled and portaged across the various rivers until they reached confluence of the Wisconsin and Mississippi Rivers at Prairie du Chien, in what is now Wisconsin. They then explored the middle section of the Mississippi River, traveling south to the confluence of the Mississippi and Arkansas Rivers. Turning back, they paddled up to the Illinois River, where they were told by the local Native Americans of a shorter route, one that would allow them to go up the Des Plaines River and then travel by foot over a short distance, the Chicago Portage, to the Chicago River, which would then bring them to the Great Lakes at what is now the site of the city of Chicago.

The trade and transportation networks of the *Pays d'en Haut* extended throughout the interior along an efficient system of water routes provided by portage-linked rivers and lakes. In short order, the transportation network filled the territory east of the Mississippi, then increasingly to the west of it. For a century and a half the Appalachian Mountains would protect the flank of this interior domain from the swarming British colonists on the Atlantic seaboard. However, the Conquest of New France, starting with the fall of Quebec City in

1759 and ending with the surrender of New France to the British with the 1763 Treaty of Paris, would end French dominance over much of the continent. In 1765, the French flag was lowered at the most distant outpost of the French Empire, Fort de Chartres along the Mississippi shore of Illinois. Though claims of French sovereignty over these territories would end, the population would remain, including thousands of French settlers—and hundreds of thousands of their descendants—spread across the continent.

By mid-eighteenth century, the population of Kaskaskia, the largest of the half-dozen French settlements in the region, was reported to be broken down as follows: around 1000 French residents; about 800 Kaskaskia Native Americans still living in the adjacent village; some 300 black slaves; and 60 indigenous slaves or *Panis* (Pawnee)—a French term alledgedly derived from the name of one tribe providing initially a significant number amongst them (Sleeper-Smith, 2001, p. 60).

Linguistic habits help illustrate the nature of this empire in which the peculiar balance of forces and demographics relegated the foreign imperial power—the most powerful in Europe—to the status of *primus inter pares* (first among equals). Other than the settlers in the *Pays d'en Bas* and those Christianized tribal remnants that relocated there, it was the French in the *Pays d'en Haut*, be they missionaries, traders, voyageur canoemen, settlers, or soldiers, who learned the indigenous languages. Though this language acquisition was usually the case in the early building stages of colonial empire, it continued for the full term of a century and a half in almost all of France's North American empire. Only later would this change with the proliferation of mixed-ancestry communities in the interior. Generally speaking, most French or *Canadien* who spent more than a year or two in the *Pays d'en Haut* became bilingual, often multi-lingual, and took local wives. Originally, some of the children of these relationships were integrated into their mother's nations or accompanied their father back to the St. Lawrence Valley. In other cases, autonomous communities began to appear where a critical mass of kinship relations and intermarriage practices developed with indigenous peoples, and more and more *coureurs de bois* opted not to return to the *Pays d'en Bas*.

It has also been recently suggested that such communities existed closer to the fringes of the St. Lawrence Valley, such as in Le Domaine du Roy (R. Bouchard, 2008b; Dawson, 2008) in Quebec's Saguenay-Lac Saint-Jean region. French may have been the written language of the empire, but it represented only one of its many spoken tongues.

In *Rites of Conquest: The History and Culture of Michigan's Native Americans*, Charles E. Cleland (1992, p. 146) summarizes the language situation in the region at the close of the Seven Years' War in the 1760s. He draws on the *Handbook of*

North American Indians, Volume 15, *The Northeast*, for which Bruce Trigger (1978) was editor:

> As heirs of the French interests, the first few British soldiers and traders who made their way to the northwest found themselves not only recent enemies of the local inhabitants, both *Anishnabeg* and French, but very much strangers confined to Detroit, Michilimackinac, and a few other remote trading forts. Most of these locales had small French settlements and it was to these communities that Indians continued to have their closest ties with the non-Indian world. Over one hundred years of contact with native people had produced frequent ties of blood and a great deal of bilingual fluency. Ojibwa/Ottawa and French not a combination of the two was the lingua franca of the fur trade. The fact that the Great Lakes region never produced a true pidgin language for the conduct of its extensive trade is an indication of the ability of a great many people to communicate in both the Algonquian dialects and French. Lacking kin ties to Indian communities and speaking neither French nor any of the Algonquian tongues, the British were, in many ways, starting a new wave of exploration. (C. E. Cleland, 1992, p. 146)

Similarly, no true fur trade pidgin would develop in either the Canadian or the American West. The Chinook jargon, the only pidgin that emerged, would come to be heavily "Frenchified" once the Pacific Northwest was integrated into the North American fur trade networks. It existed in parallel with the French language, which became the *de facto lingua franca* in the Columbia Basin and greater Pacific Northwest. Cleland (1992, p. 75) notes that to this day, "many native Americans bear French surnames, have French genes, and often greet each other with the Algonquinized French term boo-zhoo ('bonjour')." The same would be true of many of the peoples of the greater Pacific Northwest stretching to the Rocky Mountains both to the north and south of the 49th parallel.

Partition of the *Pays d'en Haut* Along the Mississippi

No longer a story of European empire building, the French-Canadian (*Canadien*) and Louisianan (*Créole*) settler and trading communities were cut loose to find their own way by the Treaty of Paris of 1763. They continued to participate fully in the development of their West, though under new flags and governors, becoming something of a story of the outer frontier.

The first partition came at the hands of the conquering enemy, Britain. The British claimed sovereignty east of the Mississippi, gaining progressively effective control over both the Indiana and Ohio Territories to the east, while the territory to the West as well as the coastal areas around New Orleans became the nominally Spanish territory of Louisiana in 1762. Britain also acquired a coastal strip that they renamed West Florida comprising the older French gulf settlements around the bays of Biloxi and Mobile. British victory over the French on the battlefield, however, did not guarantee that France's former indigenous allies would automatically realign themselves or even surrender to the British.

Following an attempt to implement the heavy-handed British occupation policies, Pontiac led a major rebellion around the Great Lakes starting in May 1763. Initially, several forts fell in a series of attacks and some two thousand settlers and soldiers were slaughtered before regular British troops were able to re-establish control by 1766, but not without British General Jeffrey Amherst having small pox-infested blankets sent to the nations allied with Pontiac. Backing off somewhat following the uprising, the British King issued the Royal Proclamation in October 1763 that granted a number of rights to the *Canadiens* and recognized the indigenous peoples as formal political interlocutors, treaty-partners, and title owners of their lands, while simultaneously claiming Dominion. The Niagara Treaty of 1764, for example, carries an important oral tradition, highlighting the specific understanding of the Royal proclamation of 1763 by the Indigenous actors of the time on much more equal terms, nation-to nation with the colonial powers (Borrows, 1998).

The proclamation also specified that the sovereign lands of the indigenous peoples to the west of the Appalachians could not be bought by individuals, but had to be negotiated by Crown officials with the sovereign indigenous nations through a treaty process, effectively repositioning many French-Métis and Halfbreed communities as mere "squatters." Here we see the precedent for enduring legacy of the American Articles of Confederation, the Northwest Ordinance.

East of the Mississippi, during the half-century following the fall of Montreal in 1760, the English and Scots gradually became dominant in the business along the northern Great Lakes and in the St. Lawrence Valley. In the void south of the Great Lakes, however, the French merchants in the interior retained a stronger position in the face of a slow assertion of regional sovereignty by the Americans between 1778 and 1795. After the British taxpayers and army had obligingly helped the colonists remove the French from the Ohio Valley in the late 1750s, the *Canadiens* of the *Pays d'en Haut* were back to assist the Americans two decades later to clear the British from the coast and the same hinterland. The collaboration of *Canadien* frontier communities like those of Illinois and Indiana with George Rogers Clark, William's older brother, greatly facilitated this task. (See Chapter 7)

With Independence, however, the United States of America were no longer restrained by the Royal Proclamation of 1763 and the Quebec Act of 1774, whose restrictions on settlement and land speculators, settlers, and assorted squatters developed quickly into one of the major grievances of the American colonists leading to up the revolution. Making its terms their own, after the War of Independence, the United States began negotiating land cessions and the removal

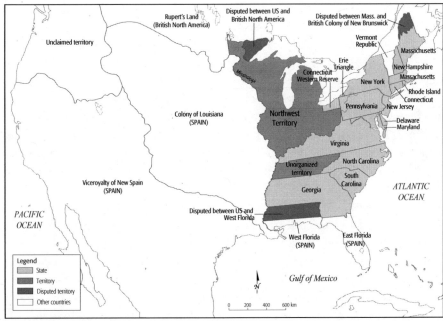

States and Territories of the United States of America August 7, 1789 to May 26, 1790. Having succeeded in gaining independence, the original Thirteen Colonies were also ceded territories to the west under the treaty signed with the British. This territory covered the lands stretching between the organized Thirteen Colonies and the Louisiana territory, then under Spanish sovereignty. These lands to the north and west of the original colonies (the Ohio, Illinois and Michigan territory) are known as The Old Northwest.

of indigenous groups on-shore, no longer restrained by distant authorities. The Native Americans and the majority of their Métis relations were increasingly isolated and vulnerable to removal by the new American authorities as settlers of European descent poured in.

Post-Conquest Demographics

Though the number of *Canadiens*, Métis, and indigenous populations of the lands to the west of the Appalachians could never compare to the millions of British colonists and other waves of immigrants coming from the East who seemed ready to spill out over the mountains, the demographic importance of the French-speaking *Canadien*, Métis, and indigenous groups is too easily glossed over in later historical accounts or popular history. Edmunds (1993, pp. 186-187) provides a useful summary of the French-speaking populations of the triangular region located between the Great Lakes, the Ohio River, and the Mississippi River—an area now known as the Old Northwest. (This 'Old Northwest', now in the United States, is not to be confused with the "Northwest" in Canada, which once meant all lands north and west of Lower Canada, later to be Ontario and the prairies).

Edmunds highlights that French was the effective *lingua franca* of the region and that the descendants of French settlers formed the majority of the non-indigenous population. As late as the War of 1812, frontier settlements such as Vincennes, Peoria, Cahokia, Fort Wayne, Prairie du Chien, and Detroit held predominantly French-speaking populations, according to Edmunds. Even in 1816, Territorial Governor Lewis Cass estimated that "four fifths" of the alleged "white" population of Michigan Territory was descended from the first French settlers. Thus, close to three generations after the conquest of New France, the children of New France and Louisiana, who often intermarried to become distinctively "French-Indians" and Métis, were still the dominant group in the American territories of the Old Northwest. Moreover, the Native Americans of the region still looked upon the memory of their French allies, lamenting after the fall of Quebec the loss of those who "used to marry our daughters." Louise Seymour Houghton (1918) honors in a book the vital role played by the Métis and the "French-Indians" in the development of the United States.

John Johnston, an indigenous agent among the Shawnees and Miamis in Ohio and Indiana, admitted that he had "seen Indians burst into tears in speaking of the time when their French father had dominance over them" (Edmunds, 1993, p. 212). In 1809, General—and future President—William Henry Harrison echoed the same sentiment when describing the throngs of Miamis, Potawatomis, Shawnees, and the remnants of the Illinois Confederacy who gathered to meet a French emissary in Vincennes in 1796: "the happiness they [the Indians] enjoyed from their intercourse with the French is their perpetual theme—it is their golden age. Those who are old enough to remember it, speak of it with rapture, and the young ones are taught to venerate it as the Ancients did the reign of Saturn" (Edmunds, 1985, p. 187; 1993, p. 212). The only nation that retained its independence and defiance during the French reign were the Foxes, who resisted the French pervasive influence; the other nations had generally maintained accommodating and cooperative relationships with the French (Edmunds, 1993, p. 213).

By the early nineteenth century, the close association between the French and the Native Americans had created a culture based upon values extracted from both groups. The new people, the Métis, dominated both the French colonial and French-Native American communities, merging facets of the rich heritage of both ancestries. Intermarriage between the two peoples had become common. Nations such as the Choctaw, Kaskaskias, Peorias, Miamis, Potawatomis, Ottawas, and Chippewas held large biracial populations, while frontier settlements throughout the Old Northwest contained significant numbers of Métis.

At Detroit, Cass reported that "many of the traders and a great many of the agents and clerks employed by the companies have Indian or half-breed wives and the mixed offspring they produce has become extremely numerous" (Russell David Edmunds, 1985, p. 188).

However, it would only be in the northern territories—those of the Red River Valley, now in Canada—that the term "French-Canadian Métis" (used by Louis Riel) would eventually be appropriated by the descendants of French voyageurs and their indigenous wives, to eventually become the basis of a "Métis" nationalistic expression. There was a perceived need to distinguish itself more sharply from the "Canadian" identity swallowed by the modern statehood project driven by Ottawa. That project, at the time, was significantly driven by Anglo-Protestant and white supremacist sentiments, hostile to the demands of French-speaking and Catholic Métis populations struggling to secure land title on the basis of their "Indian" heritage. Away from such Canadian nation-building and the dispersal of the Northern Métis Nation that followed, in the southern territories of the Ohio and Missouri rivers, and environs, the "descendants" of the French would frequently still use the ethnonym *Canadien* to refer to themselves, yet never at the cost of excluding the possession of an indigenous/non-indigenous mixed-ancestry and culture which could then also be identified by additional ethnonyms such as Métis, French-Indian, or *Bois-Brûlé*. Cases of Métis self-identification outside the area of Red River, in the Great lakes area, the U.S., and even in the Northern part of Quebec are amply documented.

As they retreated further west from the onslaught of American settlers, many of the French-*Canadien* descendants in the more northerly borderlands began to coalesce into autonomous communities. These began to appear more noticeably in the upper Great Lakes and the upper Mississippi around such villages as Green Bay, Prairie du Chien, Milwaukee, Chicago, and St. Paul in the late 1700s and early 1800s. Some stayed behind in these growing settlements to brace themselves against the rigors of dealing with the approaching wave of Americans, generally noted for their intolerance of French-speaking half-breeds and their indigenous relations. Others continued to retreat further inland across the lake country of northern Minnesota into the Red River Valley, and ultimately the plains beyond. As the beaver trade collapsed behind them, the buffalo herds of the northern plains beckoned, drawing them westward across North Dakota along the upper Missouri and ultimately into central Montana. Pembina on the Red River—soon to find itself in the crosshairs of the border lines of Minnesota, North Dakota, and Manitoba—developed into a major center for these buffalo-hunting bands of Red River Métis, with their famous squeaky two-wheeled carts. As previously mentioned, one of the names initially acquired for this particular sort of half-breed, one that had become commonplace on the north-western frontier, but also found in other regions including Quebec, was the French term for burnt wood: *bois-brûlés*—a possible translation from their Chippewa appellation, *Wisahkotewan Niniwak* (Dusenberry, 1985, p. 120).

Détroit to Detroit

With the British Conquest of New France, Detroit would eclipse the settlement of Michilimackinac, which was re-occupied after falling during the Pontiac Rebellion. The British later abandoned it, but only after the Jay Treaty in 1795. Then, with the War of 1812, Michilimackinaw was one of the first American military outposts to be taken back by the British, and one of the last re-occupied after the Treaty of Ghent in December 1814. When the U.S. Army returned, Astor's American Fur Company installed its western Headquarters on Mackinaw Island. In the interim, the native population, principally Chippewa, along with their Métis relations, continued to be the principal inhabitants of the region, including Sault Saint Marie.

Detroit benefited from a milder climate and rich soil for farming. Though the British would occupy the fort at Detroit after the Conquest in the early 1760s, the French settlers continued to inhabit the surrounding territory. Outside the fort, the narrow ribbon farm lots of the *Canadiens* and Métis were scattered along the Detroit River as far north as Lake St. Clair. In order to encourage the settling of these lands, the French commanders of Fort Detroit had given titles to the "plantations," along with gifts of oxen and seed, to French settlers from Canada between 1734 and 1753. By British and American standards, the farmers of Detroit were considered lackadaisical workers, but they did farm the land, raising sufficient surplus food to feed their kin and to provision the Lower Michigan fur trade. Simply put, any production of perishables beyond the level that the regional market could absorb was simply waste. During the French regime, therefore, many Detroit area residents engaged in both the fur trade and agriculture.

Consequently, it has been reported that there was less *métissage* than was the case elsewhere in other French forts and settlements, even though the physical appearance of the settlement and the material culture of its households differed little from those of Michilimackinac. Recent contributions provide ample evidence of the presence of Métis communities in Detroit and immediate vicinities (Karahasan, 2006; Marrero, 2011).

The layout of Detroit was reminiscent of the string of settlements along the St. Lawrence, themselves early adaptations to the needs of trade and transportation. (See Map of Detroit, p. 48.) Unlike the community within the stockade, with its rectangular grid with orderly row houses and avenues, Detroit was laid out along the water line. Each man staked out his plot, or long lot, based on the available river shoreline, with his cabin hugging the bank and his picketed garden trailing into the timber behind. The "estates" were narrow and relatively equal in size. This was the same pattern of settlement that characterized the St. Lawrence River Valley as well as the later Red River Métis settlements. After a generation or two, additional log-and-bark cabins sprang up alongside the original, occupied by sons and grandsons of the families, so that the shoreline became a continuous line of houses. Detroit was the largest town in the Great Lakes region after 1765, reflecting the greater commercial and administrative importance attached to it by the British. Nevertheless, while the British and later American merchants flocked to the urban core inside the stockade, the old *Canadien* population was forced to cope with its burgeoning population through dispersal, often accompanied by a relative shift from a mix of farming and hunting, toward a more diversified economy.

The primary challenge facing the French and Métis who remained in the British and then American territories was gaining title to land. In the case of Detroit, Peterson cites the British Governor, Henry Hamilton, who "declared at the close of 1778 that he had never granted lands at Detroit despite pressure from settlers 'whose farms [were] small and families numerous.'" As a consequence, the Governor noted that, "young men growing to age engage as canoe men, go off to distant settlements and in general become vagabonds, so that the settlement does not increase in number."

François Navarre did gain the right to settle the lands to the south of the Rivière aux Raisins (Raisin, or Grape, River) in 1784, and French and Métis settlers colonized the area. More than one hundred families had built cabins on the River Raisin over the following decades, recreating both the special pattern and lifestyle they had enjoyed at Detroit for several generations. The community at Rivière aux Raisins was an example of a second type of Great Lakes Métis settlement. (Rivière aux Raisins came to be called Frenchtown by American settlers and later Monroe after President James Monroe's 1817 visit to the region.) Unlike the commercial-military center of Detroit, whose increasingly diversified economy and strategic location allowed for potentially unlimited growth, trading towns like Frenchtown remained limited. Frenchtown was eventually able to shrug off its dependence on the fur trade, while developing into a thriving agricultural and commercial center.

Jacqueline Peterson notes that the trading towns such as Frenchtown had a simple and quite egalitarian social organization with occupational homogeneity, depending upon a local "home guard" or indigenous band for surplus food and security. These smaller settlements had none of the clear status and wealth demarcations of the growing town of Detroit. They functioned as corporate entities laid out in relatively equal-sized ribbon-shaped lots, with common fields and pastures, and were self-regulating regarding trespassing and theft, and the transfer of lands and houses—invariably without the benefit of European or American titles. They had purchased or received freely their estates from an earlier author-ity, the councils of neighboring nations with their headmen and elders (Peterson, 1985, pp. 54-55).

Of course, these transactions usually involved oral contracts, resulting in the distinct lack of a documentation trail for later arrivals to validate. In Green Bay and Prairie du Chien, for example, prominent traders formally purchased lands of the Menominee and Fox, respectively, while in smaller settlements like St. Ignace, and Sault Ste. Marie, Michigan or Fort Wayne, Indiana, and other corporate trading towns, title was not officially granted to the inhabitants until after the War of 1812, whereupon American surveyors were forced to take verbal depositions to untangle the customary rights of the Métis. In contrast, claims at Michilimackinac and Detroit carried the weight of French and British documen-tation. The principal exception to this generalization was the town of Vincennes in southwestern Indiana, which had been administered as a part of Louisiana and where many of the eighty-eight landholders of 1773 claimed pre-1763 French patents (Peterson, 1985, p. 55).

The Green Bay area, or *La Baye Verte*, had been attracting traders at least as early as 1720. In 1732, a contract to trade at La Baye was issued to Didace Mouet de Moras, the brother of Michilimackinac trader Augustin Langlade, founder of Green Bay's most illustrious Métis family. By the 1740s, several traders with Native American wives were permanently residing there, including Pierre Réaume, Claude Caron, LeBeau, and Jourdain. The Métis community at Green Bay started to grow with the transfer of Michilimackinac following the treaty of 1763. After the initial British occupation of the fort, Langlade, his Ottawa wife, and their son, Charles, abandoned their residences at the straits and settled on fifteen acres on the east bank of the Fox River opposite the fort. Charles Langlade, who later acquired considerable military acclaim, enjoyed the patronage of both British merchants and the title of Indian superintendent in the Green Bay district. Through Langlade's influence, members of other well-connected Michilimackinac trading families migrated to "La Baye" where they settled on ribbon plots, or long lots, upriver. (See map of Green Bay, p. 303.) By 1785, according to one of Langlade's descendants, the community contained at least fifty-six permanent residents— traders, voyageurs, hunters, and Indian slaves. Similar trading towns were grow-ing at Peoria, St. Ignace, Fort Miamis (Wayne) and Sault Ste. Marie on the eve of the 1763 British takeover (Peterson, 1985, pp. 55-57).

Not all French and Métis settlements could be easily separated from their native neighbors. By 1746, for example, on the lower Wabash at Post Vincennes, forty men and their families and five slaves commingled with a band of 750 Piankeshaw warriors. To the north at Post Ouiatanon (present-day Lafayette,

Indiana), twenty [Métis] households were living alongside six hundred Wea warriors and their kin. At Fort St. Joseph on the St. Joseph River near Niles, Michigan, a thriving trade with the neighboring Potawatomi had gathered forty or fifty *Canadien* families to its environs by 1750.

Many other Métis communities, of various sizes, would coalesce around trading or agricultural gatherings based upon mixed-heritage families taking up residence. Grace Lee Nute conservatively estimated that, in 1777, five thousand voyageurs plied the waterways of the greater Northwest. By the late 1820s, a population of ten to fifteen thousand residents of Métis communities south and west of lakes Superior and Huron seems a plausible estimate. Lewis Cass informed John C. Calhoun in 1819 that in the settler population in Michigan Territory alone (Michigan and Wisconsin) "there are not more than eight thousand Inhabitants" of which he estimated about four-fifths were of mixed ancestry. Indiana and Illinois also had sizeable Métis concentrations at this date, as did the region that would become the state of Minnesota. (Peterson, 1985, pp. 62-63)

A Refuge for French Colonists is Established West of the Mississippi

On the far side of the Mississippi, colonial matters had evolved dramatically. Spain, France's ally, had received Louisiana as compensation for the loss of Florida to the British. After four decades under Spanish rule, Louisiana had become much more French. Indeed, it became the principal sanctuary or refuge for over ten thousand colonists stranded by the collapsing French empire in the Americas. Refugees poured in from Acadia (via a forced exile in France), Saint Domingue (Haïti), and the Illinois Country, while a share of the 60,000 *Canadiens* continued to move west into the interior, or le *Pays d'en Haut*. After the brief restitution of Louisiana to France in 1803, the United States purchased the Louisiana territory and gained dominion over an area inhabited by several hundred thousand Native American and over 40,000 French speakers of increasingly varied ethnicity, including a few thousand descendants of African slaves and a smattering of remaining Spaniards.

As the Americans continued to move inland, they would find a significant Métis population already in place. Thomas Ingersoll (2005), in his ground-breaking study of interracial unions on the American frontier, entitled *To Intermix With Our White Brothers: Indian Mixed Bloods in the United States from Earliest Times to the Indian Removals*, downplays the scale of the French *métissage* component somewhat, arguing that the French communities appeared as one "vast mixed people" to the encroaching Anglo-American outsider. He writes, "The extent of racial mixture appeared to contemporary outsiders to be greater than it was because the French-speaking communities of the interior were so far-flung. Isolated extended family compounds loosely connected the villages," and adds that "language and religion reinforced the otherness of this veil of hamlets and family compounds that stretched across the gateway to the Far West" (Ingersoll, 2005, p. 155).

General Collot (1826, pp. 317-318) provides an inventory of the French that remained in the Illinois territory and the Missouri. Georges-Henri-Victor Collot was a French military officer who fought along with thousands of French troops allied with the American Revolutionaries in their War of Independence. The French settlements that had been located in the Spanish territory included Ste. Geneviève, Saint-Louis, Florissant, and Saint-Charles. On the American side, French remained in Kaskaskias, Prairie du Rocher, Saint-Philippe, Cahokias, Peorias on the Red River, Prairie du Chien close to the Wisconsin, in Chicago on Lake Michigan, as well as Fort Vincennes. Even though they share the same French ancestry, Collot's (1826, p. 318) description of the French inhabiting the Illinois country, the *Canadiens*, is as ethnocentric as those of any Anglo-American:

> *La plupart de ces peuples sont un composé de traiteurs, d'aventuriers, de coureurs de bois, de rameurs et de guerriers; ignorans, superstitieux et entêtés, qu'aucunes fatigues, aucunes privations, aucuns dangers ne peuvent arrêter dans leurs entreprises qu'ils mettent toujours à fin; ils n'ont conservé des vertus françaises que le courage.*

> Most of these peoples are a composition of traders, adventurers, of coureurs de bois [runners of the woods], paddlers and warriors, ignorant, superstitious and stubborn, that no fatigue, no amount of privation, no danger can stop them in their affairs, which they carry always until the end; they have kept of the French virtues only bravery.

For Collot, the French inhabitants that remained in these lands were ignorant, superstitious, and stubborn; however, he notes that fatigue, privation, and danger wouldn't stop them, and that they had kept only one French virtue: courage. However, this does not detract from his continued haranguing of the inhabitants of the *Pays d'en Haut*.

The General is clearly guided by post-Revolutionary French Enlightenment ideals, and the inhabitants of the Illinois Country are obviously quite foreign to him. He continues:

> *Mais, rentrés chez eux, et dans leur vie privée, ils tiennent du caractère des indigènes avec lesquels ils vivent; ils sont donc indolens, paresseux et ivrognes, ne cultivent que peu ou point la terre, ne parlent plus qu'un français corrompu, espèce de jargon, et ont oublié jusqu'à la division du temps et des mois. Si on leur demande dans quel temps telle chose s'est passée, ils répondent, du temps des grandes eaux, des fraises, du maïs ou des pommes de terre. Leur observe-t-on qu'ils devroient changer telle ou telle chose reconnue d'un mauvais usage? ou leur fait on quelques observations raisonnables sur l'amélioration de l'agriculture, ou l'augmentation de quelques branches de commerce, on obtient d'eux, pour toute réponse: "C'est la coutume; nos pères faisoient comme cela; je m'en suis tiré il faudra bien que mes enfans en fassent autant." Ils aiment la France et en parlent avec orgueil.* (Georges Henri Victor Collot, 1826, pp. 318-319)

But, once they have returned home, in their private lives, they adhere to the character of the indigenous peoples with whom they live; they are indolent, lazy and drunkards, cultivating little or no land, speaking but a corrupted French, a type of jargon and they have forgotten the division of time and months. If we ask them when something has happened, they will answer in the time of the great waters, [the time] of the strawberries corn or the potatoes. Do we remark that they must change this or that thing that is known to be of bad practice? Or if we make a few reasonable observations as to how to improve their agriculture or increase some branches of commerce, we always get from them the same answer: "This is the tradition, our fathers did it like this; I succeeded thus, and my children will have to do as much." They love France and speak of it with pride.

Collot's description of the behavior of the French in the Illinois Country would be comparable to that of any indigenous people of that time and place. Time was understood in terms of harvesting seasons, mostly collecting wild plants and fruits. There was also a form of conservatism whereby new innovations were not immediately embraced; instead, it was deemed preferable to carry on practices that had proven to be effective in the past.

In Collot's description, however, there is no "Noble Savage." He notes that they live with indigenous peoples (presumably their wives) and appear to share the same character traits, including indolence, laziness, and drunkenness, and to top it off, they speak (in his opinion) "corrupted" French. However, it is the final statement that is perhaps most important for our analysis. In it, he affirms that they love France and speak of it with pride. This attachment to the culture of origin is certainly an important reason why the language was so well maintained over the decades, besides other pragmatic linguistic considerations.

Surprises awaited Americans like Daniel Boone in the 1770s, and later Michigan Territorial Governor Lewis Cass during the War of 1812, and even William Keating in 1823, when they crossed the Appalachians and penetrated into "Indian Country." Among the more distasteful experiences was finding that these "mongrel" French were already there, and well entrenched. Both historians R. David Edmunds (1985) and Jay Gitlin (2009) quote from William Keating's account of his expedition to the Upper Mississippi. In passing from Ohio into Indiana, arriving at Fort Miami (now Fort Wayne, having been re-named for an Anglo-American general), Keating wrote:

Not being previously aware of the diversity in the character of the inhabitants, the sudden change from an American to a French population, has a surprising, and to say the least, an unpleasant effect; for the first twenty-four hours, the traveler fancies himself in a real Babel... The business of a town of this kind differs so materially from that carried on in our cities, that it is almost impossible to fancy ourselves still within the same territorial limits [of the U.S.] (Keating, 1825, p. 75).

Keating's sense that he had passed into a new and rather foreign country had a firm basis in reality. The French language could be heard from Detroit to St. Louis to New Orleans, and the entire western fringe of the young republic had a French or Creole flavor. Gitlin underlines that French cultural hegemony only gradually receded during the decade of the 1830s, while retaining pockets of influence in the larger cities and their suburbs—and in frontier villages such as Kansas City for decades more. He states that "it is not the ultimate demise of French hegemony that should surprise us, rather its persistence over so large a region for so many decades after the incorporation of that region into the United States" (Gitlin, 2009, p. 1).

R. David Edmunds was one of the contributing authors to Peterson and Brown's collection, *The New Peoples: Being and Becoming Metis in North America*. In Edmunds' chapter entitled "Unacquainted with the Laws of the Civilized World: American Attitudes toward Metis Communities in the Old Northwest," he had included much the same citation as Gitlin, but given his focus on the Métis population added Keating's complaints regarding not only the language of Fort Wayne, but also his distaste of the mixed heritage of the inhabitants of the fort: "[Fort Wayne] contains a mixed and apparently worthless population. The inhabitants [of Fort Wayne] are chiefly of Canadian origin, all more or less imbued with Indian blood" (Edmunds, 1985, p. 189).

The hybridity of the French-Canadian Métis culture is derided by Keating, as the Métis had been too willing in his view to adopt the dress and culture of the Native Americans: "The appearance of those Frenchmen [Métis] who had exchanged their usual dress for breech-cloth and blanket, was as risible as that of the Indian who assumes the tight-bodied coat of a white man" (Edmunds, 1985, p. 190).

The ethnocentric judgment of Keating mirrored the earlier sentiments of Adam Walker, who was serving in the U.S. Army's 4th Regiment in 1811 when his unit arrived in the frontier town of Vincennes, Indiana. Walker described the Métis as "rabble" indistinguishable from the "savages" (Edmunds, 1985, p. 190). He nonetheless indicates that they spoke French, even though the material culture was that of their Native American kin. He likewise felt the need to display his own higher standards by characterizing them in pejorative terms, writing that "many of these militia spoke the French language; their dress was a short frock of deer-skin, a belt around their bodies, with a tomahawk and a scalping knife attached to it, and (they) were nearly as destitute of discipline as the savages" (Edmunds, 1985, p. 190).

By all accounts, the Americans who first encountered the Métis of the Old Northwest came to view the Métis in a negative light. As Edmunds (1985, p. 189) recounts, the Métis had adopted many of the traits of their French forebears.

Most spoke French, and answered to French surnames. While few Métis lived lavishly, most were comfortable by frontier standards, and a small number had actually become wealthy through trade. Unquestionably, the Métis served as important instruments in the commerce of the Great Lakes and the Upper Mississippi Valley and were an important minority group, rapidly adapting to the arriving ways of the U.S. while playing a major role in the economic development of the region.

Why were many of the Métis forced out by the Americans and relocated to the lands beyond the Mississippi? Though the Métis were multilingual, many spoke no English. Worse yet, they were judged inferior (being the product of interracial unions) and generally showed little interest in becoming yeomen farmers (Edmunds, 1985, pp. 189-190). Thus, the hybridity that had been an asset during the fur trade became a liability in the new era of American hegemony, a racialized society where "miscegenation" was not tolerated. The Métis were suspect because of their culture, their race, and though Edmunds does not address it, certainly due to their superficial Catholicism as well.

The ethnocentric bias demonstrated in the writings of American settlers such as Keating and Walker was representative of what the *Canadien* and Métis settlers of the Pacific Northwest would face when the children and grandchildren of these American settlers caught up with them after traveling over the Oregon Trail. To these weary travelers, residual French and Métis settlements at trail's end were a barely tolerable irritant. Despite having been appropriately marginalized in the American Midwest over the prior generation, they were once again polluting yet another American frontier with a *lingua franca* that was French, not English. In this case, however, it would be complimented by a native pidgin known as the Chinook Jargon, one that had been linguistically infiltrated by the French language following the expansion of the fur trade in the Pacific Northwest in the 1810s.

Here too, the American newcomers would find *Canadiens* and Métis in the Columbia valley already having adopted many elements of indigenous culture. Again these "habitants" would be viewed as indolent, rather uncivilized, and definitely not "real settlers." The assimilation and removal proceedings would commence once more. Many Métis would again be pushed to the margins of society, and into the back country. Finally, having nowhere else to go, many would choose to settle with their Native American kin and friends on reservations or to blend in within the increasingly Americanized landscape. The French language would eventually become muted, but the memories remain.

The Choice: Assimilation or Removal

By the early nineteenth century, in the region beyond the Appalachians, a crusade was well underway to turn local, semi-nomadic "hunters and gatherers" into full-time, sedentary agriculturalists that would use the land more inten-sively—or not at all. In the years preceding the War of 1812, Moravian and Quaker missionaries joined the well-established Catholics working among the tribes of Ohio and Indiana. Sponsored by the government, these evangelists attempted not only to convert the Native Americans, but also to alter the ways of life of the indigenous peoples; after baptizing the indigenous peoples and their Métis rela-tions alike, they would teach their new followers the precepts of frontier agriculture.

Among certain communities of Shawnees, Delawares, Miamis, and Potawatomi, the missionaries were successful; by 1808, some of these people had cleared small fields and planted crops of corn, wheat, and barley, and were living in log cabins resembling those of their Euro-American neighbors. A period of disruption followed after the emergence of the Shawnee Prophet, an alcoholic-turned-spiritual leader (and brother to Tecumseh) who emphatically denounced all Euro-American ways—from agriculture, to manner of dress, to religion. This in turn was followed by displacement during, and immediately after, the War of 1812, which did much to undermine the influence of the missionaries. After 1815, the small communities of "civilized" Native Americans shrank in size and importance, becoming less visible (Edmunds, 1985, p. 185).

Susan Sleeper-Smith, based on later research, which was actually coordinated with Edmunds, was able to provide greater nuance to the earlier picture of how the Métis and Native Americans in the region responded to the new order. Sleeper-Smith (2001) points out that Richard White's *The Middle Ground* emphasized how the Great Lakes Region was a coherent geographical entity where a process of negotiation pervaded the early colonial period. She then examines the period that follows, one foreshadowed by White: "Although White offers important perspec-tives on a negotiation process not dominated by Euro-Americans, he also argues that the nineteenth-century dissolution of the middle ground led to indigenous demise" (Sleeper-Smith, 2001, pp. 2-3).

The end of the War of 1812 led to a definitive British withdrawal to the northern shores of the Great Lakes, and the United States was finally able to reinforce and exercise its claim to sovereignty over the region. Henceforth, new terms would be dictated to the native inhabitants as well as the *Canadiens* that remained. Negotiations might round out the sharper edges of agreements "or treaties," but there was no stopping the implementation of American policy and the associated demographics of its newly arriving constituents demanding more land. Though "the middle ground" would no longer be able to hold the line in the Old Northwest, it would shift into the newer frontier zones further north within the Great Lakes region, and then beyond the Mississippi, across the Great Plains, and ultimately into the Columbia Basin.

Canoe men camping
Sept 7 1866

Canoe Men Camping, Frances Anne Hopkins, ca 1866. Paddling all day, the voyageurs would enjoy a short respite at the evening camp with warm food, rest and sleep before taking to the waters once more the next day.

In each region the situation might be unique, but varied around some central themes. In the western Great Lakes, many Native American people persisted, despite attempts at forced removal. In the end, some were forced to relocate westward, while those located to the north often remained behind, or at least nearby. Practicing both accommodation and resistance, they used what power they could wield to either disperse in place, or endure relocation and diaspora (Sleeper-Smith, 2001, p. 3). Many *Canadiens* and other French-speaking people remained behind and played a role in the history of Michigan and points farther west.

CHAPTER 3

Accommodation in the Middle Ground

From the *Pays d'en Haut* to Illinois and Michigan Territory (1670-1818)

The roots of the continental *Canadien* and Métis are to be found in the vestiges of the *Pays d'en Haut*, the back country of New France, which, south of the Great Lakes, became the states of Ohio, Illinois, Indiana, Michigan, and Wisconsin. It is here that the iconic elements of Métis culture emerged and took root, notably the flower beadwork that came to represent the Métis of the Red River Valley and other locales in Canada and the United States.

Straddling the shifting borders of the American Indian and Euro-American worlds, the Métis and *Canadiens* of these future states were important economic and political brokers whose history has been largely buried, even though this territory had by far the largest concentration of Métis on the continent. It is in the Michigan Territory that the fur trade prospered and expanded westwards, and it is in the Michigan Country that the voyageur tradition had truly been honed.

Under the French, Fort Michilimackinac had been the central transit point where furs were brought in from distant territories before being shipped to Montreal and then Europe. The interior trade hub shifted first to Grand Portage in Minnesota and then to Fort William (now Thunder Bay), but the Michigan Territory remained a pivotal locale in the North American fur trade, and as such it had a large *Canadien*-Métis population that possibly outnumbered that of the Red River and the rest of the Northwest Territories combined. In a span of two generations, from the fall of New France and the signing of the Treaty of Paris to the onset of the War of 1812, the *Pays d'en Haut* witnessed some remarkable political changes as the political power was transferred from the French, to the

Cartes des Possessions Angloises et Françoises du Continent de l'Amérique Septentrionale," 1755. Though the French territory of Acadie in the Maritimes had been conquered, the French still controlled a vast territory that stretched to the Great Lakes, down the Mississippi to the Gulf of Mexico. Though their numbers did not match the population of the Thirteen Colonies, they had established alliances with the major indigenous nations, seeking trading partnerships as opposed to outright colonization of the territories under the control of the French. The descendants of the French—Canadien and Créole—nonetheless inhabited the forts and towns along waterways covering thousands of miles.

Voyageur Boat and Chippewa Canoe, William Armstrong, 1901. The French quickly adopted and adapted the indigenous technology of using birch bark to make light but durable canoes. The largest canoes, le *canot du maître* or "master's canoe" could measure forty feet long and carry five tons of freight (the average weight of an adult African elephant). The largest canoes were used to freight goods from the Saint Lawrence to the Great Lakes while smaller canoes would be used to fan out over continent. Though they could carry incredible quantities, even the largest canoes were light and could be carried by a few men.

British, then to the new American Republic, and in 1812 a final war would be fought that would confirm the border between the United States and British North America (later to be named Canada).

Throughout this period, in the northern region encompassing Michigan Territory that remained once Ohio and Illinois achieved statehood, the French-speaking *Canadien* and Métis were the dominant group in the settler population. For a period of sixty years they were front and center in the political and economic upheavals that would beset the Great Lakes Region. Likewise, a portion of the French-speaking populations of Illinois would remain in the new states of Illinois and Indiana, even if their demographic weight was rapidly declining with the influx of Anglo-American and other settlers.

The Montana historian Joseph Kinsey Howard, in his early rendition of the history of the Métis of Canada's Great Plains, *Strange Empire: A Narrative of the Northwest*, published in 1952, informs us that according to an estimate of an American official in 1879, half of the continental Métis still lived in Michigan. He writes: "The large Michigan group, descendants of the first of their race, had lost their Metis identity though they retained some of their French tradition" (Howard, 1952, pp. 337-338).

Howard rightly recognizes that the history of the Métis was not limited solely to the Red River, but rather stretched across the continent and began in the seventeenth century: "This was the Metis world, scattered from Michigan to Montana's Rockies, from St Louis to Great Slave Lake." The history of the Michigan Territory and the eventual state merits close analysis as it was in many ways the cauldron of a continental *Canadien* culture and tradition that became Métis.

The American official cited by Howard (1952) put the number of Métis living in the United States and Canadian Northwest in 1879 at 33,000, a figure which Howard qualified as being "far from adequate," as it underestimated the numbers of Métis living across the continent. The 1879 source estimated that half of the Métis were in Michigan. Howard is critical of the numbers assigned to Montana. The 1879 source assigned "more than a thousand" Métis living in Montana, but Howard writes that Montana had 53,000 residents at that time and some 32,000 were either American Indian or Métis. The other Métis, according to the 1879 source, lived in the Dakotas (1,300), Wisconsin (1,450), and several thousand in Missouri and Illinois. The Métis living in Canadian territory would have represented roughly a third of the continental Métis according to this source cited by Howard, with some 6,500 living in Manitoba and an equal number in the Northwest Territories, which then included Saskatchewan and Alberta.

Unfortunately, the exact sources used by Howard were not fully preserved. Howard apparently derived this information from records buried in the U.S. government archives, and though there is a bibliography for his posthumously published *Strange Empire*, Howard had not completed the full accounting of his sources cited. As explained in the Foreword to *Strange Empire*, written by his friend and editor, fellow historian Bernard DeVoto, Howard had completed the manuscript by the time he passed away, but hadn't lived long enough to fully source all elements of the text, though he had intended to do so. This includes the 1879 official government source providing an inventory of the Métis.

A more nuanced analysis of Michigan's French-speaking communities can be obtained by analyzing the work of Télesphore Saint-Pierre (1895), a journalist and writer, who had moved to Detroit as a child with his family in 1878 and who then returned to Canada and published a detailed account of the history of Michigan and the Essex County of what is now Ontario in 1895. Largely ignored by American historians, this work provides a detailed account of the history of the French-speaking people of Michigan, both during the French Regime, the British interregnum, and its eventual integration into the United States. This is both a secondary and a primary source. Saint-Pierre provides a historical analysis based on his reading of the sources that were then readily available in the public libraries of Detroit, but he also witnessed and participated in the French-speaking community in Michigan, speaking in French to the children and grandchildren of the men and women who had been in Michigan in the early years of the nineteenth century.

Télesphore Saint-Pierre (1895, p. 306) estimated that in 1890, there were some 100,000 people living in Michigan who were descended from the French-speakers that had settled in Michigan prior to 1840. Of these, he estimated that some 25,000 still spoke French and could be classified as French-*Canadien*, while the others almost all understood French, but preferred to speak English (Saint-Pierre, 1895, p. 308). Regions where French was spoken widely, according to Saint-Pierre, were in the farming communities of Monroe (formerly Frenchtown) and the larger Detroit area. He specifies that the language was maintained as these communities had much more limited contacts with the outside, and he feared that if there were any changes in the their means of subsistence, then they, too, would likely lose the language (Saint-Pierre, 1895, p. 309).

Given the demographic weight of the historical Métis community of Michigan, this territory and eventual state is an essential component of the larger history of the *Canadiens* and Métis. The history of the Métis of Michigan also reveals a number of themes that are common to the Métis communities across the continent. These themes played out in the central state of the Great Lakes region before reappearing along similar, but different lines west of the Rocky Mountains. The central theme is the prolonged presence of the French-speaking, old group of settlers of European and mixed ancestry throughout the territorial period, facing challenges of economic and political assimilation—with mixed outcomes. This parallels the experience of the old settler population of *Mestizo* in the American southwest.

A Mobile People of Dubious Loyalty

The continued presence of the French-speakers was also met with some defiance by the incoming Anglo-Americans. They suspected the loyalty of this older population, as they had been allied with their enemies over an extended period of time along the border, with much of the warfare taking place in and around their settlements. The fact that two of the bloodiest battles fought during the territorial period in both Michigan and Washington state were known as the Battle of Frenchtown is not a coincidence. These frontier "Frenchtowns," somewhat like the later "Chinatowns" in port cities and mining centers, tended to be flash points where two separate worlds met, and to the American settlers the "French" were seen as having divided loyalties, thus as not true Americans. Much of this distrust also centered on the high degree of intermarriage of this older *Canadien* settler group with the indigenous populations, whose *modus vivendi* had been based on inclusion and co-habitation, not exclusion and removal.

In contrast to their neighboring states to the south, the indigenous peoples of Michigan Territory, like Washington Territory, did not undergo wholesale removal or relocation. Subsequently, nations with their affiliated Métis relations straddling the new border between the two empires were arbitrarily split, simply to conform to straight lines drawn on a map thousands of miles to the east that did not reflect human reality on the ground. Many Indians never were consigned to a reservation, and remained with their Métis relations in a "no-man's land" off-reservation, and often these same tribes continued to be unrecognized by the Federal authorities. Elsewhere, it is the *Canadien* and Métis who relocated to the reservations, taking allotments of land in the 1880s and later choosing to live close to their kin, as was the case in much of the Pacific Northwest. In turn, they lived in a form of cultural limbo, having to remain largely quiet as to their *Canadien* antecedents.

The other recurring theme is the mobility of the *Canadiens* and omnipresence of a number of *Canadien* and Métis families in the earliest exploration parties and settler populations in both the Old Northwest and the Pacific Northwest— be it different branches of the same *Canadien* clan like the Drouillard, Charbonneau, Rainville, Picard, and Petit families, or a later generation of descendants, like those of the Montour, Campau, and Nadeau families. These families were in turn followed by the Catholic Church—also dominated by French-speaking priests and bishops until there was a large-scale influx of Irish migrants later in the nineteenth century. These priests played a leadership role during this difficult transition period among these disenfranchised groups—be they Indians, *Canadiens*, or Métis.

How this history was buried across the United States is the other common thread. The historiography of the Old Northwest and Michigan still recognizes the early presence of the *Canadiens* and Métis, and of course the Indians, but then generally writes them off, suggesting that they had disappeared. In the Pacific Northwest, for example, the numerous *Canadien* settlement areas and their deeply rooted tribal affiliations are generally ignored. The exceptions are limited to the early *Canadien* trading posts, which are treated as British, plus the existence of a French Prairie settlement in the Willamette Valley, which is dissolved in a sequence of departure, death, and assimilation of the residual fragments. In either case, there is supposedly little or no demographic legacy.

The Fascinating Montours

One Métis family story, briefly referred to in the introduction, stands out. The Montour clan was founded near Trois-Rivières by the marriage of Pierre Couc to his Algonquin wife, Marie Miteouamigoukoue in 1657. Many of their children and grandchildren followed their son, Louis, in adopting the name of Montour. As Serge Bouchard (2009) observes, the French settlement of Trois-Rivières, founded in 1634, was an important Algonquin locale, and numerous indigenous women were eligible for "marriage" to French settlers; as such mixed marriages were quite common there. Some of the Montour children stayed on in the Trois-Rivières area, while others left for the *Pays d'en Haut*. One daughter, the widowed Isabelle Montour, was in Michilimackinac by the late seventeenth century, actively participating in the trade with her husband, while another son of Pierre Couc, Louis, ranged all over the region from Michilimackinac to Detroit, upstate New York, and all points between. Pierre Couc's sons and grandsons would take indigenous wives from a variety of nations, while the daughters and grand-daughters, with the exception of Isabelle, would marry new French settlers or their children. The Montour family thus expanded both geographically and numerically, and continued to speak French, but was not necessarily subservient to the French authorities even at the height of New France's power.

The Montours were irascible traders, pushing boundaries, even before the fall of New France. With the colonial administration of Louis XIV applying an ever more heavy-handed approach to licensing, Louis and Isabelle Montour, like Groseilliers and Radisson, also from Trois-Rivières, and an increasing number of their countrymen, each began trading independently with the British, defying the self-serving authorities catering to the prerogatives of New France's landed and commercial gentry. Louis soon had a price on his head, and was assassinated in upstate New York, along the Niagara River. The multilingual Isabelle, now going by the title of Madame Montour, evaded capture, and re-married an Iroquois chieftain by whom she had a number of children. Her son, Andrew, followed her footsteps and became a prominent frontier diplomat and interpreter for the British and Iroquois (S. Bouchard, 2009).

A central characteristic of the Montour family, and other trading families, is the close ties developed and maintained with their indigenous allies and the mixed culture being created, hence the French term *métis*. As Denis Vaugeois (2009) writes, citing Simone Vincens' biography of Madame Montour, the interests of the American Indians were their interests, the Indian cause their cause, and over time this would become stronger as the two groups would continue forging stronger ties and alliances. Vaugeois recalls that this was Champlain's dream but in the inverse, as a number of Frenchmen were becoming culturally closer to their Indian allies with time, as opposed to the various indigenous nations becoming more French.

Not only do the Montours figure prominently in the history of the Great Lakes, they also ventured far West, reaching the Pacific. In 1806, the Métis clerk Nicolas Montour, Jr., son of a North West Company partner, was on the upper Columbia with fellow Métis Jaco Finlay, preparing the way for David Thompson in establishing a permanent presence for the Montreal-based North West Company on the Columbia River. In addition to Thompson, Nicolas and Jaco were soon joined by their colleagues Joseph Bercier, Bucher, Le Camble, Lussier, Clement, Michel Boulard, Beaulieu, Augustin Boisverd, and Finan McDonald (Nisbet, 2005, pp. 35-41).

By the second half of the nineteenth century, children and grandchildren of Nicolas were living in the Métis communities of the Willamette and Umpqua valleys, while others had relocated to the Grand Ronde and Flathead Indian Reservations at opposite ends of the Columbia River system, in territory that had since been acquired by the U.S. By then, one of his sister's daughters, Letitia, had arrived with her husband from the Red River and established another extensive line in the Willamette (Jackson, 1996).

Close scrutiny of the history of the Métis, and by extension the history of French in North America, with an eye on the two intertwined paths, shows the crucial role women played. The French voyageurs and *coureurs de bois* were by no means ascetic, much to the chagrin of some groups in the region. One of the challenges faced by the Catholic Church of French North America—whether in Canada, the *Pays d'en Haut*, or the *Pays des Illinois* —was the libertine and slightly rebellious nature of the men. Louis-Armand de Lom d'Arce, baron de Lahontan (1703, pp. 147-148), relates the ongoing battle between the men and the clerics:

> *Les Sauvagesses aiment plus les François que les gens de leur propre Nation, parce que ces premiers se soucient moins de conserver leur vigueur, & que d'ailleurs ils sont assídus auprès d'une Maîtresse. Cependant les Jésuites n'épárgnent rien pour traverser ce commerce; & pour y réüssir, ils ont de bons Vieillards dans toutes les cabanes, qui comme de fidèles espions leur raportent ce qu'ils voyent, ou ce qu'ils entendent. Ceux qui ont le malheur d'être découverts; sont nommez publiquement en Chaire, dénoncez à l'Evêque & au Gouverneur Général, Excommuniez & traitez comme des Infrácteurs de la Loi. Mais malgré toute l'adresse & toute l'opposition de ces bons Pères, il est constant qu'il se passe dans les Villages quantité d'intrigues dont ils n'ont aucune connoissance.*

> The Savage women love the Frenchmen more than the people of their proper Nation, because the former are less preoccupied with conserving their vigor, & that they are very attentive to their lovers. However, the Jesuits stop at nothing to stop these transactions and to do this they have good old men in each cabin like faithful spies who

report to them all that they see. The ones who have the misfortune of being discovered are named publically from the pulpit, denounced to the bishop and to the governor general, excommunicated and treated like criminals. However, in spite of all the opposition of the good fathers [priests], it is a constant that there are many illicit affairs in the village of which they have no knowledge.

The men were even threatened with excommunication for entertaining any relations with Native American women, though this does little to stop the nocturnal activities of either the men or the women. Having left Canada, the men in the *Pays d'en Haut* often did their best to stop the spread of the Jesuits and discourage the indigenous peoples from accepting the Black Robes. The Jesuit Father Jacques Gravier wrote in his account of life in the Illinois Country that the son-in-law of the Kaskaskia chief, almost certainly Michel Accault, had tried his best to discourage his future father-in-law from converting, giving him an extremely negative account of the missionaries. In his words:

> *Leur gendre contraint par les reproches de sa conscience a avoué à son beaupere et à sa bellemère que toutes les fables qu'ils avoient raconteés au desavantages des missionnaires n'etoient que des fictions que la médisance et la calomnie lui avoient fait inventer pour empescher les gens d'embrasser notre sainte foi, et pour plaire à certains libertins, qui l'avoient gagé pour débiter des mensonges et m'obliger s'il avoit été possible à quitter le pays* (Gravier, 1857, pp. 20-21.)

> Their son-in-law, forced by the reproaches of his conscience, admitted to his father-in-law and to his mother-in-law that all the fables that he had told concerning the missionaries were nothing but fiction having invented malicious gossip and slander to prevent the people from embracing our blessed faith and [thus] to please certain libertines who had him pledge to utter a stream of lies and force me if possible to leave the country.

Thus, a number of Frenchmen, "*français,*" in the *Pays d'en Haut* were seeking to drive out the Jesuits, forcing the Jesuits to seek out unlikely allies, the indigenous women of the region, as a means to convert their nations as well as to control the "*libertins*" who had strayed from their faith. Gravier (1857, pp. 62-63) recounted how the son-in-law, Marie's husband, had changed after his marriage and had become as zealous to convert the Native Americans as he had been a contrarian working against the Jesuits. Marie, according to Gravier (1857, p. 40), told him that she was merely turning the Illinois into the French ("*Je ne fais que changer l'Ilinois en François*"). Consequently, an alliance of women and priests helped to shape the settlements that would become *Canadien*.

In her book, *Indian Women and French Men: Rethinking Cultural Encounter in the Western Great Lakes,* Susan Sleeper-Smith (2001) relates another gender-focused central theme: how indigenous women, in their traditional roles as the designated family agriculturalist, also successfully responded to the new market opportunities in selling agricultural surplus. This would free up their husbands to pursue their trading and transport activities without the distraction of running a farm. Sleeper-Smith, gleaning information from the records of the Catholic Church, fur trade companies, the associated correspondence, and secondary sources, examines in detail the lives of several women of Potawatomi, Illini (Illinois), and Odawa (Ottawa) origins, whether "pure blood" or mixed. She found this assumption of agricultural responsibilities to be the case for Marie Rouensa Accault (Illini); Marie Madeleine Réaume L'Archeveque Chevalier (Illini-Potawatomi métisse); Magdelaine Marcot Laframboise (Odawa métisse); Madeleine Bertrand (Potawatomi); Kakima Burnett (Potawatomi); and Marie Bailly (Odawa). All except one of these women were married to *Canadien* or Métis men. All of them were also active partners in their husbands' business operations.

To begin with, Marie Rouensa's close relations with the local Jesuit, Father Jacques Gravier, played a critical role in the conversion of indigenous families and other Kaskaskia tribal members to Catholicism. Sleeper-Smith (2001) illustrates the significance of these kinship networks in matters not only of trade in furs and agricultural goods, but also of survival, accommodation, and even prosperity during challenging times. In providing a more nuanced view of the region during its "middle ground" years (1650-1815), one that would later become the American Midwest, we focus on the story of only the first three of these six women.

The term "middle ground" is derived from Richard White's (1991b) work, *The Middle Ground: Indians, Empires, and Republics in the Great Lakes region, 1650-1815*. Sleeper-Smith (2001, pp. 2-3) specifies that White's work has "drawn attention to the importance of the western Great Lakes as a coherent geographical entity and more important, as a region where encounter entailed a process of negotiation, where neither Europeans nor Indians could win through force." Sleeper-Smith diverges from White, however, in arguing that in the western Great Lakes, Indian people persisted, practiced both accommodation and resistance so that even "[i]n the face of overwhelming odds, Indian people were still far from powerless," whereas White, according to Sleeper-Smith (2001, p. 3), argued that the American Indians were powerless after the middle ground era.

The same is true of those French-speaking *Canadien* and Métis who remained in the region and played an important role even as they gradually came to assimilate to the new hegemonic language in the second half of the nineteenth century. Unlike Sleeper-Smith, we believe that *Canadien* identity emerged. Essentially, the mixed-heritage descendants of the indigenous women and their fur-trading husbands became, for the most part, *Canadien*, forging a culture that drew upon both French and indigenous cultures, but kept the French language and Catholic faith. Popular and academic historians easily forget that French remained the dominant language of trade long after the fall of New France. In the region located between the Appalachians and the Mississippi, from the seventeenth century to the early nineteenth, "Pidgin French, not English, was the *lingua franca* of the trade" (Sleeper-Smith, 2001, p. 160). The same applies to the Potawatomi who had occupied the western and southern shores of Lake Michigan and adjoining inland areas.

Cleland (1992, p. 218) notes that the the bands around Lake Michigan were quite close to the French: "This latter group was intermarried with the French-Canadian community at Niles and South Bend; some spoke French as well as Potawatomi, and many were inclined toward Catholicism." These close ties continued even after the British Conquest of New France and the signing of the Treaty of Paris that transferred New France to the British in 1763.

Historians overlook too easily the continued influence of the French-speaking traders, be they *Canadien*, Métis, or to a lesser extent Créole, who remained in the former French territories after dominion over these lands had been ceded to the British. R. David Edmunds (1978, p. x) writes: "Indeed, the close Potawatomi-French relationship continued well after the official French withdrawal from the Midwest, playing a major role in tribal acculturation patterns in the nineteenth century." Edmunds infers, however, that the "mixed-bloods" were not culturally *Canadien*: "A product of two (and sometimes three) cultures, many of the mixed-bloods subscribed more to the value systems of the Creole French traders than to either Potawatomi or American ideals" (Edmunds, 1978, p. x).

It is not surprising that such "mixed-bloods" conformed to the values of the "Créole French traders," as they certainly would have identified as *Canadien*, which a number of scholars seek to confound with "French Créole" in the North. Being a "mixed-blood" did not disqualify an individual in the early nineteenth century from identifying as *Canadien*, Métis, or *Bois-Brûlé*. They could describe themselves as one or more of the three and use their alliances with Native Americans to act as mediators to their own benefit or that of their kin. As Edmunds writes: "They served as mediators between the red and the white communities, often protecting Potawatomi interests, but also amassing personal fortunes in their negotiations with the federal government" (Edmunds, 1978, p. x).

Edmunds suggests rightly that they provide an interesting "study in acculturation." However, different conclusions can be drawn from the historical data. Some of the descendants of these Michigan "mixed-bloods" ended up in the Pacific Northwest and they identified as *Canadien*, while others eventually became Métis. These "mixed-bloods" must therefore be included in the analysis of the emergence of a *Canadien*, *Canadien*-Métis, and eventually simply Métis identity across the continent (See Chapter 9).

Treaties are marked by dates and lines that can represent traps for those who look back. Regardless of earlier treaties, the U.S. authorities were not able to reach and occupy Detroit until 1796. Moreover, the British only definitely withdrew to the northern shores of the Great Lakes after the War of 1812. That was when the dynamics of the middle ground were dramatically altered. The United States was finally able to exercise its sovereignty over the region, which had previously only been theoretical. New terms would henceforth be virtually dictated to the Native Americans.

Negotiations might round out the sharper edges of agreements "or treaties," but the implementation of American policy and the associated demographics of its newly arriving, land-hungry constituents would not be stopped. Though "the middle ground" would no longer be able to hold the line in the Old Northwest, it would shift into the newer frontier zones further north within the Great Lakes region, and then beyond the Mississippi, across the Great Plains, and ultimately into the Columbia Basin. In each region the situation might be unique, but varied around central themes associated with accommodation. The emergence of these new identities is evident in the history of the individuals, starting with Marie Rouensa, who is in many ways the godmother of Kaskaskia and its historical *Canadien* community.

Marie Rouensa and Kaskaskia

Marie Rouensa grew up in the primarily indigenous village of Kaskaskia in the early eighteenth century, a village that attracted such neighbors as Michel Accault, who had entered the region with La Salle in 1679. After the wars between the Illini and Iroquois and the relocation of the surviving Kaskaskia bands to Peoria, Cahokia, and Kaskaskia, the area acquired a mission manned by French Jesuits. Under its austerity-driven fiscal strategy, the French authorities shut down all the outer posts that had been so hard to control in order to consolidate the *Pays d'en Haut* around two new centers located at Detroit and Kaskaskia, in Illinois Country on the Mississippi. The Jesuits also supported this policy for the reasons cited above. These two new outposts coincided with another set of expeditions to establish ports of entry for the Mississippi River along the Louisiana coast line, beginning with Biloxi in 1699 and Mobile in 1701.

Regardless of colonial policies formulated across the ocean, in all these settlements local traders would remain dependent on the indigenous people for food. With agriculture being women's work in the indigenous world, fur traders who married into indigenous households had an advantage over those more transient traders who did not. Throughout the region, a general decrease in inter-nation warfare stimulated a demographic recovery and the fur trade, resulting in increased agricultural production by Indian communities in the eighteenth century. The agricultural surplus produced by native women kindled an expanding and ever more diversified trade. With furs, grain, and livestock being traded for household utensils, cloth, guns, and ammunition, native agriculture could now support military operations for extended periods. Yet since agricultural communities were more vulnerable to the repercussions of warfare, they generally had a vested interest in maintaining peace and prosperity (Sleeper-Smith, 2001, pp. 25-30).

These communities would nonetheless be forced into an infernal cycle of resistance or relocation in the face of periodic outbreaks of colonial warfare as the eighteenth century progressed and by the relentless encroachment of American squatters, settlers, and speculators, and their militia that followed in the early nineteenth century.

Marie Rouensa, the daughter of a prominent Kaskaskia headman, initially resisted her parents in their choice of the fifty-year-old fur trader, Michel Accault, for a husband. Since these outsiders provided access to cloth and other trade goods—crucial to forming or reaffirming indigenous alliances—a fur trader was viewed as a welcome addition to any household or village. Marie Rouensa eventually consented, but only if her parents agreed to convert to Catholicism, which they did (Sleeper-Smith, 2001, pp. 25-30). Michel Accault died after seven years of marriage, and Marie remarried shortly thereafter to another trader, Michel Philippe. He was a more recent arrival, less prominent than her first husband, but he and Marie remained married for twenty years and had six more children together descendants of which live in Prairie du Rocher today.

The appeal of Catholicism to Illini women was rooted in the continual decline over several generations in the number of eligible Illini men resulting from continual warfare in the seventeenth century—first with the Sioux and Winnebago, then the Iroquois. The number of polygamous marriages thus increased, which, according to reports of the earliest French missionaries and explorers, became increasingly oppressive (Sleeper-Smith, 2001, pp. 25-30). Conversion to Catholicism, with its requirement for monogamous relationships, offered an attractive alternative for women such as Marie Rouensa. As Sleeper-Smith (2001, p. 26) relates, "Father Gravier told stories of female Catholic saints and provided native women with very powerful models of assertive behavior." Before Catholicism, the only option that unmarried women had was to join the warrior society; now they could devote their lives to the Church.

In this contested middle ground Christianity would also offer a channel through which recent male converts could reassert their authority. As Sleeper-Smith recounts, Father Gravier, in his most lavish testament to Marie's miraculous power, noted that with Marie's campaigning, two hundred Kaskaskia were baptized between March 30 and November 29, 1693. His letters were published in the Jesuit Relations and later translated into English.

Marie's success, however, did create new challenges for Father Gravier. As more senior and higher status individuals converted to Catholicism, they expected to be accorded greater status within the church, even challenging the priest's authority. Gravier had to resort to closing the church doors and refusing access in his struggle with the village elders (Sleeper-Smith, 2001, pp. 28-29). However, with the decline of the Jesuits disbanded by the Pope in 1773, soon there would be no priests left to contest the elders. Lay leaders of the Indian and Métis communities that had adopted Catholicism filled the void during the second half of the eighteenth century across the Great Lakes and Illinois Country and increasingly asserted themselves in sustaining the religion. Later examples would include Madame Laframboise among her Odawa neighbors along the Grand River and then in Michilimackinaw, as well as chief Pokagon in the St. Joseph River Valley of southwestern Michigan.

Marie Rouensa, in addition to her community religious leadership role, also ran an extensive farming operation throughout her adult life. While raising her family, Marie had accumulated an estate valued at 45,000 *livres* when she died in 1725, nine years before Daniel Boone was born in Reading, Pennsylvania. An inventory of her property along the Mississippi shore of Illinois included two houses, complete with stone fireplaces, in the Kaskaskia village. Though the maize or corn remained to be harvested, two barns on the family farm were already filled with wheat and oats, along with hay to feed the livestock, which included a team of oxen, thirteen cows, three horses, thirty-one pigs, and forty-eight chickens. She owned five slaves, including two African-American couples and one indigenous woman. There were also iron ploughs, axes, oxcarts, and horse carts (Sleeper-Smith, 2001, pp. 31-32). The inventory at Marie's death provides a glimpse of the household's economic structure:

Marie's wealth rested on her household's agricultural productivity, and because she left sufficient property to inventory, we also see the material evidence of her second husband's continuing employment as a fur trader. Among the goods inventoried inside Marie's house were prodigious amounts of cloth, emblematic of a household that was directly engaged in the trade. Michel Philippe was a fur trader—he was not a French peasant farmer (Sleeper-Smith, 2001, p. 32).

Marie's will, drafted by a Jesuit priest, included a number of clauses seeking to discipline a wayward son. With the assistance of Jesuit missionary Antoine-Robert Le Boullenger, a codicil was added to her last testament specifying that he could claim his inheritance if he repented and re-entered life in society, abandoning his life "among the *sauvage* nations" (Sophie White, 2013, p. 131).

During Marie's lifetime, Kaskaskia was still an Indian village with a French mission, a small number of fur traders, and a growing number of families with children of mixed-ancestry. Only one French woman lived amongst them then. Sleeper-Smith (2001, p. 32) argues:

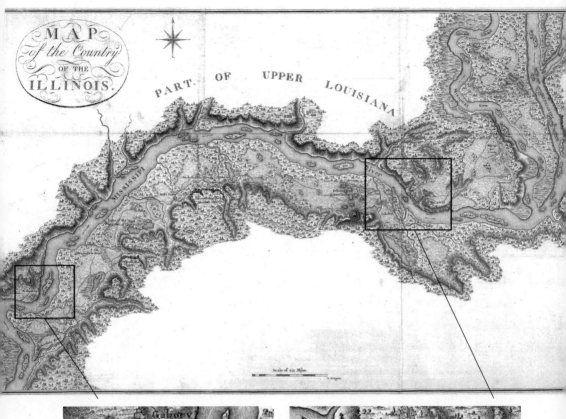

Map of the Country of the Illinois, Collot, ca. 1800. Georges-Henri-Victor Collot, effectively a French spy, traveled from the Great Lakes to the Missouri and down the Mississippi to New Orleans where he was arrested by the Spanish who still had possession of Louisiana before it was transferred a few years later to the French and then sold to the United States. A military officer, Collot was focused on providing an account of the military installations of the territory. Nonetheless, he provides some interesting insights into the population inhabiting these territories. This particular map provides a detailed accounting of not only the settlements, but also windmills in ruins as well as the site of the salt works. St. Geneviève, Bourbon and Kaskasias are on the left. Cahokia and St. Louis, on the right.

Neither Catholicism nor involvement in the trade transformed Native woman into French housewives. Native women resisted the division of labor associated with European households. There were none of the tools that characterized home industry (spinning wheels, looms, or even knitting needles) among probated wills and inventories of these river community residents. Since Kaskaskia remained part of an indigenous universe in which agriculture remained a female responsibility, the viability of evolving matrifocal households was ensured through an ever expanding labor pool that incorporated adult children and their offspring, as well as Native American and African American slaves and their children. Indigenous gender roles gave women the management and allocation of productive resources.

She notes, however, that the Jesuits taught the Indians to use the *charrue*, a wheeled plough. And again, in such a household enterprise, as the women oversaw agricultural production, this allowed the men to focus on the family business.

The author failed to acknowledge, however, the early expressions of *Canadien* identity would prevail in the growing settlement of Kaskaskia. She refers throughout her work to "Frenchmen," which is erroneous in most cases as the men would have self-identified as *Canadien* in its original and often strongly indigenized acceptation of being "country-born." She also writes, "Marie Rouensa was not French. The Kaskaskia village population grew owing to the intermarriage of Frenchmen and Native women, forming a French-Canadian-Metis population, not Frenchmen and Frenchwomen" (Sleeper-Smith, 2001, p. 35). Marie was not French, but her children and grandchildren would become *Canadien*.

A century later, Auguste Levasseur, General Lafayette's private secretary, describes Kaskaskia in 1825 during a stopover made during Lafayette's farewell tour of the states of the union. Levasseur (1829, p. 290) described the crowd that had gathered to listen to the speeches by the governor and General Lafayette:

> *A côté d'hommes que la dignité de leur contenance et l'exaltation patriotique de leurs regards faisaient facilement reconnaître pour Américains, étaient d'autres hommes dont les vêtemens plus grossiers, la vivacité, la pétulance des mouvemens, la joie expansive de leurs visages, me rappelèrent beaucoup les paysans de ma patrie; derrière ceux-ci, près de la porte et sur le piazza qui entoure la maison, se tenaient debout, immobiles, impassibles, de grandes figures rouges, à demi-nues, appuyées sur un arc ou sur un long fusil; c'étaient des Indiens du voisinage.*

> Next to the men whose dignified countenance and patriotic exaltations of their gaze made it easy to recognize them as Americans were other men whose clothing was more coarse, whose vivacity, petulance of their movements, expressive joy on their faces, reminded me greatly of the peasantry of my homeland; behind these men, close to the door and on the veranda that surrounded the house, standing upright, immobile, impassive, were tall red figures, half naked, leaning on a bow or a long rifle; these were Indians of the neighborhood.

The *Canadiens* are depicted as being somewhat more shabbily dressed, but their countenance and the joy expressed in their faces reminds Levasseur of the peasants of his country, France. Once the speeches are completed, he walks around the milling groups and discovers French being spoken around him. He writes how, "*dans toutes les parties de la salle, ou formaient quelquefois de petits groupes au milieu desquels on entendait éclater, en langue française, les expressions de la joie la plus franche, la plus animée*" (Levasseur, 1829, p. 292). [Throughout the room, where there occasionally formed small groups in the middle of which we could hear bursting out, in the French language, expressions of joie the most frank, the most lively.]

Once it is known that he is French, Levasseur is bombarded with questions by the men about their historic homeland, "*la mère-patrie.*" Levasseur (1829, p. 294) specifies the term used by the men to identify themselves: "*Je fis de mon mieux pour répondre à la question de mon Canadien.*" [I did my best to answer the question of my Canadien.] The men are *Canadien*, though they still carry an emotional attachment to their paternal homeland, France. Clearly, though, they would have had ancestors such as Marie. They had remained attached to the French culture that had been passed down the paternal line, while developing strongly indigenized ways of life that blended elements of both French and indigenous cultures within this "*Canadien*" collective identity, puzzling European visitors for whom these two identities could only be mutually exclusive. Levasseur meets a man who is the product of a much more recent *métissage* and whose description provides perspective:

> *Son visage, sans être cuivreux comme celui des indigènes, était cependant très-basané. Ses vêtemens courts, sa large ceinture à laquelle pendait une poudrière, ses longues guêtres de cuir qui montaient au-dessus de ses genoux, tout son équipage enfin annonçait un chasseur des forêts. Il était appuyé sur une longue carabine.*

> His face, without being coppery as those of the indigenous peoples was however very bronzed. His clothes were short, his large belt to which hung a powder horn, his long leather gaiters that went up to his knees, all his apparel finally announced that he was a hunter in the forests. He was leaning on a long rifle.

The man explains in French that his father was a white man from Canada and his mother from the tribe of the Kickapoos. Levasseur thus symbolically contrasts the four principal groups inhabiting Kaskakia in the 1820s: the Americans, better dressed and very patriotic; the *Canadiens*, most certainly the product of an earlier métissage, but often depicted as resembling the lack of refinery associated with the French peasantry, mingled with undeniable influences from the Native Americans often living among them; the image of a hunter with deeply tanned skin, yet not copper-colored like the indigenous peoples, dressed in leather leggings and a wide belt (possibly a sash) from which hung his powder horn, and leaning on a long rifle; and the Native Americans, depicted as red-skinned, half-naked, and leaning in turn on either rifles or long bows. All told, it provided a gradation of sorts from the "civilized" to middle-range to the "savage," distinctions that would ultimately be used by the Andrew Jackson Administration to justify the policies of forced relocation during the next decade.

A new influx of *Canadiens* would continue after the Conquest of Canada by the British, as *Canadiens* from the St. Lawrence Valley would join the older *Canadien* community in Kaskaskia.

Between Conquest and Revolution: Migration of the *Canadien*

The increasingly isolated *Canadiens* of the lower St. Lawrence continued to move inland to their Northwest, "*leur Pays d'en Haut*," despite the conquest and absence of priests. Unsubdued, they were involved at multiple levels in a wide range of activities. A politically and commercially astute class of men picked up the baton and headed inland to join the descendants of the *coureur des bois*. Here, they met and mixed with French-speaking people from all over.

One of them, Jean-Gabriel Cerré, would be instrumental in helping the American Republic establish itself both economically and militarily in the Northwest. Information drawn from the published journal of the American commander in the field, George Rogers Clark, highlights the important role played by Gabriel Cerré in cementing the precarious position of the American militia deep in Illinois Country (Harrison, 2014, pp. 27-29; Nester, 2012, pp. 80-83). The case of Jean-Gabriel Cerré, along with that of Pierre-Louis Lorimier, the Robidoux clan, and Étienne Provost are representative of hundreds of other *Canadien* families that continued to move into the *Pays d'en Haut* through the 1760s and 1770s.

Robert Englebert (2014) tells the story of the life of Jean-Gabriel Cerré and the impact of the Conquest of New France on his trading and commercial interests. Though he writes about one individual, Englebert (2014, p. 48) stresses that Cerré's life resembled that of many others following the Conquest:

> *Pendant la seconde moitié du XVIIIe siècle, Gabriel Cerré, ce quasi-inconnu originaire des rives du fleuve Saint-Laurent, parvient à se tailler une place parmi la classe d'opulents marchands de la moyenne vallée du Mississippi. Né en Nouvelle-France, il passe son existence a naviguer entre les écueils d'un paysage impérial changeant, en s'adaptant a une série de régimes successifs qui contrôlent les territoires de l'Amérique du Nord: français, britannique, espagnol, américain.*

> During the second half of the 18th century, Gabriel Cerré, this quasi-unknown person originating from the shores of the Saint Lawrence River, succeeded in carving out a place among the class of opulent merchants of the middle valley of the Mississippi.

> Born in New France, his existence was devoted to navigating between the pitfalls of a changing imperial landscape, in adapting to a series of successive regimes who controlled the territories of North America: French, British, Spanish, American.

Jean-Gabriel Cerré was born in 1734 on the family farm near Lachine just outside of Montreal, the oldest son of an *habitant*. Under contract to a merchant named Raymond Quesnel, Cerré headed up the Ottawa River to Michilimackinac in the *Pays d'en Haut* for the first time in 1753 (Englebert, 2014, p. 50). At this point he was a simple voyageur, hired to paddle and portage. He soon entered the fur trade on his own, joined by a younger brother, Antoine. Relations between France and Great Britain in the contest for control of North America were souring once again. Warfare in the Ohio Country and deportation of the Acadians would commence in 1754 and 1755 (Englebert, 2014, p. 56).

Jean-Gabriel and Antoine Cerré did not enlist during the war and ran a trading operation between Montreal and the interior via Michilimackinac, though some evidence suggests they were engaged in a battle or two along the way. By the end of the war, Jean-Gabriel had established himself in Kaskaskia in the Illinois Country, while his brother Antoine handled his end of their business out of Montreal. Following the Treaty of Paris in 1763, a bloody sequel engulfed the *Pays d'en Haut,* triggered by the Pontiac uprising against the British. Commerce was totally disrupted for two years.

In the interim, Gabriel married the daughter of a local settler, Marie-Catherine Giard in 1764. At the same time, LaClède and his young step-son, Auguste Chouteau, were founding St. Louis just upriver on the opposite shore of the Mississippi. Jean-Gabriel and Marie-Catherine's first child, Marie-Anne, was also born that year. The following year, in 1765, the French flag was lowered at nearby Fort de Chartres, when a small British garrison finally showed up. In 1769, Jean-Gabriel began farming as well, on land bequeathed by his father-in-law, near the Mississippi River fort, now occupied by the British, at least for a few more years (Englebert, 2014, p. 52). Different flags would be lowered and raised in the area over the following decades.

In 1767, Jean-Gabriel Cerré took on a French merchant named Jean Orillat in Montreal as his business associate. Orillat supplied financing, manpower, and trade goods to Jean-Gabriel via Michilimackinac, while delivering furs to the London firm of Brook, Watson, and Gregory Olive. Englebert explains how this relationship was able to take advantage of the sudden integration of transatlantic commerce under the British, one that had been previously fractured: "*L'accord entre Orillat et Cerré illustre bien comment certains marchands canadiens font des affaires entre l'Illinois et Montréal, en exploitant les réseaux commerciaux britanniques d'outre mer après la cession du Canada à la Grande Bretagne.*" He says essentially that most French and *Canadien* traders lacked the necessary networks to establish markets in Great Britain, but traders like Cerré managed to find overseas associates to link the Illinois Country, Montreal, and international markets. Soon Cerré was shifting his routes to south of the Great Lakes, utilizing the portages of the Ohio-Wabash-Maumee corridor, returning periodically to Montreal himself to handle business matters directly (Englebert, 2014, pp. 53-54).

As his stature in the *Canadien* community of the Illinois Country grew, Cerré soon began settling estates back in Montreal for those Illinois frontiersmen, more recently arrived from the St. Lawrence Valley—some twenty-six in total (Englebert, 2014, pp. 54-55). Though the Illinois Country had been ceded to the British with the Conquest of New France, Great Britain was never able to maintain more than a nominal presence in the region. So when the War of Independence began, General Clark requested Cerré's help as one of the leading figures of Kaskaskia and the Illinois Country to provide supplies for the revolutionary troops that had recently penetrated the region. Cerré cooperated with Clark but decided to leave the region the following year for St. Louis on the other side of the Mississippi, in La Haute Louisiane, or Upper Louisiana Territory, then under the Spanish monarchy. From St. Louis, Cerré maintained his trade ties with Montreal, but equally developed new trade networks via New Orleans (Englebert, 2014, p. 55).

The continued trade originating from Canada and then pushing deep into the continent frustrated the American traders. Major Stoddard (1812, pp. 301-302) describes the frustration in his account of the Louisiana Territory in the early nineteenth century (Also See Chapter 5):

> The Canadian traders annually rendez vous at Prairie des Chiens, where they have built a small village. From this place they dispatch their goods in various directions, particularly to the Rivers des Moins and St. Pierre, which fall into the Mississippi from the west, and no small proportion of them find their way across to the Missouri. If circumstances will not allow us to prohibit the Canadian trade at present carried on at the Mandan nation, and other Indians on the upper parts of these two great rivers, still we have it in our power to check them below the points just mentioned.

Particularly frustrating, from Stoddard's (1812, p. 302) perspective, are those *Canadiens* (we can safely say that he is referring to French-speaking *Canadiens*) or their dependents who move to Michilimackinac, become naturalized citizens of the United States, and effectively act as agents for merchants based in Montreal and Quebec. In all likelihood, Stoddard would thus have seen Jean-Gabriel Cerré as an example of a *Canadien* serving as an "agent" for foreign merchants in Canada. To Captain Stoddard, the geo-strategic implications of this ongoing trade by *Canadiens* were self evident.

Englebert concludes by summarizing Jean-Gabriel Cerré's life, one which was ended by pneumonia in 1805 after returning from a final trip to Montreal, via

Generations of Cerrés

For his children's further education, Gabriel sent his oldest daughter, Marie-Anne, and his only son to Montreal. Much to her father's delight, another daughter, Marie-Louise, would marry a son of the prominent Panet family of Montreal and Quebec City, Pierre-Louis Panet. A younger sister married Auguste Chouteau of St. Louis in 1786. When Auguste Chouteau in turn decided to send their oldest son to Montreal to study, he entrusted their son to Marie-Louise Panet and her husband. Again citing Englebert (2014, p.56), marriage alliances and the education of children and grandchildren contributed to reinforcing the networks that were woven since the end of the French colonial period in North America. Successive generations of Cerrés would be active as traders, translators, negotiators, and leaders in their frontier community. In addition to his Chouteau grandchildren, the later generation of Cerrés included, for example, Gabriel Pascal Cerré (1800-1855) and Michel Sylvestre Cerré (1802-1860). They showed up in the Missouri River trade as two of the eight partners who signed on to create P. D. Papin and Company in 1828. This company was bought out by John Jacob Astor's American Fur Company in 1830. Michel Sylvestre Cerré was one of the trail captains working for French native Capt. Bonneville several years later. (LeCompte, 1982, p.38; Todd, 1982, pp.282-283) After retiring from the trade, Michel Cerré entered politics and got himself elected to the Missouri state legislature in 1848, and county sheriff in 1858.

Detroit and Michilimackinac. Cerré was a man who spent his life navigating the rivers of the St. Lawrence and Mississippi basins. He started as a simple voyageur earning some two hundred pounds per year, but managed to borrow the funds to ship merchandise to Illinois that he then traded for furs. In an era when the *Canadien* merchants were largely pushed aside in the fur trade of British North America, he nonetheless succeeded in carving out an important place in the market. He was able to build upon his *Canadien* commercial and familial ties while accommodating the sequential imperial regimes and realities that governed the territories (Englebert, 2014, p. 57). Generations of Cerrés would contribute to the developing American society as it pushed westwards.

After the Conquest, like the Cerré family, other *Canadiens* would head out West. Some would hold positions of leadership in economic development and re-settlement of the region, which ultimately became the American West.

Marie Madeleine Réaume

Marie Madeleine Réaume was born in circa 1710. Her mother, Simporose Ouaouagoukoue, was an Illini woman one generation removed from Marie Rouensa's time, while her father was Jean Baptiste Réaume, a *Canadien* who spent most of his working life as an interpreter based out of Fort St. Joseph. The region had become increasingly dominated by the Potawatomi, and their autonomous villages scattered around what is now southwestern Michigan and northeastern Indiana. They collected refugees and spouses from all the region's nations, including Illini, Miami, Shawnee, Huron, Ojibwe, Odawa (Ottawa), and, of course, *Canadiens*. After retreating down the Illinois River to the Mississippi during the late seventeenth century, the remnants of Illini that had survived the prior Iroquois onslaught, reformed and began to head back up toward Lake Michigan. As this migration progressed in the eighteenth century, these Illini bands increasingly intermixed with other Algonquian-speaking nations returning after having sheltered from the Iroquois storm west of Lake Michigan, especially the Potawatomi.

Sleeper-Smith (2001) demonstrates how Marie Madeleine Réaume's life illustrated the formation of kin networks that became integral to trade. As daughter of an Illini woman and a *Canadien* father, Marie Madeleine Réaume provides a perfect case study of how these kin relationships work themselves in matters of religion, commerce, and broader society during a transition period in a frontier zone, between an expanding agrarian society and a retreating society still based heavily on foraging, with limited horticulture.

Marie Madeleine's father, Jean Baptiste, like most employees of the government with an official function, also ran a quasi-illegal trading operation. He operated this side business as a partnership with his brother, Simon Réaume, who was likewise employed as an interpreter. By 1732, Jean Baptiste had relocated to Green Bay, where he continued to trade covertly while being employed as the post's interpreter. As was the norm, the far-flung operations of this family business included the wives as active partners, providing the necessary alliances for trade. "Jean Baptiste Réaume's marriage to Simphorose Ouaouagoukoue," Sleeper-Smith writes, "assured both brothers access to the Illinois Country fur trade and protection while traveling and trading" (2001, p. 45). Their daughter, Marie Madeleine, like all her siblings, was raised to be fluent in both languages. This was the norm for such families: "The female and male children of Indian women and French men were raised biculturally. From an early age, they functioned effectively as part of an indigenous world, while at the same time being raised in the French world of the fur trade" (Sleeper-Smith, 2001, p. 46).

The majority of Métis would, however, be Catholic, and religious traditions allowed the families to create extensive networks through the careful and often strategic selection of godparents. Marie Madeleine became the godparent of several Indian and mixed-ancestry children at age eighteen, entering into what would be a life-long role. She soon became an important member of the emerging Catholic kin networks of the Great Lakes. Quite often, the commanders at French posts were also the favored godparents as it allowed parents to create kinship ties with a high ranking official. This relationship also allowed the commander to cement alliances with indigenous allies essential to his success both as the commander of the fort and in his own commercial pursuits in the fur trade (Sleeper-Smith, 2001, p. 46).

In 1849, widowed and in her late thirties, Marie Madeleine assumed the initiative in securing her family's future. She took her teenage daughters and young son to the far end of Lake Michigan to further expand her kin network at Michilimackinac. This included reorienting the family's trading operations. She had found suitable husbands for her two daughters: a Trois-Rivières trader for seventeen-year old Marie-Catherine L'Archevêque, and a trader with Montreal trading connections for fifteen-year-old Marie-Joseph Esther L'Archevêque. Both sons-in-law returned with the family to Marie Madeleine's St. Joseph household. While in Michilimackinac, she enlisted two of the region's most prominent trading families, the Langlades and Bourassas, signing them on as godparents for her son and as witnesses at her daughters' weddings.

Within two years, at the age of forty-one, Marie Madeleine further extended her trade ties and Catholic kin network by giving birth to a son and subsequently marrying the child's father, Louis-Thérèse Chevalier. Louis was several years younger than his new wife, one of sixteen Chevalier children raised mostly around Michilimackinac. Members of the Chevalier family had been in and out of Fort St. Joseph since its original establishment; Louis' father had even been legally involved in the trade, having purchased a permit in 1718. In short order another of Marie Madeleine's daughters married one of Louis' younger brothers. In fact, all five of Marie Madeleine's *Métisse* daughters ended up marrying fur traders, be they of French-Canadian or Métis origins. Meanwhile, "kin linkages established by marriage were then reinforced by the godparent roles that siblings played to one another's children" (Sleeper-Smith, 2001, pp. 47-48).

This historically representative family network was significant:

> Although the fur trade entailed a continual influx and outflow of people, identifiable core families emerged. The Catholic kin network at Fort St. Joseph was integrated into the networks of other Great Lakes communities. Mixed-ancestry offspring identified themselves by kinship, but they might simultaneously identify themselves as either Indian or French. Initially, someone like Marie Madeleine could function both alternatively or simultaneously in two cultures. Ironically, in the smaller communities like St. Joseph, mixed-ancestry offspring such as Marie Madeleine came increasingly to resemble their indigenous kin rather than their French relatives. Madeleine's world bore the imprint of the Illini world in which she was raised and the Potawatomi community in which she would live for almost seventy years. Not surprisingly, her son Louison married among the Potawatomi (Sleeper-Smith, 2001, p. 49).

This passage contains an inherent contradiction, however. Sleeper-Smith states that the "mixed-ancestry offspring" identified themselves based on kinship, yet they simultaneously identified as "French," which is an ethno-national identity, not a kin-based identity. In rereading the primary texts, it is evident that the "mixed-ancestry offspring" who chose to live in the shadow of the French, British, or American fur trading posts identified themselves as *Canadien*, which was an ethno-national designation. While the Fort St. Joseph community was reclaimed as a predominantly indigenous settlement by the mid-eighteenth century, with Marie Madeleine increasingly identified with her indigenous heritage, other Métis families were beginning to move on to other settlements of *Canadiens* within the broader region where they would identify as solely *Canadien* in turn.

For the Potawatomi and Métis families who stayed behind, the women continued to produce an abundance of agricultural produce that supported local communities but was also sold to more distant posts and settlements. The women had integrated a number of European livestock species into their agriculture mores, thus raising chickens, cattle, oxen, and horses for sale in the larger regional market (Sleeper-Smith, 2001, p. 76). French colonial authorities had originally tried to minimize dependence on Indian foodstuffs, with Robert de la Salle ordering his men to plant "French grain, Indian corn, peas, cabbages and other vegetables, when he established Fort St. Joseph."

Yet men quickly began to take local wives and these families would begin producing surpluses for the fur trade being sold in portage villages (Sleeper-Smith, 2001, p. 75). This dependence would remain well into the American era and the early nineteenth century as "American troops garrisoned at Detroit were supplied with cattle by the Indians. Traders were now brokers of foodstuffs as well as furs" (Sleeper-Smith, 2001, p. 76).

In an effort to consolidate the growing settlement around Detroit, the authorities of New France had offered land and tools to the *habitants* and mixed-ancestry Métis as an inducement to relocate eastward. The St. Joseph Valley families that relocated to the Detroit area would eventually coalesce into one of the local *Canadien* communities. South of Detroit, one important resettlement area would ultimately be the Rivière aux Raisins, with another along the Detroit River on the eastern shore, now in Canada. Following the Seven Years' War, the Spanish Bourbons assumed control west of the Mississippi and similarly offered inducements to the *Canadien*, Métis, and affiliated Indian communities to relocate westward. Marie Madeleine's daughters and their families chose to join other families resettling near St. Louis, which provided new markets for the St. Joseph River valley Potawatomi.

Detroit: The *Canadien* City

On both shores of the Detroit River, the *Canadiens* would establish farms reminiscent of those found in the St. Lawrence Valley. According to one first-hand account:

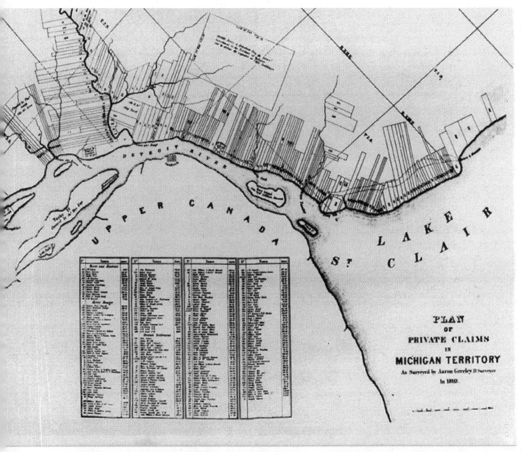

Plan of private claims in Michigan Territory as surveyed by Aaron Greeley, D. surveyor in 1810.
Detroit remained a largely French-speaking settlement up to the War of 1812 and the French presence
would remain vibrant well into the nineteenth century. The French language held on longest in the more
rural settlement of Monroe (formerly Frenchtown) where the French-speaking *Canadiens* continued to
use French well into the twentieth century.

*Les maisons sont si nombreuses et si rapprochées les unes des autres, sur les bords de
la rivière Détroit, que pendant plus de dix milles, on croit voir une suite de plusieurs
villages. Les fermes sont très-étroites sur le devant, et s'étendent considérablement par
derrière. On donna aux lots cette forme bizarre, afinque les colons pussent s'aider les
uns les autres dans le cas d'une attaque de la part des Indiens, qui jadis étaient extrême-
ment nombreux et in commodes dans ces cantons reculés* (Ledoux, 1835, p. 434).

The houses are so numerous and so close together on the shores of the Detroit River
that for more than ten miles, we could believe it were the succession of many villages.
The farms are very narrow in front and spread out considerably in back. The lots had
this bizarre shape in order to ensure that the settlers can help each other in case of
attack by the Indians who once were extremely numerous and troublesome in these
distant lands.

Living on the narrow plots of land stretching along the Detroit River are the descendants of the French who settled there during the French Regime and became *Canadien*, though many would have an indigenous maternal ancestor. On what became the American side of the River, the descendants of the French soldiers and traders also came to define themselves as *Canadien* (de Saint-Père, 1861).

Magdelaine Marcot Laframboise of Michigan

The Grand River Odawa community was much like the Potawatomi villages along the St. Joseph River to the south. The Odawa living on the Grand River had more than three thousand apple trees and almost two thousand five hundred acres of corn and vegetable crops. Magdelaine was actually born at Fort St. Joseph, but when her father, Jean Baptiste Marcot, left for the region beyond the far northwest shore of Lake Michigan (Wisconsin), her mother, Thimotee, returned to the Grand River Valley village of her father, Chief Kewinaquot, or Returning Cloud. Magdelaine and her siblings were raised among the Odawa, and when they had traveled to Michilimackinac for baptism, they were identified by the priest as Odawa.

> Magdeleine and her sisters married young. When she was fourteen, Joseph Laframboise paid the bride's price required by the Odawa. Magdeleine and Joseph remained in the Grand River valley, where her indigenous kin network ensured access to peltry. Joseph Laframboise's access to trade goods came through Michilimackinac, probably from his brother in Montreal (Sleeper-Smith, 2001, p. 151).

At some point, Joseph was killed by an irate Odawa. His widow did not remarry, choosing instead to take over her husband's trading business. Madame Laframboise, as she preferred to be called, established a lock on local trade, selling the majority of furs exported from the Grand River area during and immediately after the War of 1812.

In his book, *Grand Times in Grand Rapids*, Gordon G. Beld identifies Magdelaine Laframboise with a sub-chapter heading as "Our First Businesswoman" at the rapids of the Grand River, now the city of Grand Rapids, Michigan. After her husband's demise, "Magdelaine continued the business alone, usually earning between $5,000 and $10,000 per year when most traders netted only $1,000" (Beld, 2012, pp. 23-25). Each June, Madame Laframboise hired voyageurs to take her to Michilimackinac to sell her furs and resupply her outfit. She obtained trading licenses originally from the British, then later from the Americans. When the latter arrived on the scene, the American Fur Company became her customer.

Her daughter, Josette, married a U.S. Army officer stationed at Fort Mackinac named Benjamin Pierce (whose younger brother, Franklin, became U.S. President in 1853, the same year Washington territory was created). In 1822, after her daughter Josette's death left behind two orphaned children, Magdelaine Laframboise sold her business and relocated to Mackinac Island. Here she became an active parishioner of Ste. Anne's Catholic Church, providing educational opportunities for Native American and mixed-ancestry children and housing many of the area's orphans. There were no nuns yet in this part of the continent. At her island home, today's Harbour View Inn, she also hosted traveling dignitaries—including, in 1831, a traveling lawyer from France by the name of Alexis de Tocqueville.

Magdelaine's life was intersecting a number of disparate worlds and is one of nuance, as Sleeper-Smith (2001) points out. Simply put, it is a case study in social complexity and human resilience in the face of political and economic change. Faithful to her people, the Odawa, she played a vital role in keeping them in Michigan as "Catholic" Indians. She was also an inveterate trader, taking over the family business after her husband's death, and, to boot, she assumed the role of a French widow after the British relinquished control of the territory to the United States. When Fort Michilimackinac was transferred to the United States following the Treaty of Ghent that ended the War of 1812, she forged new business ties with John Jacob Astor's fur trading company to ensure that she maintained her trading interests. In this she was like many other Métis in the nineteenth century. No fundamental contradiction prevented her from assuming multiple roles and affiliations so she could play it both ways over time.

Life in Detroit Under British Rule

The Conquest of New France was a grim period for *Canadiens* living along the St. Lawrence and in the *Pays d'en Haut*. During the summer of 1759, the inhabitants on the south shore of the St. Lawrence had to endure Wolfe's scorched earth campaign. After the war, the British noted that their new subjects were relieved to see the war end as they were suffering from famine and had to provide much of their food to feed the French troops, but also that in their hearts they remained loyal to France. Saint-Pierre notes (1895, p. 180) this ambivalence: "*Les Canadiens, réduits à la famine par les contributions pour le soutien des armées, étaient heureux d'avoir un moment de trève pour ce ravitailler, mais leur cœur restait fidèle à la France.*" In the *Pays d'en Haut*, they soon faced another war when the Pontiac Uprising in 1763 put the French and *Canadien* settlers that remained in a thorny and dangerous position.

Unsure of who were their friends, since they had only recently been at war with the same British and American forces, the French and *Canadiens* who remained in Detroit and elsewhere generally sought to remain neutral as British forces fought Pontiac's Uprising. The British forces greeted this with contempt. Major Gladwin wrote in his correspondence: "*On verra bientôt que la moitié des habitants méritent un gibet, et que les autres devraient être décimés.*" [We will soon see that half of the inhabitants deserve the gallows and that the others should be decimated.]

The *Canadiens* during the uprising generally tried nonetheless to convince the indigenous nations not to rise up; they advised the British, guided them from Niagara to Detroit, and also lent a supporting hand in defending the fort (Saint-Pierre, 1895, p. 180). All told, in spite of their misgivings, the *Canadiens* and Métis who remained in the *Pays d'en Haut* contributed to the British success in containing Pontiac's Rebellion.

With peace, the settlements gained in population and Fort Michilimackinac, re-baptized Fort Mackinaw, regained its status as an important hub in the fur trade. In the fort's stores, one would find up to 100,000 pounds of flour, 50,000 pounds of pork, 1000 gallons of "fire water," and large quantities of other trade goods (Saint-Pierre, 1895, pp. 181-182). For the *Canadiens* that remained in the colonies, the Conquest of New France immediately disrupted everything and replaced their former trading networks. Traders were now cut off from French markets and market networks and did not have easy access to British capital and trade networks. Incoming Scottish and English traders gradually capitalized on this vacuum to establish themselves over the next four decades as the primary intermediaries in trade, as both importers and exporters. New companies eventually emerged, such as the North West Company and the American Fur Company, among others, including the latter's short-lived Pacific Fur Company subsidiary. Some who had remained in the trade had to absorb heavy losses due to the paper currency that France had issued but would not honor or redeem after the loss of the colonies.

The British who settled in Detroit and the other former French forts soon came to establish cordial relations with the French majority that remained and even came to be assimilated, as noted by Saint-Pierre:

> *Les colons de Détroit donnèrent si bonne opinion d'eux-mêmes par leur conduite que les meilleurs hommes parmi les premiers colons anglais, tels que le gouverneur Hay, le lieutenant George McDougall, les Macomb, les Meldrum, les Brush, ne dédaignèrent pas de s'allier aux Campeau, aux Navarre et à d'autres familles canadiennes. Ces premiers anglais adoptèrent si bien les idées et les habitudes de la population canadienne qu'encore aujourd'hui il y a de leurs descendants dans la ville de Détroit qui parlent mieux le Français que l'Anglais (1895, p. 177).*

The settlers of Detroit acquired such a good reputation by their conduct that the best men among the English settlers, notably governor Hay, the lieutenant George McDougall, the Macombs, the Meldrums, the Brushes, were not averse to allying themselves to the Campeau, the Navarre and other *Canadien* families. These first English adopted so well the ideas and habits of the *Canadien* population that to this day many of their descendants in the city of Detroit speak better French than English.

A similar trend will also be seen elsewhere, notably at Fort Vancouver, where English migrants working in the Hudson's Bay Company fort surrounded by the

Canadiens and Métis of the Pacific Northwest were in turn being acculturated through adoption of the French language.

The people and the ways in the *Pays d'en Haut* and the St. Lawrence Valley were quite similar, with one exception: slavery. Saint-Pierre (1895, p. 179) notes that while there were few slaves in the French colony along the St. Lawrence, there were many more in Detroit and the other forts of the Great Lakes Region:

> *Les premiers esclaves furent des Panis, sauvages d'une tribu lointaine de l'Ouest. Des traiteurs de Michilimackinac avaient jusqu'à trois et quatre de ces esclaves. À Détroit leur nombre était relativement moins grand, cependant le recensement de 1773 constate la présence de 83 esclaves. Dans l'inventaire des biens de Dequindre, 1768, la valeur d'un Panis de douze ans est portée à 300 livres. En 1793 un jeune nègre se vendit £213.*

> The first slaves were the Panis [Pawnees], savages from a distant western tribe. The traders at Michilimackinac had up to three or four of these slaves. At Detroit, their numbers were relatively less great, however the census of 1773 ascertained the presence of 83 slaves. In the inventory of the goods of Dequindre, 1768, the value of a Pani [Pawnee] of twelve years of age is valued at 300 pounds. In 1793, a young negro would sell for £213.

The *Canadiens* who remained in the British-controlled territory retained their property, land rights, and slaves, but the Catholic Church imposed restrictions on Catholic slave owners. Slaves were baptized and married, and quite often slave owners married their former slaves. The Catholic rite of marriage also had to be respected, and Catholic slave owners were discouraged from separating wives from husbands or children from parents (Saint-Pierre, 1895).

Saint-Pierre goes to great lengths to demonstrate that the *Canadien* settlers in what would become the Michigan Territory had not simply hunted and traded, but had also been efficient farmers:

> *Mais il est faux de dire qu'ils négligeaient l'agriculture et se contentaient de vivre au jour le jour, du fruit de la pêche, de la chasse ou de la traite. Les renseignements les plus précis nous font voir que l'élevage des bestiaux se faisait sur la plus grande échelle possible. Un recensement de 1778 démontre qu'il y avait 1425 têtes de bétail dans la colonie. D'autre part, du fait qu'un seul cultivateur avait près de mille minots de blé en grenier en 1763, on peut conclure que la culture des céréales n'était pas négligée.* (Saint-Pierre, 1895, p. 177)

> But it is false to say that they neglected agricultural pursuits and were content to live day to day from the fruits of fishing, hunting or trading. The most precise information we have makes it clear that the raising of animals was done at the largest scale possible. A census of 1778 demonstrates that there were more than 1425 head of cattle in the colony. Additionally, the fact that a single farmer had close to one thousand bushels of wheat in storage in 1763, leads us to conclude that the cultivation of cereals was not neglected.

He explains in detail how the 1778 census had tallied 1,425 head of cattle in the colony, and how, in 1763, one farmer had 1,000 bushels of wheat in his granary. He then provides information from the last wills and testaments and the lists of goods that were left behind by the deceased to demonstrate the relative prosperity of some of the more successful families. He is addressing clearly what he believes are commonly held misconceptions or prejudice.

The Early Settlements of Southeastern Michigan Territory

The town of Ecorse (from *écorce,* meaning bark) provides an intriguing case study of an early European and *Canadien* settlement in what became southeastern Michigan. Kathy Covert Warnes (2009) traces the history of the small village in her book *Ecorse Michigan: A Brief History.* The French history of this village traces back to 1701, when Antoine Cadillac landed at what is now Detroit. As the French established forts, settlers would occupy the lands surrounding the fort. Farmers wanted to ensure access to the rivers for transportation so the land would be divided into long lots running up from the rivers. Farms therefore lined both sides of the Detroit River from Ecorse to Lake St. Clair. The farmers used canoes to travel along the various rivers to visit other farmers and friends and to bring produce and furs to market (Warnes, 2009, p. 9).

In a little over a half century, between 1760 and 1815, the region was transferred through conquest from France to Great Britain and then to the United States. The Treaty of Paris of 1763 gave the British sovereignty over the territory, while the 1783 Treaty of Paris transferred it to the new American Republic. The British were reluctant to transfer their western posts in Michigan to the United States. Only following General Anthony Wayne's defeat of The Western Indian Confederacy in Ohio at the battle of Fallen Timbers in 1794 did the British finally agree to completely withdraw from Michigan. Under the Jay Treaty, they retreated by June 1, 1796, after which American forces occupied Detroit that same year (Gilpin, 1970, p. 2). The American Congress, still operating under the Articles of Confederation, created the Northwest Territory through the Northwest Ordinance of 1787.

Michigan became a separate territory in 1805 as Ohio achieved statehood, and the southwestern part of the Northwest Territory became Indiana Territory. Ominously, the old French town of Detroit caught fire and burned to the ground in 1805, days before the new Territorial delegation arrived. Only stone chimneys stood to greet the incoming Territorial Governor (Gilpin, 1970, p. 2). Other than the charred remnants of Detroit, Frenchtown, located where the Rivière Raisin empties into Lake Erie, was the main settlement in the new territory. Gilpin notes that "possibly as many as one hundred and twenty-five families, all holding land by Indian grants, were scattered along its banks" (Gilpin, 1970, p. 12).

The first "French" inhabitant of Frenchtown had been François Navarre, who moved there from Detroit in the 1780s. Francois is known as the official town "Father," though its most famous son would be the one to enter the history of the American West almost a century later: George Armstrong Custer, whose family did not arrive until the 1840s. Navarre built his cabin on land deeded to him by the local Potawatomi Indians in 1785. The next year the Potawatomi also deeded land on the opposite shore for a church, St. Antoine's. In the following years, almost one hundred *Canadien* and Metis families set up farms along the banks of the Rivière aux Raisins, inter-marrying with Potawatomi families. Living until 1826, François would rise to the rank of Colonel in the local unit of the Michigan territorial militia. During the War of 1812, in this one family alone, thirty-six Navarres enlisted and fought in the Michigan militia. One of the more famous members of the clan was a cousin of François named Pierre, who lived in Presque Isle. Pierre Navarre served as a scout and courrier during the War of 1812, managing to escape across a frozen lake after Colonel Winchester surrendered his troops at Frenchtown in January 1813. British General Proctor offered a 200-pound reward for his scalp, but it was Pierre who would deliver later that year Commander Oliver Hazard Perry's well-known message after the naval battle on Lake Erie, "We have met the enemy and they are ours."

The process of re-building Frenchtown after its wartime destruction took about six years. In 1817, as the town was slowly being re-built, the settlement was renamed Monroe in honor of the new President then visiting the much neglected region (Hutchison & Hutchison, 2004, pp. 10-30). Among the tribal leadership of the southern Potawatomi who were relocated west of the Missouri were several Navarre descendants.

Un Village des Canadiens: Ecorse, Michigan

Between Detroit and Frenchtown there were several clusters of cabins, one of which was the future town of Ecorse. Warnes provides details of Ecorse's origins. It's name is said to stem from the French word for bark, *écorce*, and the fact that the Huron-Wendat had buried their chiefs near the sandbanks of the river after having wrapped the bodies in birch bark. The river would thus have been named the "Rivière aux Écorces" (Warnes, 2009, pp. 9-10).

Warnes describes a population whose roots clearly lie in the French colonial period and notes how "residents reading the deeds to their properties often found the first pages in French and even some pages with drawings of fish, turtles or birds." The original owners, the Potawatomi and Huron-Wendat, would have signed the first deeds giving French settlers permission to settle the land at the mouth of the Rivière aux Écorces (Warnes, 2009, pp. 9-10).

Canadiens arriving in Ecorse in the late 1700s include Pierre St. Cosme, Pierre LeBlanc, Jean Baptiste Salliotte, a branch of the Labadie family, and Pierre Michel Campau. Several days before the United States released its Declaration of Independence, the Potawatomi nation granted Pierre Saint-Cosme and his sons, Amable and Dominique Saint-Cosme, land in recognition of their "Love and Affection" for this family, with the deed dated July 1, 1776. The land grant gave Saint-Cosme and his descendants the land facing the Detroit River and the Rivière aux Écorces (Warnes, 2009, p. 13). The first settlers would then receive their deeds from the heirs of Pierre Saint-Cosme (Warnes, 2009, p. 13).

Another early *Canadien* settler to the region was Pierre LeBlanc, probably a descendant of Acadians, who married a woman from the Fox nation, and together they established a homestead farm on what is now West Jefferson near the Detroit River. Though they were "settlers," the homestead was in fact but a part of their larger economic activities. The fur trade still reigned and the LeBlancs were trappers who traded with neighboring nations maintaining good relations with them. The Métis son of Pierre, Pierre LeBlanc *fils* (Jr.) was the town constable by age twenty, later serving as a road commissioner (Warnes, 2009, p. 12).

Frontier settlement and disruptive warfare sparked litigation on right of precedence and property rights. One set of documents contend that the Labadie family settled in 1764, near the mouth of the Ecorse River. An 1821 lawsuit referred to Pierre Michel Campau and Jean Baptiste Salliotte as among the first to cultivate farms along the Detroit riverfront.

Michel Campau is cited in the first, 1710 census of Detroit as a farmer born in Montreal in 1667. His numerous descendants would soon scatter to all corners of Michigan Territory, starting with the nearby Ecorse River settlement. The 1710 census of Detroit also refers to some three dozen settlers. They included: Pierre Roy, born in Laprairie in 1677; Joseph Parent, farmer, master toolman, brewer, born in Quebec in 1669; François Fafard dit Delorme, farmer and interpreter, born in Trois-Rivières circa 1660; Jacques Langlois, born 1667; Pierre René Poirier dit Lafleur, farmer and soldier; Étienne Esteve dit Lajeunesse, in the army, born in France, died in Detroit, 1736; and several Lemoyne brothers: Alexis, Jacques, and René.

Reflecting a lack of growth in the population in the interim around Detroit, only about two dozen settlers are listed in the 1743 census, including such newer names as Robert Navarre, Pierre Morriseau, Antoine Beaubien, Pierre St-Pierre, Zacharias Chicot, and Jean-Baptiste Godet. The 1750 census includes new arrivals such as St. Cosme, LaForest, and a growing Campau clan including Claude, Nicol, Baptiste, Antoine, Louis, and Michel. The latter Campau, Michel, uses the alternate spelling of Campo, however. A Charles Campo using this spelling would appear eighty years later as one of the earliest settlers in the Walla Walla and

Willamette Valleys of the Pacific Northwest. Though born in the U.S., this Campo would serve as the original translator and general assistant of the American Presbyterian ministers of Samuel Parker and Marcus Whitman, who actually referred to Charles Campo as a French-Canadian Catholic (Josephy, 1965, pp. 132-180).

Another old settler family were the Cicottes. The first generation in Ecorse were Joseph and François Cicotte. According to Detroit historian Friend Palmer, the Cicotte family has a 150-year-old tradition in Ecorse. Warnes (2009, p. 18) describes Francois X. Cicotte as "a fine specimen of the early Frenchmen possessing that rare charm of manner which seemed a peculiar legacy to those descendants of the first pioneers." Télesphore Saint-Pierre (1895, p. 156) notes that the Cicotte surname had been Chiquot.

After the Conquest in 1760, *Canadiens* continued to move west into the *Pays d'en Haut,* which was still *de facto* "their West," in spite of the British inroads. George Rogers Clark had been successful in co-opting only the *Canadien* residents of the Illinois Country and Vincennes, Indiana, in his 1778-1789 military campaign. The *Canadiens,* in what would become Michigan, had been reticent to join the American revolutionaries, as their commercial and political ties were even more closely linked with the province of Quebec.

Further inland, other *Canadiens* were more willing to side with the revolutionary forces. Saint-Pierre explains that in the colonies of Illinois and Indiana, under the exhortation of the priest Gibault, the *Canadiens* sided with the American forces against the British (Saint-Pierre, 1895, p. 182); (See Chapter 7). Nonetheless, the limited contribution of some *Canadiens* in Michigan had been enough to secure the territory on the west side of the Detroit River for the young republic. Yet under the 1783 peace agreement, the British wouldn't actually withdraw from the northern territories until 1796, two years after the Jay Treaty was signed.

In the meantime, the British had actively encouraged the *Canadiens* to relocate to British territories. Saint-Pierre (1895, p. 184) lists a number of families, some fifty individuals, who had left the American side of the new divide to settle on the left bank of the Detroit River, in British North America. Jean Salliotte and, his wife, Marie Magdalene Jourdain, appear in the 1779 Detroit census. Of the four Salliotte children, the two daughters, Marie and Thérèse, married two *Canadien* brothers, Joseph and Dominique Bondie. The two Salliotte boys were Jean-Baptiste and Alexis Moses. The latter, Alexis Moses, was the first member of the family to move into the Down River area, building his first log cabin on the shore of the Detroit River near the mouth of the Rivière aux Écorses. Alexis Moses married Archange Bourassa. The Salliottes had two sons, Moses (1807-1892) and Hyacinth. Moses Jr. and his wife had five children together in Ecorse. Moses Jr., who lived until 1892, reportedly never learned more than a few words of English. His brother, Hyacinth, born in 1810, married Adelaide Labadie, and they had seven children. In short, the *Canadiens* of Michigan and their language didn't just vanish when the Americans showed up.

Michigan Territory Established (1805), the *Canadiens* Remain

The 1801 census for the Wayne County area in the southeastern corner of Michigan around Detroit sets the population at 3,206, excluding Indians (Gilpin, 1970). This census highlights the French character of the territory. The population was primarily of French ancestry, while the British were next in terms of demographic importance. French farms consisted of long lots along the waterways, with no farms behind them. Waterways, instead of wagon roads, were the transportation routes in the territory. The population and layout of the farms was mirrored on the British side, as the *Canadiens* had settled on similar long lots along the waterways. If anything, the British territory by then had a larger number of English-speaking settlers than the American territory, as British Loyalists who fled the Thirteen Colonies settled in the western part of the Province of Quebec, which became Upper Canada in 1791 (under the British, the Province of Quebec included the Michigan Territory before the American Revolution) (Gilpin, 1970, p. 13).

The Anglo-Americans and the British might appear to have replaced the French-speaking leadership of the community, yet many maintained their roles. This is apparent in both the officer ranks of the Michigan territorial militia and commercial families in Detroit. On both sides of the new boundary separating the U.S. from British North America along the Detroit River, a number of prominent Anglo-Americans and British newcomers married into these older families. The *Canadien* and the Métis community in place also drew from the old country, France, for reinforcements.

After 1763, French immigrants to North America continued to choose either the United States or Louisiana, under the Spanish Bourbons, for a while longer. Two leading Michigan citizens among the Euro-American population in the early nineteenth century were Father Gabriel Richard and Judge Pierre Audrain, both born in France and buried in Ste. Anne's Cemetery in Detroit. Michigan's first newspaper published articles in both languages, and one of the first judges appointed to the Michigan Supreme Court in 1805 was the bilingual John Griffin of Virginia. Having studied law at The College of William and Mary, Griffin had previously been appointed as judge for Indiana Territory in 1800. "With five years experience on a territorial court and a fluent command of French, John was a wise choice," notes Gilpin (1970, p. 25).

In the first years of the American administration of the area, a *de facto* bilingualism imposed itself, remarks Télesphore Saint-Pierre: "*Comme les Canadiens ne parlaient pas encore l'anglais, les législateurs firent publier leurs ordonnances en français"* (1895, p. 194). [As the Canadiens did not yet speak English, the legislators had their ordinances published in English.] This need to publish the ordinances in both French and English was certainly facilitated in the first years by having judges and other territorial administrators fluent in French. Michigan remained a *de facto* bilingual Territory among the settler population. "There were still in 1810 so many French in the Territory unable to read English that they petitioned to have the laws of the United States published in the French language," noted Almon Parkins (1918, p. 131). This can be compared and contrasted with Louisiana, and to a lesser extent Missouri, where the French language, law, and custom retained legal status through the territorial period on into the early decades of statehood and into the middle decades of the nineteenth century.

Also, lest we forget, the earlier Indian population still represented the large majority of the residents of the future Territory of Michigan. In contrast to the two written languages—one was official—a larger population still spoke one or more of the region's three Algonquian languages: Odawa, Chippewa, or Potawatomi. The French had called these loose tribal groupings "The Three Fires." These three groupings spilled out in all directions from the current territorial limits of Michigan. The Potawatomi had a special relationship with Miamis, located just to the south.

The Iroquoian-speaking Wendats (Hurons) living along the Detroit River were a displaced nation. They had formed one of several Huron refugee enclaves after the Iroquois, in mid-seventeenth century, effectively dispersed them from their homeland located to the southeast of Lake Huron (now the Georgian Bay region of Ontario). Another Huron refugee reserve had been created some thousand miles downriver on the outskirts of Quebec City. Other surviving bands of the extended Huron/Wendat/Wyandotte diaspora would eventually end up in Oklahoma.

Charles Cleland published a summary of the figures from Michigan's first Indian census in the late 1830s in *Rites of Conquest: The History and Culture of Michigan's Native Americans* (1992). They indicate that some 20,000 Indians were living in what is now Michigan and northern Wisconsin, with between 12,000 and 15,000 living in the Lower Peninsula and the remainder in the north. These are probably conservative estimates. When Michigan's Potawatomi are factored in, the numbers would certainly be closer to 30,000 (C. E. Cleland, 1992, p. 194).

Father Gabriel Richard, who had arrived in Baltimore from France in 1792, had been performing Mass in a Detroit warehouse pending the rebuilding of Ste. Anne's Church that had burnt down along with most of the town in 1805. Richard had been performing his clerical duties in this town since 1798, when he moved there from Kaskaskia, Illinois. Although the sending of Catholic priests from France had been severely restricted in Canada after the Conquest, there were no such limitations in the overwhelmingly Protestant nation to the south.

In 1807, Father Richard also began a series of Sunday afternoon meetings for Protestants in the Council House, where he concentrated on themes common to both Catholics and Protestants. "These were not official services but lectures on general Christian principles," notes Gilpin (1970, p. 19), and he continued these ecumenical lectures until his death a quarter of a century later.

Pierre Audrain, the other prominent local Frenchman arriving directly from the "old country," had accompanied General Anthony Wayne to Detroit in 1796, with the first contingent of U.S. officials to arrive in this northern part of the Northwest Territory. Wayne appointed Audrain to be the Wayne County notary. Serving in this capacity from 1796 to 1809, Audrain, who was both bilingual and skilled in administration, landed a critical position in the new Michigan territorial government once it was formed in 1805. He served as both Clerk of the territorial Supreme Court and Secretary of the Legislature. He turned eighty in 1805 and served in government for another fourteen years in positions such as City Register and Secretary of the Land Board.

Born in Normandy, France, Pierre Audrain (1725-1820) was already middle-aged and working in Paris as a teacher and a professional translator of English when he met Baron von Steuben who was on his way to America to join George Washington's Continental Army. Like any educated Prussian of the day, the baron spoke only two languages: French and a northern German dialect. He hired Audrain to accompany him to America in 1777. Audrain left the Continental Army in 1779 and settled with his wife and three children in Pennsylvania (Historic Fort Wayne Coalition, 2015). In a territory where the majority of the Euro-Americans still spoke French and a significant number of those with mixed backgrounds also spoke some French, the services of such men as Gabriel Richard, Pierre Audrain, and the bilingual John Griffin were in demand, and they effectively participated in the orderly transition from British to American rule.

The United States had incrementally reaffirmed prior land grants in the Northwest Territory by several treaties signed between 1785 and 1795 with various nations, despite several notable military disasters. In Michigan, these land grants comprised only those that had been made to the French authorities at an earlier date, as well as to the British. This included a six-mile-wide strip of territory running from the Rivière Raisin in the south up to Lake St. Clair just north of Detroit, where most of the European population of the territory still resided. Further north, there was also a grant to Mackinaw Island, plus the land along the strait on both its northern and southern shores where the modern day cities of Mackinaw City and St. Ignace are located near the sites of the original French forts and missions (Gilpin, 1970, pp. 38-39).

William Hull, the First Territorial Governor of a Bilingual Michigan 1805-1812

William Hull, a veteran of the Revolutionary War from Massachusetts, was the first federally appointed territorial governor of the Michigan Territory, created out of the northern tier of the Northwest Territory in 1805, which the British had only evacuated in 1796. One of his primary responsibilities was to command the Territorial Militia. As Detroit was in the process of rebuilding following the fire, Hull issued his General Orders providing for the organization of the militia on September 10, 1805. The First Regiment consisted of eight companies of militia, and the second, seven companies. The chosen officers had little in the way of military experience, but were notable citizens who included influential people in the French-speaking community. Colonel Augustus Woodward, along with Lieutenant Colonel Antoine Beaubien and Major Gabriel Godfroy, were appointed field officers for the First Regiment. Colonel John Anderson, and his colleagues, Lieutenant Colonel François Navarre and Major Israel Ruland, commanded the second. Lieutenant Colonel Elijah Brush and Major James Abbott headed a Legionary Corps. Hull counted his total militia strength at 1,316 men (Gilpin, 1970, pp. 47-48).

Having established a militia, the governor was ready to begin negotiating treaties with the indigenous nations for surrender of land for settlement. He held a council with the nations in June 1807 at the Foot of the Rapids, though the Saginaw Chippewa had refused to attend; the Americans suspected the British had influenced their decision. The Saginaw Indians ultimately showed up in Detroit the following month for the distribution of annuities, along with other Chippewa bands, the Odawa, and the Wyandot. Despite opposition, the territorial governor went ahead planning for a treaty that he estimated would add approximately five million acres to land previously ceded by the Indians.

The Treaty of Detroit was signed in November 1807, despite a last minute message from President Thomas Jefferson that Governor Hull should hold off on negotiations until a later time. Father Gabriel Richard had written a cautionary letter to Bishop Carroll in Baltimore, who forwarded it to Secretary of State Madison, who in turn had passed it on to the president. The letter highlighted the simmering resentment among the Indians over the terms of Swan Creek Treaty of 1805 (Fort Industry) and the subsequent speculative land sales. In any event, Jefferson's letter had arrived too late; the treaty ceded most of the land in the southeastern quartile of the Lower Peninsula. In addition to the usual guarantee of hunting and fishing rights and the services of two blacksmiths for ten years, the treaty agreed to a lump sum of 10,000 dollars: one-third each to the Odawa and Chippewa; and one-sixth each to the Potawatomi and Wyandot. Subsequent annual payments of 2,400 dollars would also be distributed in similar proportions.

Relations between the U.S. and Great Britain had meanwhile deteriorated and war appeared imminent in 1807. The British ship of war, the HMS Leopard, had attacked and boarded the American ship the USS Chesapeake, looking for British deserters. The incident contributed to the ill-will eventually leading to the War of 1812. The United States Secretary of War, Henry Dearborn, became concerned about the situation in Detroit and asked Governor Hull to ensure he was stocked for the winter months and to gather intelligence about the British and Canadian forces. As the British and Americans prepared for an eventual war, both looked warily on the *Canadien* population living on both sides of the border (Gilpin, 1970, p. 52).

The leadership of the *Canadien* community in Detroit, which no longer represented geo-strategic alliances and empires, was trying its best locally to solidify the uneasy peace. Father Richard in particular was showing a great deal of initiative in the area of education, to try to demonstrate the loyalty of the *Canadiens* in Michigan Territory. Whereas influential French residents had customarily sent their children to Montréal or elsewhere for an education, Father Richard had taken it upon himself to establish a school in Detroit. This school, Spring Hill, was meant to educate both European and indigenous children, encouraging their integration into American society at an earlier age (Gilpin, 1970, p. 44). To ensure success, Father Richard took the matter directly to President Thomas Jefferson, who endorsed the program. A request was sent to Congress in January 1809 to approve funding for Richard's plan for additional primary schools (Gilpin, 1970, p. 45). However, the incoming administration of James Madison did not support the project and the funding request fell to the side, leaving Richard with no funds to pay the rent for the Spring Hill school and saddled with debt. Perhaps having learned a crucial lesson as to the vagaries of politics, Father Richard returned to Congress after the War of 1812 as a newly elected Congressional representative. This would raise hackles in Washington, D.C., a city not used to seeing French and Catholic clerics in Congress.

By the 1810 census, Detroit and the surrounding settlements still represented an isolated pocket in Indian Country, connected only by Lake Erie to Buffalo (Beau Fleuve), New York, and the rest of the the United States and British North America. Other than the water routes, only a very exposed and soggy trail led south via Frenchtown on the River Raisin to the Ohio settlements. These very tenuous connections would depend on whose navy controlled Lake Erie, as well as the strength of either party's alliance with the local nations in any given year. As of 1810, the British had the upper hand on both accounts, and would retain that advantage for several more years, through the first half of the coming war.

On the U.S. side of the Detroit River, the 1810 census identified 4,762 "white" settlers, over two-thirds of whom lived in the southeastern corner of the territory.

This encompassed two of the territory's four districts: Detroit at 2,227 (the town itself numbering 1,650); and Erie at 1,340. The balance of 1,200 settlers were scattered along the shores of Lake Huron up to Saginaw Bay—the Huron district covering the more remote portions of the Michilimackinac territory to the north and west. Michilimackinac was the former French, then British post, where the Odawa, Chippewa, and Métis populations constituted the large majority of the community. Twenty-four slaves reportedly lived there, too (Gilpin, 1970, p. 19).

The Indian majority had mixed loyalties towards the prior colonial authorities, who both remained either through their residual colonial population or their neighboring outposts just across the river. Since Americans had a tenuous hold on the area, the territorial government's primary responsibilities in case of war included dealing with the indigenous population. Though local conflict had been rare in the past, the threat lingered. The indigenous nations were seen as a threat as they not only had close contacts with British traders, but also traveled to British North America to receive presents. Moreover, a growing movement in the indigenous populations of the Great Lakes Region and beyond favored returning to tradition, refusing to sign treaties and to retake control over the land and their lives. This movement was headed by Tecumseh and his brother, the Prophet, who had a Shawnee father and a Creek mother (Gilpin, 1970, p. 39).

The fear, certainly legitimate, that the bands of the region would be relocated motivated the rise of active resistance. The American military struck with a preventative attack on November 7, 1811, when the settlement of Prophetstown was destroyed. The perpetrators of the Battle of Tippecanoe sought to destroy a growing confederacy of Indians seeking to stop American expansion into their territories. The violence escalated until Tecumseh was killed in 1813. After the battle of Tippecanoe in November 1811, William Harrison returned to Vincennes, leaving only a small garrison behind in northeastern Indiana, near the Michigan border.

The War of 1812 in Michigan Territory

As tensions with Great Britain increased again in 1812, Hull went to Washington to offer his services and advice to the nation's leaders. To prepare for war, Hull urged the Madison Administration to build a naval force on the Great Lakes to challenge British control and stockpile provisions at Detroit. The Madison Administration ignored his advice but they did appoint him Brigadier General, while retaining his governorship. Hull organized three regiments of Ohio volunteers under Colonels Duncan McArthur, James Findlay, and Lewis Cass, and was joined by a regiment under Colonel James Miller that had fought at Tippecanoe. Madison's Secretary of War, William Eustis, failed to inform Hull that war had been declared, and so while on his return trip to Detroit, he forwarded his baggage and papers to Detroit by ship on Lake Erie. The British Army officers on the opposite shore, knowing that war had been declared, captured the ship and acquired full knowledge of American plans.

Upon return to Detroit, Hull delayed his planned invasion of British North America, and then, lacking proper artillery, withdrew a month later on August 11 shortly after it began, without ever attacking Fort Malden. By then, the land route between Detroit and Raisin River was cut off, and the British controlled all ship-bound transportation on the Great Lakes (Gilpin, 1970, p. 59). Back in Detroit Hull sent out a third expedition to reach the depot at Frenchtown on the Raisin River. Learning that the British had also taken the unsuspecting Fort Michilimackinac—as the nearby British garrison had once again gotten the word first of the American government's declaration of war—Hull realized that the northern Indians would soon be reinforcing British forces around Detroit. Hull panicked and surrendered Detroit and its garrison, as he believed he was out-numbered, successfully bluffed by the British and their First Nation allies who were in fact less numerous than Hull's forces stationed at Detroit. Hull was later court-martialed accused of cowardice, neglect of duty and unnofficer-like con-duct. Found guilty and sentenced to be shot, Hull later saw his sentence com-muted by President James Madison because he had been a distinguished soldier in the American Revolution (Adams & Harbert, 1986, p. 906; Dearborn, Peckham, & Brown, 2009, p. 26; Gilpin, 1970, p. 59).

Télesphore Saint-Pierre describes how the *Canadiens* had been divided as to which side to support. The leading *Canadien* citizens on the west side of the Detroit River, however, did raise funds to buy gunpowder for the benefit of Detroit and the American cause. They included Denis Campeau, J. B. Piquette, Pierre Desnoyers, Joseph Campeau, Henri Berthelet, Barnabe Campeau, Antoine Dequindre, and Pierre Audrain (Saint-Pierre, 1895, p. 202). The Navarres were particularly supportive of the war effort, as François Navarre, his son, Robert, and nephew, Pierre, all enrolled at the request of Governor Hull. A Detroit mer-chant, Hyacinthe La Salle, gathered enough men to establish a company of mounted scouts. Likewise, at the outbreak of the war, a company of *Canadien* volunteers was organized under the command of captains François Cicotte, Antoine Beaubien, and Antoine Dequindre (Saint-Pierre, 1895, p. 203). On the British side of the border, the *Canadiens* were also active in supporting the British war effort. Some 400 French-Canadian volunteers contributed to the taking of Detroit by General Brock on August 16, 1812 (Saint-Pierre, 1895, p. 204).

Five months later, in January 1813, Americans incurred their highest casual-ties of the War in a battle fought on the River Raisin at Frenchtown. After they initially forced the British and their Indian allies to retreat from Frenchtown on January 18 as part of a campaign to retake Detroit, the British forces pulled off a

Pierre (Peter) Navarre (1787-1874). Born in Detroit, Peter Navarre was the grandson of Robert de Navarre, a French officer who settled in New France. When war broke out pitting Tecumseh's Confederacy against the Americans, Pierre and his brothers sided with the Americans and Peter was reportedly among those who killed Tecumseh in battle. Pierre distinguished himself in the War of 1812 against Great Britain, serving as a scout and messenger carrying military missives across enemy lines. He took part in the General William Hull's failed attempt to invade Canada in 1812. After the war, he returned to the River Raisin.

surprise counterattack on January 22. Caught completely unprepared, the Americans lost 397 men, with 547 taken prisoner. Several dozen wounded American prisoners left behind by the British were killed the next day by Indian allies, along with others who could not keep up or who tried to escape during the subsequent forced march.

The *Canadiens* on both sides of the new border had demonstrated great loyalty to their respective states. To ensure the loyalty of their subjects, the British brandished the threat of reprisal should the *Canadiens* side with the Americans. A proclamation issued by Major-General Sir Isaac Brock on July 12, 1812 stated: "Every Canadian freeholder is, by deliberate choice, bound by the most solemn oaths to defend the monarchy, as well as his own property; to shrink, from that engagement is a treason not to be forgiven" (Brock & Tupper, 1847, p. 210). The *Canadiens* of the American Northwest could have sided with the British, yet they chose to be loyal to the American authorities. This is summarized by Saint-Pierre:

> *Malgré la tyrannie dont ils avaient à souffrir et les abus qu'ils voyaient partout, les Canadiens de l'Ouest firent preuve durant la dernière lutte contre l'Angleterre, de la plus grande loyauté et prouvèrent leur valeur sur plus d'un champ de bataille. Les habitants de Détroit et les traiteurs de Michilimackinac se retrouvent partout durant cette guerre, entraînant à leur suite les nations sauvages au milieu desquelles ils vivaient.*

> In spite of the tyranny under which they had to suffer and the abuses they witnessed everywhere, the *Canadiens* of the West demonstrated during the final struggle against England their great loyalty and they proved their mettle on the battlefield. The inhabitants of Détroit and the traders of Michilimackinac were to be found everywhere during this war, bringing with them all the savage nations among whom they lived.

The *Canadiens* proved their mettle both for the British fighting the Americans, and for the Americans fighting the British. The American Civil war is often depicted as brother fighting brother, yet for the *Canadiens*, the War of 1812 was equally fratricidal, though the contribution of the *Canadiens* on either side of the border is rarely fully recognized or acknowledged.

The British withdrew from Detroit after losing the Battle of Lake Erie to a naval force under the command of the American Commodore Oliver Hazard Perry in September 1813. A couple weeks later the retreating British force was defeated at the Battle of the Thames in southwestern Ontario, along with its Indian allies under the leadership of Tecumseh, who died in the battle. With the end of an Indian and British threat on land, the Detroit region was suddenly placed back under U.S. control, but the naval threat remained on Lakes Erie and Huron. Taking back Fort Michilimackinac far to the north would have to wait, however. Colonel Lewis Cass replaced Hull as territorial governor at the end of October 1813, a little over fourteen months after Hull's surrender, and once the British occupation ended.

As the war wound down in late 1814, the territory's reconvened legislature set out to build a road through the Black Swamp of northwestern Ohio to secure an overland connection to the rest of the United States and ensure that Detroit and surrounding territory would never again risk being cut off from the rest of the country (Gilpin, 1970, p. 66). Whereas Hull had received little aid from the Madison Administration, Cass got most of what he asked for. He also received strong support over subsequent years as territorial governor, from the Monroe, John Quincy Adams, and Jackson Administrations. Cass took initiatives early on to hire a force of friendly Indians and offer a job as an interpreter to any white man who knew an Indian language. He knew that each interpreter would cost

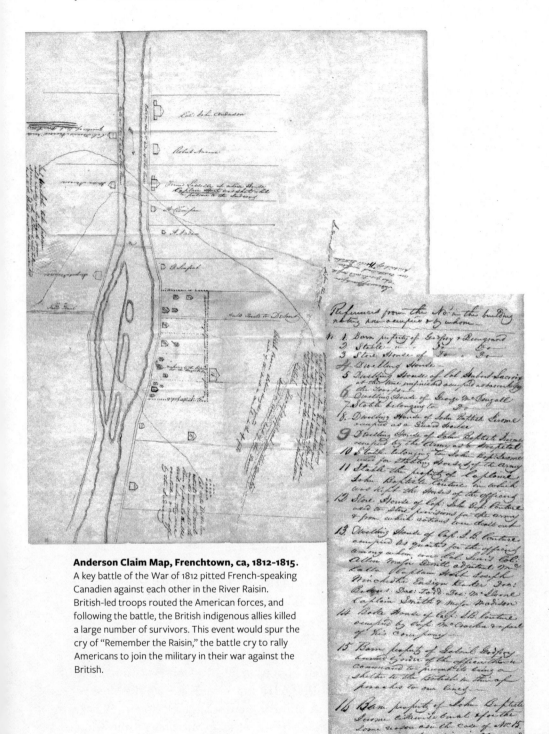

Anderson Claim Map, Frenchtown, ca, 1812–1815.
A key battle of the War of 1812 pitted French-speaking
Canadien against each other in the River Raisin.
British-led troops routed the American forces, and
following the battle, the British indigenous allies killed
a large number of survivors. This event would spur the
cry of "Remember the Raisin," the battle cry to rally
Americans to join the military in their war against the
British.

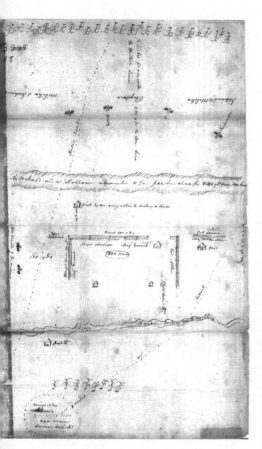

...etch of the battlefield, 1813, Lieutenant Colonel ...estler

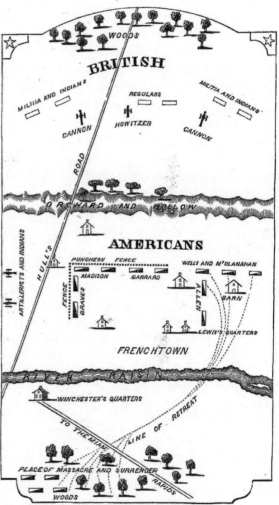

Movements at Frenchtown. From the sketch by Lieutenant Colonel Boestler sent to Colonel William H. Winder. Boestler wrote: "a hasty sketch of the situation of the troops at Frenchtown."

less than the support of two soldiers and accomplish more. Cass also emphasized that in its Indian policies, the federal government made the same mistake the British had originally made of practicing false economies. Generosity with the Indians was less expensive than military force. Once in Detroit, Governor Cass hired two Indian agents: Gabriel Godfroy, a *Canadien* (1758-1832) and Whitmore Knaggs, an American.

Godfroy was a Major in the territorial militia and succeeded Judge Woodward as Colonel in the First Michigan Regiment. The entrepreneurial Godfroy with his two partners, fellow *Canadiens*, purchased two mills in Detroit and ran a ferry across the Detroit River. They also established a trading post in 1809 where the Potawatomi Trail leading out of Detroit crossed the Huron River in what is today Ypsilanti, just east of Ann Arbor. In 1815, after the war, Gabriel Godfroy and his partners also established a tannery in Detroit.

In spite of the wars and the transfer of sovereignty from one crown to another, and then to the new American Republic, the *Canadiens* who remained in the *Pays d'en Haut* that became part of Michigan Territory managed to thrive. Their farms were producing cattle and grain, but they derived the main wealth from the fur trade, as they maintained close ties with indigenous trading partners and often took indigenous wives. A shift occurred in the later half of the nineteenth century when the fur trade life came to be reviled by the *Canadien* elites of Quebec. For example, Saint-Pierre (1895, p. 215) writes:

> *L'indifférence affichée par les Canadiens pour les choses de la politique, laquelle devait être fatale à leur influence dans les affaires publiques, correspondait malheureusement à une décadence quasi générale des vieilles familles canadiennes. Les enfants des anciens colons avaient été éloignés de l'agriculture par les profits que le commerce des fourrures offrait durant le commencement du siècle. Gagnant gros, ayant beaucoup de loisir, ils contractèrent dans la ville des habitudes incompatibles avec la vie agricole. Lorsque le commerce des fourrures disparut, les uns suivirent le castor et les Sauvages dans l'extrême Ouest, d'autres, possédant des terres près de la ville naissante, les vendirent à des prix qu'ils croyaient fabuleux; et ils mangèrent leur capital avec la rente en s'amusant.*

The indifference displayed by the *Canadien* for all things political, which became fatal to their influence in public affairs, corresponded unfortunately to the widespread decadence of the old *Canadien* families. The children of the ancient settlers were estranged from agriculture by the profits that could be made from the fur trade at the start of the century. Earning large sums, with plenty of leisure, they acquired in the city habits that were not compatible with agricultural life. When the fur trade disappeared, some followed the beaver and the Savages to the extreme West, while others owning lands close to the growing city sold them for what they thought fabulous prices and squandered their capital amusing themselves.

Saint-Pierre is highly critical of the old *Canadien* families who abandoned agriculture for trade and were too intent on spending their wealth on frivolities than preserving their capital. His tone is particularly disdainful of those who trekked farther westwards to follow the beaver and the "savages" in search of profit. Marrying women who were "savages" would also have been seen as disdainful. This might explain why Saint-Pierre rarely uses the term "Métis" when discussing the identity of those who were mixed. When listing the ancestors of the old established families, he often specifies which men married a sauvagesse or Native woman, but does not necessarily comment as to the children and how they would be defined. The one notable exception is when Saint-Pierre (1895, p. 205) describes Mackinaw in 1820, specifying that *"L'élément canadien-métis y dominait de beaucoup"* [The Canadien-Métis element dominated by large.] The *Canadiens* and Métis continued to live in Great Lakes Region after the War of 1812 as Alexis Tocqueville witnessed on his trip into the American wilderness in 1830s. But despite de Tocqueville's stature, historians have paid little attention to his observations.

Alexis de Tocqueville, Théodore Chassériau, 1850

In some of Tocqueville's least known writings, he made sharp and surprising—even for him—observations about the Canadiens or bois-brûlés.

"It was an Indian canoe roughly ten feet long and formed from one single tree. The man who was crouched at the bottom of this fragile embarcation was dressed as and had every appearance of being an Indian. He spoke to our guides who at his direction took the saddles off our horses and disposed of them in the canoe. As I was preparing myself to get in, the so-called Indian came to me, placed two fingers on my shoulder and told me with a Normand [French from the region of Normandie, in France, prevalent in Quebec] accent that made me quiver: "Ah! You come from the old country of France!... Wait, don't go too quickly; there are some who sometimes drown here." Had my horse spoken to me, I would not have been less surprised. I studied the one who had spoken and whose figure bathed in the first rays of the moon glowed like a ball of copper: Who are you? I asked him; you speak French, yet you have all the airs of an Indian? He answered that he was a bois-brûlé, that is to say the son of a Canadien and an Indian woman. I would often have the opportunity of speaking of this singular race of métis who cover all the frontiers of Canada and part of those of the United States. For the moment, I did not think more than of the pleasure of speaking my mother tongue."

CHAPTER 4

Michigan Territory From the War of 1812 to Statehood in 1837

War ravaged the Great Lakes Region and inhabitants of the devastated territories were boiling hay to stave off starvation. In the decades following the War of 1812 the fur trade in the Michigan Territory boomed. It made John Jacob Astor tremendously wealthy, but much was built upon the work of *Canadien* and Métis traders and boatmen who worked or were co-opted by Astor's American Fur Trade Company. By the 1830s, however, signs of decline were evident. In Detroit, the French-speaking population was becoming a minority even among Catholics, and the *Canadiens,* not willing to support only their own in elections, effectively neutered the political power they had when they were still a majority among the electorate in the Michigan Territory. Anglo-American settlers moved in as the governor signed treaties to have Native Americans cede lands to be redistributed to homesteaders. In this transitional period, two men from France traveled to the United States and visited the Michigan Territory before going to Canada. Alexis de Tocqueville and Gustave de Beaumont depicted life in the Western regions before they were opened to wide-scale settlement and described the lives of the French-speaking *Canadiens* and Métis whom they were surprised to meet in these distant lands. Their very significant work has largely gone under the radar of historians analyzing the origins of the Métis in the Great Lakes Region, a process that was underway when the region would be transformed by the forced removal of many of the indigenous nations that inhabited the region to the south of Michigan Territory in the late 1830s.

Post War Reconstruction: Frenchtown and Father Gabriel Richard

With the River Raisin having been the scene of one of the War of 1812's deadliest battles, the largely French-speaking inhabitants bore the brunt of the ravages of war. Battles had been fought, crops destroyed, livestock killed or rustled. Caught in the crossfire of the British and the American forces, the inhabitants of the River Raisin were left with little food and supplies and faced a largely indifferent American response. Although President James Madison had authorized the issue of food and provisions from the public stores and the temporary relocation of the inhabitants to Ohio where more food was available, none of this had been carried out (Gilpin, 1970, p. 69).

By spring 1815, the situation was critical. Judge Woodward, who had lived in the River Raisin area for a number of years, made his case to the Secretary of War describing depleted supplies, destroyed fences, stolen clothing, and inhabitants forced to eat boiled hay and bereft of seed grain. He recommended that provisions be sent to the region to be distributed by the military under the supervision of Father Gabriel Richard. Not only did the region lack the basics, the territory was debt-ridden and unable to pay the militia. The war had also ravaged the territory's trade in furs, maple sugar, and fish (Gilpin, 1970, pp. 69-70).

The *Canadien* and Métis descendants, after the Indians, were the principal victims of the depredations of war. Washington, D.C. responded slowly. The territorial officials, however, were working with Father Richard, who was serving as an unofficial arm of local government. Funds were set aside, but the conditions led to a major upheaval in the socioeconomic organization of the territory. Though some *Canadiens* and Métis had become dedicated farmers and relied on agriculture to ensure their livelihood, many others relied on a mix of hunting, trading, and horticulture. Growing food in gardens would have been under the supervision of women, as was the case for the Native American societies that had inhabited the region.

The ruins of war accelerated an economic shift in the region. Though the conditions were critical in spring 1815, a formal plan for relief was not approved until September. Moreover, relief would only be provided if proven justified because of infirmity or demonstrable inability to support oneself. Those applying for funds had to present certificates signed by two justices or one justice and Father Richard. The measures were thus ineffective in helping the families still struggling after the war. They in fact hastened what would certainly have been an inevitable shift. "The basic long-range problem for the French descendants," notes Gilpin (1970, p. 70), "was that they would be almost forced to change their way of life to the more typically American farming and domestic economy."

Under the scrutiny of territorial officials, the *Canadiens* and Métis were reprimanded for what would be seen as inferior farming practices. In a letter sent by the territorial governor to the officials in Washington, "Cass mentioned the decline of the Indian trade, the comparative ignorance of the French regarding agriculture, the large numbers of people who had lost most of their property during the war, the rise of prices, poor growing season, and the number of indigent widows" (Gilpin, 1970, pp. 70-71). President Madison informed him that only Congress could help, thus deflecting the issue to another branch of government. Various petitions requesting payment for war damage were sent to Congress, but only a small number of claims were paid out in 1816 (Gilpin, 1970, pp. 70-71).

The War of 1812 and its ravages pushed the *Canadiens*, Métis, and others to adapt to the shifting political, social, and economic landscape. Some families joined the growing English-speaking society, while others relocated northwards and westwards to lands where the fur trade was still viable. Integration was the norm for those families who remained in Detroit, and intermarriage was a means of building ties with the newcomers. John R. Williams, the leading candidate in the early 1830s of the Jackson supporters who called themselves Democratic Republicans, was an example. Williams was a Catholic, whose mother was Joseph Campau's sister. After serving in the Tennessee Militia at Fort Massac in 1799, Williams joined his uncle, Joseph Campau, in his successful mercantile business in Detroit. The bilingual Williams later became president of a local bank, mayor of Detroit, Major General of the Michigan Militia, and one of the first trustees of the University of Michigan. One of Williams' ten children became a general in the Union Army during the Civil War, and was killed in action (Gilpin, 1970, p. 139).

James Monroe became the fifth president of United States in 1817, the same year Michigan's first newspaper, the *Detroit Gazette*, was launched. Though it was an English-language newspaper, in the early years an occasional article in French appeared. President Monroe toured the north and west, including Detroit, following his inauguration. He followed a more activist and inclusive approach to executive responsibilities. Clearly impressed by the incoming president, the Governor of Michigan named the second newly organized territorial county Monroe after the president. Located in the southeastern corner of the territory, it required a county seat that was to be chosen by a local citizens' committee. The old Frenchtown located in this new county was so ravaged by war that many of the structures were not rebuilt. The acting governor named this new village Monroe while Cass was back east (Gilpin, 1970, p. 100).

When the successes of the Battle of New Orleans supplanted the memory of the Battle of Raisin River, the memory of Frenchtown was buried. The site of the old town did not disappear from the maps altogether, however. An 1876 map of Monroe still identifies Frenchtown as the district of Monroe lying north of the River Raisin, while the bay at the southeast corner of town is called La Plaisance Bay (Hutchison & Hutchison, 2004). Another clearly visible legacy of yesteryear is that property outside of the center of town, where the smaller town lots prevailed, still shows the long lot pattern of *Canadien* villages. An amazing number of Navarres, plus other early families such as the Duval and Nadeau clans, were amongst the owners of these long lots in 1876 (Hutchison & Hutchison, 2004, p. 47). Moreover, French thrived for many more generations. Even as late as the 1890s, it was still strong in Monroe county, as the farmers of the region continued to speak French (Au, 2007; Saint-Pierre, 1895).

The collective memory of local families also stayed alive. Interestingly, a century later in 1916, one of the more prominent sons of this old settlement, Ira Nadeau, still identified his home town to have been Frenchtown, Michigan. Living in Seattle, Ira came to the Pacific Northwest with the railroads late in the nineteenth century. Shortly after the turn of the century he became a leading businessman in Seattle, which had passed Portland, Oregon, in 1907 as the largest city in the Pacific Northwest. Nadeau became Seattle Chamber of Commerce Executive Vice President before taking over as the Director General of Seattle's first world's fair, the Alaska-Yukon-Pacific (A-Y-P) Exposition, held in 1909. In *The History of Seattle* (Bagley, 1916, p. 191), Nadeau claimed to be from "Frenchtown, Michigan," even as later histories of the A-Y-P went with "Monroe, Michigan."

The year after Frenchtown was renamed, the borders of Michigan Territory were shifted, adding other old French settlements further west. With the admission of Illinois to the union as a state in 1818, the upper Mississippi region west of Lake Michigan, which had been the northern part of Illinois Territory, was now joined to Michigan Territory. This meant that the old French towns of Green Bay (Baie Verte) and Prairie du Chien were now included in Michigan Territory (Gilpin, 1970, pp. 74-75).

Thus, while the southeast corner of the territory became less *Canadien*, Indian, and Métis as new American settlers moved into the farmlands surrounding Monroe leaving a French enclave in an increasingly English-speaking territory, the hinterland expanded westward, deeper into the remaining lands still dominated by the Indians with their *Canadien* or "French" and Métis populations (Wyman, 1998, p. 165). The territory now embraced what remained of the old *Canadien* hinterland west of Lake Michigan, in what is now Wisconsin and eastern Minnesota. Moreover, the continued hunger for land pushed the territorial government to sign new treaties requiring that the American Indians cede their lands.

Peace Consolidated

In 1819, the Indians living in proximity to the growing settlements were becoming embittered. Governor Cass and others believed the British were to blame by providing more of the customary gifts to Indians visiting Fort Malden than in the past. To counter this perceived threat, stricter controls were applied to the movement of Native Americans from Michigan Territory to British North America. The military garrison at Fort Detroit was strengthened and Governor

Cass was authorized to increase spending both in support of his territorial Indian Superintendency and to allocate funds for a land cession treaty at Saginaw. To accomplish this, Cass called upon the assistance of an old *Canadien* family to serve as intermediaries.

Louis Campau was one of the richest traders in the Michigan Territory, with some one thousand horses pasturing on his lands close to Detroit (Saint-Pierre, 1895, p. 206). He had been running a trading post at Saginaw with Henri Campau and Benoit Brunel, and was tasked by Cass to make arrangements for hosting the treaty council. Most of the thousand Indians assembled were Chippewa. After three councils the treaty was signed on September 24, 1819, with more than a hundred Chippewa signing. In return for land cessions and the right to build roads through their reservations, annual annuities would be distributed amounting to a thousand dollars, paid in silver, with the usual commitment to provide a blacksmith, farm equipment, livestock, and farmers to teach the Indians more intensive farming techniques. According to Saint-Pierre, Campau was to receive 15,000 dollars following the signing of the treaty, but an American trader by the name of Smith plotted to ensure that Campau did not receive the sum promised. In revenge, Campau reportedly intoxicated the Native Americans and sent them to attack Smith's fort, and Smith had to flee (Saint-Pierre, 1895, p. 206).

In 1826, Campau bought some lands and built a house on the site of the future city of Grand Rapids. In spite of his early wealth, he finished his life destitute, and in 1883 the citizens of Grand Rapids raised one thousand dollars to come to his financial assistance. He died shortly afterwards (Saint-Pierre, 1895, pp. 206-207).

The following year, in 1820, during his expedition to the northern and western parts of Michigan Territory, Cass signed another set of treaties with the Chippewa at Sault Ste. Marie, then at Michilimackinac and L'Arbre Croche. None of these treaties involved significant tracts of land, but they did reinforce American control of northern Michigan, while ensuring the Chippewa and Odawa their fishing and camping rights (Gilpin, 1970, p. 122).

A *Canadien* boatman who propelled Cass into the wilderness hinterland of Michigan Territory during this expedition, or possibly an earlier one, would reappear on the Cowlitz River a couple of years later in what is now western Washington: Simon Plamondon is just another example that belies the image of French-speaking settlements as isolated historical curiosities. These settlements should in fact be seen as an important network spanning the continent and underlying the later Anglo-American expansion. Plamondon grew up in one of the increasingly mixed communities of Lower Canada (Quebec), that of the Abenaki First Nation, located on the south shore of Lac St. Pierre at the mouth of the Saint-François River.

Commodore Charles Wilkes, commissioned to lead a global naval exploration expedition, visited the Pacific Northwest in the early 1840s and was guided by Plamondon along the lower Columbia. The 1841 visit to the Pacific Northwest of the six-ship expedition headed by Wilkes represented the first official U.S. exploring and mapping party to visit the region since Lewis and Clark had completed their sprint down and then back up the Columbia between late fall of 1805 and early spring of 1806. Wilkes (1856, pp. 316-317) provides a gratifying account of Plamondon:

> The guide that Mr. Forrest [the officer then in charge of an HBC subsidiary with an operation located at Cowlitz Farm] has sent for was one Simon Plamondon, whom I engaged to carry us to Astoria. He proved to have been the cockswain of general Cass's canoe, when on his trip to the lakes in the Northwest Territory; and a more useful person I have seldom met with, or one that could be so well depended on. He had been for several years in this territory, having left the Company's service, married an Indian wife [the eldest daughter of the Chief of the Cowlitz] and is now living on a farm of about 50 acres, at Cowlitz, independent and contented. I have seldom seen so pretty a woman as his wife [a métisse daughter of Jaco Finlay, Emilie, now his second wife] or more cheerful and good housewife: before her marriage she was the belle of the country, and celebrated for her feats of horsemanship.

Plamondon was among an increasing number of *Canadiens* heading out to the Columbia River via the Upper Missouri. They were the precursors of the Anglo-American settlers who would traverse the Oregon Trail. Plamondon was later cited as the first settler of western Washington Territory. (See photo of Simon Plamondon, p. 46.)

The U.S. census of 1820 showed that Michigan's non-Indian population had almost doubled since the 1810 census, reaching 8,896. The Métis, however, would often be classified as either non-Indian or Indian, quite often shifting from one census to the next. Much was left to the discretion of the individual census enumerator. In 1830, the incentive would have been greater to classify Métis as non-Indian, thereby boosting the number of settlers to favor the case for Michigan statehood. Lifestyle, social standing, literacy, scale of farming, length of residency, and ability to speak some English would also weigh in on the rather arbitrary, binary categorization. Métis living with the Indians or having a similar lifestyle with a focus on horticulture, hunting, trapping and trade were more likely considered Indian, regardless of their self-identification. The census data nonetheless highlights the continued demographic weight of the *Canadiens* and Métis in Michigan Territory.

Father Richard's Catholic census of his parishioners recorded 926 Catholic families in the Territory: "These were mostly French, but with a few scattered Irish" (Gilpin, 1970, p. 85). The Michilimackinac county census shows only thirty-two names in 1820; a few are Anglo-Saxon but the large majority are still *Canadien*. Many Métis were very likely excluded. The *Canadien* and Métis included had such names as Picard, Brisbois, Laplante, Petit, Archambeau, Cadotte, Gauthier, Morrin, and Fontaine.

In stark contrast to Michilimackinac, Frenchtown in Monroe County in the southeast corner of the territory was a major settlement. Hundreds of old *Canadien* settlers co-existed with a substantial inflow of new settlers, with an assortment of Anglo-Saxon names. Some of the *Canadiens* were Joseph Montour, Jean Baptiste Lature, Alex Gardipier, Louis, Etienne, and Claude Couture, Laurent DuRocher, Robert, François, and Jacques and Isadore Navarre, among many others. Cleavages were nonetheless evident in the French-speaking community.

Though the French-speakers remained an important force while being joined by new settlers from Lower Canada (*Pays d'en Bas* or Quebec), American laws prevailed. One telling case involves a legal dispute between Father Gabriel Richard and a recent *Canadien* settler, when the former, who had been a driving force for decades, overreached his authority and fell deeper into legal troubles. On the American side of the border, the Catholic Church lacked the authority they had retained in Lower Canada and the more conservative rural communities of France and Belgium. After the War of 1812, François Labadie was with the newer wave of *Canadiens* arriving from the *Pays d'en Bas*. He moved from Montreal to Detroit, leaving his wife behind. Once in Detroit he asked for and received a divorce from the civil authorities in Michigan on the grounds of her supposed adultery, and married a local widow. Father Richard warned Labadie that it was he who was the adulterer and asked him to leave his new wife three times, which Labadie refused. Father Richard, with Bishop Flaget's permission, excommunicated Labadie. Labadie in turn charged that Richard's excommunication cost him his job as Justice of the Peace and as a clerk for John Roby and sued Father Richard for five thousand dollars in damages in civil court in 1817. Both parties lined up prominent attorneys. The jury found for Labadie in 1821, awarding him 1116 dollars, plus costs. Father Richard, wiped out by the unfunded Indian school project, could not pay (Gilpin, 1970, pp. 80-81).

Downriver in Ecorse, one Métis family was clearly integrating into Anglo-American society. While others chose to join their mother's or grandmother's people, the LeBlanc family settled down as farmers and their descendants remained in the community. Kathy Warnes provides an intriguing case study as to the process of integration, one that saw the Métis becoming *Canadien* and then American. The story begins with Pierre and his Fox Indian wife, who had a son named Pierre who was raised in a log house on the family farm. This house served as a community rallying point, as it was here that the first Catholic Mass would be held. Pierre, the son, served as a constable and a road commissioner, laying out the first roads in southeastern Michigan, but these first generations still relied on trapping, hunting, and fishing for a livelihood. The two Pierres, father and son, would build pitfall traps for wolves, which preyed on the sheep that provided farmers with meat and wool. The old log house was replaced by a new house built in 1850 where Pierre's son, Frank X. LeBlanc, was born (Warnes, 2009, p. 12). The LeBlanc story was paralleled by others; the 1827 township census included, among others, Michel and Jean-Baptiste Compo, Peter Lafferty, Dominique Boucher, Peter (Sr. and Jr.) LeBlanc, and Alexander Labadie.

In 1821, the Territorial Government pressed the local Native Americans to sign treaties to cede their sovereign lands and make room for settlers. Cass signed the Treaty of Chicago in August with Sibley and representatives of the Odawa, Chippewa, and Potawatomi. The land ceded was located between the Grand River and the St. Joseph River in southwestern Michigan. This territory had a considerable *Canadien* and Métis population and, as the Jesuits proselytized in the region during the French regime, was the site of a Catholic Church. Given their historic ties, the Indians had invited Father Richard to the treaty signing, apparently to aid in setting up an educational facility. Traveling by boat, Father Richard stopped along the shores of the lakes to minister to the Indian, Métis, and *Canadien* populations and stayed in Michilimackinac for several weeks. Consequently he didn't arrive in Chicago until after the treaty had been signed.

In his absence, however, the Baptists were able to obtain the rights to establish a mission among the St. Joseph Potawatomi, who, like the other Indians in the region, had already absorbed a certain amount of Christianity during a previous wave of missionary activity by French Jesuit priests. The Baptists chose to locate their Carey Mission on the St. Joseph River (now the city of Niles) near the site of an earlier Catholic Mission. Once in Chicago, Father Richard held the first Mass the settlement had witnessed in several decades (Gilpin, 1970, p. 123).

Much as would happen in the Pacific Northwest in the following decade, the Protestant missionaries' superior financial and manpower resources enabled them to initially pre-empt an overextended Catholic church in reclaiming its own. This signaled the beginning of a continental competition between Catholics and Protestants that stretched across the northern borderlands to the Pacific. A pattern emerged: French-speaking *Canadien*, Métis, or Native populations (Iroquois and Abenaki, among others) brought popular Catholicism to their Native American peers, with priests and pastors following to compete for worshippers.

A Priest Goes to Congress

In 1823, Father Richard, at the suggestion of several parishioners, decided to run as candidate for Michigan's territorial delegate when the incumbent Sibley decided not to run for re-election. To qualify, he belatedly became a citizen. John

R. Williams, a prominent Catholic whose mother was a Campau, also seriously considered running for the position. Williams expected to win the French vote, but with Father Richard in the race he clearly would not. Williams withdrew from the race, and Father Richard became Congressional delegate. When he appeared in Congress in December, an opposing candidate, Biddle, showed up to contest the election on the grounds that Richard's naturalization was invalid as he had not been a citizen for a year. The House Committee on Elections ruled that Richard was a citizen as the usual membership requirements did not apply to territorial delegates. Richard did make history, and as Gilpin (1970, p. 85) notes: "Thus the only priest in the history of Congress was seated."

The ongoing Labadie legal dispute was a motivating factor in Richard's decision to run. Unable to pay the monies owing to Labadie, Father Richard was incarcerated and had to spend several weeks in prison (Saint-Pierre, 1895, pp. 209-210). Seeing his predicament, his friends encouraged him to seek office. Elected to Congress, he could not be imprisoned and he could then use earnings in Congress to pay his debt to Labadie (Saint-Pierre, 1895, p. 210). Religion and politics were never far apart on the American frontier.

Cass was reappointed governor for his fifth term in February 1824. The same year, bilingual John R. Williams wrote the Detroit city charter and became the first official mayor of this city. He was re-elected in 1830 and again in 1844. Construction projects underway in 1824 included a new capitol building in Detroit, and a lighthouse was authorized at the southern tip of Lake Huron where it empties through the St. Clair River into Lake St. Clair. Planning ahead for opening up the north country, commissioners chose the route for a territorial road from Pontiac to Saginaw (Gilpin, 1970, p. 86). Governor Cass and the Legislative Council in 1824 granted Peter Berthelet of Montreal permission to build a new wharf, provided he also build a public pump at the end of the wharf to draw water from the Detroit River for city residents. This became the city's first public water distribution system and a sign that Detroit was on its way to becoming a modern city. However, as Alexis de Tocqueville's journey to the "wilderness" illustrates, it was not necessary to venture far from the city to enter into the world of fur traders, Métis, and Native American communities living side by side on their traditional lands.

Roads were essential to the continued development of the territory. Father Richard actively lobbied Congress for federal grants for both roads and education, which prompted Congress to authorize the building of a graded and drained road between the Detroit River and the Rapids of the Miami (Gilpin, 1970, p. 88). When Richard returned to Detroit in September to deal with the Labadie affair, the original verdict was confirmed and he was briefly locked up. He protested that the government had no right to interfere in an ecclesiastical matter. Back in

Washington, D.C. for the December session of Congress, Father Richard was credited, following his only speech in Congress, for having Congress vote to allocate three thousand dollars for a survey of the road that would link Detroit and Chicago (Gilpin, 1970, p. 88).

He lost the following election by four votes to Austin Wing, with Biddle trailing in third place. Richard and his supporters charged that many of the French had been physically intimidated to prevent them from voting. Wing and Biddle supporters replied that this alleged intimidation was only an attempt to keep the voting lines orderly (Gilpin, 1970, pp. 89-90). Richard's appeal to the Congress was unsuccessful. Saint-Pierre (1895, p. 210) submits that Richard surely lost the election because a number of *Canadien* electors voted for his English-language opponents

Writing to a friend, the Catholic missionary priest Pierre Dejean noted that Richard's loss was also a loss for the Catholic Church as had he won the election he could have continued paying off his debts and finished his cathedral in Detroit (Saint-Pierre, 1895, p. 210) Only after Father Richard's death did Detroit get its cathedral and bishop. Although they bore witness to the continuing presence of a French-speaking Catholic population in Detroit, they also heralded its decline. In 1832, Father Richard died of cholera after ministering to the sick when an epidemic was raging. Father François Vincent is named as his successor and the next year, Monsignor Frédérick Résé is named as as Bishop of Michigan. Upon his arrival, the question of what to do with Saint Anne's Churh and parish came to the fore immediately. Though burdened with debt, the parish was quite rich in property. Saint Anne Parish was a legally incorporated entity since 1807 and owned much of Detroit's prime downtown land, but under Richard's leadership, was left with a debt of $16,723. The corporation negotiated with the new Bishop the transfer of lands to his new bishophric. In exchange for paying off the parish's debt, the episcopal authorities would be given the lands that Saint Anne Parish owned under a 999 year lease. It was also requested that the episcopal authorities maintain the church, exempt parishioners from paying the *dime* (tithe) or the "tenth" of their earnings as a church tax, and finally that one priest be assigned to the parish who spoke French (Saint-Pierre, 1895, p. 211). Clearly, the French-speaking Catholics understood that they risked losing their established French-language church services. Though the deal reached was criticized, Saint-Anne remained one of the most important French-language churches for decades. In turn, Bishop Résé immediately built a new church to serve English-speaking Catholics in 1834 (Saint-Pierre, 1895, p. 211).

The Contested Reelection of Gabriel Richard

After review, the three candidates in the 1825 election to be territorial representative to Congress, Austin Wing, Father Gabriel Richard, and John Biddle obtained 728, 724, and 689 votes respectively. An earlier count had thrown out all but nine of the 61 votes cast in Sault de Sainte Marie. A backlash occurred at the same time as masses of Anglo-American settlers arrived. Though well documented, the violence and intimidation targeting the *Canadiens* has been buried by modern historians, as has the debate on voting rights of the "half-breeds." The "Report of the Contested Election for Delegate to the Nineteenth Congress from the Territory of Michigan" addresses complaints about manipulation of *Canadien* voters and early closing of the polls at Frenchtown and includes the sworn testimony of ten witnesses as to targeted acts of violence and intimidation by the constables directed at *Canadiens* in Detroit. "... he observed (...) many persons struck over the head with a big stick when they attempted to go up to the polls to give in their votes, which caused much disturbance; (...) constables (...) opposed the Canadians in particular, when they attempted to vote, but appeared to suffer the Americans to vote without molestation (...) This deponent has no hesitation in believing (...) in consequence of the outrageous conduct those persons called constables (...) that Mr. Richard lost at least sixty votes by the terror and alarm..." (19th Congress, 1825:49/759). Another nine sworn affidavits testified along the similar lines. In Sault de Sainte Marie Wing received only three of the 61 votes cast, with the balance going to Biddle who also swept the territory's even more remote western settlement, Prairie du Chien on the upper Mississippi where the Metis, still a large majority, practiced consensus block voting under Joseph Rolette and Michel Brisbois, formerly of Quebec. The Wing campaign attempted to get one block of Biddle votes disqualified by challenging those of Sault de Sainte Marie (Murphy, 2014:33) and particularly on half-breed voting rights. The Congressional Committee on Elections examined the charges and reconfirmed Wing's election. The final report entitled "Michigan Election" Report No.69 refused to second guess the Detroit public authorities who had denied reelection to Richard. The Committee was less categorical on Métis or half-breed voting rights in Sault de Ste Marie, focusing on mode of life and the society to which the party by his own voluntary act attaches himself. Yet they gave equal weight to the testimony of a small partisan core of Wing supporters, summarily dismissing the overwhelming testimony as to the 'civilized' character of those half-breeds who had voted in Sault Ste. Marie. These Metis included a Francois Dufeau, Francois Goulet, J-B Piquet, and Charles Roussain. Half-breed voting rights were thus re-confirmed 'in principle' by both the Indian Department and the U.S. Congress, be it in a qualified manner.

Legacies and Themes in the History of Michigan Territory

Over the following decades dozens of other French-speaking priests from Europe and eastern Canada would pour into the northern borderlands of the U.S. to pick up where Father Richard had left off. These included Father Lucien Galtier at St. Peter's and St. Paul on the upper Mississippi; Father Belcourt at Turtle Mountain Reservation of the Chippewa Metis in North Dakota; Fathers Pierre-Jean De Smet, Nicolas Point, and Joseph Joset on the upper Columbia; Fathers Blanchet and Brouillet on the lower Columbia; Fathers Eugene Chirouse and F. X. Prefontaine on Puget Sound: and Fathers Modeste Demers and Pierre Rondeau in British Columbia. During a difficult transitional period, they would provide leadership to the politically disenfranchised communities of *Canadien* and Métis settlers. They would also support the traditional Indian leadership associated with their missions in their efforts to mitigate the encroachment of American settlers, squatters, and speculators assisted by their ever compliant government officials.

A typical historiography of Michigan includes Bruce Catton's (1976) history of Michigan. Though he cannot ignore the contribution of French-speaking people to the bicentennial history of Michigan, he presents them as a vanishing population, there at the beginning but quickly giving way to what he viewed as the more advanced Anglo-American settler population. He refers regularly to characters that amplify certain themes he chose to weave through the text: Étienne Brulé and Tocqueville. Brulé is presented as the prototype for the appearance of the *coureurs de bois* and their subsequent disappearance (along with their progeny apparently), while the traveling Tocqueville receives full credit for his astute observations and clairvoyance prior to his return to France. The French come, and they go, their subsequent history neatly buried. *Les Canadiens* are mentioned often in the book into the early nineteenth century, but heavily intermixed with terminology involving termination. There are numerous self-fulfilling flourishes scattered with words that begin with the letter 'd,' such as death, defeat, disappearance, and destroyed. Catton (1976) takes the reader down the parallel paths and forks in the road of history involving *les Canadiens*, leading the broader readership along, while ensuring that the dead-end signs are well posted. The last individuals mentioned in his work are the Métisse entrepreneur Madame Laframboise and her husband Joseph, and the frontier town founder from Detroit, Louis Campau. Although Catton presents a detailed history and analysis of the French contribution to Michigan's history, they are a dead-end group whose main contribution was facilitating the later settlement of Americans.

Catton provides a thorough summary of the first half of the nineteenth century and he introduces John (Johann) Jacob Astor to the history of Michigan. Though never a resident of Michigan, Astor's business interests certainly shaped the territory and state. During the War of 1812, Astor redeployed two key men from his failed venture in the Pacific Northwest to the expanded and reorganized operation centered in Michigan. As will be seen, many of *les Canadiens* employed by these same men along the Columbia made the opposite choice, staying put and signing on with the North West Company, later merged with the Hudson's Bay Company between 1821 and 1824.

Catton's analysis of Michigan's history includes the on-going viability of the independent fur traders from the earlier era who continued to work the retail end of the fur trade. This aspect is often overlooked. As independent contractors or employees, many of these traders reached a *modus vivendi* with the much more visible giant American and British chartered firms that came to dominate the wholesale end of business — and historical notoriety. The Laframboise family operation along the Grand River, for example, illustrates the social and economic forces shaping Michigan that other historians have largely ignored or underplayed.

Forced to sell his Pacific Fur Trade Company during the War of 1812, Astor focused on those territories that would eventually fall within American jurisdiction. Astor quickly re-established his fur-trade empire in the Great Lakes Region, pushing out the British competitors and developing a new trade network that dominated the region. Catton argues that Astor's work facilitated that of Governor Cass. As overtrapping emptied regions of fur-bearing animals, the Native Americans who had relied upon these furs to obtain trade goods and for food were left with little choice but to negotiate treaties with Cass. "Without intending to do anything of the kind, [Astor] cleared the way for Cass's program to induce the Indians to give up title to their land; through his agents, he destroyed the wild animals that were the mainstay of the Indians' way of life, and by the time Astor sold out—just before the boom collapsed—the Indians could do nothing but make the best deal they could and let the whites have the land that ceased to be fruitful wilderness on which Indian society was based" (Catton, 1976, p. 65). Cass in turn was promoting Michigan's land to the restless potential settlers to the east who yearned for homesteading lands.

A visionary who had become momentarily over-extended, Astor moved immediately to consolidate his commercial empire within the re-affirmed territorial limits of the U.S. as of 1815. It was more feasible to take on the North West Company closer to home, while letting them monopolize the Pacific Northwest. Before the War of 1812, British companies such as the North West Company continued to trade actively in American territories. Following the war, the Monroe administration actively pushed the British traders out of American territory, to the advantage of Astor's commercial interests. Astor deployed his two chief lieutenants returning from the Columbia, Ramsay Crooks and Robert Stuart, to Michigan's Mackinac Island, while a third, Gabriel Franchère, also from Montreal continued in the employ of the American Fur Company as well. Aware of Franchère's loyalty, Astor appointed him to be his agent in Montreal when he returned from the Pacific. Franchère published his famous journal in French in Montreal in 1820. The English version came out several decades later, in part to rebut insinuations by Washington Irving in his *Astoria* denigrating the contributions of Franchère's fellow *Canadiens*. After Astor sold out to Ramsey Crooks and partners in 1834, Franchère moved inland and took over the company's operation in Sault Sainte Marie, Michigan. Franchère served in northern Michigan until 1842, before joining Crooks in the New York office. While in New York, Franchère co-founded the New York branch of the Société Saint-Jean Baptiste becoming its first president, seeking to bring together the *Canadiens* of the growing metropolis and founding as well a literary institute to promote his French language.

Astor is often cited as a pioneer in the development of modern managerial techniques. The structure he set in place to ensure the profitable trade in furs still stands as a model for business organization. Alfred Chandler and Richard Tedlow (1985) provide a study of John Jacob Astor as their third case study in their work which has served to train generations of MBA students. Catton outlines how Astor structured his American Fur Company to aggressively corner the fur trade market. He organized the territory in districts and each of these districts was assigned a manager who would oversee the district headquarters: a log cabin and warehouse located at the mouth of a river. From there, outposts would be located as far as could be traveled by canoe. In addition to the district managers, Astor's company relied on the organization of fur brigades who used open boats—"Montreal barges" that were towed or powered with sails by wind—to transport trade goods and furs between Mackinac and the district headquarters. Trade goods would be stored in district warehouses and from there would be distributed to outlying posts where isolated traders would spend the winter trading for furs before traveling down stream to the district headquarters in the spring by canoe loaded with furs (Catton, 1976, pp. 66-67).

Given Astor's capital, organization, and access to markets, his American Fur Company gradually pushed aside independent traders who often would then be incorporated into Astor's network. This would include not only *Canadien* and Métis men, but quite often their wives. As Susan Sleeper-Smith (2001) notes, the indigenous wives of *Canadien* and Métis traders were invariably active partners in the family enterprise. If widowed, they would often take over the commercial activities, continuing the family's business. Magdelaine Marcot Laframboise, introduced in Chapter 3, is but one example.

Saginaw: Louis Campau, Jean-Baptiste Desnoyers and Alexis de Tocqueville

The Treaty of Ghent in December 1814 officially ended the War of 1812. As peace gradually returned to the northern frontier, the American Fur Company assigned its employee Louis Campau to establish a trading post at the site of the future city of Saginaw. When trade picked up, the American Fur Company sent another employee, Jean-Baptiste Desnoyer, to assist Campau in Saginaw. By 1831 when Alexis de Tocqueville and Gustave de Beaumont from France arrived to document what they saw in the Chippewa village on the Saginaw River, they also found 30 or 31 inhabitants on the opposite shore of the Saginaw River where the city would soon stand. One had two houses built with boards plus two or three log houses. By this time Louis Campau had moved on to found the city of Grand Rapids in Western Michigan (Lamarre, 2003, p. 30). Campau arrived on the heels of Mme Laframboise who by then moved north to Mackinaw Island.

Tocqueville and the *Canadiens* of the *Pays d'en Haut*

Alexis de Tocqueville is one of the most renowned scholars of nineteenth-century American history, and students and scholars alike continue to study his writings. Yet his work on the *Canadiens* and the Métis of the *Pays d'en Haut*, the Great Lakes Region, has largely escaped the gaze of scholars and the general public in both the United States and Canada. During his impromptu, month-long excursion to the Great Lakes (mid-July to mid-August, 1831) de Tocqueville and his traveling companion Gustave de Beaumont visited five sites in Michigan Territory via two steamers. The first steamship, the *Ohio*, crossed Lake Erie from Buffalo to Detroit. Then two weeks later, on a second leg they headed north up Lake Huron on the *Superior,* allowing for a glimpse of Lake Superior, then across northern Lake Michigan, and finally back to Detroit. The first half included an overland trip in southeastern Michigan, from the major settlement around Detroit to the nearest Indian village Tocqueville deemed to lay beyond the frontier, one which, as it turned out was located on the Saginaw River. The primary goal of the detour to Michigan had thereby been reached: to find Indians that remained relatively "uncontaminated" by exposure to the European settlements. But even here, across the river from the Indian village was the tiny hamlet of a half dozen structures occupied by a mix of 30 or 31 *Canadiens*, Métis, and American families, where the lumber town of Saginaw, Michigan would soon appear. A significant percentage of the population of the future city of Saginaw would be composed of *Canadiens* working primarily in its sawmills. This early hybrid settlement also benefited from the analysis of Tocqueville.

The second half of the Michigan loop was similarly unplanned, involving a two week excursion on the steamer *Superior* whereby Tocqueville and Beaumont were able to spend time among the Indian and Metis communities that had emerged from a century and half of fur trade activity at Sault Ste. Marie, Michilimackinaw, and Green Bay (la Baie Verte). The first two were located on the straits where lakes Michigan and Superior empty into north western Lake Huron, and the third was at the head of the long bay on the western shore of Lake Michigan extending in a southwesterly direction and leading to the Fox-Wisconsin river portage route to the upper Mississippi. Published posthumously and subsequently largely ignored by historians, Alexis de Tocqueville's account of this voyage to the "wilderness" deserves close analysis. It provides an informative account of the life in Michigan in the transition from a largely French and Algonkian speaking territory focused on the fur trade to a largely Anglo-American settler society that would become an American agricultural, and later industrial heartland.

The *Canadiens* and the Fur Trade in Tocqueville's Account

When Alexis de Tocqueville was in Detroit seeking to negotiate his travel through the forests of Michigan, his interest in the area baffled locals; at the time (1831), the forest began only a short distance north of Detroit, with most of Michigan still lying beyond the American frontier. At that point, the most distant settlements had been established in the St. Joseph River region, the mouth of the river being less than 200 miles (320 km) due west from Detroit. When Tocqueville left Detroit for the "wilderness," he entered into another world where the *Canadien* is omnipresent. In his journal, he describes an indigenous market he comes across:

> *Un Anglais, froid trafiquant, au milieu d'une foule de Canadiens et de sauvages qu'il mène commercer avec les Indiens du lac Supérieur. Les Canadiens nous entourent avec la franchise et la bonhomie des Français. Ils paraissent charmés de voir des Français. Nous leur demandons des renseignements sur les Indiens. Les Indiens vont tous les ans jus qu'à fond du lac, portent le même habillement que ceux que nous avons vus. Bons et hospitaliers en paix. Bêtes féroces à la guerre, brûlent leurs prisonniers. Antipathie des Indiens pour la langue anglaise. Leur goût pour le français. Dans les déserts les plus éloignés, les Indiens saluent les Européens en disant: Bon jour.* (de Tocqueville, 1865, p. 245)

> An Englishman, a wily trader, in the middle of a crowd of *Canadiens* and Savages that he leads to trade with the Indians of Lake Superior. The *Canadiens* surround us with the frankness and affability of the French. They seem charmed to see Frenchmen. We ask them for some information on the Indians. Each year the Indians go to the far reaches of the lake wearing the same clothing that we have seen. Good and hospitable in peace. Ferocious beasts in war, burning their prisoners. The antipathy of the Indians for the English language. Their taste for French. In these most distant deserts [forests] the Indians greet the Europeans in saying: *Bon jour* [Good day].

Here, Tocqueville describes a scene where one Englishman, a trader, is leading a large number of *Canadiens* to trade with the indigenous inhabitants. He takes the opportunity to question the *Canadiens* as to the nature of the Native

Americans, and he is told that they do not want to speak English and much prefer French. Even in the most distant wilderness, Indians will greet Europeans by saying *"Bon jour,"* meaning "Good day." This echoes the favorable sentiments expressed by many "Indians" toward the French, as reported in Louise Seymour Houghton's book, *Our Debt to the Red Men* (1918, pp. 7-8).

Alexis de Tocqueville meets Magdelaine Laframboise at that point, as the priest accompanying the group wishes to visit the settlement of *l'Arbre-Crochu [or l'Arbre-Croche],* home to "Catholic Indians." He commends the *Canadiens* as they guide the canoe down the river through rocks and rapids like an arrow. As he is looking for the priest, he comes across Madame Laframboise. He notes in his journal that they had a conversation, and that she was a respectable woman who told him her story.* Unfortunately, he records nothing of that conversation. Instead he went to speak to a group of *Canadiens* camped on the shore and recorded their conversation at great length on the fate of the Hurons and the nature of the Native Americans.

All told, the fifteen days that Alexis de Tocqueville spent in the "wilderness" were in reality spent visiting the territory that large numbers of *Canadien* traders and settlers called home. He started from Detroit, a city of two or three thousand inhabitants where he observes "a very large number of French families." The "wilderness" he then visited was teeming with *Canadiens,* with the French language still central to the fur trade. These forays would shape Tocqueville's understanding of those *Canadiens* that lived in the St. Lawrence River Valley. He saw the *Canadiens* as having the French national character and as being comparable to the French peasantry, though morally superior: *"vifs, railleurs, aimant la gloire et le bruit, intelligents, éminemment sociables. Le peuple y est seulement plus moral, plus hospitalier, plus religieux qu'en France"* (Tocqueville, 1865, p. 267). [Lively, derisive, loving glory and noise, intelligent, eminently sociable. The people there is only more moral, more hospitable and more religious than in France.] He commented on how the French were tied to home and hearth, but when they happen to leave they quickly and passionately adopt the vagaries of savage life: *"Le Français est tout à la fois l'homme le plus attaché naturellement au foyer domestique, et, quand par hasard il l'a quitté, le plus prompt à se passionner pour les accidents de la vie sauvage"* (Tocqueville, 1865, p. 267). [The Frenchman is both the man most attached by nature to the domestic hearth and, when, due to shifting circumstances, he leaves it, the quickest to become passionate for the unexpected encounters of a savage life.] The *Canadien, habitant* and

---

* Tocqueville commented: *"Madame [La]Framboise, Sang indien. Détails intéressants sur sa vie. Femme très respectable. Lettre d'une jeune Indienne.* Livre de prières indien" (Tocqueville & Vallée, 1973, p. 49).

voyageur, are thus the two sides of the French coin, representing both their desire to stay tied to their homes and villages as well as the ease with which they adopt the "savage" way of life when given the opportunity.

This lesser known work of Tocqueville provides significant insight into an emerging Métis collective identity, one still tied to a larger *Canadien* nationality. In the modern Canadian political context, however, it developed as an independent and formal Aboriginal identity. A significant segment of the Métis populations of the Northwest, particularly in Canada, came to see themselves as a new nation. This stemmed in part from the mounting pressures associated with "Canadian" statehood-building, which included the hijacking of the early *Canadien* identity that initially served to identify the "country-born" or French-indianized inhabitants both north and south of the later line of partition along the 49th parallel. The Canadian ethnonym came to be politically rerouted to identify all newcomers as "Canadian-citizens," including the settlers who encroached on the Western territories upon which the Métis claimed an inherent right due to the "Indian blood" flowing through their veins (de Tocqueville, 1865, p. 267). In speaking of the Métis of the Northwest, Riel also writes, "that they were peoples that had the North-Western Territories to themselves. The Indian blood flowing through their veins established their right or title they had to the Land itself. They had joint-ownership to the Land with the Savages" (Riel, 1985, p. 279). (Our translation).

In their own way, the *Canadiens* of the *Pays d'en Haut* also provided Tocqueville with some insights as to how the French can easily adopt the ways of life of the "savage" and even rejoice in the freedom this provides. His observations of the *Canadiens* in both the "wilderness" and the already densely populated farmlands of the St. Lawrence Valley helped crystallize his thoughts on what it means to be both French and American, and how the two nations also differ. This in turn would influence the writing of his best-known work, *Democracy in America*.

His writing sheds light on the emergence of a Métis identity as a means of describing some of the *Canadiens* who have mixed French and aboriginal ancestry. One intriguing passage in Alexis de Tocqueville's description of his voyage illustrates the population he encounters in Sault Ste Marie: "*Caractère singulier de cette population. Mélange de tous les sangs. Les plus nombreux, les Canadiens. Bois brûlés ou métis; nuances depuis l'Européen jusqu'au sauvage*" (de Tocqueville, 1865, p. 244). [The singular characteristic of this population. The mixture of all the bloods. The most numerous, the *Canadiens. Bois brûlés* [burnt wood] or métis; with nuances ranging from the European to the savage.] A first read would seem to suggest two distinct populations—one *Canadien*, the other Métis, with the former being closer to the European and the latter being closer to the *sauvage*. However, another interpretation is that it is the *Canadien* population that is characterized as being

Chief Guide and Rapids Pilot John Boucher, ca. 1905. Boucher was a "Chippewa half-breed," his father, a wealthy fur trader and a descendant of Pierre Boucher. Chief John Boucher was one of best known of the rapids pilots who would take tourists with him in his "Indian canoe" to "shoot the rapids" in St. Mary's River.

bois brûlés or *métis* within a certain continuum of indigenized identities allowing new collective identities to emerge, although not yet fully distinct from early expressions of *Canadien* identities. His next passage implies this, as Tocqueville (1865, p. 244) specifies how at either end of the canoe was a half-savage *Canadien*, "*Aux deux bouts un Canadien demi-sauvage,*" reinforcing the perception that the early *Canadien* was already a mix of European and indigenous. If the mix was not solely in terms of ancestry, it was certainly in terms of culture. And who was going to sort this all out for each individual, at the time and place, or at any time since? Then again, this was before the invention of the arbitrary and bureaucratic precision of "blood quantum," and the associated special prerogatives. The blood quantum was instituted with the intent to "quantify" how much native ancestry an individual had based on ancestry, usually with the goal of denying indigeneity to some and granting it to others. Thus, for example, having one grandparent who was "pure blood" would have given a blood quantum of one-quarter and other combinations would result in other proportions of "blood" that person was deemed to have in this bureaucratic measurement of indigeneity.

"Indians Fishing at the 'Soo'," ca 1901. The rapids of Saint Mary's River (rivière Sainte Marie) separate Sault Ste. Marie, Ontario and its namesake in Michigan. The word sault in old French designated rapids or waterfalls. Though a risky proposition, fishing in the rapids would have provided an abundance of fish, notably the spring rainbow trout, Atlantic salmon, whitefish and pickerel.

The publication authored by Alexis de Tocqueville that provides the greatest insight into the life of the *Canadiens* and Métis of the Great Lakes Region is *Quinze jours au désert,* also known as *Quinze jours dans le désert,* later translated as *A Fortnight in the Wilderness* (Pierson, 1938). In this posthumously published work, de Tocqueville describes his travels with a Chippewa Indian guide named Sagan-Ruisco, through a stretch of primeval forest to the edge of America in Saginaw, Michigan. The "desert" is in fact the forest wilderness that Alexis de Tocqueville longs to see. Here he meets Native Americans as well as the *Canadien* traders working and living side-by-side with the indigenous populations. In this account, certainly one of the least well-known of his works, Alexis de Tocqueville (1860, pp. 594-595) describes his first encounter with a man that he first thought to be native as he and Beaumont were preparing to cross the Saginaw River. It is undoubtedly one of the most revealing passages.

> *C'était un canot indien long de dix pieds environ et formé d'un seul arbre. L'homme qui était accroupi au fond de cette fragile embarcation portait le costume et avait toute l'apparence d'un Indien. Il adressa la parole à nos guides qui à son commandement se hâtèrent d'enlever les selles de nos chevaux et de les disposer dans la pirogue. Comme je me préparais moi-même à y monter, le prétendu Indien s'avança vers moi, me plaça*

deux doigts sur l'épaule et me dit avec un accent normand qui me fit tressaillir: "—Ah! Vous venez de la vieille France!… Attendez, n'allez pas trop vitement; y en a des fois ici qui s'y niyent." Mon cheval m'aurait adressé la parole que je n'aurais pas, je crois, été plus surpris. J'envisageai celui qui m'avait parlé et dont la figure frappée des premiers rayons de la lune reluisait alors comme une boule de cuivre: —Qui êtes-vous donc? lui dis-je; vous parlez français et vous avez l'air d'un Indien? Il me répondit qu'il était un bois-brûlé, c'est-à- dire le fils d'un Canadien et d'une Indienne. J'aurai souvent occasion de parler de cette singulière race de métis qui couvre toutes les frontières du Canada et une partie de celles des États-Unis. Pour le moment je ne songeai qu'au plaisir de parler ma langue maternelle.

It was an Indian canoe roughly ten feet long and formed from one single tree. The man who was crouched at the bottom of this fragile embarcation was dressed as and had every appearance of being an Indian. He spoke to our guides who at his direction took the saddles off our horses and disposed of them in the canoe. As I was preparing myself to get in, the so-called Indian came to me, placed two fingers on my shoulder and told me with a Normand [French from the region of Normandie, in France, prevalent in Quebec*] accent that made me quiver: "Ah! You come from the old country of France!… Wait, don't go too quickly; there are some who sometimes drown here." Had my horse spoken to me, I would not have been less surprised. I studied the one who had spoken and whose figure bathed in the first rays of the moon glowed like a ball of copper: Who are you? I asked him; you speak French, yet you have all the airs of an Indian? He answered that he was a bois-brûlé, that is to say the son of a *Canadien* and an Indian woman. I would often have the opportunity of speaking of this singular race of métis who cover all the frontiers of Canada and part of those of the United States. For the moment, I did not think more than of the pleasure of speaking my mother tongue.

Historian George Pierson provides additional insight into this seminal moment in de Tocqueville's nine-month sojourn in America. Descended from a long line of Yale scholars, George Wilson Pierson led the effort among historians to rescusitate interest in Tocqueville's writings during the twentieth century. Based upon his PhD thesis, Pierson (1938) published his seminal study, *Tocqueville and Beamont in America*. Pierson (1938, pp. 268-269) cites Tocqueville: "Following the counsels of our compatriot the savage, I seated myself in the bottom of the canoe and held myself as steady as possible; my horse, which I held on my bridle, entered the river and began to swim, while the Canadian propelled the craft with his paddle, all the while singing softly, to an old French air, the following couplet, the first lines of which alone I caught: Entre Paris et Saint Denis[;] Il etait une fille, etc."

---

* Normandie in France provided many of the French settlers in New France and their dialect would influence the language spoken by the French in the colonies and the future *Canadiens* who would eventually become *Québécois*. Tocqueville notes that the *Canadiens* of the St. Lawrence Valley as speaking French with a Normand accent.

Apparently this moment made a powerful impression upon Tocqueville. After referring to this scene, some twenty pages later, George Pierson ends his chapter entitled "A Fortnight in the Wilderness" with the following sentence:

He was often to refer to its incidents in conversation with his friends – especially to the 'delighted wonder' with which he had heard the Canadian Indian at Saginaw begin to sing:

> Entre Paris et Saint Denis
> Il etait une fille. . .

This particular song, *Le Message de l'infidèle*, is derived from a medieval French song (Laforte, 1981, p. 36) that was quite common throughout the Great Lakes region on both sides of the border and in Quebec, and versions were also recorded in the folklore of France in the nineteenth century (Rosenberg, 2014, p. 104). This man Tocqueville thought to be Indian, who called himself *Bois-Brûlé* and Métis, spoke French and sang songs common to the folklore of France, would certainly have astounded him.

In the text that follows, Tocqueville significantly refers to the man as a *Canadien*, suggesting that both collective identifiers could be used interchangeably in a non-mutually excluding fashion. Tocqueville never capitalizes the term Métis; instead, he lists those he encounters as "*des Canadiens, des Américains, des Indiens et des métis*" (Tocqueville & Vallée, 1973, p. 36). This suggests that the early usages of the expression "*Canadien*" (noun) didn't require the suppression or the plain assimilation of this other collective identifier, the "métis." It can, however, be inferred that the term "métis" remained closer to an adjective rather than describing a capitalized noun (indicative of nationality) in Tocqueville's writings. Yet it remained simultaneously and surprisingly "distinct" enough to stand apart among an enumeration of different capitalized nationalities, both apart yet compatible with the *Canadien* ethnonym. If we consider the "métis'" close relation to *Canadien* parentage, the term stands interestingly in a non-mutually excluding yet distinct fashion.

Tocqueville biographer André Jardin attributes the posthumous publication of *Quinze jours dans le desert American* or *A Fortnight in the Wilderness* to Tocqueville's desire to withhold this part of his journal in order to allow Beaumont to cover the "Indian question" in his own words in the book he was authoring, entitled *Marie*. His close friend de Beaumont himself later published *Quinze jours au desert* (de Tocqueville, 1860) in the *Revue de deux mondes* (Jardin, 1984, pp. 117-118). George Wilson Pierson (1938) was the first to provide a complete and literal translation in English of Tocqueville's "Fortnight in the Wilderness" in his work *Tocqueville in America*. Fortunately, this work was published because of its detailed discussion of identity, ethnicity, and race in Michigan in the early 1830s when the fur trade was still going strong and the Native Americans had not been relocated. In Tocqueville's own words, the village of Saginaw was the last point inhabited by Europeans in the North West located in the middle of the Indian nations. He describes thirty individuals, men, women, elders, and infants, a small embryonic society that was just taking root in the wilderness. He specifies: "*On remarquait parmi elles des Canadiens, des Americains, des Indiens, et des métis*" (Tocqueville, 1998, pp. 67-68). Here, too, Tocqueville uses the term Métis, but not capitalized, indicating that it is an adjective and not a noun. This reinforces the use of métis to designate a specific type of *Canadien*.

Astonished to discover the "savage" that spoke his native tongue, Alexis de Tocqueville then discusses the nature and character of these individuals in the American wilderness. He notes that it would be easy enough at first glance to mistake them for an Indian submitting to a savage life, as he has adopted voluntarily the habits and customs of the Indians, yet he remains European. In Tocqueville's estimation: "*Cet homme n'en est pas moins pourtant encore un Français, gai, entreprenant, glorieux, fier de son origine, amant passionné de la gloire militaire, plus vaniteux qu'intéressé, homme d'instinct, obéissant à son premier mouvement mieux qu'à sa raison, préférant le bruit à l'argent*" (Tocqueville, 1998, p. 69). [This man is nonetheless still a Frenchman, merry, entrepreneurial, glorious, proud of his origins, a passionate lover of military glory, more vain than interested, a man of instinct, obeying his first reaction more than reason, preferring passion (noise) to money.] This man, the métis *Canadien,* is still French, proud of his origins and otherwise conforming to the character and personality of the French. Or, as Tocqueville (1998, pp. 69-70) phrases it, the most civilized of Europeans has become the adulator of the savage life and they have become exceptional hunters almost as if God created them to live in the cabin of the savage and live in the wilderness.

Along similar lines, after providing excerpts from Alexis de Tocqueville's own words, his biographer, André Jardin (1984, p. 125), expands on Tocqueville's take on *le Canadien.* "*Il se plie sans effort à la vie sauvage, traite les Indiens avec une cordialité sans mépris, copule sans préjugé avec les sauvagesses, parfois recrée avec une Indienne ce foyer domestique pour lequel il garde malgré sa vie errante un atavique attachement.*" [He bends without effort to the savage life, treating the Indians with cordiality without scorn, copulates without prejudice with the savage women, occasionally recreating with the Indian woman that domestic sphere for which he kept, in spite of his nomadic life, an atavistic attachment.]

Alexis de Tocqueville inadvertently explains why the "civilized life" is not inherently better. He notes that the Indian in Saginaw smiles bitterly seeing the European being tormented in life, seeking to acquire useless riches. He write: "*Ce que nous appelons industrie, il l'appelle sujetion honteuse.*" (Tocqueville, 1998, pp. 70-71) [That

Peter Barbeau and his Métisse wife Archange Lalonde, ca. 1865. Born Pierre Barbeau in LaPrairie (Quebec), Peter Barbeau arrived in Sault Ste. Marie in about 1817 where he worked first for the Hudson's Bay Company then John Jacob Astor's American Fur Trade Company. After working in Wisconsin, he returned to Sault Ste. Marie, Michigan and worked under Gabriel Franchère in the ranks of the American Fur Trade Company. A naturalized American, he worked for this company until 1842 when he resigned over a question of salary. He opened a general store in Sault Ste. Marie and became one of the city's distinguished civic and business notables.

which we call industry, he calls shameful subjugation.] Here Tocqueville hints that he himself understands the attraction of the life of the Native Americans, and his biographer stresses the fascination he had for the *Canadien* métis: "*A Saginaw même, il est attiré par les bois-brûlés, ces métis franco-indien. Leur destin n'est pas facile, il est fait de contradictions tragiques*" (Jardin, 1984, p. 126). [Even in Saginaw, he is attracted by the bois-brûlés, these Métis Franco-Indian. Their destiny is not easy, as it is comprised of tragic contradictions.]

Furthermore, in Tocqueville's own words:

> *Enfant de deux races, élevé dans l'usage de deux langues, nourri dans des croyances diverses et bercé dans des préjugés contraires, le métis forme un composé aussi inexplicable aux autres qu'à lui-même. Les images du monde lorsqu'elles viennent se réfléchir sur son cerveau grossier, ne lui apparaissent que comme un chaos inextricable dont son esprit ne saurait sortir. Fier de son origine européenne, il méprise le désert; pourtant il*

aime la liberté sauvage qui s'y règne. Il admire la civilisation et ne peut complètement se soumettre à son empire. Ses goûts sont en contradiction avec ses idées, ses opinions avec ses mœurs (Tocqueville, 1998, pp. 72-73).

A child of two races, raised in the use of two languages, nourished by diverse beliefs and cradled in contrary prejudices, the Métis form a composite as inexplicable to others as to themselves. The images of the world when they come to be considered in their crude minds appear to him as an inextricable chaos out of which his spirit would not know how to escape. Proud of his European origins, he despises the desert [forest]; yet he loves the savage liberty that rules there. He admires civilization, yet he cannot submit himself to its rule. His tastes are in contradiction with his ideas, his opinions and his mores.

Jardin felt compelled to caution his readers at the end of his partial quotation from the above text, in which Tocqueville describes the Métis as having a chaotic, tumultuous psychological existence, torn between the love of savage liberty while hating the wilderness, admiring civilization yet unable to submit himself to its constraints. Jardin prefers to point out that the contradictions in the soul of the Métis do not condemn his existence from Tocqueville's perspective. Beaumont, not Tocqueville, informs us that the *Canadien* Métis hates the domination of the English and hopes that he will be able to realize his autonomy in the American Republic. This experience will shape how Tocqueville will see the inhabitants of Lower Canada (Quebec) (Jardin, 1984, p. 126).

Returning to Detroit from Saginaw, Tocqueville and Beaumont had to visit the territorial prison, as they were officially a two-man commission sent by the French government to study such institutions in America. As they prepared to catch a steamboat for Buffalo at the eastern end of Lake Erie, another option presented itself. A steamboat, the *Superior*, was preparing to head north across Lake Huron for the old Indian and *Canadien* settlements of Michilimackinac, Sault Ste. Marie, and Baie Verte (Green Bay, on the far side of Lake Michigan). This afforded them the opportunity to further penetrate the frontier in pursuit of a better appreciation of the plight of the surviving Indians, and as a matter of course, the Métis (Jardin, 1984, p. 126).

While in Detroit, Tocqueville met and spoke with Father Gabriel Richard, known for his somewhat ecumenical leanings. Then, on the steamboat, he conversed with a priest of Irish origins. From this meeting he reached the conclusion that religious ardor becomes much more passionate in the West (Jardin, 1984, p. 126). Tocqueville is stunned by the beauty of the Great Lakes and when the boat docks, Beaumont paints and Tocqueville hunts. Both go down the rapids at Sault Ste. Marie in a birchbark canoe, guided by a Métis man who sings old French songs (Jardin, 1984, p. 127). Tocqueville and Beaumont noted that everybody spoke French at Sault Ste. Marie and that Fort Mackinac was more populous and there, too, the dominant language was French. The 1830 census recorded the names of the inhabitants of Fort Mackinac, some of whom Beaumont and Tocqueville would certainly have encountered: Jean-Baptiste Marchand, Jules Lachance, Jean-Baptiste Durocher, and Joseph Gauvreau, among many others.

Beaumont does note, "The Canadians call metiches (metis) those who come of this double origin. I have seen some young metiches girls who seemed to me of noteworthy beauty." He goes on an excursion to the Pointe aux Pins and also remarks the songs being sung: "While paddling they did not stop singing to us a number of old French songs, some of whose couplets are altogether droll." Spending an hour or two at Pointe aux Pins, the French visitors were introduced to the local chief, who was fascinated with studying their guns. The chief told them that "he has always heard that the French were a nation of great warriors." On their return trip, descending the rapids in the canoe Beaumont remarked, "There is no danger because you are guided by skillful boatmen who know the river and its rocks marvellously well" (Pierson, 1938, pp. 296-297).

Tocqueville had a great deal to say about his encounters with certain *Canadiens* and Métis, and likewise specific Americans and Indians, yet he only recorded the nature of discussion with others summarily or not at all. His meeting with Madame Laframboise on Mackinac Island was, unfortunately, one such case. When he dropped by to visit the local curé at Ste-Anne's Mission, he found that the priest was out making his rounds. Madame Laframboise, however, was in. Failing to meet the priest, they had a chat. Historian George Pierson described what little Tocqueville noted down in *Tocqueville and Beaumont in America* (Pierson, 1938, p. 302). An interesting sampling of the ethnic attitudes of the day is reflected in Pierson's choice of terms:

> Instead he met with Madame La Framboise, a respectable woman partly of Indian extraction, whose family was well known at Mackinac and in the adjoining regions. Nothing loath, the half-breed lady gave her French visitor some interesting details on her life and family history. She then showed him a letter written by an Indian girl, and some Indian books of prayer.

Neither Tocqueville nor Pierson provided further details. Other sources fortunately provided an outline of her story. As described above in Chapter 3, Madame Laframboise was an orphaned Métisse raised by her mother back in her Odawa village, who then married a *Canadien* and became a prosperous trader in her own right following her husband's murder. Later she retired north to care for her grand children and to devote her life to working with the missionaries in establishing her own school and orphanage to educate Indian and Metisse girls. Madame Laframboise became an icon of Michigan history, to some degree straddling both the Sacagawea and Mother Joseph legacies of the Pacific Northwest.

Fortunately, Tocqueville's next encounter after Magdeleine Marcot Laframboise was recorded in some detail. Among all the tens of thousands of campfire gatherings of *Canadiens* and Métis all across North American in the course of the seventeenth, eighteenth, and nineteenth centuries, one was about to benefit from a systematic interview in their common native language by a man intent on deciphering their world, as it was being swallowed up by the expanding republic. He was there to interpret that world's legacy for posterity, including especially their unique role in, and observations of, Indian Country, including Indian-Euro-American relations at that time and place.

While Beaumont was off sketching, Tocqueville, after giving leave to Madame Laframboise, wandered on and came to a bivouac of *Canadiens* along the shore (Pierson, 1938, p. 302-303). The chief of the band of traders was a *bois-brûlé*, with the air and manners of the French, gay, open, and energetic:

"I sat down at their fire, and I had with their chief the following conversation: I have only taken in this conversation," Tocqueville noted in his diary, "what accorded with all the notions I had already received."

"Q. What has become of the Hurons and the Iroquois who played so great a role in the history of the colonies?

"A. The Hurons have almost disappeared. The Iroquois, half destroyed also, have almost all mingled with the Chippewas. Many are established at Green Bay and its neigborhood. The Iroquois form an astute nation, always ready to join our side or the English, as fortune seems to incline.

"Q. Have you something to fear from the Indians in trading with them?

"A. Almost nothing. The Indians are not thieves, and besides we are useful to them.

"Q. Do you think the Indians are better or worse, in proportion as they are nearer or further away from Europeans?

"A. I think they are much better when they have no contact with us, and certainly happier. There is more order, more government among them as one advances further into the wilderness. I make an exception, however, for the Chrisitian Indians and especially for those who are Catholic. Those are the best of all.

"Q. Have the distant Indians, of whom you speak, chiefs?

"A. Yes, sir, they have chiefs whose power is very respected in peace. They are hereditary, and their origin is lost in the night of time. They name a special chief (the bravest) to lead them in war. They don't exactly have a system of justice. However, when a murder is committed, the murderer is delivered to the family of the dead. Often he succeeds in buying himself off. More often still, he is killed and buried with his victim.

"Q. How do the Indians you speak of live?

"A. In an ease absolutely unknown near European establishments. They do not cultivate the land. They are much less well clothed, and use only bows. But game is in extreme abundance in their wilderness. I imagine it was thus all the way to the Atlantic before the arrival of the Europeans. But the game flees toward the west with unbelieveable rapidity. It precedes the whites by more than a hundred leagues. The Indian peoples which surround us die of hunger if they do not cultivate the ground a little.

"Q. Is it that the Indians do not realize that sooner or later their race will be annihilated by ours?

"A. They are unbeleivably careless of the future. Those who are half educated already, or on whose heels we tread, see with despair the Europeans advancing toward the west, but there is no longer time to resist them. All the distant western tribes (I have heard said that there were a good three million of them) do not seem to suspect the danger that is menacing them.

"A. Is it true that the Indians love the French?

"Q. Yes, sir, extremely. They do not consent to speak anything except French. In the furthest wilderness, the quality of being a Frenchman is the best recommendation with them. They always remember our good treatment of them when we were masters of Canada. Besides many of us are allied to them, and live almost as they do."

It was late when Tocqueville returned. He must have been smiling to himself at the recollection of how the chief of the voyageurs had "sirred" him. As he passed a savage hut, an Indian family was chanting a canticle of the church in its native tongue (Pierson, 1938, 302-303).

Leaving Michilimackinac on the evening of August 7, the *Superior* crossed northern Lake Michigan and arrived at Green Bay on the morning of the ninth. During the 24-hour stay, Gustave de Beaumont adapted his artistic interests to interacting with the Indians. He ventured off alone, visiting one Indian hut after another along the river bank, noting that he talked as much as possible with the local Native Americans and that a few knew a little French, enough to say *bonjour*. Slowly, Beaumont's preconceived notions of the "savages" was being modified, and as he notes: "I have learned the ways of the Indians better in half a day thus passed in their midst than I should have done in reading thousands of volumes," and he even remarks that they seem an excellent people. Meanwhile, Tocqueville nearly drowned while hunting along the river nearby (Pierson, 1938, p. 304).

Surviving his brief encounter with the Fox River, later in the day Tocqueville and his friend went together to interview the Major in charge of the local U.S. Army post, Fort Howard. Beaumont asked whether the Indians would ever "bend themselves" to civilization, and the Major replied, "No," adding, "They feared work, despised the comforts of the white man, and were too proud to change." Beaumont also asked whether they would ever unite to attack the whites. The major replied: "Too few realize the danger; and they are too busy with their private wars." Beaumont was satisfied with the discussion that followed as "[t]he rest confirmed what the Canadian fur traders had said" (Pierson, 1938, pp. 304-305). The two then returned to the *Superior*, where Beaumont reverted to sketching the harbor and fort with the steamship moored at the pier.

One Métis teenager present during their brief visit to Green Bay in 1831 would appear in the Pacific Northwest later in the decade. His name was Alexandre Guérette, dit Dumont. Alexandre would later be cited as one of the earliest settlers of southwestern Oregon, Douglas County, in Umpqua country in particular. A photo of Alexandre sitting with his hunting rifle leaning diagonally across his lap, would eventually become the most familiar of all photos of early Métis settlers in the Pacific Northwest. Tracing the movement of individuals across the continent shows that the history of the Michigan Territory was intimately tied to the larger continental story of the *Canadien* and Métis stretching both west and north.

Several years after the two French travelers had returned home, another *Canadien,* who had relocated further down the west shore of Lake Michigan on the trail heading northwest from the town of Chicago, co-founded Milwaukee: "Solomon Juneau, Milwaukee's leading trader, laid out one town east of the river, while surveyor Byron Kilbourn planned another west of the river. In the spring of 1835 Milwaukee already had '20 to 30 houses,' and by August 1836 the sheriff there counted a population of 2,893" (Wyman, 1998, p. 158). A decade or so later a son (or nephew) of Solomon Juneau named Joseph Juneau would head further west, as did so many others. The California mines were his first stop. Later, in the 1850s and 1860s, he would follow the gold into mining camps along the rivers of Oregon and Washington territories, up into British Columbia and ultimately to the Alaskan panhandle, where he finally made his mark.

Removal and Resistance

Tocqueville and Beaumont visited Michigan Territory in the summer of 1831, on the eve of a critical development in American history. The Jackson Administration soon began implementing the Indian Removal Act, which led to the systematic removal of the Indian populations of the trans-Allegheny region of the southeast and lower Midwest, to the prairies located west of the Mississippi River. In Michigan Territory, however, which included Wisconsin at this point, only the southernmost regions were caught up in the manhunt intended to clear out the region's original inhabitants. A major theme of Susan Sleeper-Smith's *Indian Women and French Men* focuses on how these women and their multi-ethnic, Catholic family networks helped many of their Métisse and indigenous relations avoid removal and hide out instead in small pockets on the periphery of the Midwest. Those who more successfully entrenched themselves usually lived on more marginal lands further north avoided by the American settlers, such as small enclaves in swampy or heavily wooded areas along the St. Joseph or Grand Rivers. This included communities sustained by some mix of farming, hunting, and the final stage of the fur trade in that part of the country, that of the black raccoon. Though some were landless squatters on the move, these Native American and Métis communities were generally located on private property or private reserves. Many communities were heavily Potawatomi, with some remaining Miami and Odawa groups, each including a diverse mix of indigenous and Métis refugees from all over the region. Significantly, the Catholic communities among them acquired the critical institutional assistance of the Catholic Church in successfully resisting the final sweep of territorial militia and bounty hunters working under contract to capture and remove them.

The larger and better-established Native American agricultural communities further south would feel the brunt of the removal policy in the 1830s. This scenario had started earlier in a more piecemeal manner north of the Tennessee River, and especially above the Ohio River. In the meantime, the close ties of the Métis with the Native Americans would continue to facilitate their work in the fur and related trading, as pointed out by Edmunds (1985). As cultural brokers, the Métis spoke the languages of their trading partners and kin, and were welcome in the camps and villages of their Native American relations.

Michigan Territorial Governor Lewis Cass, who worked on the American frontier and in public service for close to half a century, was instrumental in shaping the destiny of both the Métis and the Native Americans of the Old Northwest. Appointed by President Madison in 1813, Cass was governor until 1831, when Jackson appointed him Secretary of War. Cass became a leading proponent of Native American removal—along with any non-compliant Métis relations. He also became a spokesman for the Popular Sovereignty Doctrine in the 1850s, appeasing slave-holder interests in settling the Kansas-Nebraska territory, and eventually served as Secretary of State on the eve of the Civil War under Democratic President Buchanan.

The Indian Removal Act signed in 1830 would lead to the expulsion of almost all southern indigenous peoples. They were to be relocated, forcibly if necessary, west of the Mississippi. That same year, Lewis Cass reported to officials in Washington, telling his superiors what they wanted to hear. Cass reported that "so far as respects the three great tribes of the Northwest, the Chippewas, Ottawas, and Potawatomis, I am not aware that any improvement has taken place in their condition within the last eight years… On the contrary, I believe every year adds to the moral and physical evils which surrounds them" (Edmunds, 1985, p. 188). The Métis were clearly part of the indigenous problem in his view, and thus their removal would have to be part of the solution.

Superintendent of Indian Affairs Thomas L. McKenney, a former champion of assimilation and integration, toured the Old Northwest and, not surprisingly, also concluded that the government's "civilization" program had failed; the Native Americans and Métis had not become small farmers. Rather, he castigated them and pointed out how they "pretend to do nothing more than to maintain all the characteristic traits of their race. They catch fish, and plant patches of corn; dance, paint, hunt, get drunk, when they get liquor, fight and often starve" (Edmunds, 1985, pp. 185-186).

The Native American and Métis people had apparently not become the type of small farmers that the Americans wanted them to be. This type of reporting and documentation would provide all the excuses needed to continue relocating Native Americans further west, the policy that the United States Government pursued in the 1830s. Most of the indigenous peoples would be pushed out of the Old Northwest, either farther to the west or into British-controlled territories to the north. Sleeper-Smith (2001, p. 163) explains:

> Removal reduced but did not eliminate Michigan's Native American population. Out of a population of 7,600 to 8,300 [enumerated] Indians, only 651 Indians were officially removed. The most persistent focus of removal was the Potawatomi of southern Michigan, where emigrants were very intent on transforming prairies into farms. But river valleys, with their less desirable lands, continued to shelter and sustain many native communities. The Indians of northern Michigan were less threatened with forcible removal than their southern neighbors were. Again, the northern lands were considered unproductive agriculturally.

At Detroit, William Hull explicitly complained that the Métis had adopted much of Native American culture, even openly fraternizing with them: "From their infancy they have been in the habit of friendship with the Indians—and in a variety of respects there is a great similarity and connection between them. The Indians are as familiar and as much at home in the homes of these people, as the people themselves."

Hull also denounced the Métis farms as being no better than those of the Indians, thus helping to justify the long-range policy of their eventual forced removal. However, it was the highly partisan Lewis Cass who was the most critical of the Métis, as he accused them of being indolent traders, spending "half of the year in labor, want and exposure, and the other in indolence and amusements." Not only were the men seen as poor agriculturalists, their wives were accused of being substandard in their tasks. Cass complained that Métis women refused to spin or weave their families' clothing. In his words, "a pound of wool is not manufactured in the Territory by any person of Canadian descent" (McLaughlin, 1891, p. 25).

What Governor Cass failed to say was that they were masterful seamstresses, using cloth obtained from the local fur traders to develop their own unique fashions—fashions subsequently captured in the paintings of George Winter. Susan Sleeper-Smith points out an under-appreciated fact of considerable import: during the eighteenth century, "Cloth represented well over half of all the goods traded at Great Lakes fur trade posts" (Sleeper-Smith, 2001, p. 125).

In *Rites of Conquest: The History and Culture of Michigan's Native Americans*, Charles Cleland lays out the region that the far-flung Potawatomi people occupied, wrapping around the western and southern shores of Lake Michigan and adjoining inland areas. It included the Prairie bands of Wisconsin and northern Illinois, "the Lake bands around Lake Michigan, and the St. Joseph bands in southwestern Michigan and northern Indiana. This latter group was intermarried with the French-Canadian community at Niles and South Bend; some spoke French as well as Potawatomi, and many were inclined toward Catholicism" (Sleeper-Smith, 2001, p. 163). Yet when Cass sent his team of observers into southwest Michigan during the late 1820s to prepare the ground for land cession negotiations, they were surprised to find a growing number of Potawatomi agricultural villages. By 1830, the number had reached thirty-six villages, many newly established, comprising an estimated total of 2,500 residents, with another thousand in twenty-three other nearby Miami villages.

The Governor's representative, identified as Mr. Reed, told Cass: "The Indians uniformly said they wished to keep small reservations for each family, to have provisions in the treaty for supplying them with cattle and farming implements" (C. E. Cleland, 1992, p. 218). Land concessions in the resulting agreement were considerable but enraged the governor. Sleeper-Smith notes that "Lewis Cass was infuriated by the large tracts of land retained by the Potawatomi" (Sleeper-Smith, 2001, pp. 96-97). The Potawatomi were aided in their negotiations by the *Canadiens* who helped to organized the bands.

At this time, Joseph Bertrand and his Potawatomi wife, baptized Madeleine, were the St. Joseph Valley's most prominent traders. With such status, Joseph coordinated the position of multiple Potawatomi villages as they negotiated with the American state. Joseph and Madeleine Bertrand had re-established the type of Catholic fur trade community that had existed during the lifetime of Marie-Madeleine L'Archevêque Chevalier, with kinship, Catholicism, and trade inextricably intertwined. Bertrand replaced William Burnett, an outspoken American murdered near the end of the War of 1812. Burnett's widow, Kakima, a Catholic Potawatomi, continued to do business out of the St. Joseph trading post for a number of years before relocating into Indiana. The Bertrands were able to embed themselves in the local community in the wake of Kakima Burnett's departure:

> Bertrand's newly established post drew on the associations of the pre-nineteenth-century fur trade world. His house was constructed from logs from the old Fort

St. Joseph mission. His wife actively promoted Catholicism and reestablished the Catholic kin networks that had long forged social links in the exchange process. Bertrand... was able to offer the Potawatomi better-quality goods [than those offered by the Burnetts] that he had acquired through John Jacob Astor's American Fur Company (Sleeper-Smith, 2001, pp. 97-98).

The governor's representative, Reed, excluded from the meetings in the interest of confidentiality, frustrated and under pressure from Cass, soon became outraged with Bertrand. Referring to Bertrand's *Canadien* and indigenous ancestry, Reed was soon resorting to ethnic slurs. He disparaged the Potawatomi spokesman as "a sinister half-breed" (Sleeper-Smith, 2001, p. 94).

Though this agreement greatly reduced their land by 1832, the multiple Potawatomi enclaves still totaled more than five million acres. This predictably led to a call for another round of negotiations and agreements. The Potawatomi and Bertrands still controlled some of the most fertile acreage in the valley, known as *Parc aux Vaches*—meaning cow pasture, or cowpens (Sleeper-Smith, 2001, pp. 98-99). However, Cass was politically ambitious and sought opportunities for advancement in the Jackson Administration. He refused to leave this rich land under Potawatomi control.

As the situation heated up, the Potawatomi turned to the Catholic Church for intervention, sending a delegation to meet with Father Richard in Detroit. Several generations had passed since the St. Joseph Mission had been shut down. Pokagon, one of the Potawatomi village headmen whose family had a long Catholic tradition, delivered the plea for once again sending a missionary priest to his people:

> I implore you to send us a priest to instruct us in the Word of God... We still preserve the manner of praying as taught our ancestors by black robes at St. Joseph. Morning and evening with my wife and children, we pray together before the crucifix ... according to the traditions handed down to us by our fathers, for we ourselves have never seen a black-robe. Listen to the prayers we say, and see if I have learned them correctly (Sleeper-Smith, 2001, pp. 99-100).

A final round of negotiations was conducted in Chicago during the winter of 1832-1833. Through threats of force and offers of increased annuity payments, resistance was whittled down. The Potawatomi were nonetheless able to ensure that some additional language of note made it into the supplemental agreement. Although Cass obtained the concessions he wanted, thus forcing an agreement on relocation of the Potawatomi, Sleeper-Smith notes that they were allowed to remain on their lands for two years following the ratification of the treaty. What's more, Catholic converts would be allowed to remain in the Great Lakes Region, with the American negotiators understanding this as northern Michigan. Consequently, by the end of 1832, all the St. Joseph River headmen as well as 360 adults and 160 children were baptized as Catholics.

A number of other baptisms were carried out among the other peoples of the Great Lakes Region. Father De Jean, for example, baptized ninety-seven Odawa farther to the north (Sleeper-Smith, 2001, p. 101). When the two-year deadline came, the Catholic Potawatomi refused to move, and with the assistance of the Catholic Church and lawyers out of Detroit, they successfully won concessions from the state, and stayed (Sleeper-Smith, 2001, p. 106).

The non-Catholic Potawatomi agreed to removal within three years of the treaty's ratification by the Senate, which occurred in 1835. Indigenous groups in the states of Ohio, Indiana, and Illinois were rounded up further south for removal. Federal troops and state militia were assisted by private "conductors" hired by the government to collect and transport the Native Americans west. In the northern country, however, over the course of the decade implementation lost steam. Following the Chicago negotiations, many Potawatomi returned to their Michigan villages or temporary reservations, doing their best to ignore government pressure to move westward. Further north, some five hundred Ottawa and Ojibwe opted to cross the straits into Canada to seek refuge among their relatives located across the porous border on Manitoulin Island. Many later returned to Michigan. One notable case was that of the Potawatomi headman, Pokagon, who acquired legal title to Michigan land following its admission as a state, purchasing 874 acres in the vicinity of Silver Creek (Sleeper-Smith, 2001, p. 107).

In the face of the American settler encroachment during the early nineteenth century and the aggressive removal program, Catholicism assumed a more political dimension; it was no longer simply the religion of a minority of indigenous people within the larger majority. As one more accommodation strategy, village headmen saw the need to supplement and eventually supplant the earlier female catechizers working among the Potawatomi in the St. Joseph region—women such as Marie-Madeleine Réaume L'Archevêque Chevalier during the eighteenth century (see Chapter 3), or more recently, Madeleine Bertrand. Given Catholicism's historic malleability and the ability of converts to integrate elements of their older faiths under the guise of saints and religious practices, the headmen embraced Catholicism while using it to promote a form of religious blending that provided them continued status through skillful use of a charismatic leadership style.

Pokagon was one such individual who served as an influential lay Catholic, deftly fusing practices that could either be construed as the devotion of a Catholic or as traditional Potawatomi religious practices. Fasting was central to both Potawatomi traditional beliefs and Catholic Lent. The priests even described Pokagon's fasts as more lengthy and disciplined than those of the clergy. Pokagon thus fused the traditional and the new to acquire both power and spiritual guidance in his village (Sleeper-Smith, 2001, p. 106).

The Western Great Lakes and Looming Statehood

In Michigan and northern Wisconsin, the first census of the region's indigenous peoples in the late 1830s recorded about 20,000 people. About 60-75 percent, between 12,000 and 15,000, lived in the southern third of the Lower Peninsula of Michigan. The remaining 5,000 to 8,000 were sparsely scattered across the central and northern part of Michigan into Wisconsin. Anthropologist Cleland qualifies this tally, however: "These are likely conservative figures, and, adding in Michigan's Potawatomi [those who didn't relocate beyond the Mississippi], it is likely that the total count was closer to 30,000" (C. E. Cleland, 1992, pp. 193-194). Four treaties involving various Potawatomi bands were signed between fall 1832 and fall 1833 in Michigan Territory. They can be found in the National Archives' Microfilm Publications under the "Ratified Indian Treaties" of the Jackson Administration's Removal Program. The first three were signed at an encampment on the Tippecanoe River in the new state of Indiana in October 1832 and the latter one in Chicago in September 1833. The high rate of métissage, or mixing, both biological and cultural, is apparent in four areas within the treaty documents, addenda, and supplements, which are characterized by the following features:

- Individual land grants in Michigan, instead of the usual wholesale "half-breed" tracts west of the Mississippi
- Individual payments to traders for the accumulated debts, running at about one-third of these payments going to *Canadiens* & Métis
- Individual payments to settle with tribal leaders and affiliated Métis to get the necessary signatures on the agreements
- Signatures of key participants.

These were clearly very complex negotiations. It is evident that concessions had to be made in the treaties, to gain the support of key traders and community members. People had to be compensated. A certain amount of "divide and conquer" would be required.

The *Canadiens* (including the *Canadien* Métis) were generally reasonably well-compensated for helping the process along, while they also tried to balance business and kin relationships. Mark Wyman (1998) notes how the Métis were seen as a complicating factor by American officials seeking to negotiate treaties. Often officials sought to deal with the Métis first before negotiating treaties with Native Americans. "Especially numerous around fur trade centers, whether large or small, they showed up in large numbers at treaty sessions and from 1817 onward they were usually included in the final agreements—obtaining small reserves of land at first, after 1833 given money" (Wyman, 1998, p. 165). Wyman refers first to the presence of itinerant Iroquois bands on the western shore of Lake Michigan. Family names that appear throughout the official treaty documents for the Potawatomi include such names as Chevalier, Bertrand, Langlois, Ducharme, Laframboise, Bourassa, Rolla, Navarre, Nadeau, Drouillard, LeClerc and LeClare, Bousee (Bousie, Boucher), Duret, Gambin, Bobeaux (Barbeau), Chapeau, Bourbonnais, Ouimet, Vieux, Menard, and Beaubien. These people received either land concessions, ranging between one-quarter to ten sections of land, or cash payments of between 100 and 1,200 dollars.

Four treaties signed in 1832 and 1833 with the various Potawatomi bands from the territory surrounding the lower end of Lake Michigan provided compensation for the cession of their lands and removal westward:

- Treaty with the Potawatomi Indians of the Prairie and Kankakee, concluded on October 20, 1832 and ratified January 21, 1833, by the U.S. Senate.
- Treaty between the U.S. and the Potawatomi of the Wabash, concluded October 26, 1832, and ratified January 21, 1833.
- Treaty between the Potawatomi of the State of Indiana and Michigan Territory, concluded October 27, 1832, and ratified January 21, 1833.
- Treaty with the Chippewa, Ottawa, and Potawatomi Indians, concluded in Chicago September 26, 1833.

The names listed on the treaties illustrate both the breadth and depth of the *Canadien* presence in the tribal lands of the Great Lakes Region. Many of the *Canadien* and their Métis families were clearly not dispossessed without compensation. They were instead bought out in order to ensure the peaceful removal of the Native Americans from the Michigan territories, and as such were dealt with in a different fashion than "Indians" with pre-existing title to the land.

Amending Treaties, Forceful Relocation

In 1836, the Jacksonian Democrats in control of the U.S. Senate unilaterally amended the negotiated treaty that had been ratified the year before. President Jackson proclaimed a new treaty that limited the existence of reservations to five years. Hence, the land would revert to the public domain in 1841. If the Native Americans agreed to move west, they would be given land there. Indian Superintendent Schoolcraft summoned the original delegations to Mackinac Island in order to ratify these changes. He made it clear that he would suspend all payments under the treaty unless the Native Americans assented to the revised treaty. They reluctantly accommodated him, but only after Schoolcraft assured them that the government would not need the land for many years. Michigan indigenous groups, who faced removal in five years, thus had little incentive to clear or make improvements on their lands, as agents and missionaries were suggesting.

Cleland cited the Grand River Ottawa, mostly located downstream from the modern city of Grand Rapids, as facing a particularly difficult dilemma in this

regards. Faced with increasing encroachment from the growing settler population, many Ottawa began to hedge their bets by using their share of annuity
money to purchase land on the same basis as the settlers from the federal government's land office. Native American leaders petitioned the new state's first
governor, Stevens T. Mason, to clarify whether land ownership implied Michigan
citizenship. The positive answer made another option for permanent residence
available (C. E. Cleland, 1992, pp. 228-229).

Michigan became a state in 1837 while Jackson was preparing to turn the White
House over to his former Vice President, Van Buren. In January, the new
Michigan state legislature petitioned Congress to authorize removal of all the
state's indigenous peoples to the west. That same year, the irresponsible populist
financial policies of the Jackson Administration finally precipitated an economic
crisis. As the depression dragged on, prospects in the national elections of 1840
did not look good for the incumbents. Moreover, on the frontier, some people
were contemplating voting with their feet. Even remote Oregon seemed like it
was worth a long and difficult trail.

With the election approaching, the push to forcibly remove all Native
Americans came to a head. General Hugh Brady organized four companies of
soldiers and settlers to carry out the military round up and escort for deporting
the indigenous peoples. Though the Catholic Native Americans were supposed
to be spared, the soldiers and settlers initially made no distinctions. "Unaware
of the exclusion of the Catholic bands," notes Cleland (1992, p. 223), "Brady had
to be served with a court order obtained by Pokagon to permit them to remain.
Many others were not so fortunate."

Those who remained faced uncertain ownership of their lands. The year 1841
came and went with no resolution as to the lands still occupied by the remaining
Potawatomi. A large portion of the compensation for surrender of the enormous
tracts of land involved in these treaty arrangements was delayed, or siphoned off
over subsequent decades. Cash payments were again redirected to settle existing
debt on the accounts of traders, both Euro-American and Métis. Individual allotments of land could take years or even decades to receive, and then were either
sold off or acquired by fraudulent means—often involving local tax authorities.
In the end, thousands of Native Americans remained in Michigan with very little
land or annuity payments to show for the transfer of title to the U.S.: they were
not removed, but rather dispossessed.

Potawatomi headman Pokagon, like some others, was able to acquire legal
title to land in Michigan. Following Michigan's admission to the union as a state
in 1837, Pokagon began purchasing land incrementally, building his property
holdings up to 874 acres in the vicinity of Silver Creek (Sleeper-Smith, 2001,
p. 106). Pokagon's private property would serve as a safe haven for the commun-

ity centered on his band of Potawatomi, at least for a while. In spite of dispersal and generally hostile government policies at both state and federal levels, the Pokagon Potawatomi (as they became identified) constituted one of two Potawatomi bands that had been able to avoid removal while at the same time maintaining their identity.

The Federal Government only recognized the Pokagon Band of the Potawatomi, however, a century and half later, in 1994. Tribal land and facilities are located at Dowagiac and New Buffalo in southwestern Michigan, while tribal membership, according to their website, stood at 4,563 individuals in 2009 from among 60,000 Michigan residents self-identified as Native Americans. The other Potawatomi band remaining in the state was located at Hannahville, in a far corner of Lake Michigan, north of Green Bay, Wisconsin, just inside the border of Michigan's Upper Peninsula. At a more remote location, this Potawatomi band had been able to obtain federal recognition in 1913.

Michigan's current tally of ten federally recognized bands and tribes were able to regain federal acknowledgement one by one over the course of the twentieth century. About half of them received recognition between the 1930s and 1970s, followed by three more in the 1990s. Those bands and tribes induced to sign regional treaties in the 1820s and 1830s, and who were also on the more peripheral lands, were generally able to avoid relocation west of the Mississippi. One way or another, however, the new authorities officially dissolved the bands that remained over the following decades. Putting them back together again was a long, slow, and painful process, which contemporary Métis-American associations also know quite well.

The Ojibwe/Chippewa account for the large majority of the bands and tribes in Michigan today. Among these, the Sault Ste. Marie Tribe of Chippewa account for more than all the other bands and tribes combined. As of 2013, Sault Tribe of Chippewa Indians' website placed tribal membership at over 44,000. Other Ojibwe/Chippewa bands include the Saginaw Chippewa Tribe of Michigan; the Lac Vieux Desert Band of Lake Superior Chippewa, located just north of the Wisconsin border; the Keweena Bay Indian Community on the copper-filled peninsula of the same name which juts out into Lake Superior from the south shore; and the Mills Bay Indian Community which is located thirty miles to the west of Sault Ste. Marie on Lake Superior near the town of Brimley.

There is also the Grand Traverse Band of Ottawa/Chippewa Indians on the shores of a Lake Michigan bay, and a strong presence of Métis descendants in all these localities. Under the Clinton Administration, in 1994, during the final round of negotiations with the Pokagon Potawatomi, two other Odawa (Ottawa) bands succeeded in obtaining federal recognition: the Little Traverse Bay Band, and the Little River Band of the Ottawa.

A bit to the south of Sault Ste. Marie, in the area of St. Ignace and Mackinac, the Ottawa community has also maintained a significant presence. "There is no better evidence of the influence of the Métis traders than at Mackinac, where mixed-blood Ottawa families formed a very large community," notes Cleland. It was not only large but powerful, and a community where sex and race were not impediments to success" (C. E. Cleland, 1992, p. 179). Charles Cleland adds that in order to get the money owed to them, Ottawa descendants had to sue the Unites States government, as government officials regarded the Ottawa as a small group of assimilated "mixed-bloods," (C. E. Cleland, 1992, p. 270). This again shows the stigmas associated with Métis or Half-Breed identities, especially in the United States and parts of Eastern Canada where the existence and rights of Métis/Half-breeds are still being challenged. Various arguments are utilized suggesting their lack of collectiveness, culture, historic communities, or nationhood, portraying them as either assimilated or individuals of merely mixed heritage.

These few examples show just how the Americans of the day, overly confident of their increasingly self-reinforcing manifest destiny, could dismiss the accomplishments of the Native Americans in adapting to a newer set of circumstances. It is even easier to see how the mainstream settler population and its elected leadership at the time—and American and Canadian historians ever since—would tend to overlook the contributions of the French-Canadians and their descendants, the Métis (also identified as "French-Indians" in the United-States). Jay Gitlin emphasizes that in the American territory, though dotted as it is with French place names in testament to the past importance of the French and Métis, the true contribution of the French is actually overlooked: "the true legacy of the French in the American West does not reside in a collection of names on our maps. Rather, it is the role they played in western expansion, in negotiating the course of American empire, that we must acknowledge" (Gitlin, 2009, p. 122).

Of course, the "new Empire" was being built largely at the expense of the Indigenous Peoples living in North America. This included the indigenized-*Canadiens*, the Métis or "French-Indians," more or less "recognized" or "compensated" due to later bureacratic distinctions referring to blood quantum and other Eurocentric conceptions of indigenous identities, that would serve to undermine their tribal affiliations. After a generation had passed, American politicians and settlers could overlook the contributions the French of the Old Northwest had made in fighting the British during the American Revolution, then later generally assuming a more neutral posture during the War of 1812, thereby helping to ensure that the Old Northwest would remain American. The British threat gone, the Métis and Native Americans could now be pushed aside—or the scattered remnants ignored—to make way for "properly" American, English-speaking, Protestant settlers.

Despite their relative demographic decline, the evidence indicates that much of French culture was maintained in the communities of the Great Lakes and other more northerly regions, including cultural folklore. Dennis Au (2007, pp. 171-172) conducted research on the folklore of Monroe County (Michigan's former Frenchtown) and discovered that as late as 1898, French was the home language of most families, and that even as late as the 1930s, some families continued to speak French. Au's (2007, p. 174) discussion of folklore identifies how much had been retained of the culture of the *Canadiens*: all the classic folktales involving the *loup garou* (werewolf), the Devil at the dance, and others were part of the repertoire of the descendants of the *Canadiens* in Monroe. The food Au ate was entirely reminiscent of what would be traditional fare in French Canada, including *tourtière* (meat pie) that was simply called "tut" in Monroe Country and, like in French Canada, would have been featured at the *réveillon,* or the awakening, on New Year's Eve and then later Christmas Eve as well (Au, 2007, pp. 175-176).

The case of Monroe County highlights that much of the original *Canadien* culture was maintained until the twentieth century, including songs, folklore, food preferences, and recipes as well as the language. To overemphasize the indigenous to the detriment of the French heritage is potentially misleading, as it is certainly not what the evidence suggests further north. Interestingly, the French population in Detroit and its vicinities was described pejoratively by officials as imbued with Indian blood, and as entertaining close family ties and alliances with local Indian peoples, to the point of questioning their loyalty in case of conflicts. Karen Marrero (2012) notes how visiting Quakers echoed this sentiment, as reported in their journal. "It was obvious that the Quakers hailing from New Jersey and Philadelphia considered Chene and other metis at Detroit as a culturally distinct and almost entirely inscrutable collective following their own political agendas, and who therefore could not be trusted."

The historical account will now continue westwards to St. Louis and the territories of what had been Upper Louisiana (La Haute-Louisiane) to explore the history of the *Canadien* and *Créole* who would meet along the Missouri. *Canadien* and Métis traders would push westwards and became the "Mountain Men" par excellence, though American popular history has given them short shrift.

CHAPTER 5

La Haute-Louisiane and the Far West

The French had pushed deep into the continent and down the Mississippi in the seventeenth and eighteenth centuries, while the descendants of the *coureurs des bois* who remained after the Conquest of New France established families and settlements in the Old Northwest. After the American Revolution, these *Canadien-Métis-Bois-Brulé* communities served as intermediaries between the American authorities and their indigenous kin and relations as treaties were signed. Some of the merchants and go-betweens profited handsomely for these efforts, while others were dislocated by the waves of Anglo-American and immigrant settlers that followed. They nonetheless played a vital if overlooked role in the history of this region.

This is also true of those French-speaking people farther west who were the backbone of the American fur trade that produced the wealth that financed the investments of the Astor family, while New York City emerged as the United States' first metropolis. They scoured the continent, establishing kin and friendship networks with the indigenous populations.

French place-names scattered across the continent bear witness to their forgotten history. To demonstrate the continental—as opposed to local—scope of the *Canadien* and Métis of the United States in the region located between the Mississippi and the Rockies in the nineteenth century, this history must be pieced together. To do so, the works of renowned authors and persons of the nineteenth century, including their lesser-known works or overlooked passages in monumental works, must be re-examined. A documentary archaeology must be conducted to find artifacts of the French past that can be reassembled to provide a new reading.

As discussed in Chapter 3, the War of 1812 conducted in the Great Lakes Region placed the *Canadien* population on both sides of the border in the crossfire of the American and British forces. That war had no clear winner, but it did go a long way toward determining where the border between the United States and British North America would lie.

Less than a decade earlier, however, American expansion had made its greatest leap. In 1803, the United States bought the Louisiana Territory for a paltry sum. This territory passed from the French to the Spanish Crown before the Treaty of Paris was signed in 1763, under which the rest of New France was ceded to Great Britain. The Spanish held Louisiana until the end of the eighteenth century, before returning it to France. A few years later, Napoléon Bonaparte would sell this newly reacquired territory to the Americans. The United States annexed lands that not only allowed expansion westwards but also included a large French-speaking population spread out from the Louisiana Delta, up the Mississippi to St. Louis and beyond.

The history of this French-speaking population of La Haute Louisiane (Upper Louisiana), like that of the thousands living in the Great Lakes Region and the Michigan Territory, has been buried. One crucial account of the Upper Louisiana Territory is that of Amos Stoddard (1812, p. 219), the commandant of the military district of Upper Louisiana after the Louisiana Purchase. His description of Louisiana (Upper and Lower) was published in that decisive year of 1812. He participated actively in the War of 1812, was wounded at the British Siege of Fort Meigs, and died of tetanus in 1813. He would also have met Lewis and Clark as they recruited among his company when he was stationed at Fort Kaskaskia, and the following year participated with them in the ceremony in St. Louis transferring La Haute-Louisiane to the U.S. (Clarke, 1970, p. 17).

The French in New Spain

The French-speaking people who lived south of the porous and ever-shifting U.S.-British North America border when the U.S. was expanding westward experienced a different situation from those to the north. In what was gradually becoming the U.S., the French colonial merchant and upper classes remained very active in the fur trade, along with general transportation and financing, expanding their reach across the Great Plains. They opened up the Santa Fe trade route, where a number of Missouri Créoles settled in, moving on to Mexican California. French-speaking families include Robidoux, Chouteau, St. Vrain, Beaubien, Pratte, Gratiot, Cerré, Fontenelle, Provo(st), Bonneville, Boudreaux, Fremont, Lajeunesse, and Lorimier, among so many others.

These families were also disproportionately well represented among the cadets of West Point, where the only foreign language admission requirement prior to the Civil War was the necessity of being able to at least read French—many of the engineering professors and most of their text books were still from France. One of the most famous of these Franco-American graduates came from Lower

Canoe Party Around Campfire, Frances Anne Hopkins, ca. 1870. The *Canadiens* or Métis and descendants made up the vast majority of the labor force in the transport of furs across the continent. Without them, the fur trade could not have existed.

Louisiana, Civil War General Pierre Gustave T. Beauregard. In the West, some of the French Creoles were also investing in the ever-larger set of opportunities in manufacturing and transportation, be it riverboats or, later, the railroads. Even French Huguenot descendants began to enter the frontiersman picture with characters such as Davy Crocket, Governor Sevier of Tennessee, and the Sublette brothers spilling over the Appalachian Mountains. As with their voyageur predecessors, water transportation was the choice of the ten thousand plus Frenchmen arriving in California in the late 1840s and early 1850s, where together with their *Canadièn* cohorts, they outnumbered Spanish speakers for a number of years in the 1850s.

On the American frontier and in what remained of British North America, the ranks of the fur trade and the labor force of the transport sector retained a very large French-speaking contingent. This linguistic group comprised an ever-broader ethnic mixture. In the run-up to the Civil War, many of these people, by their professional and investment choices, and their ethnicity and language, increasingly integrated into the evolving American mainstream. Others identified more and more with their Native American relations. Whichever path a family or individual took, these French-speaking people, by their disproportionately large role and numbers, were crucial to the opening of the American West and its extension to the Pacific coast until the end of the nineteenth century. While Gitlin highlights the important role played by some of the Creole French bourgeois in negotiating the course of western expansion, Peterson, Edmunds, Sleeper-Smith, and to a lesser extent Ingersoll underscore the role many French-speaking Métis (as well as the English-speaking "country-born" equivalent in the case of Ingersoll) played in the American colonial expansion westwards.

English-speaking scholars have produced abundant evidence that the social structures of all mixed-ancestry communities in the Far West were primarily Native American rather than French or Anglo-American, an argument made by Ingersoll (2005, pp. 155-156). To demonstrate this, Ingersoll cites the work of Tanis C. Thorne who described the Métis communities of the Missouri River with careful attention to detail. Thorne brings cartographical order to an array of these mixed-blood clans, especially at Côte Sans Dessein, Halley's Bluff, Three Forks, Flat Rock Creek, and Kasmouth (Kansas City). She argues that despite white Americans' expectations that mixed-ancestry treaty reserves would separate and become "civilized" over time, by 1830 it was obvious that those of mixed ancestry identified themselves fundamentally as Indigenous rather than European. Few converted fully to Christianity in spite of the efforts of Protestant and Catholic clergy, and most, but not all, refused to become dedicated farmers. The Métis had served as intermediaries (workers and retail merchants) for the fur trade and they continued to prefer this way of life, but then this tended to be ever deeper into Indian Country, further to the southwest.

One reason for the bias is that the historical record, in which the Anglo-American writings are taken at face value, produced a slanted account, reinforcing the ideological interests of white Anglo-American Protestant settlers. As a new cultural hegemony was their goal, they had an interest in emphasizing the "savage" and "uncivilized" nature of the French speakers, be they Canadien, French Créole or Métis. Edmunds (1985, p. 190) explains this succinctly: "Although American leaders complained that they were indigent, many Metis maintained a standard of living comparable to that of American settlers. But to the Americans, they had accepted the *wrong* European culture, that of the Creole French."

True, the French-speaking Métis had maintained close ties with the remaining Native American communities, but it is quite plausible that they were undesirable both for being French *and* for having mixed heritage, and it was simply easier to justify their removal by affirming that they were "unacquainted with the laws of the civilized world" (Edmunds, 1985, p. 190).

They posed a potential political threat, as the Métis had children who could be integrated into Native American communities, where they often became prominent leaders. The French army officer Sabrevoie Decarie, for example, founded a family with Glory of the Morning, which gave the Winnebagoes a succession of Métis chiefs and many additional descendants. The same was true of a number of other leading Native American-allied families, including those of Lucien Fontenelle, Laforce Pappan, and Augustin Grignon. In fact, Jeffersonian and Jacksonian policy makers were increasingly concerned about the expanding "mixed-blood" population, especially those adopting bourgeois and European values. Adding to the threats of political alliances and charismatic leaders, the Métis could also form distinct communities, such as the Fort St. Louis community in what is now central Illinois, noticed by French colonial authorities as early as 1687 for asserting their political independence and ownership over their lands. It has been suggested that virtually all "mixed-bloods" displayed an irritating propensity toward defending local Native Americans and their own land claims (Ingersoll, 2005, p. 157), which reflects an ongoing tendency that characterized even the early Métis settlements.

Russell Bouchard (2005) cites a letter from Denonville to the Minister whereby he derides the behavior of the French stationed at St. Louis: "*Mr. de la Salle a donné des concessions au fort St. Louis a plusieurs françois qui y sejournent depuis plusieurs années sans vouloir dessendre, ce qui a donné lieu a des desordres et abominations infinies. Ces gens a qui Mr. de la Salle a concedé sont tous garçons qui n'ont rien fait pour cultiver la terre. Tous les 8 jours ils epousent des Sauvagesses à la mode des Sauvages de ce pays là, qu'ils achetent des parens aux depens des marchands. Ces gens se pretendent independans et [maîtres] sur leurs concessions* (Emphasis is ours.)." ["Mr. de la Salle gave concessions at Fort St. Louis, has several François [French] staying there for several years, and they no longer wish to come back [descend to the colony], which gave rise to endless disorders and abominations. Those people are boys who have done nothing to cultivate the land. Every week they marry the savages according to Indian custom, they pay off parents at the expense of our merchants. These people claim to be independents and [master] on their own concessions."]

The Métis were vulnerable on another front. As a mixed people living in a frontier zone and prone to considerable mobility, be it by chosen profession or lifestyle, they were susceptible to dispersal and assimilation once the frontier had "disappeared," and a large percentage of the indigenous people had been confined to more remote reservations. Often, the only question scholars would ask was which of their ancestral ties would prevail. This might be characterized as something along the lines of, "pick one yourself, otherwise it will be done for you."

Unlike the "full-bloods," the Métis and other "mixed bloods" had a choice, although it was likely only theoretical for the large number who were closely affiliated with their tribes. The geographic mobility of Great Lakes Métis was crucial to the spread of the fur trade and Catholicism, but also a liability, according to Peterson. The very diffuseness of the Catholic fur trade communities, whose members had married among, and were related to, more than a dozen tribes of Algonquian, Siouan, and Iroquoian speakers, is said to have made group solidarity and combined action difficult to sustain under pressure. In the end, the identity of the Great Lakes Métis, like the transitional economy associated with it, was a fragile construction, suggests Peterson (1985, pp. 63-64). As itinerant petty merchants with little attachment to a specific plot of land, the early Métis have been described as vulnerable to both displacement and eventually re-assimilation into either one of their native ancestral ethnic groups, or into the larger hegemonic American society. To do the latter they first had to shed both their stigmatized *Canadien* and Native American past, a process that ordinarily would be a matter of several generations.

Bridging East and West: Prelude to the Louisiana Purchase

Following the Conquest, in the *Pays d'en Bas* along the St. Lawrence Valley, the heavy hand of British colonial patronage with its privileges and prerogatives set in. From there, British influence slowly extended into the *Pays d'en Haut*. Over an extended period of two generations, much of the *Canadien* commercial elite that remained in North America was gradually marginalized to lesser roles by the new set of insiders. An accommodation was quickly reached with the Catholic Church that would reinforce the new social hierarchy in the *Pays d'en Bas*. On the other hand, inland, especially south of the Great Lakes and along the Mississippi, social and business relations were quite different. Here the residual colonial population of La Nouvelle France was left to its own devices, and generally doing quite well, be it under the thinly spread nominal authority of the British east of the Mississippi, or the Spanish Bourbons west of the river. In 1778, the Americans began to push the British north, opening the way for both *Canadiens* and Americans. French families were instrumental in the push west, when the United States incorporated the Louisiana Territory (Upper and Lower) into the Republic.

In the interim, the predominance of Créoles and *Canadiens* was reinforced by a significant refugee population gathering from the far corners of the collapsing French Empire in the Americas. After the loss of the North American continent came the Revolution and the loss of most of the remaining West Indies. And with each change of regime in the 1790s in France, and then the Napoleonic Wars and the Bourbon Restoration, more political refugees flowed in from the old country. The large majority of them chose the U.S. over British North America, where at this time the port cities of New York, Philadelphia, Baltimore, Charleston, and New Orleans, along with a number of back-country settlements were teeming with new French-speaking arrivals from Europe. The British did not even allow French ships to go up the St. Lawrence, the first being *La Capricieuse* in 1855 (Villemure, 2005). Consequently, whether on the Atlantic seaboard or in the interior of the continent, more and more of the French-speaking population, be they of the older or more recent types dislocated by the turmoil of the French Revolutionary and Napoleonic periods, were choosing the United States, not Canada.

St. Louis, a French Citadel, Capital of Upper Louisiana

An intriguing account of Upper Louisiana at the end of the eighteenth century comes from Georges-Henri-Victor Collot, a distinguished French military officer who had fought under Jean-Baptiste-Donatien de Vimeur de Rochambeau, along with thousands of French troops allied with the American Revolutionaries in their War of Independence. Collot later served as Governor of Guadeloupe. In the spring of 1796, he was given the secret mission of mapping the Ohio and Mississippi Rivers—Spanish territory—and providing a military reconaissance of this former French territory now under Spanish dominion. He was promptly arrested and imprisoned when arriving in New Orleans that autumn. Freed, he returned to write an account of his voyage, completing his manuscript before his death in 1805. It was published in 1826.

General Collot, for example, had a strikingly different opinion of the inhabitants of the newer St. Louis settlement located on the Mississippi just south of its confluence with the Missouri River, as he critically compared the descendants of French living on the right bank of the Mississippi—a larger Créole population—and those who remained in the American territory on the left bank of the Mississippi and those of the Illinois Country and the Great Lakes Region who were largely *Canadien*, seeing the former in a much more favorable light. Saint-Louis, the core settlement of the Spanish Upper Louisiana territory at the time of his visit toward the end of the eighteenth century had a population numbering 600, of which 200 were capable of taking up arms—and they were all French (Collot, 1826, p. 338). He describes the men of Saint-Louis in patriotic terms: "*Ces hommes sont moins dégénérés que la race qui existe sur le côté américain. On y trouve encore cet esprit qui caractérise la nation française, d'excellens patriotes dont la vie et la fortune appartiennent à la France; des familles aisées de labour-eurs, de bons négocians, et le peuple en général y seroit heureux sans le vice d'admi-nistration qui accorde à des étrangers des privilèges exclusifs pour la traite des pelleteries; privilèges toujours odieux au peuple et ruineux pour les Etats, parce*

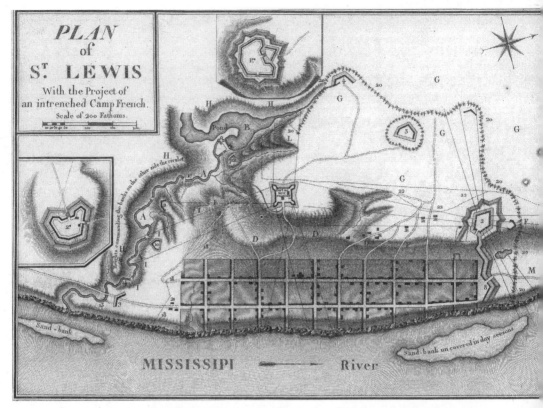

Plan of Saint-Lewis, Georges-Henri-Victor Collot, ca. 1796. Collot traveled on the Ohio, Illinois, Missouri and Mississipi rivers in 1796. Saint-Louis, located on the West Bank of the Mississippi, was not in the United States until the Louisiana Purchase of 1803. It remained an important French-speaking city after the Louisiana territory was transferred to the U.S. Given its pivotal location, it served as a staging ground for pushing westwards. The French-speaking inhabitants include people from the *Canadien* settlements in the Old Northwest and French-speaking Créoles who had come up the Mississippi from Lower Louisiana. Pierre Laclède who had come up the Mississippi from New Orleans is credited with founding the city in 1764. His lieutenant was his stepson René Auguste Chouteau.

qu'ils anéantissent l'industrie, et tuent l'émulation" (Collot, 1826, pp. 338-340). [These men are less degenerate than the race that exists on the American side. We still find the spirit that characterizes the French nation, excellent patriots whose lives and fortunes belong to France; prosperous families of laborers, good traders and the people would be in general happy if it was not for the vice of administration that gives to foreigners exclusive privileges for the trade in furs; privileges that are always odious and ruinous for the States as they destroy industry and kill competition.]

Collot also notes (1826, p. 345) that the settlement of Florissant is comprised of thirty or so families, mainly Americans, but a bit farther away in the community of Marais des Liards, he counted one hundred French families, the last settlement being Saint Charles with two hundred families of traders and hunters. To the south was the small city of Ste. Geneviève, called Misère by its inhabitants because of the frequent flooding. Here, Collot (1826, p. 346) notes that the city had some 1,200 inhabitants, 240 armed, composed of people of all colors, some free, some slaves.

The American Annexation of Upper Louisiana as Recounted by Stoddard

Amos Stoddard was a Captain when he presided over the official transfer of the territories of Upper Louisiana to the American forces in 1804. He was later promoted to Major. St. Louis was the capital of Upper Louisiana. Following the transfer, Stoddard spent five years in the territory as well as five months along the Red River section located in American lands south of the 49th parallel (Stoddard, 1812, p. v).

Stoddard's description as to how he collected the data to write about of Louisiana is revealing (1812, p. vi.). He is clearly dismissive of what the locals might have to offer: "The writings of missionaries at least those I have seen, and the accounts published by French officers who were employed in the country during part of the two last centuries, are mostly of an uninteresting nature." Stoddard wrote this even though he had access to all the written records left behind by the Spanish colonial authorities, which were precisely the accounts that provide a balanced perspective on the history of Upper Louisiana. He also trivializes the inhabitants' oral accounts:

> No detailed accounts of the interior are to be found in the records of Louisianian literature: On Indian traders, and other transient persons, we are obliged in most instances to rely for what limited information we possess. They present us indeed, with an exuberant mass of materials, but extremely crude, confused and contradictory; and it requires no small share of patience and attention to distinguish truth from fiction. (Stoddard, 1812, p. vii)

He relies instead on "respectable men" to provide him with the information needed to write his account (Stoddard, 1812, p. vii). The inevitable result is bias, as the voice of the marginalized, and those in the process of being marginalized, are less likely to be heard. It also helps explain how some history is buried and forgotten.

Cape Girardeau from Girardot to Lorimier and Stoddard

Cape Girardeau had the geographical peculiarity of being an inland rocky cape overlooking the Mississippi River. It was named for Sieur [Lord] Jean Baptiste de Girardot, who was stationed at Kaskaskia in the early decades of the eighteenth century. He is said to have established a trading post on top of the cape. In any event, this post would have been abandoned by the time Pierre-Louis de

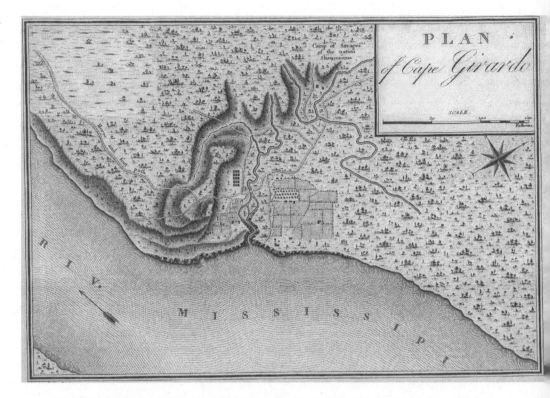

Plan of Cape Girardo, Georges-Henri-Victor Collot, ca. 1796. Pierre-Louis de Lorimier, founder of Cape Girardeau was born under the French crown, lived successively a British subject, then as a Spanish subject, and finally as an American citizen. His was a typical course for many thousands of *Canadiens* and Métis of the mid-eighteenth and early nineteenth centuries.

Lorimier established the community that Major Stoddard would visit in the early years of the nineteenth century. The name Girardot was kept alive in the oral tradition, though the spelling was transformed to Girardeau. Stoddard (1812, p. 214), however, refers to it as Cape Girardeau, and he simplifies the history to a short statement: "The first house built in this district was in 1794 at the cape, and by a Frenchman," and follows by stating, "Since that period settlements have been rapidly formed by emigrants from the United States." He then specifies that "Not more than three or four Frenchmen live in this district; the rest are English Americans, who were organized into three large companies of militia soon after we assumed the government" (Stoddard, 1812, p. 214). A closer examination of Pierre-Louis de Lorimier, one of the "Frenchmen" in question, is warranted, as it shows again how easily history is effectively buried and forgotten.

This "Frenchman" of so little account in Stoddard's eyes, Pierre-Louis de Lorimier, was born a subject of the French Bourbons in 1748 at Oka, Quebec, where his father, Captain Claude-Nicolas de Lorimier was stationed at the time. Oka is located at the mouth of the Ottawa River on Lac des Deux Montagnes, where it empties into the St. Lawrence just west of Montreal. Pierre-Louis de Lorimier would serve the British as a tribal war leader in Ohio and Indiana, then moving further inland, serve as Indian agent and war leader under the Spanish Bourbon authorities in Upper Louisiana (Missouri) where he founded the Cape Girardeau settlement, before becoming the highest-paid U.S. Indian sub-agent serving in the department headed by Auguste Chouteau in Missouri under Superintendent of Indian Affairs, William Clark. He also benefited from the appointment by President Thomas Jefferson of two of his Métis sons to West Point.

After *La Conquête*, Pierre-Louis joined with his father, Claude-Nicolas de Lorimier, in establishing a trading post in 1769 along a twenty-five-mile portage trail in northwestern Ohio between the Maumee and Au Glaize Rivers to the north and the Great Miami to the south, an area then under British rule. Once the American Revolution had started, Pierre-Louis aligned himself and the local tribe with which he was by then inter-married (the Shawnees, or les Chaouanon) with the British, and assumed a military role in the war (Nash, 2012, p. 26).

The first of the three Journals translated in *The Journals of Pierre-Louis de Lorimier* (Nash, 2012) provides a clear picture of the costs, risks, and benefits of running a combined trading and military post during a period of warfare in a frontier zone. This first journal is a petition for compensation for loyal service, including the provisioning of war parties, translation services, and losses incurred during the revolutionary war in the Indiana-Kentucky borderlands. In the journal (or report), he details his communication and coordination with the British commandant in Detroit and the trips this entailed. He also details his participation in war parties, and raids of the allied Shawnee and Delaware (Loups) bands on the Ohio and Kentucky settlements, with reference to the numbers of prisoners and scalps taken, as well as the costs of hosting and supplying other multiple Indian war parties passing through, with the general pilfering that accompanied their presence and departures (Nash, 2012, pp. 83-85).

During the last official military campaign of the Revolutionary War in November and December 1782, George Rogers Clark led roughly 1,050 Kentucky militia across the Ohio River to put an end to Shawnee raids on their settlements, and proceeded to burn and loot their winter villages and stores, including "the Frenchman's Store" belonging to Pierre-Louis de Lorimier (Nash, 2012, pp. 36-37). Pierre-Louis and the Shawnee band with which he was closely associated withdrew westward immediately thereafter during the winter of 1782-1783, toward the Wabash and Vincennes.

Pierre-Louis had married a Métisse named Charlotte Penampieh Bougainville of her mother's Shawnee tribe. Charlotte is believed to be the daughter of Louis

Antoine de Bougainville who had been General Montcalm's *aide-de-camp* during the Seven Years' War. De Bougainville later transferred to France's Navy to become an early explorer of the South Pacific in the 1770s before returning to America as a squadron commander under Admiral De Grasse. Captain de Bouganville took the lead in beating back the British fleet trying to relieve the besieged British forces at Yorktown, Viginia, in October 1781. Pierre-Louis de Lorimier's first two of six children by Charlotte were born during the years in Indiana (Nash, 2012, p. 60).

Forty to fifty years before the Trail of Tears associated with the removals under the Jackson Administration, bands of mid-western and eastern Indians, including the bands of Shawnee and Delaware with whom de Lorimier was associated, were already relocating across the Mississippi on their own initiative. The ongoing contest between the British and Spanish Bourbon authorities for the loyalty of Indian tribes of the Old Northwest after the American Revolution shifted further in favor of the Spanish, after the British had failed in 1794 to provide promised support at the battle of Fallen Timbers. Operating as an intermediary between the tribes and now the Spanish authorities, de Lorimier acted as a recruiting agent "to encourage defeated and displaced peoples" of the Old Northwest to relocate west of the Mississippi. This task was facilitated by the fact that it had become obvious to the Native Americans that it was in their best interest to leave: "They began to see the same benefit that earlier native emigrants had seen in the great potential offered by the Spanish government west of the Mississippi" (Nash, 2012, p. 106).

Several years later, de Lorimier relocated to the far side of the Mississippi, while negotiating with the local French Creole authorities representing the Spanish Bourbons in allowing many of his wife's Shawnee relations and neighbors to relocate to the west side of the river to re-establish their community based on a mixed agricultural and hunting economy .

This was an arduous process as the resettlement was challenged by both the local Native Americans and a variety of officials, French and Spanish, in the Spanish-held Upper Louisiana. Along with the Shawnee came numerous Delaware refugees, and they soon found themselves under attack from the Osage, the tribe into whose former territory they had resettled. Likewise Pierre-Louis de Lorimier had initially settled immediately to the south of Ste. Geneviève, on the Saline River, but chose to move further south with the Shawnee to avoid further conflict. The commandant of Nouveau Madrid, Thomas Portelle, challenged their presence. Fortunately, the Lieutenant Governor of La Haute Louisiane (Upper Louisiana), Zénon Trudeau, valued de Lorimier's leadership role with the Shawnee and endorsed their relocation to Cap Girardeau.

De Lorimier soon proved his worth in organizing a band of six hundred Shawnee warriors, some of whom carried out a pre-emptive strike against an advanced post of the armed American group who were attempting to invade Spanish Louisiana by land and sea in the 1793-1794 period. The group was part of a larger filibustering force being organized by the disgruntled George Rogers Clark, who enjoyed the financial support of Edmond Genet, the French Revolutionary government's Ambassador to the U.S. President George Washington ultimately intervened to suppress the planned invasion in 1794, while the French government recalled Genet. The Spanish in turn eased tensions by re-opening the port of New Orleans for the export of produce from the American settlements west of the Appalachian Mountains.

De Lorimier's journals raise several interesting points, such as the diplomacy and logistical challenges of mobilizing and sustaining a militia on the frontier in the 1790s comprising mostly Indians and the actual ethnicity of the supporting white settler population. A case in point is the text of the harangue delivered to the Shawnee, Delaware, Miami, Peoria, Ottawa, and Piankashaw bands assembled in council by Don François Vallé of Ste. Geneviève on behalf of Don Zénon Trudeau, in the name of the Governor General of Louisiana. It was delivered in French but de Lorimier also translated it into the Algonkian languages of those present. It refers to *"votre Père le Grand Chef de la Louisiane"* (your Father, the Great Chief of Louisiana), and seeks to cajole the Native Americans into supporting the war plans of the colonial authorities representing the Spanish Crown. The speech reminds the Native Americans gathered that they were given lands and asylum in the Spanish controlled territories. They are being warned not to listen to those who are trying to gain their support: "Do not listen, my Children, to evil persons who daily flutter about your ears, and who do not cease to entertain you with an evil song."

What is particularly interesting in the speech are those who are singled out as these "evil persons." In the French version, they are labeled as *"mauvais Français"* and *"de mauvais Amériquains."* [Bad Frenchman and bad Americans.] There is also the standard monarchist characterization of republics, whatever their national language, as representing anarchy and the rule of mobs, emphasizing that *"votre tranquilité... va etre troublé par des gens conduits par eux-memes et non pas des véritables chefs"* [your tranquility... will be troubled by those people who are leading themselves and not by true leaders] (Nash, 2012, pp. 142-144).

The speech and the description of those present reveal the demographic composition of the territory. Even though in maps of the 1790s, the territory is depicted as being American to one side and Spanish to the other, the population of European background is largely French-speaking on both sides of the river, especially on the western bank, which was still predominantly Indian territory. The names of a variety of couriers, boat builders, and militiamen enumerated include L'Empeigne, La Chance, La Deroute, La Chapelle, Langlois, Laplante,

Beaubien, Menard, Bonneau, Racine, Drouillard, and many others. It sounds much like a standard cast of characters in a western movie, but one that recognized the true demographic weight of those present.

The following year, Cap Girardeau was established as an independent post with de Lorimier appointed as its commandant. De Lorimier ultimately received land grants from the Spanish authorities for 30,000 arpents, or somewhat over 25,000 acres. A condition of this appointment and the land grants was further development of the area that included enlisting new settlers. This ended up providing mostly unruly Kentuckians from the opposite shore of the Mississippi River prospects for recruiting in the region.

Living in close proximity with the Shawnees, who had resettled nearby several years earlier, soon strained relations (Nash, 2012, pp. 42-47). By the census of 1803, the last year under the Spanish Bourbons, among the 185 Euro-American householders listed, the core of French Créole and *Canadiens* included only those of the Lorimier, Largeau, Godair, Berthiaume, and Mariot families (Nash, 2012, p. 50).

In addition to his public responsibilities and real estate projects in Cap Girardeau, Pierre-Louis de Lorimier continued to operate a profitable fur trade business, two mills, and a Mississippi ferry service. Since he had obtained a license to operate a ferry, the settlement at Cap Girardeau was referred to for a time as de Lorimier's Ferry. De Lorimier also oversaw an extensive agricultural operation, which he left in the hands of his oldest *Canadien*-Métis son, Guillaume, for day-to-day management. (The relationship with Guillaume's mother had preceded the one with Charlotte Bougainville.) The farm produced wheat, corn, and maple sugar, with almost two hundred head of cattle, as well as horses and pigs (Nash, 2012, pp. 57-58).

Lewis and Clark later visited the thriving though turbulent settlement in 1803 on their way up the Mississippi to winter across from St. Louis at Campement du Bois. Lewis, until recently President Jefferson's secretary, wrote several pages in his journal describing a horse race he witnessed at Cape Girardeau and a visit to the de Lorimier home. Lewis's journal first includes his negative comments about the more recently arrived American settlers, using such terms as "it is not extrawdinary [sic] that these people should be disorderly they are almost entirely emigrants from the fronteers of Kentuckey & Tennessee, and are the most desselute [sic] and abandoned even among these people." These comments can be contrasted with those of Captain Stoddard. Meriwether Lewis then interestingly makes positive comments about Pierre-Louis, his wife, and especially his eldest daughter. Several excerpts from his journal for the November 23, 1803 encounter include the observation that "a party under the command of Genl George Rogers Clark of kentuckey burnt the store of this man—the value of the property lost on this occasion is estimated at 20 thousand dollars; this broke him as a merchant but he seems to have entirely recovered his losses and is now a man of considerable property."

Lewis continues: "this man agreeable to the custom of many of the Canadien Traders has taken to himself a wife from among the aborigines of the country his wife is a Shawnee woman, from her complexion is half blooded only. She is a very decent woman and if we may judge from her present appearance has been very handsome when young, she dresses after the Shawnee manner with stroud leggings and mockinsons, differing from them in her linin—with long sleeves more in the style of the French Canadian women; by this woman Lorimier has a large family of very handsome Children [sic]."

Finally, Lewis notes: "the daughter is remarkably handsom[e] & dresses in a plain yet fashionable stile or such as is now common in the Atlantic States among the respectable people of the middle class [sic]" (Nash, 2012, pp. 54-55; Quaife, 1916, pp. 58-62). Here we see a cultural fusion: de Lorimier's wife is clearly dressed integrating cultural norms that draw from both a Shawnee and *Canadien* tradition, while the daughter is following the norms of the middle-class elite.

Upon arriving, Lewis delivered a letter from a Shawnee relation of Mrs. de Lorimier, a nephew named George Drouillard (spelled Drewyer by Lewis), who was serving at the U.S. Army post of Fort Massac on the opposite shore, downriver. Lewis and Clark were intent on recruiting George, the Métis son of Pierre Drouillard and a Shawnee woman, to join them as their principal translator and scout, to which he agreed, shortly thereafter. Clark did not accompany Lewis during the visit, but stayed behind on the shore with the men. He was apparently feeling sick, but it is also entirely likely that he would not have been welcome. Bad blood had poisoned relations between de Lorimier and the Clark family for over a quarter of a century of frontier warfare, as it was troops under the command of William Clark's older brother, George Rogers Clark, who had previously destroyed Lorimier's commercial operation in Ohio. Becoming Superintendent of Indian Affairs for Upper Louisiana after his return from the Pacific, William Clark being a practical man, would later accept Pierre Louis de Lorimier to serve as one of his principal Indian sub-agents (Nash, 2012, pp. 52-53; Quaife, 1916, pp. 58-62).

In 1812, Pierre-Louis de Lorimier succumbed to the river fever, what appears to have been malaria. His eldest son, Louis Jr., was the twenty-fifth officer to graduate from West Point, but he resigned his commission three years later in 1809 and returned home from Fort Osage, where he had been serving in the Army, in order to help his father run the family business. In 1812, Louis Jr. accompanied a Manuel Lisa trading expedition up the Missouri. After the passing of Pierre-Louis de Lorimier, Pierre Menard of Illinois would assume much of his role vis-a-vis the local bands of Shawnee and Delaware. A decade later, during the early 1820s, Menard would be the key figure in negotiating with the U.S. Government on their behalf, leading to their re-location to the Kaw River Valley, just west of the future Kansas City (Thorne, 1996, 150).

Amos Stoddard (1812) in his account of life in Upper Louisiana makes absolutely no mention of any de Lorimier, nor does he refer to any individual. Rather, he occasionally refers to the ethnic composition of various locales, emphasizing the distinction between the Créoles and *Canadiens*. He notes, as a case in point: "The village of Carondelet is situated on the Mississippi about five miles below St. Louis. It contains forty or fifty houses, inhabited by Creoles and Canadians" and "This district presents us with only two compact villages, St. Charles, and Portage des Sioux; and these are almost wholly peopled with Creoles and Canadians" (Stoddard, 1812, p. 219 and 223).

Stoddard thus makes the point that Créole and *Canadien* are distinct identities and though both would have been born in the country, Créole and *Canadien* are not interchangeable by the nineteenth century. Neither appear to Stoddard, however, to be of sufficient interest in Upper Louisiana to be referred to as individuals. The stories of particular *Canadiens* or Créoles he may have met in the territory he was overseeing as military commander that still harbored a considerable French-speaking population simply failed to pass muster. Over two centuries later, apparently, little has changed in St. Louis in matters of whose history counts. A visitor to the Museum at the National Historic Site will learn that the history of St. Louis and Upper Louisiana begins in 1803. Fortunately, local and State Museums tell the rest of the story.

The American Fur Trade

Though the fur trade era of the United States has received less attention than the later era of the cowboy, those people immortalized in popular writings, movies, and songs have invariably been Anglo-American traders, trappers, and mountain men such as Jim Bridger and Kit Carson. The story had to be kept simple, and thoroughly American. (The Hollywood film, *The Revenant*, though the work of a Mexican filmmaker, is a case in point.) They were credited with the exploration of the American Northwest, even though French-speaking *Canadiens* had invariably preceded them, sometimes by a century. Jim Bridger is often credited as being the first European American to see Great Salt Lake, but it is just as likely that Étienne Provost, a *Canadien* fur trader born in Chambly, Quebec, deserves this honor.

However, as the writers who would write the history and epics of the old Northwest would be Anglo-Americans, the men they chose to glorify first in print, then later in cinema, would be the Bridgers and not the Provosts; the Carsons, and not the Lajeunesse brothers. John Charles Frémont features Bridger and Carson in his *Report of the Exploring Expedition to the Rocky Mountains in*

John Charles Frémont, William Momberger, ca 1862-1864. A renowned explorer and mapmaker, John Charles Frémont was sent to explore the Rocky Mountains in 1842 and the Oregon Territory and Northern California in 1843-1844. He grew up speaking French and English and was comfortable commanding the *Canadien* and Créole in his western expeditions. Frémont was instrumental as a military officer in the conquest of California when the Southwest was wrested from Mexico in 1846. He served as military governor of California for two months, and then as an elected Senator of California before being the first Republican candidate to run in the American presidential elections in 1856. He was a high-ranking officer in the Civil War, commanding the Department of the West and the Western Armies.

the Year 1842, and to Oregon and North California in the Years 1843-44, but shows both playing relatively minor roles even though they had already achieved a great deal of notoriety. Christopher (Kit) Carson was known for his exploits in the mountains, and was likely hired to the group because of that, but he certainly did not distinguish himself in the expedition. Frémont notes instead that his "favorite man" was Basil Lajeunesse. On another occasion Frémont (1845, p. 47 and 72) enumerates five of his best men, including Basil Lajeunesse, along with four other French-speaking voyageurs, but not Carson.

These French-speaking explorers, trappers, cartographers, and western artists, alas, would be set aside in favor of those icons that could pass for being more American. Unless, of course, they were of a better class, such as Army officers who descended from French émigré families, like Bonneville or Frémont, or even one that was born in the French colony of Saint Domingue (Haiti) and grew up in France but arrived in the U.S. as a teenager escaping enlistment in Napoléon's Navy, like Jean-Jacques Audubon. For future generations of Americans, a Bridger and a Carson were certainly more palatable as heroes of the early American West than French-speaking voyageurs with their Gallic names and their "race-mixing" habits. Despite the presence of *Canadien* and Métis all around them, it was Bridger and Carson who would be lionized in all forms of popular culture, including Johnny Horton's song, *Jim Bridger* which begins as follows:

> Once there was a mountain man who couldn't write his name
> Yet he deserves the front row seat in History's Hall of Fame
> He forgot more about the Indians than we will ever know

In this song from the 1950s, Horton even ranks the pantheon of American heroes, lyrically placing Bridger above Kit Carson: "compared to Jim Bridger, Kit was civilized and tame." Bridger is even credited with having ensured the very existence of the United States and thus must be remembered "as long as there's the USA."

As Horton's song correctly notes, Bridger's and Carson's fame rested on poems and legends. These men are seen as "deserving" a front row in history, whereas the French speakers (*Canadien*, Métis, and others) would be effectively relegated to the back rows, as the poems and the legends that would be written would be in English, and destined for an Anglo-American audience.

To understand the breadth and depth of the French-speaking presence in the continent in the first half of the nineteenth century, it suffices to read the accounts written by a host of individuals ranging from naturalists to painters, and princes to military officers. They did not set out to tell the story of the *Canadien*, Métis, and Créole they encounter, but invariably refer to those French-speakers they encountered in their voyages in an "American" West that was still more Indian and French than American. A critical rereading of these texts can resuscitate the buried history of the United States.

Jean-Jacques Audubon and Edwin Thompson Denig

Jean-Jacques Audubon (later John James) was sent as a teenager from France to Pennsylvania by his father to avoid probable impressment into Napoléon's Navy. Though Audubon's name is well-known, few would likely know that he was French. A small number of English-speaking authors have nonetheless provided accounts that hint to the French-language presence out West. Edwin Thompson Denig, a Pennsylvania-born American, is an example. Jean-Jacques Audubon's experience is significant, as he traveled up and down the Ohio and Mississippi Rivers during the 1810s, 1820s, and 1830s, and the Missouri in the mid 1840s, when French-speaking *Canadiens* and Créoles were the dominant group of

European descent. French-speaking settlements would have been found all along these rivers, and French would have been the *lingua franca* of the region. One stopover in 1811 included Cape Girardeau.

Though Audubon's Journals were written in English, a large percentage of the people in them spoke French like him. His fluent French certainly facilitated his work as a naturalist and he would have been able to draw upon the knowledge of those people whose families had been living in the territory for generations. However, the edited and published versions destined for English-speaking readership, beyond the names of individuals, the occasional idiomatic French expression, and the odd reference to the names of wildlife originating from French-speaking "Creoles," "French-Canadians," or "Missouriens" contain very few references to the language spoken by these people. One would not want to offend the sensibilities of the mostly English-speaking audience.

An exception involved an encounter on the upper Missouri with a number of Métis women. Here, Audubon describes a scene in which, after having a breakfast comprised of bison meat, peas, and pudding, he goes to Fort Mortimer with his party. He describes five "squaws" and notes that these women speak French as well as they speak Cree (Audubon, 1990 [1897], p. 236). This is a recurring observation: the wives and daughters invariably speak French and they sometimes speak French on par with Cree and other indigenous languages. French thus continued to be used over generations without the need for a pidgin or linguistic créole language.

Créoles and *Canadiens* are prominent characters in the Audubon journal, including Chouteau family members, Cerré, plus Chardon, Picotte, Michaux, Charite, Primeau, and Bonaventure. Alexander Culbertson and Edwin Thompson Denig, from Pennsylvania, were two of the numerous Americans featured in the Audubon journal. Denig spent his adult life in the fur trade on the upper Missouri where, like his mentor, Culbertson, he worked as an employee of the American Fur Company, mostly out of Fort Union, where Denig's children by two Indian wives grew up. The name of his Assiniboine wife was translated as Deer Little Woman.

Fort Union is located on the Missouri River near its confluence with the Yellowstone (still referred to by some at that time as "La Pierre Jaune"), not far from the modern Montana-North Dakota state border. In the 1850s, Denig authored an important study, *Five Tribes of the Upper Missouri: Sioux, Arickaras, Assiniboines, Crees, and Crow,* not published until 1961. He rose to the position of chief clerk at Fort Union, serving there with Charles Larpenteur under fellow Pennsylvanian Alexander Culbertson.

Denig also assisted Audubon in the summer of 1843, when the naturalist visited Fort Union collecting fauna for his next book. Audubon later provided information to Father Pierre-Jean De Smet on the local tribes during an 1851 visit. De

Smet was publishing his own books back in Europe in French, all part of his ongoing fund-raising and recruitment drive on behalf of the Jesuit missions to the Indians across the Great Plains and the Northwest (P.-J. de Smet, 1848, 1853; P.-J. de Smet & van Iseghem, 1844).

The editor of Denig's posthumously published work, John C. Ewers (1961, pp. xiii-xiv), emphasizes the importance of Denig's work in his preface. Ewers notes the contribution of French speakers to the historical record of the region, particularly Pierre de la Verendrye's account of his visit to the Mandan Indians in 1738, Jean-Baptiste Trudeau's description of the Arikaras penned six decades later in *Journal de voyage sur le Haut-Missouri*, 1794-1796 (2006), and in 1805, the first report on the customs of the Crow Indians, written by François Larocque, a *Canadien* working for the North West Company. Ewers nonetheless argues that no other trader-writer provided the wealth of detailed information on the Indian tribes of the Upper Missouri as did Edwin Thompson Denig, who devoted twenty-three years of his life to trade with the Indians of this region.

Regardless of the origins and language of his predecessors in the initial European penetration of the region, Denig was clearly ready to actively forget the French past and rewrite it to conform to America's Manifest Destiny. Despite his efforts, even he was unable to completely erase the history and contribution of French-speakers to the region. The place-names he provides and the designation of various American Indian nations make this evident. At other times, he derides the French in order to showcase his own sagacity. In his chapter on the Sioux, for example, Denig starts out describing the topography of the region, its fauna and flora, the native peoples, and the art of surviving and thriving there. Showing respect for the skills of the native peoples, with whom he was allied through marriage, he needed to provide a telling example of those newcomers who would not listen to the advice of the locals. Denig first mentions the people behind the French-sounding names that he uses for the rivers and highlands (Denig, 1961, pp. 9-10). He introduces three *Canadiens* who were "new hands in the country" and would not listen to their Indian guide's advice in weathering a snowstorm when caught suddenly out in the open. The Indian survived with minor injuries, and made it through to the fort. A search party was immediately sent out which located the other three. One of the *Canadiens* died several days later, having been "frozen to the top of the thigh," a second lost both legs below the knee, and the third lost his feet.

Denig (1961, pp. 26-27) cites a second example. He describes how Chief Little Bear of the Honcpapas had hated the white man since his youth and describes how his hate "has been manifested and his rule commenced with killing one of the principal traders of the American Fur Company, Mr. La Chapelle. This gentleman, though married into their band, consulting their interest, and speak-

Dog-Sledges of the Mandan Indians, Karl Bodmer, ca. 1833. The Mandan were Siouan speakers. Before feral horses arrived from Spanish colonies, dogs were used to pull the travois, a term derived from French. Pierre Gaultier de Varennes, sieur de La Vérendrye first made contact with the Mandan in 1738. Close trading ties between the Mandan and the French and their descendants persisted as they served as crucial intermediairies in the fur trade. The Mandan numbered 15,000 when Pierre de La Vérendrye first met them, but were devastated by a smallpox epidemic later in the century. Lewis and Clark wintered with them in 1804 as their expedition headed west.

ing their language, was murdered in his own house on Grand River by the Honcpapas."

Throughout the book, there are constant references to the French traders, whether it was the fur trade that was opened on the Missouri River by the American Fur Company with its itinerant French traders (Denig, 1961, p. 32) or the large war excursion by the Yanctonnais to the Mandan and Gros Ventres villages that stopped at the trading post run by Primeau, who refused to provide ammunition to the war party (Denig, 1961, p. 34). This unfortunate trader was then, according to Denig, killed by the unsuccessful war party who, on their return, exacted revenge on Primeau and robbed the post of all its merchandise (Denig, 1961, p. 34). As is often the case, the earliest witnesses are unable to completely erase the French from their accounts, as they were too close to the events,

Horse Racing of Sioux Indians near Fort Pierre, Karl Bodmer, ca. 1833. The Great Sioux Nation, now known as the Lakota, comprised seven smaller groups, members of the confederacy called the Seven Fires Council. Other Siouan speakers were not members of this confederacy. The first contact of the French and the Sioux date back to the mid-seventeenth century. The French established "La Compagnie des Sioux" in 1727 to trade with them, but when this endeavor failed many men remained and settled in the West and North. Relations with the Sioux were not always easy. A Sioux war party killed Pierre de la Vérendrye's son Jean-Baptiste and some twenty companions in 1736. Jean-Baptiste had established a number of forts in the Red River in what is now Manitoba. The French continued to push for trading relations, which continued beyond the Conquest. There were unions between the *Canadien* and the Sioux in the decades that followed.

but later historians with greater temporal distance from the events—and dexterity—would complete the task in later publications.

Denig's account illustrates not only how topographical terms were being translated from French to English, but also how the names applied to native peoples were also based on the translations of the French terms that had been assigned to them by earlier generations of French-language traders. Denig preserves the French designations given to the peoples he is actively trading with, notably the Lakota (Sioux) known as Brûlées, the Black Feet, who were first known as Pieds Noirs, the Two Kettles people from Deux Chaudières, and the Lakota population known as Without Bows from Sans Arcs.

Then there were the Sioux known as the Têtes Coupées, the Gens du Pins, and the Gens des Perches. There is also the litany of Assiniboine designations that were all French: Gens du Gauche, Gens du Lac, Gens des Roches, Gens des Filles, Gens des Canots and Gens du Nord. The Crows had likewise derived their English language name via an interim Gens des Corbeaux. These designations bear witness to the long ties they had with French traders, including the many cases of métissage with French-speakers, *Canadien* and Créole, marrying into the Lakota or Sioux nation. Moreover, the Sioux name came from *Nadouessioux,* a French rendering of the Odawa word *Nadoüessioüak,* first recorded by a European in 1640, namely the Jesuit Jean-Nicolet.

Denig's topography indicates eloquently the impact of French-speaking people on the history of the region. In addition to the well known French names straddling the Oregon trail, such as the Platte or Laramie Rivers, Denig also refers to the Mauvaises Terres (Bad Lands), Butte de Mince, the Coteau de Prairies, Lac qui Parle, Lac du Diable (Devil), and Traverse Lake. There are the assorted *coulees* [from the French *coulées* for canyon or literally flowing or poured], and the following rivers: la Rivière aux Jacques (translated as the James River, though the French designation logically should designate a type of fish than a name as the "aux" signifies a plural designation, as opposed to the *à* signifying singular possession), la Rivière aux Souris, la Rivière du Parc (Saskatchewan), la Rivière aux Trembles, L'eau qui Court (Rapid), Couteau (Knife), Moreau, and the Qu'appelle. Denig was not exceptional in this regard. The journals and maps authored by Lewis and Clark (2002) are also rife with French topographical terms. Were one to rely solely on the topographical maps of the expedition, notably the Rivière aux Jacques, one could conclude that the French were the sole inhabitants of the lands visited by this American expedition.

Not only did the French language seep through the topographical descriptions, it also worked its way into biological designations. Providing the Sioux and English terms in listing "The fruits and esculent roots indigenous to this section," for two of them Denig also inserted French words in widespread use during an interim period in the American West in order to ensure that he would be fully understood. Denig (1961, pp. 11-12) takes great care to point out that the prairie turnip called by the Sioux, *teep se nah,* was known in French as *pomme blanche,* and is found everywhere on the high prairies, while choke cherries were known as *grain de boeuf* in French or *mush tim poo tah* in the Sioux language. Finally, the nicknames given to chiefs and prominent individuals are often French, as attested by Denig, who records the name of "Hai wah ze chah" of the "Min ne con zus Sioux," also known as *La Corne Seule* as well as *La Main qui tremble,* chief of the "Gens du Gauche" band of the Assiniboines.

Prince Maximilian of Wied-Neuwied

A number of primary accounts in addition to Frémont's shed light on the role of the French-speaking *Canadiens* and their descendants. A notable early account is that of the German Prince Maximilian of Wied-Neuwied, who traveled in the old Northwest in the 1830s accompanied by the artist Karl Bodmer. Together they provided a detailed written and illustrated account of life in the Missouri and Great Plains region of North America.

Prince Maximilian was very much an anthropologist and a naturalist, traveling through the territory after arriving in the United States in 1832, on the heels of Tocqueville and Beaumont. He noted, "It is incredible how much the original American race is hated and neglected by the foreign usurpers" (Maximilian, 1843, p. 20). His account seeks not to excessively glorify the American expansion, but to examine the impact of the settlement of the territory by the Americans, notably in observing first-hand the spread of a smallpox epidemic that decimated the indigenous population across the plains and over the Rocky Mountains in the 1830s. His notes and observations are thorough. Knowing French, he recorded his encounters with French speakers and provides a relatively objective insight into the history of the region, which does not completely remove the French-speaking *Canadien*. As he traveled west from Boston through Philadelphia and Pittsburgh, Maximilian recorded the presence of French settlements. He first passes through Cape Girardeau, a settlement that was a village when he traveled through it. He then proceeds to Kaskaskia and Ste. Geneviève:

> St. Genevieve, an old French settlement, now a large village, with 600 or 800 inhabitants, is about twenty minutes' walk from the landing-place, and appears to be in a state of decline; it was founded at the same time as Kaskaskia. The streets are at right angles, unpaved, and bordered with hedges. The houses, which are of one story, are separate from each other, and have, in general, a verandah in front. The church is built of red brick. French and English are spoken, and there are several German inhabitants. Caravans go every spring from hence to the interior of the western prairies, to Santa Fe and the Rocky Mountains; they consist of many armed men, with their horses and wagons. The well-known lead mines are further up the country (Maximilian, 1843, p. 100).

These settlements were located not too far from the old Fort de Chartres. Other French settlements dotted the countryside; Maximilian notes that they passed the French settlement of Vide-Poche or Carondelet on their way to St. Louis. He describes how the settlement was founded one hundred years earlier and that it was a large and scattered village. Maximilian (1843, p. 101) wrote that the inhabitants were "reported to be not very industrious," but this is certainly a third-party accounting owing perhaps to Anglo-American settler stereotyping of the Native American and Métis people.

Encampment of the Travellers (voyageurs) on the Missouri, Bodmer, ca. 1833. Prince Alexander Philipp Maximilian of Wied-Neuwied traveled with the Swiss Painter Karl Bodmer to the Great Plains of the United States journeying up the Missouri River. On his return, he published an account of his travels featuring Bodmer's artwork. Maximilian's account provides a description of the voyageurs and other French-speaking people encountered. These paintings provide rich first-hand insight into the lives of the peoples of the region, including the voyageurs.

St. Louis was a growing town in the early 1830s, with a population ranging between six and eight thousand people. The French founded it as a trading establishment with construction dating from 1764. The settlement was ideally situated for trade, and by the 1830s steamboats traveled daily down the Mississippi to New Orleans and back, and also to Pittsburgh, Cincinnati, Louisville, and Prairie du Chien (Maximilian, 1843, p. 101). The legacy of slavery was evident, as many of the men working in the ports of the city were "negroes and their descendants," and Maximilian reported the brutal and inhumane treatment reserved for slaves. He wrote, "One of our neighbours at St. Louis, for instance, flogged one of his slaves in the public streets, with untiring arm. Sometimes he stopped a moment to rest, and then began anew" (Maximilian, 1843, p. 102). St. Louis was nonetheless memorable for Maximilian as the first location where he met Native

Americans. He also met General Clark, formerly half of the titular Lewis and Clark expedition, now superintendent of Indian Affairs. In a meeting organized by Clark with the local indigenous peoples at his home, Maximilian (1843, p. 107) notes, "We strangers sat at the General's side, and near him stood the interpreter, a French Canadian." Maximilian also recounts how *Canadiens* established the fur trade in the newly independent United States:

> The first regular company of this kind in the United States was the Michilimackinac Fur Company, established in 1790. Its capital belonged chiefly to some persons in Canada; but as foreigners were not allowed to trade with the Indians in the United States, some citizens of the latter gave it the sanction of their names. The last war with England dissolved the company, and during that time no trade was carried on with the Indians. About 1816, Mr. Astor, of New York, a countryman of ours, formed a fur company, under the name of the American Fur Company (Maximilian, 1843, pp. 109-110).

In St. Louis, two competing companies had been formed: the Missouri Fur Company and the French Fur Company. Both were later bought out by the American Fur Company, leaving but two continental rivals for the final years of the fur trade while Maximilian was traveling through North America: the American Fur Company and the Hudson's Bay Company. Both relied on French Canadian voyageurs, and occasionally partners, to ensure their success.

The success of Maximilian's journey rested with his reaching out to the fur traders, in particular one Pierre Chouteau, a director of the American Fur Trade Company. Gaining Pierre Chouteau as a benefactor, Maximilian had access to the resources needed to travel up to the indigenous territories where he would spend a winter with the Mandan and other neighboring peoples. It is here that he would also encounter the voyageurs of the American fur trade:

> On the 10th of April, at eleven o'clock, all our company having collected, the Yellow Stone left St. Louis; Mr. Pierre Chouteau, and several ladies of his family, accompanied us to St. Charles. Some guns were fired, as a signal, on our departure, on which numbers of the inhabitants assembled on the shore, among them the Saukies and some half-civilized Kikapoo Indians. Mr. Bodmer made some interesting sketches of the former, of which the plate gives a specimen. (Vignette X.) There were about 100 persons on board the Yellow Stone, most of whom were those called engages, or voyageurs, who are the lowest class of servants of the Fur Company. Most of them are French Canadians, or descendants of the French settlers on the Mississippi and Missouri (Maximilian, 1843, p. 112).

Prince Maximilian (1843, p. 172) had called upon the service of "the old interpreter, Charbonneau" who would certainly have been none other than Toussaint of Lewis and Clark fame. As they travel from St. Louis to St. Charles, the French presence is felt in the topography Maximilian describes: Belle Fontaine, Tavern Rock or Taverne de Montardis, Isle and Rivière au Boeuf, the River Gasconade,

Portrait of Auguste Chouteau, artist unknown. Auguste (sometimes referred to as René Auguste) Chouteau was a founder of St. Louis, second only to his stepfather Pierre Laclède Liguest. Jean-Pierre Chouteau was Auguste's half brother: Auguste's father René Chouteau had abandoned his family, including his son, and Auguste's mother Marie Thérèse Bourgeois Chouteau. Marie Thérèse referred to herself as a "widow," which gave her more rights over property and her children, and then she had four children with Pierre Laclède, three daughters—Marie Pélagie, Marie Louise and Victoire—and a son Jean-Pierre. All bore the family name Chouteau. Born and raised in a Créole setting in New Orleans, the Chouteau siblings and their children came to be the leading family of St. Louis. Jean-Pierre's son Pierre, Jr. bought John Jacob Astor's western interests in the American Fur Company, and his company, Pierre Chouteau, Jr., & Company, dominated the fur trade. The Chouteaus later diversified into steamboats, railways, and mining. Pierre, Jr. died a multimillionaire. Fort Pierre was named after him as was the city of Pierre, South Dakota.

the old French settlement of Côte-Sans-Dessein with six or eight houses, Little-au-Vase Creek that fuses both English and French, as well as the Bonne Femme Creek, Isle au Bon Homme, and the whirlpool named Remoux à Baguette. The terrain was riddled with French names and old French settlements. As was the case across the continent, French names were often anglicized. Maximilian (1843, p. 115) often notes the name with the French in parentheses afterwards—for example, Arrow Rock (*Pierre à flèche*). In this case, the French name came from the flint used by the local indigenous peoples to make arrowheads.

St. Charles was one of the oldest French settlements on the Missouri and had some three hundred houses when Maximilian passed through it. The town still features an old stone tower that had been part of the defenses built by the French against hostile indigenous peoples. The town possessed a massive church with a low tower, various European fruit trees, and brick houses built in a "modern" part of the town (Maximilian, 1843, p. 113). Though he does not mention specifically what language was being spoken in Saint Charles, French was definitely still being used by the voyageurs traveling with them on the steamboat. Maximilian (1843, p. 114) reports, "At night-fall we lay to on the right bank, where a cheerful fire of large logs was soon made, round which our engagés assembled and chatted incessantly in French." Clearly, French was still a dominant language in this region in the 1830s. It is thus not surprising that even Jim Bridger spoke conversational French, as well as Spanish and a number of indigenous languages.

Unlike what was happening farther north, the descendants of the *Canadiens* seemed to have maintained an identity characterized by a more inclusive approach to the various indigenous heritages that individuals may carry as "country-born," including Métis or "Bois-Brulé" identity. It is not that the term "Métis" was not known by *Canadiens*—Father De Smet (1875, p. 61) uses the term *enfants métis* (Métis children) when referring to some children he had baptized at Fort Union—but the men themselves often refer to themselves as *Canadien* in ways that such identification does not force the exclusion of Métis identity, which could sometimes even be used interchangeably with the "*Canadien*" identity. This is evident in the event that Maximilian (1843, p. 119) describes as follows:

> We were here joined by a couple of canoes, with some Canadian engagés from the Upper Missouri, who brought to Mr. Mc Kenzie news from Fort Union, at the mouth of the Yellow Stone River. Their half Indian costume, which is usually worn, was new to us. One of them, named Defond, a tall, slender, brown man, was a half-breed Indian, and one of the best and most experienced pilots of the Missouri.

Here, men who clearly identified as Métis are also referred to as *Canadien*. This is not necessarily an oversight by the author. Whereas in the British-controlled territories, the "Canadian" march to statehood pressured the "French-Canadian Métis" (as Riel would call them) and the Half-breeds to unite and define themselves as a "new nation"—arguably adopting republican and nationalistic ideals articulated by the 1837-1838 *Canadien* Patriots of Lower Canada—the descendants of the French in American territory could much more easily be both *Canadien* and Métis. Indeed, many voyageurs or *Canadiens* were of mixed Euro-Indigenous heritage. They would, however, have retained the language and important cultural traits of their French ancestors, for example, often mixed with various indigenous ones inherited from their close cultural connections or simply kinship ties with Indigenous peoples. This gave rise to the cultural specificity of the Métis, which embraced different cultural modulations according to circumstance, including nationalistic expressions in the midst of Patriotic early Canadian culture in the Northwest.

The Travellers (voyageurs) Meeting with the Minatarre Indians near Fort Clark, Bodmer, ca. 1833. Fort Clark was located on the Upper Missouri. Maximilian and his artist companion Bodmer wintered at this fort. Pictured to the far right are Prince Maximilian and Karl Bodmer. It has been suggested that the man depicted pointing to Prince Maximilian was in fact Toussaint Charbonneau.

John Charles Frémont (1845, p. 9) does however make a clear distinction between two types of American-born French speakers. "I had collected in the neighborhood of St. Louis twenty-one men," he writes, "principally Creole and Canadian voyageurs, who had become familiar with prairie life in the service of the fur companies in the Indian country."

The term Créole in Louisiana at this time was used to define French who were born in the colonies as opposed to the European French. Frémont's use of the term suggests a distinction being made between the French who had originated in the colony of New France (*Canadiens*) versus those who had come up from the heartland of Louisiana (Créoles). Sadly, Frémont does not specify how precisely the two differed, though in his memoirs he does mention that he had grown up with the children of a Créole family, refugees from Saint-Domingue, the French colony that became Haïti. Allan Nevins (1992, p. 16), writing Frémont's biography, explains how, "Like himself [Frémont], they [the Créole refugee family] spoke French." The refugees would have been the descendants of the French born

Republican Ideals

Historian Alexander Ross (1957 [1856], p. 239) notes the influence of the Patriots of Lower Canada on the development of national and republican ideals espoused by the "new nation" as expressed by Louis Riel, Sr. O'Toole (2010, p. 147) cites Ross: "The Papineau rebellion which broke out in Canada about this time, and the echo of which soon reached us, added fresh fuel to the spirit of disaffection. The Canadians of Red River sighed for the success of their brethren's cause. Patriotic songs were chanted on every side in praise of Papineau. In the plains, the half-breeds made a flag, called the Papineau standard, which was waved in triumph for years, and the rebels' deeds extolled to the skies" (Ross, 1957 [1856], p. 256). O'Toole (2010, p. 147) also recalls the political rapprochement between the Patriots' republican ideals and the Canadien-Métis resistance in the Red River colony. A member of a committee organized by Louis Riel, Sr. to resist the HBC's monopoly in 1849 was "the Métis François Bruneau, who 'was a first cousin of Julie, wife of Louis-Joseph Papineau, and a nephew of Pierre Bruneau, member for Chambly, Lower Canada'" (Dorge, 1974, p. 18).

in the Americas—those who were the elite plantation owners, the slave owners. In the biography, Nevins (1992, p. 43) interestingly notes that on the other hand the Half-breeds (the Métis) called themselves the *"gens libres."*

Slavery and the Fur Trade

As elsewhere, the participants in the fur trade were not all *Canadien*, and indeed, some slaves—some black, but mostly Native American slaves—worked in the industry. Maximilian (1843, p. 301) provides this account of the men who left St. Louis on an expedition to the Indian territories: "Our party consisted of Mr. Bodmer, Chardon, and myself, and the half-Indian hunters, Dechamp, Marcellais, and Joseph Basile, a negro slave belonging to Mr. McKenzie, with three or four more who led the horses that were to carry the meat."

Black slaves were thus as much integrated to the fur trade as the plantations, and some free men of African descent would in turn become traders and voyageurs. In his autobiographic account, Charles Larpenteur provides an intriguing account of one such freed slave, John Brazo. In the footnotes, the anthropologist who edited Larpenteur's handwritten autobiography (in preparing it for publication) provides the following account that was furnished to him by Dr. Matthews:

There was a white Brazeau (John, I think) and a colored Brazeau on the Upper Missouri. It was the latter that I knew. He used to say he was the first 'white man' that ever came into the country. I think he came as a servant or slave to the former. My John Brazeau was a full-bloode Æthiopian, apparently, of small stature and intelligent, though not handsome, face. He must have been 70 or over when he died. He enunciated his English well and had a good command of it for an uneducated man. He spoke French better than most Canadians; also Sioux and other Indian languages. He was hardy, courageous, and on the whole a creditable specimen of his race. He served the A. [American] F. [Fur] Co. and its successors for many years. About 1868, the company he had been working for at Fort Berthold sold out to an opposition concern, which had houses outside the fort. The people of the latter firm moved in and turned all the old hands out, including Brazeau, who was now too old, feeble, and rheumatic to work. He was literally turned out to die; no white man offered him anything. Then the Indians took pity on him and gave him such shelter and food as they could afford; but they were, themselves, very poor at this time (Larpenteur, 1898, p. 121).

This description is indicative of racial relations during the fur trade and is a telling account of the fate that awaited the traders once the fur trade came to an end. Brazeau could claim to be the first "white man," as the distinction was not racial, but rather an affirmation that he was the first man who was not Native American to visit the territory. Also, Brazeau demonstrated the linguistic prowess common to the voyageurs: the ability to learn and speak many languages. Naturally, the Anglo-American doctor does get one jibe in, noting that Brazeau spoke "French better than most Canadians," which was an indirect denigration of the French language that the *Canadiens* spoke. Finally, the fate of Brazeau and the Native Americans is indicative of the fate of these indigenous people who would be relocated to reservations, and the fate of the fur traders and voyageurs who would be left unemployed and penniless if they did not succeed in reinventing themselves when the fur trade economy eventually collapsed.

Métis and Halfbreed identities are especially visible when a mixed population settles down in a given territory and its neighbors are contrasted as Native Americans. Here, Maximilian (1843, p. 124) provides one revealing example:

We came to the mouth of the Grand Nemahaw river in a beautiful romantic country, from which, to the Little Nemahaw, the territory of the people called Half-breeds extends. Among the Omaha, Oto, Joway, and Yankton (Sioux) Indians, there lived from 150 to 200 of their descendants by white men, to whom they assigned this tract of land as their property.

What is remarkable in this passage is that the population is referred to as a *people* and are named "Half-breeds." As was the case elsewhere in the United States—and as we will examine, in the Pacific Northwest—the American settler-Native American mixed heritage people, unlike their Métis counterparts in Canada, would often be pressured to join reserves and integrate into Native American communities. The Half-breeds described by Maximilian are likely ancestral to some of the modern Ioway who had intermarried with French traders and American farmers. Hailing from that union, the "mixed bloods for a time had their own reservation in Nebraska, called Nemaha Reservation" (Ioway

Cultural Institute, 2013). Some examples of Ioway arts listed on the Ioway Cultural Institute website interestingly include a woven sash reminiscent of the voyageur sash, and intricate beadwork that certainly suggests Métis or French-Canadian cultural inputs.

Accounts abound about Native Americans who have no French ancestry learning the French language. John Charles Frémont (1845, p. 11), in his report, provides one such example:

> A number of Kansas Indians visited us today. Going up to one of the groups who were scattered among the trees, I found one sitting on the ground, among some of the men, gravely and fluently speaking French, with as much facility and as little embarrassment as any of my own party, who were nearly all of French origin.

Frémont explains later that the Native American who was speaking French had spent time in St. Louis as a child, having learned French as a boy some twenty-five or thirty years earlier. This passage reveals the continued importance of the French-speaking *Canadiens* in the region: any serious expeditions leaving from St. Louis would in fact by necessity need to recruit *Canadiens* whether they originated in American territory, or in the St. Lawrence Valley.

The French and *Canadiens* are moreover omnipresent in Maximilian's account. They include the commercial and somewhat bourgeois Chouteau family of Louisianan and French Créole origins, *Canadien* traders dispersed throughout the countryside in trading posts, French *Canadiens* serving as interpreters and cultural mediators as well as Native Americans who have French-Canadian ancestry. Frémont's account demonstrates that not only were the *Canadiens* working for the fur trading companies, they also continued to operate as *coureurs des bois,* be it across the open expanse of the Great Plains (1845, p. 40). These are the itinerant free traders who seek trade for personal profit. Frémont (1845, p. 40) is critical of these unlicensed traders, as they invariably pursue their trade with kegs of liquor, plying alcohol for furs with little regard for the future well-being of either their trading partners or even future trade: "the coureur des bois has no permanent interest, and gets what he can, and for what he can, from every Indian he meets, even at the risk of disabling him from doing any thing more at hunting." The *Canadiens* thus permeate every sphere of the fur trade from the unlicensed individual trader to the directors of the large fur trade companies.

Though the story of the voyageur is better known in Canada, the life of the "*voyageur Canadien*" in American territory was nearly identical to that of the voyageur to the north of the 49th parallel. This haunting passage from Frémont (1845, p. 75) summarizes the toil and dangers that defined the voyageur life as well as the shared culture:

We placed ourselves on our knees, with the short paddles in our hands, the most skilful boatman being at the bow; and again we commenced our rapid descent We cleared rock after rock, and shot past fall after fall, our little boat seeming to play with the cataract. We became flushed with success, and familiar with the danger; and, yielding to the excitement of the occasion, broke forth together into a Canadian boat song. Singing, or rather shouting, we dashed along; and were, I believe, in the midst of the chorus, when the boat struck a concealed rock immediately at the foot of a fall, which whirled her over in an instant. Three of my men could not swim, and my first feeling was to assist them, and save some of our effects; but a sharp concussion or two convinced me that I had not yet saved myself. A few strokes brought me into an eddy, and I landed on a pile of rocks on the left side. Looking around, I saw that Mr. Preuss had gained the shore on the same side, about twenty yards below; and a little climbing and swimming soon brought him to my side. On the opposite side, against the wall, lay the boat bottom up; and Lambert was in the act of saving Descoteaux, whom he had grasped by the hair, and who could not swim; "Lache pas," said he, as I afterward learned, "lache pas, cher frère." "Crains pas" was the reply, "Je m'en vais mourir avant que de te lacher." Such was the reply of courage and generosity in this danger.

Of particular note are the *Canadien* boat songs that the men sang in the rapids—songs that would have been shared by the *Canadien* voyageurs from the St. Lawrence Valley to the Great Lakes and across the Great Plains and Rocky Mountains to the Pacific and up to the Arctic.

French voyageurs (*engagés*), traders, merchants, and the French living in indigenous communities—often called upon to serve as interpreters—were clearly all playing an essential role in an American fur trade still going strong in the 1830s and early 1840s. However, by the latter decade, the trade had switched over to a high volume extermination of another fur bearing animal, the buffalo. Not only had they made alliances with Native American nations, they had also named the territory and founded a number of settlements stretching from the Great Lakes to the Rocky Mountains. However, little of their story is told; only the faintest of traces of their contribution to the history of the western United States remain.

In the 1840s, the waves of migration would begin pushing westwards. De Smet (1875, p. 8) describes the movement of peoples on a steamboat ride up the Missouri River in 1840 thusly: *"Le navire ou j'étais embarqué était (comme ils le sont tous dans ce pays où l'émigration et le commerce ont pris une si grande extension) encombré de marchandises et de passagers de tous les Etats de l'Union je puis même dire de différentes nations de la terre, blancs, noirs, jaunes et rouges, avec les nuances de toutes ces couleurs. Le bateau ressemblait à une petite Babel flottante, à cause des différents langages et jargons qu'on y entendait."* ["The ship, where I had embarked, was (as they all are in this country where emigration and trade had extended its reach) cluttered with goods and passengers from all the States of the Union, I can even say the different nations of the earth, white, black, yellow,

Half Breed [Métis] Hunters' Camp near the Three Buttes, ca 1873, artist unkown. Idaho straddles the Columbia Plateau and the Rocky Mountains. It provided prime trapping territories that attracted fur traders and freemen. Among those who came to the region were the Iroquois recruited as employees and trappers by the North West Company. Some Iroquois left Québec to trap for the North West Company, eventually settling down among the Flathead Indians in the Bitter Root Valley of western Montana. Pierre's Hole Idaho was named after one of these Iroquois, le Grand Pierre Tivanitagon. Pierre's Hole is located where the Teton River flows down from the Grand Teton Mountains into a beaver rich basin. It is here that Pierre was killed in 1827 in a battle between his fellow trappers and the Blackfeet Indians.. French-speaking Catholics, these Iroquois appealed for priests and promoted both trade and missionary activities among the Native Americans with whom they lived. Indigenous people from territories now part of Canada traveled and settled throughout the interior of the American Pacific Northwest both before and after partition in 1846.

and red, with all the nuances of all these colors. The boat looked like a small floating Babel, because of different languages and pidgins you could hear there."]

The migrants would continue pouring in as the fur trade came to an end, marking also an end to the preeminence of the French language. Whereas in the past some of the older French inhabitants of St. Louis could have taken pride in never learning any English (Karel, 1992, p. 317), their descendants became bi- or tri-lingual before they would come to speak only English in the generations to follow. The Chouteau family dynasty, however, deserves greater attention before we go on.

A Family Enterprise on the Missouri: The Chouteau Family

The French government and military completed their withdrawal from North America with the transfer of Fort de Chartres on the Mississippi River to the

Buffalo Hunting, Western Prairies (Kansas), Henry James Warre, ca. 1840. The shared culture portrayed stretched across the continent. The Red River Cart was not limited to the Red River region and many elements of what is now thought of as Métis culture—including the sash (*ceinture fléchée*)—were found across the plains and forests along with the French language.

British in 1765, five years after the surrender of Montreal and six years after the fall of Quebec City. Fort de Chartres was located a short ways downriver from the town of St. Louis on the opposite shore. The town was established the year before the final French Army contingent surrendered the old Fort. The Fort was located across the river from the west bank settlement of Ste. Genevieve. The Bourbon cousins sitting on the Spanish throne had in the interim been asked to take over Louisiana and the region west of the river for safekeeping, or until developments dictated otherwise. In reality, relieved of the heavy hand of the French monarch's government administration, the self-appointed elite of the Créole French trader class assumed the mantel of authority, or much of it. Not all these merchants of the ever-shifting frontier zone were relegated to the class of petty traders. The Chouteau clan of St. Louis were among a number of families that rose to prominence.

While a flag was lowered and another raised at Fort de Chartres in 1765, upstream on the far shore of the Mississippi River, a French merchant named Pierre Laclède, working with his stepson Auguste Chouteau, began building what would become the town of St. Louis in an area that was technically Spanish territory. No Spaniards had appeared yet, though. As the overextended Spanish Bourbon rulers were assuming a defensive posture in North America, the Spaniards left the actual governance of Upper Louisiana to local notables. Laissez-faire rule, even by default, was the new policy in practice on the western frontier. To a lesser extent, this was also true of the French traders trapped behind British and then American lines east of the big river. There, however, they had to compete with the hordes of squatters, speculators, settlers, and their lawyers. After much of the groundwork had been laid, the American government showed up on the right, or west, bank of the Mississippi two generations later, in 1803. Once there, they endorsed the "*liberté de commerce*" or laissez-faire as the official economic policy, but only after a brief attempt at enforcing a government trading monopoly.

By that time, the Chouteaus were quite experienced at managing political appointees from distant capitals and navigating the legislation and laws of the growing American state. As Jay Gitlin writes, "In Indiana and Missouri, Illinois and Michigan, French traders with the means to do so accumulated parcels of land that they assumed would rise in value as droves of American immigrants headed west. They also held political capital as their connections to a variety of Indian tribes ensured their usefulness in the decades after the War of 1812 that saw local and federal officials desperate to sign treaties and obtain one land cession after another" (Gitlin, 2009, p. 83).

On both sides of the Mississippi, many of these *Canadien*, Créole, and Métis traders continued in the fur trade, later diversifying their interests to include timber, canals, steamboats, and railroads (Gitlin, 2009, p. 83). One successful Métis businessman, Antoine LeClaire, a refugee from the Potawatomi and Métis settlement of Peoria that had been destroyed by the Illinois militia under Governor Ninian Edwards in 1812, developed the town of Davenport, Iowa, while, as mentioned above, Louis Campeau of Detroit was central to the establishment of both Saginaw and Grand Rapids, Michigan. Their stories are disconnected anecdotes that are known locally, but have failed to gain the attention of historians more broadly.

In St. Louis, the Chouteau-Laclède clan displayed both entrepreneurial flair and political acumen. The family comprised initially the children of Marie-Thérèse Bourgeois (1733-1814) by two husbands, René Auguste Chouteau (1723-1776) and Pierre Laclède (1729-1778). The latter founded the city of St. Louis in 1764 and fathered most of Marie-Thérèse' nine children; however, oddly enough, his children kept the surname of their mother by her first husband, Chouteau. The Chouteau children married into nearby French-Canadian and Métis clans such as the Cerré, Labadie, Gratiot, Kiersereau, Dubreul, Ménard, Saucier, and

Cabanne families, most of which joined in the Chouteau enterprise in one capacity or another. The Chouteau sons, and several of the grandsons, also had "country wives" from the Osage tribe, while two grandsons had Shawnee wives. The Métis children of these parallel families were numerous. As time went on, exogamy set in as more familiar sounding names such as White and Carpenter entered the picture as spouses for grandchildren, including also a grandchild of close friend William Clark. The family expanded, becoming instrumental in founding Kansas City, and thus helping to shape much of the American Midwest.

Gitlin (2009) documents the successive generations of children and grandchildren who preserved French names and fostered the continued use of French well into the nineteenth century as their economic interests expanded into Kansas, Nebraska, and Oklahoma. Gitlin (2009, p. 84) states, "Here and elsewhere in the Far West, the French were often the first in the field, the advance guard of U.S. expansion pursuing a variety of economic opportunities though often starting with furs. In following the activities of the French and their role in this story of western expansion, [we] hope to provide a case study not only of the dispersion of the French, but also the French in the process of middle-grounding, of occupying a cultural and social space of accommodation while pursuing an economic agenda of development and change." A number of other French families joined the Chouteaus to form the elite of St. Louis by the 1820s, most notably the Ménards, the Papins, the Sarpys, and the St. Vrains. Eventually withdrawing from the original waterfront, they regrouped in a neighborhood of the growing city which became known as Frenchtown.

From St. Louis, other French bourgeois families moved farther afield, up and down the Missouri River, West to the Rocky Mountains, and South to Texas and New Mexico. Others moved down into Lower Louisiana, notably Natchitoches. These families often greeted the arrival of the Americans as an opportunity to expand their economic activities. The Chouteaus focused their interests on consolidating their position in the central portion of the valley from the mouth of the Kansas River to the area north of the Platte around Council Bluffs near present-day Omaha.

As fate would have it, there were other ways for these French-speaking people to be relevant to the new overlords. In 1808, with war looming between Great Britain and the United States, many of the Native American nations were threatening to join forces in a pro-British alliance directed against the American settlers. The Chouteau clan, however, decided to side with the Americans and worked to ensure the peace between the American state and their Native American allies. Gitlin (2009, p. 85) describes the actions of Pierre Chouteau, Sr. (1758-1849), who, acting as the U.S. government's agent for the Osages, negotiated a treaty that secured the land between the Missouri and Arkansas Rivers that the Osages had ceded to the American state. Many of the Osages agreed to move to the west and southwest in search of better hunting grounds, and this treaty ensured that the Osages, a still formidable group, were moved safely away from British influence. The treaty negotiated by Chouteau had the consequence of opening central Missouri for white American settlement, but also included a provision that guaranteed that Chouteau family members would receive title to thirty thousand *arpents* (acres) of land. That same year, the first town in central Missouri, Côte Sans Dessein, was settled, the residents of the town being mostly Métis families who worked as interpreters, hunters, and voyageurs in the fur business, and who were closely tied to Chouteau interests.

What is notable of the Chouteau family was not that they spoke French, but that they strove to become educated in it, seeking a high level of literacy in the French language. A history of St. Louis written by Auguste Chouteau, of which only the first dozen or so pages survive, uses French to relate the founding of the city—and a reasonably high level of literary French at that. These preserved pages are a testament to the desire of the Chouteaus to participate in a larger French culture and civilization extending far beyond the Missouri Valley. Likewise, Frémont's wife, Jesse, who was the daughter of Missouri Senator Bent, spoke French, having been sent as a child to a convent school in St. Louis that "had a staff of accomplished teachers, models of French breeding and refinement" (Nevins, 1992, p. 65). The Chouteaus were at the heart of a French community that was literate and cultured—a community that could extend *en français* a civil and proper welcome to both princes and senators.

The Americans pushed further and further West and negotiated treaties to remove the indigenous peoples from lands coveted by incoming settlers. Between 1818 and 1825, the U.S. government negotiated land cession treaties removing all of the indigenous peoples from what was to become the State of Missouri. The relocated groups included both those native to the region, including the Osages, Ioways, the Sac, Foxes, and Kansa Indians, and those immigrant tribes from east of the Mississippi, like the Shawnees and Delawares who had been previously dispossessed of their homelands. Here, too, French Métis were closely involved whatever the outcome.

A half century before the Shawnee band associated with de Lorimier had crossed the Mississippi, another group of Shawnee, under the leadership of Métis war chief Pierre Chartier, had moved south. These Shawnee chose in the 1740s to live in Creek Country in defiance of both the French and British governors (R. White, 1991b, pp. 189-192). Two generations later, a group of Shawnees and affiliated Delaware located in the Ohio region had tired of fighting against the Americans and had begun moving to southeastern Missouri. The main Shawnee bands had been in an almost continual state of warfare with the Americans since the War of Independence, culminating with the resistance organized by the Shawnee war leader Tecumseh and his younger brother, "The Prophet," defending their Ohio homeland in one battle after another. In the run-up to the War of 1812, the brothers sought to create a Native American confederation in the Midwest that would have been under British rule and independent of the United States. Tecumseh's dream died with him in 1813, when he was killed in combat during one of the skirmishes occasioned by the British Army's retreat from the Detroit area after their supply lines had been cut off by the American victory at the Battle of Lake Erie. Tecumseh's confederation subsequently disintegrated and the defeated Shawnee bands continued their retreat to the Mississippi, and beyond. Those Shawnee that had crossed the Mississippi a generation earlier under the sponsorship of Pierre-Louis de Lorimier, would soon find themselves forced to relocate once again further west.

By 1815, more than twelve hundred Shawnees occupied comfortable cabins along Apple Creek (north of Cape Girardeau) with flourishing fields, land rich in game, livestock, and slaves. White squatters, however, soon began to make life miserable for these migrant Native Americans. Despite protests on their behalf by local notables, such as traders Pierre Ménard and Auguste Chouteau, and despite attempts by territorial governor William Clark to create a new reservation for the Shawnees and Delawares in western Missouri, the majority of American Missourians would have none of it. Clark's attempts to protect Native American rights secured his defeat in the first gubernatorial election of 1820. A final land-cession treaty was negotiated in 1825 that forced the Shawnees to exchange their lands in Missouri for 14,000 dollars and a tract of land beyond the western border of the state, near the junction of the Kansas and Missouri rivers (Gitlin, 2009, p. 86).

By 1822, a new sense of structure and permanence began to emerge in the region. It was a pivotal year, as a newly consolidated family firm known as the French Fur Company signed a marketing agreement with German immigrant John Jacob Astor and his American Fur Company. Astor had also played a crucial role in establishing a preliminary American presence in the Pacific Northwest, as shall be examined later on in this book. This same year, the Chouteaus' political ally, Senator Benton, pushed Congress to abolish the governmental factory system for the fur trade, thus allowing private companies like those run by Astor and the Chouteaus free reign to trade with the Native Americans. The Chouteaus' privileged trade position was reinforced by the creation of the Superintendence of Indian Affairs headquartered in St. Louis, directed by a Chouteau family friend, William Clark. François Chouteau was placed in control of the family operations at the junction of the Kansas and Missouri rivers in what would become a second Chouteau town, Kansas City (Gitlin, 2009, p. 90), which allowed the Chouteau family to cement its commercial and business empire. The family was also instrumental in ensuring the spread of the Catholic Church, actively sponsoring the building of Kansas City's first church served by Father Benedict Roux, who arrived in 1833. Chouteau's Church was built in 1835, located on the site of the present day Cathedral of the Immaculate Conception.

Canadien Merchants, across the Mississippi and Beyond

The Chouteau clan and most of their closest associates were Louisiana Créoles that had come upriver from New Orleans during the second half of the eighteenth century—but not all. As demonstrated, though the Créoles were distinct from the *Canadiens*, inter-marriage was inevitable over time, e.g., the marriage of Auguste Chouteau to one of Gabriel Cerré's daughters.

The elite of the new community deep in the interior of North America was in fact quite cosmopolitan. St. Louis also drew on the French Huguenot diaspora scattered across northwestern Europe, as exemplified by Charles Gratiot. Gratiot married one of Auguste Chouteau's sisters, Victoire. They had thirteen children together. Born in Lausanne, Switzerland, Gratiot joined the business of one uncle in London, before joining another who had emigrated to Montreal after *La Conquête*.

In 1777 he moved inland to Illinois Country setting up his business in Cahokia, where he proved to be another source of supplies for George Rogers Clark's American and *Canadien* militia men. By 1781, Gratiot joined the Cerré and Chouteau families in St. Louis. Thoroughly bilingual, after the U.S. takeover of Louisiana Gratiot was appointed as judge of the court of common pleas, justice of the peace, and clerk of the board of land commissioners. The latter had a critical role in sorting out the tangled property rights of the pre-American settlers and those of the newcomers.

Other founders of leading St. Louis families included Jean-Pierre Cabanne, who arrived directly from France and married a Gratiot daughter, Julie, in 1799; French-speaking Bartholomew Berthold, who was born in Italy and married Pélagie Chouteau in 1811, the only daughter of Pierre Chouteau, Sr; and finally Bernard Pratte, Sr., who was born in 1771 downriver from St. Louis in the older community of Ste. Geneviève, from an early *Canadien* frontier family—his father was Jean-Baptiste Sebastien Pratte. Bernard married Émilie Sauveur Labadie in 1771. John Jacob Astor's chief lieutenant in running the American Fur Company, Ramsay Crooks, married one of their daughters, Pélagie Émilie Pratte. Bernard Pratte, Sr. served as a general in the Missouri militia in the War of 1812, while one of his sons, Sylvestre, was a major participant in the Santa Fe Trail trade, and another son, Bernard Jr., was elected mayor of St. Louis in 1844 and 1846.

Joseph Robidoux III, date and photographer unknown. The first Joseph Robidoux was born in Laprairie, just southwest of Montreal. The Robidoux set up in St. Louis and became a successful trading family in the Missouri. Joseph Robidoux, the grandson, was born in St. Louis, son of Joseph Robidoux and Catherine Rollet. He first established a trading post at Fort Dearborn Illinois (current site of Chicago), but was driven out by competitors. He then established a trading post at Council Bluffs in Iowa and married Angélique Vaudry in 1813. The American Fur Trade Company bought him out, paying him $1,000 not to compete with them. He then moved back to St. Louis with his family. The American Fur Trade Company hired him to establish a trading post at the Black Snake Hills in Missouri. In turn he hired other French-speaking traders who then pushed westwards. It is close to this post that he founded the town of Saint Joseph, Missouri. Mount Rubidoux near Los Angeles is named after the family.

Other influential trading families of *Canadien* origins in the West included the Robidoux family, for example. Much like the Cerré family who helped the Americans push west into the Louisiana Territory, the Robidoux family would in turn facilitate American expansion over the Rockies on the Oregon Trail, although that was probably not their intention when they arrived in what was Spanish territory. It is important to note that at the time, the future of the West probably appeared to the people there to be up for grabs with Spain, France, and Great Britain being possible contenders along with the U.S.

The history of these families demonstrates the continued expansion westward of the *Canadiens*, always followed by American settlers. The Robidoux emigrated from Montreal during this post-Conquest period and later moved well beyond the Missouri to the Pacific. Joseph Robidoux and his son, also Joseph, left Montreal in 1771, heading inland to St. Louis. By the late eighteenth century, Joseph II was working the middle stretch of the Missouri River in Dakota Territory. Over the following decades the six sons of this younger Joseph along with three of his grandsons would be swarming all over the Santa Fe, Oregon, and California Trails of the American West, while making a great deal of money. The grandson, also Joseph, took over and expanded the family business in the third generation, taking on his younger brothers as they came of age.

As early as 1799, Joseph III and several of his brothers were trading out of their first trading post in the Black Snake Hills, not far from the of the future town site of St. Joseph, in the northwestern corner of Missouri, where he founded a permanent post sometime between 1826 and 1831. Out of St. Joseph, Joseph III, with the help of younger brothers François, Isadore, and Michel, were soon running a major business operation extending up what was becoming the Oregon Trail to Scott's Bluff in western Nebraska. His son, Joseph IV, and two nephews joined them in running a series of trading posts in the Scott's Bluff region. Joseph III also became a real estate developer in 1843, having laid out the new town of Black Snake Hills, renamed St. Joseph for his patron saint, two years later.

Even though the first names of the individual Robidoux family members were rarely identified in the journals of numerous Oregon Trail travelers, those of another set of family members are still visible in the names of nine streets in today's downtown St. Joseph, the eighth largest city of Missouri. They are named for eight of the children of Joseph III (but not Joseph IV) and his second wife: Faraon, Jules, François, Félix, Edmond, Charles, Sylvanie, Messanie, and Angélique. For the Oregon Trail, "St. Joe" became the other major "Jumping-Off Point," after Westport and Independence, Missouri, located some forty miles to the southeast. St. Joseph was also the westernmost terminus of the national railroad network until after the Civil War, while having served as the easternmost terminus of the short-lived Pony Express system, which incidentally was founded by François-Xavier Aubry, who was born in St. Justin, Quebec. Today, St. Joseph offers a complex of historic sites of western Americana including the residence of Joseph Robidoux III, which has since been converted into a museum, the "Patee" house where Jesse James was killed ("Patee" from the French *Pâté de maisons*" or block of houses), and a Pony Express museum. Though there was no street named for him back in "St. Joe," Joseph IV, commonly called Indian Joe, left a different legacy. He had numerous descendants from his three Indian wives. Then there is the chiefly line among the Ioway, descending through the marriage of an older métisse daughter of Joseph III by another Indian women, born at "la Post du Serpent Noir." Named Mary Robidoux, she married Ioway Chief White Cloud.

Brothers Louis and Antoine Robidoux had long since gone off on their own, establishing themselves independently on the upper Rio Grande by the early 1820s, while working the expanding commerce along the Santa Fe Trail. By then, Santa Fe and Taos were under the tenuous authority of a sequence of Mexican governments. In 1843, Louis Robidoux, by then known as Don Luis, after two prosperous decades in New Mexico, moved his Mexican wife and their children to California and set up in San Bernardino County near Riverside, east of Los Angeles. There he re-established his milling and ranching operations. Several years later, his brother, Antoine, made a name for himself leading Colonel Kearny and his U.S. Army troops across the deserts of New Mexico and Arizona into southern California. Increasingly disenchanted with the chaos and arbitrary behavior of the authorities in New Mexico, like most of the sizable *Canadien* community resident on the upper Rio Grande at the time, both brothers opted to support the American invaders (Mattes, 1949, 1965-1972, 1966, 1988).

In summary, the six Robidoux brothers in the third generation became major players in the American expansion into the far west between the 1820s and 1850s. They became one of the more famous *Canadien* families in the history of the West. This involved, first, penetration of the southwest both commercially and ultimately militarily along the Santa Fe Trail, and on to California during the Mexican-American War (Antoine and Louis); and second, the history of the Oregon Trail, especially along its eastern portion between St. Joseph, Missouri, and the Scott's Bluff area near the Nebraska-Wyoming border, where the other brothers worked for their elder brother, the entrepreneur Joseph III, founder of St. Joseph, Missouri.

Other *Canadien* and Créole settlers followed, including Étienne Provost, known as "*l'homme des montagnes*," ("The Man of the Mountains"). He was one of the few *Canadiens* that American journalists and historians actually included among the acclaimed American Mountain Men. Étienne Provost was born at Chambly on the Richelieu River southeast of Montreal in 1785. Amongst other feats, he has been credited with the "discovery" of the Great Salt Lake, that he called "*Le grand lac salé*." A city and river in Utah bear his name, spelled Provo. His activities as a trader and leader of trapping brigades made him a close associate of the Chouteau, Pratte, and Cabanne families. He married Marie-Rose Salle, dite Lajoie, in 1829. Provost served as guide and translator for the expedition of Jean Nicollet and John Frémont in 1839, when they mapped the region between the upper Mississippi and Missouri rivers, and he assisted J. J. Audubon in 1843 when he ascended the Missouri River some three decades after his original Mississippi travels. The comings and goings of the trader Provost appear in journals almost everywhere, from Santa Fe in 1815 to the Missouri trading posts of Fort Union in 1844, and Fort Pierre in 1845 (Hafen, 1965).

Lucien Fontenelle, raised on his family's plantation south of New Orleans, is one other Créole worth mentioning. Like Provost and the Robidoux brothers, Fontenelle appears in virtually all tales of the mountain men and early travelers heading west including those of Captain Bonneville recounted by Washington Irving (1886a). Bonneville, accompanied by his two lieutenants, Joe Walker and Michel Cerré, and managing an expedition of 110 men to the Rocky Mountains in 1832, "now considered himself as having fairly passed the crest of the Rocky Mountains; and felt some degree of exultation in being the first individual that had crossed, north of the settled provinces of Mexico, from the waters of the Atlantic to those of the Pacific, with wagons" (Irving, 1886a, p. 46).

Bonneville's exultation was short-lived as he saw a cloud of dust rising in the distance and soon discovered that the cloud was formed by fifty or sixty mounted trappers: "They were headed by Mr. Fontenelle, an experienced leader, or 'partisan,' as a chief of a party is called in the technical language of the trappers" (Irving, 1886a, p. 47). Fontenelle informed Bonneville that they were riding from the company's trading post on the Yellowstone to the annual rendezvous. Fontenelle proved to be a shrewd negotiator and Bonneville, in Irving's (1886a, p. 48) account, gives him his due: "The captain was somewhat astonished when he saw these [Delaware Indian] hunters, on whose services he had calculated securely, suddenly pack up their traps, and go over to the rival camp."

Three years later in 1835, when two missionaries named Samuel Parker and Marcus Whitman were getting ready to head up the Missouri to scout out and found the Presbyterian mission complex in the Pacific Northwest, they hired Lucien Fontenelle for the first leg of their journey. Thomas Fitzpatrick took over from Fontenelle once they reached Fort Laramie.

When they reached the Green River rendezvous, they no longer needed a paid guide. Two of the tribal groups present had been seeking missionaries for several years and offered to escort them further west. What the missionaries needed was a translator, so they hired the multi-lingual Charles Campo (as in Campeau) whose wife was a Nez Percé. Parker and Campo then followed the Flatheads and Nez Percé back over the Rockies to the Columbia Basin.

In order to accelerate their plans, they agreed that Whitman would return with one of the caravans heading back down to St. Louis to organize the team of missionaries coming out the following year, while Parker would proceed alone on his scouting mission with Campo. Campo was rehired the following year by Whitman, along with Henry Spalding, continuing his working relationship as translator and general assistant for years to come as they established their missions amongst the Nez Percé at Lapwai near the confluence of the Snake and Clearwater rivers, and with the Cayuse at Waiilatpu in the Walla Walla Valley (Josephy, 1965, pp. 130-139, 180). Charles Campo would reappear in the Willamette Valley in May 1843 as one of the French Prairie settlers who was now reidentified as among the "Americans," voting in favor of organizing a Provisional Government.

Tanis C. Thorne cites the Robidoux, Fontenelle, and Chouteau families to make several points (Thorne, 1996) in reviewing relations between the central Siouan nations along the lower Missouri in the eighteenth and early nineteenth centuries and the white traders and the numerous mixed-ancestry families. The mixed-ancestry families discussed also included other families with *Canadien* and Creole antecedents such as the Mongraine, Gonville, Vasseur, Menard, Dorion, Cabanne, Roy, La Flesche, Marchesseau, Sarpy, Revard, Blondeau, Deroin, Derouin, and Papin families (as in Papinville along the Marais de Cignes River of eastern Kansas).

Thorne describes the factors that were both pushing and pulling "the burgeoning French bicultural population of the lower Missouri" up river. "Many, like Robidoux and the second-generation Chouteaus, were drawn into closer residential and kinship relations with native people as a result of their fur-trading activities." One factor pulling them up river was the insistance of the native leadership; "… these alliances were deliberate attempts by chiefly lineages to monopolize the flow of trade goods and thus secure political status by marrying daughters or sisters to merchant-traders" (Thorne, 1996, 127-28). Thorne continues, these "… mixed-blood children knew who their parents were." Even "… the mixed-blood issue of short term relationships … invariably carried their father's names and their mother's status as a badge of their identity" (Thorne, 1996, 157-70).

Thorne notes that "… to move back and forth between Indian and French relatives, as many of the French-Osage appear to have done, was a surprisingly common childhood experience for many biracial persons born between 1800 and 1830. Lucien Fontenelle and Rising Sun's children, for example, stayed close to their mother's people during their early years" (Thorne, 1996, 166-67). Meumbane, whose name had been translated to Rising Sun, was the daughter of Big Elk, the principal chief of the Omaha, while her mother was Pawnee (Thorne, 1996, 157). Their older boys were eventualy sent to St. Louis for schooling, while the younger boys, after their father's death in 1842, learned the trades of blacksmith and wagonmaker at the Indian Manual Labor School at Fort Leavenworth. The oldest son, Logan Fontenelle, by mid-century would become a sometime collaborator, and sometime competitor, for tribal leadership of the Omaha with a fellow mixed-blood, Chief Joseph La Flesche (Thorne, 1996, 167, 225).

This sampling of individual stories should suffice to re-establish the imprint of *les Canadiens* in the history of what is now the American West. Their descendants, and those of many more *Canadiens*, remained and proliferated. They, too, have a right to identify with a history in which their forebears were active participants, along with those of the later arrivals who have succumbed to the usual tendency to write those who were there earlier, out of history.

Following the British Conquest, contrary to the commonly portrayed image, *Canadien* merchants actually continued to play a major role in the North American fur trade, be it ever deeper into the continent and increasingly oriented toward the southwest and out of British North America, into a region which became American territory in 1803. The destiny of the region was certainly not foreseeable and American expansion to the Pacific was not a foregone conclusion. The *Canadien* traders pushed farther west to ensure their livelihoods, not to build empires. Their ties of family, education, and commerce with Montreal continued while, after living under the French crown, they operated first as British, then Spanish subjects, and finally as American citizens.

As British North America receded northward over a half-century of wars and treaties, *Canadien* merchants continued to play a significant but gradually declining role into the early nineteenth century, in the face of their British competitors. The latter had been able to leverage themselves increasingly by insider access to the patronage of British colonial authorities and financial institutions.

In spite of the advantages enjoyed by British entrants to the north, one positive outcome for *Canadien* merchants such as Cerré, de Lorimier, Robidoux, and Étienne Provost, among others operating in the interior during this period, was that they now had equal access to cheaper British trade goods, be it through Montreal, or increasingly the French-speaking port city of La Nouvelle-Orléans near the mouth of the Mississippi. Here, of course, with these *Canadiens* we are speaking of American history: not only were Créole merchants of the older established élite families of Upper Louisiana such as the Chouteau, Gratiot, St. Vrain, and Pratte families able to thrive in the expanding U.S. market place, but *Canadien* and Métis traders and merchants as well. The presence of both Créole and *Canadien* in St. Louis complicates these too-rigid conceptions by which some scholars define the presence of Créole or Métis in the American West based on their theoretical presumptions that limit the emergence of an identity to tightly defined geographical spaces or specific populations that they see as intermarrying over generations. The historical reality of St. Louis, generally overlooked, shows quite clearly that various ethnic groups could co-habitate and still retain their distinctive characteristics. Thus, the *Canadien* and the Créole identities co-existed even if they were intermarrying and shared much in common.

Philipe de Trobriand and the Dakotas

Each work cited alone provides only dribs and drabs of the past that needs to be rewritten, but taken as a whole they reveal how the French-speakers, Creole, *Canadien,* and *Canadien-*Métis, had deeply infused themselves into the social and physical landscape of what became the American West. To illustrate how French survived well after the Americans purchased the Louisiana territory from France, suffice it to quote a U.S. Army officer stationed on the upper Missouri after the Civil War and who happened to be French. Philipe de Trobriand was a French national who fought in the United States Army during the Civil War and wrote an account of his experience in which he provides insight into the presence of French-speaking people in the American West. As a U.S. Army Colonel who had served in the Dakotas during the late 1860s, he had the vantage point of a commander of one of the scattered Army outposts in Sioux country. The de Trobriand family had had a long military tradition. Most recently, his father, Joseph de Trobriand, had been an émigré aristocrat who returned to serve under Napoléon, and then later, with the Restoration and Charles X, he reached the rank of General.

The Colonel's journal was originally published in France as *Vie Militaire dans le Dakota* and later in English as *Military Life in Dakota.* During the Civil War, de Trobriand had been the highest-ranking Frenchman serving in the Union Army, eventually earning the rank of Major General.

After the war he returned to France to publish a book on his experiences with the Union Army during the Civil War, entitled *Quatre Ans de Campagne à l'Armée du Potomac.* In 1867, he came back to the U.S. where he was assigned to a fort on the upper Missouri, in Sioux Country. A significant percentage of the characters identified by Colonel de Trobriand in his description of life around the outpost are French, French-Canadians, *Canadiens,* or "half-breeds" in the English translation. Little background is given on many of them. However, whenever "the half-breeds from the Red River" are mentioned, they usually remain nameless and are often associated with the trouble they cause by selling whiskey to the Indians. Arriving at his new posting in 1867, de Trobriand (1951, p. 48) is struck by the prevalence of the *Canadiens* and the French language:

> There are many French-Canadians here. The traders at Berthold are French with the exception of one. Their people are all of French-Canadian origin. French is their language. The interpreters speak it much better than they do English. The contractor and almost all the carpenters and masons are either French or Canadians. The half-breeds are all sons of Canadian fathers. My native language will certainly be a great help to me here.

Not only do the *Canadiens* and Métis occupy leading roles in trade, the French language had also made important inroads into the Lakota community.

According to de Trobriand (1951, p. 85): "It is notable that the French language is a good deal more common among them in these parts than English, which is a result of a great infusion of Canadian blood in the tribes." The account provided by de Trobriand uncovers the lasting influence of the *Canadiens* and Métis on the Dakotas and the broader American West. When de Trobriand was writing his journal, sixty-four years had passed since the United States acquired the territory with the Louisiana Purchase, and sixty years since Lewis and Clark traveled through, yet French was still the *lingua franca* of the Dakotas. Other *Canadiens* would follow, notably those who would settle in the Frenchtown of Montana, and still others would settle in increasingly isolated pockets in the Dakotas and even Kansas. Their history, not entirely overlooked, however, appears too often to be studied in isolation.

The descendants of the French-speaking *Canadiens* of the Old Northwest continued to push westwards, eventually reaching the Rocky Mountains; however, it would be another branch of French and *Canadien*-Métis who would establish a French-speaking presence in the new Northwest, with the region later taking its name from the ocean bordering its western edge as the Pacific Northwest. Sailing from New York, French-*Canadien* voyageurs would travel to the mouth of the Columbia, while other French-speaking *Canadiens*, their Métis sons, Iroquois, and even a few Scots would cross British North America and the northern Rocky Mountains to the headwaters of the Columbia and Snake Rivers, then down to the Pacific. This territory would be contested by commercial surrogates of the competing empires; Astor's Pacific Fur Company was soon bought out by the North West Company of Montreal, merging a decade later with the Hudson's Bay Company.

In the next chapter we will examine the history of the British (and later Canadian) fur trade and, in doing so, take the role of a latter-day witness to the arrival of French-speaking peoples in the Pacific Northwest.

CHAPTER 6

The Fur Trade and the Métis
of the New Northwest

French names dot the countryside of the Pacific Northwest, dropped in the landscape much like the boulders wistfully discarded by the melting ice of an earlier epoch in the fields of Washington State. In that, the Pacific Northwest differs little from the rest of the continent except east of the Appalachians. Locales such as Coulee City, Coeur d'Alene, The Dalles, or Malheur National Wildlife Refuge are among the dozens of names of clearly French origin in the region, yet the true depth of the French linguistic substrate is masked by the translation of many more topographical designations from French into English. The Bitterroot River and Mountains were the Racine Amère before being translated into English. The French terms were thus kept, albeit often translated, replacing older French designations and even older indigenous names in the region. The French topographical artifacts are the buried linguistic remains of an era when the French language was heard across the continent, stretching from Montreal to the Pacific.

Americans and Canadians often forget that although the officer or bourgeois class in British North America increasingly marginalized the French-speaking *Canadiens* over the late eighteenth and early nineteenth century following *La Conquête*, this did not apply across the board. The North West Company partners and clerks, such as François-Antoine Larocque, Nicolas Montour, Sr., Jules Maurice Quesnel, and HBC officers and clerks such as François Noël Annance, Jean-Baptiste Gagnier, and Pierre Pambrun were good examples of this. There were also men with British and Irish names, such as Richard Grant and John McLoughlin (baptized Jean-Baptiste), whose mother tongue was the French spoken by *Canadiens*.

Secondly, in the United States the *Canadiens* and Upper Louisiana Créoles retained a significantly greater percentage of representatives amongst the bourgeois

Hudson's Bay Company Officials in Express Canoe, Peter Rindisbacher, ca. 1825. Hudson's Bay Company officials whether Governor Simpson or his lieutenants would travel the width and breadth of the fur trade territories inspecting posts and ensuring that business was properly being managed in forts and far flung trading locales.

managing the fur trade than in British North America. In this era, even the English-speaking "bourgeois" or the largely English-speaking, predominantly Scottish factors and administrators of the fur trade under the British were mostly obliged to speak French in the forts and on the trails all across the continent. The French songs of the voyageurs (the French word for travelers) rang across the Columbia, the Walla Walla, the Fraser, and other rivers and tributaries of the Pacific Northwest. Though the employees of the fur trade were not exclusively French-Canadian voyageurs, they were the dominant group that shaped the culture of the fur trade and associated activities on both sides of the eventual border.

In addition to the voyageurs, whose children and grandchildren came to be known as Métis, the largely French-speaking and Catholic Iroquois must be included. Sandwich Islanders, as the indigenous Hawaiians were called in the nineteenth century, were also brought to the Pacific forts to work in turn in the fur trade. Despite this ethnic diversity, French became increasingly the *de facto lingua franca*—truly, a unifying tongue binding the realm of the fur trade. The Oregon Territory came to be an extension of the northern fur trade, its history interwoven with the old *Canayen* and nascent Métis culture.

The fur trade progressed unevenly across North America. The British, the Americans, and their traders were seeking a route to the Pacific. The fur trade in some ways leapfrogged over the continent. In short, the Americans—the state and its leading fur trade baron, John Jacob Astor—sent an overland and a naval contingent to find a more practical route to the lower Columbia. The tortuous, dangerous routes of earlier explorers overland to the Pacific coast included that of Alexander MacKenzie in 1793, as well as that led by Meriwether Lewis and William Clark, the fabled expedition across the continent that reached the Pacific in 1805. John Jacob Astor commissioned a ship that sent clerks and voyageurs from New York in 1810 on the sea route to find the mouth of the Columbia and set up a fur trading outpost for his Pacific Fur Company. Oddly enough, Astor's outpost on the Pacific was staffed primarily by former North West Company partners and *Canadiens*. Shortly after Astor's men established Fort Astoria, David Thompson of the North West Company, who had crossed the Rocky Mountains several years earlier and built a network of trading posts along the tributaries of the middle Columbia River, descended with a party of voyageurs to reach the mouth where they encountered the Astorians. Astor's overland expedition then also reached the Pacific.

The Pacific Northwest fur trade history ties into that of all the other regions of the continent. Even though many older *Canadien* and Métis families were established in the United States, some of whom moved to the Pacific Northwest, many voyageurs came directly from Lower Canada. They included the *Canadiens* from the St. Lawrence, but also the Iroquois and other indigenous voyageurs and "freemen" from Canada. Based on the large amount of quality material published describing daily life in the forts of the Pacific Northwest, it is possible to recount the early history of the Pacific Northwest, describe the fur trade and voyageur culture, and also tie this history, and its political economy, into that of the rest of North America.

Two Accounts: One French, One English

Two published works provide first-hand accounts of the fur traders' lives in the Pacific Northwest and the challenges facing the fur trade companies in establishing control over a territory hotly contested by multiple interested parties. Gabriel Franchère wrote the first, in French. A clerk hired by the Pacific Fur Company, Franchère sailed from New York in 1810 on the first ship John Astor sent to the Pacific coast, the *Tonquin*. Franchère kept a diary and published his account of life in the Pacific Northwest in 1820 in a work entitled *Relation d'un voyage à la*

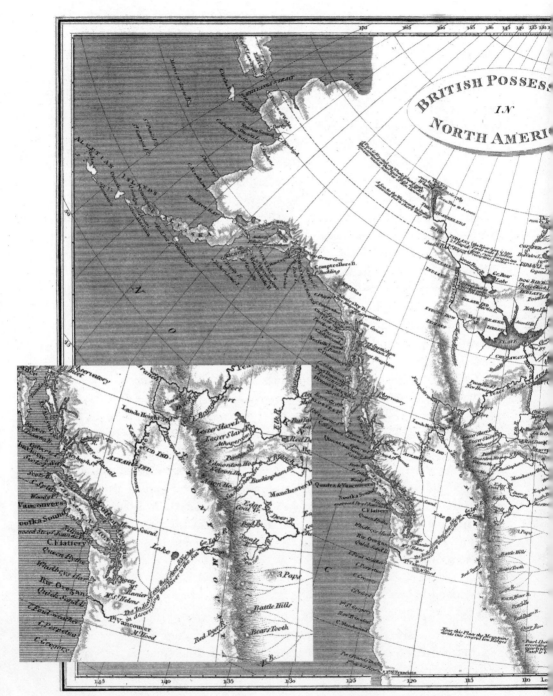

British Possessions in North America, 1809. Though Lewis and Clark preceded the arrival of David Thompson, the British laid claim to the Oregon country. The Hudson's Bay Company acquired the Pacific Fur Trade Company through the North West Company and conducted a flourishing business in the Pacific Northwest with Fort Vancouver as capital of the large Columbia Province. The United States however pushed its claims in the 1840s and eventually the British-American was set in 1846.

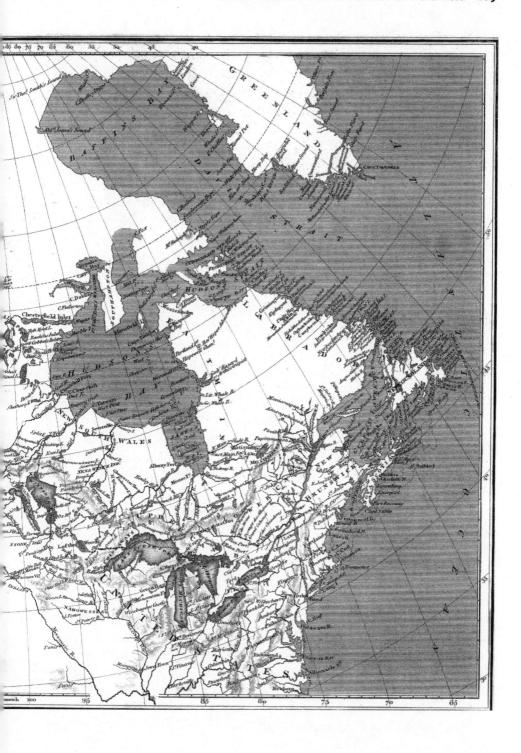

côte du Nord-Ouest de l'Amérique septentrionale, dans les années 1810, 11, 12, 13 et 14. First published in 1820 in Montreal, this work provides a detailed and historically accurate account of the early history of the fur trade in what would become Washington State and Oregon.

Ross Cox, a young Irishman who embarked on Astor's second ship, the *Beaver*, sailing to the Pacific in 1811 from New York, wrote the other account. Cox's book was first published in London in 1831, and was republished later in London and New York in 1832; its long title is *Adventures on the Columbia River: Including the Narrative of a Residence of Six Years on the Western Side of the Rocky Mountains, Among Various Tribes of Indians Hitherto Unknown: Together with a Journey Across the American Continent.* Printed close to two decades after he embarked on the *Beaver*, Cox's work suffered from some historical inaccuracies, notably in dates, and he certainly inflated his role in events; it is nonetheless an informative account of the lives of the men and women working and living in the fur trade of the Pacific Northwest. The importance of French leaves no doubt whatsoever, as the long-suffering Irishman complains that he was losing his English since he was forced to speak French and local indigenous languages while serving as a clerk at one of the outposts of the North West Company.

Coureurs des bois

The history of the fur trade in the Oregon Territory can be traced back to the sixteenth century, when the French sailed up the St. Lawrence River in the 1530s. This river, also called the Rivière du Canada, bore the name applied to the territory of New France surrounding the St. Lawrence Valley. The French hoped to find riches in the Americas, like the gold and silver the Spaniards had discovered in Central and South America. Jacques Cartier brought back what he thought was gold and diamonds that proved to be merely quartz and iron pyrite (better known as fool's gold). The sought-after veins of gold and silver actually lay much further inland and would only be exploited in the nineteenth century .

With religious wars between the majority Catholics and protestant Huguenot minority raging in France for much of the later half of the sixteenth century, the French presence was limited to fishermen continuing to take a share of the harvest from North America's off-shore fisheries. Only in the early seventeenth century did France again seek to establish a permanent settlement—first in Acadia (1604) and then in Quebec (1608) under the leadership of Samuel de Champlain. Though the lands of New France did provide arable lands for settlers, the more valuable commodity of fur and beaver pelts in North America would serve to create the rich felts used to make hats coveted by Europe's elites. The beaver had been over-hunted in Europe and so North America quickly became the primary source of beaver pelts for European consumption.

The colonists brought to New France, few in number compared to the British on the Atlantic coast, quickly understood that more money and adventure could be had from the fur trade than in trying to cultivate the soil. The *coureurs des bois,* or the "forest runners," began to emerge; French colonists would head out into the surrounding forests to trade for furs with the indigenous populations, bringing the pelts back to the colony for personal profit, often to the consternation of New France's Governor. The *coureur des bois* was an unlicensed trader often condemned by French officials, facing either heavy taxation or confiscation of their furs. The colony sought to contain the movement of these *coureurs des bois* and keep a monopoly on trade. Two such individuals would be harshly rebuked by the colonial authorities, leading them to betray France and provide their services to the English resulting in the creation of the oldest of corporations, the Hudson's Bay Company.

In 1659, Médard Chouart des Groseilliers and his brother-in-law, Pierre-Esprit Radisson headed out into the forests to the north of Lake Superior and returned in 1660 with one hundred canoes loaded with furs. Upon their return to the colony, the Governor Pierre Voyer d'Argenson fined them and confiscated their furs for having obtained them without a trade license. Infuriated, the brothers-in-law went to France to seek justice. When their appeal failed, they went to New England and then to London. Radisson and des Groseilliers capitalized on stories that the French had been hearing from the indigenous peoples, stories of the rich supply of beaver pelts and furs available for the taking in the lands south of Hudson Bay.

With this information, English ships guided by des Groseilliers and Radisson sailed to Hudson Bay. Radisson's ship had to return prematurely after being damaged in a storm, but des Groseilliers' ship reached Hudson Bay and returned to London with a shipload of furs. Seeing the success of this first expedition, the King of England created the Hudson's Bay Company in 1670 and granted a Charter to The Governor and Company of Adventurers of England trading into Hudson's Bay. All the territory surrounding Hudson Bay was claimed, including those rivers which drained into Hudson Bay, and the area came to be known as Rupert's Land, after the first Governor, Prince Rupert, cousin of the King. The company was granted an English monopoly over this territory, with des Groseilliers and Radisson leading several more expeditions for the Hudson's Bay Company, although the French sought to push them out of the region. France later enlisted the help of des Groseilliers, who was convinced to return to New France to help the French in their on-going struggle against the English.

The French, in the meantime, seeking to maximize the profits of the fur trade, continued to push deep into the continent to establish forts and to trade directly with the indigenous peoples. By the 1620s, the French had already reached the

Fort William, Lake Superior, Canada West, William Henry Edward Napier, ca. 1857. To ensure their main central transport depot would remain on British territory and avoid paying import or export duties, the North West Company had relocated it from Grand Portage to Fort William following the Jay Treaty of 1796, which ceded Grand Portage and surrounding territory to the United States.

Great Lakes and the territory that is now Michigan, claiming them for France. The Jesuits established a mission at Sault Ste. Marie in the 1660s. Other forts as well as settlements were established in the decades that would follow, including Fort Kaministiquia on the northern shores of Lake Superior where Thunder Bay is now located. Fort Pontchartrain du Détroit was founded in 1701. By the time Detroit had been founded, the French had explored the Ohio Territory, found the headwaters of the Mississippi, and made their way down to the Gulf of Mexico.

The ethos of the *coureurs des bois* would shape the soon-to-emerge voyageur culture. Few women came to New France in the early decades so the *coureurs des bois* would often take indigenous women as wives, adopting the technology and ways of life of the surrounding peoples to ensure their success in trade. The *coureurs des bois* as free traders declined relatively following the British conquest of New France but also owing to the increasing distance that had to be traveled for furs. *Voyageurs* as employees came to replace them somewhat, but this assertion must be qualified.

In what became the Canadian West, over time, the growing Métis communities, especially those living off of the buffalo herds of the northern prairies, were operating more as indigenous bands or as "*les gens libres*," while continuing to trade with the increasingly consolidated larger companies by contracting as independent suppliers or customers. This would also be true but to a much lesser extent in the territory claimed, but not yet effectively occupied by the U.S., where the situation was much more fluid. Partnerships formed, dissolved, competed against each other, then re-formed, or merged. Individuals would often contract with one partnership one year and another the next.

The documentation available is also revelatory. Those employees whose names show up in the registers of the large American and Canadian firms, as multi-year or seasonal workers, are only the tip of the iceberg. Catholic Church records on both sides of the eventual border and the U.S. census show that these increasingly independent communities, working themselves ever deeper into the continent, included a broader population base than simply an assortment of families of current and former employees of these enterprises.

Furthermore, as the volume of trade increased and the economy of the west diversified it penetrated the regions west of the middle Missouri and the Rocky Mountains where alternate modes of transport were called for. The son or grandson of many a voyageur became a plainsman, working as a packer with horses and mules, doing more mundane and settled chores offered by small-scale ranching or getting hired on as someone else's cowhand.

The distances the fur trade had to cover were so great that an individual trader with limited capital could not compete head-on with larger, better-capitalized trading consortia. Some voyageurs, for instance, would never return to their original homeland once they had successfully worked and lived in the upper *Pays d'en Haut*, while others would retire and go back to the St. Lawrence Valley in Quebec. Political, economic, and geographical forces thus encouraged the emergence of a consolidated partnership such as the unwieldly North West Company, one that would become the main competitor to the Hudson's Bay Company as they expanded further inland.

Français to Canadien

The term "Canada" from the outset of the colony of New France designated the colony along the banks of the St. Lawrence River. The term "Acadie" was used to designate the colony centered on Port Royal in what is now Nova Scotia. Originally composed of soldiers, administrators, and settlers, the local inhabitants in the colony of Canada were calling themselves *Canadien* (often pronounced *canayen*) by the end of the seventeenth century, while those in the Maritimes called themselves *Acadien*. *Canadien* was used well into the twentieth century in Quebec and elsewhere in North America, and was the ethnonym of the country-born inhabitants of French or Métis ancestry living in the distant reaches of the continent and the St. Lawrence Valley. It was a self-identification distinguishing someone from people born in France, England, or in English-speaking North America. The settlers in French Louisiana who would refer to themselves as Créole, a term also used to designate those born in the colonies, were an exception. The term "Métis" or "*Bois-brulé*" became more popular in the nineteenth century to identify the children and grandchildren of the *Canadien* voyageur and their indigenous wives. In 1849, Bonnycastle (1849, p. 144) wrote:

> To this day, where, in the interminable wilderness, all trace of French influence is buried, the Indian reveres the recollections of his forefathers respecting that gallant race; and, wherever the canoe now penetrates, the Solemn and silent shades of the vast West, *the Bois Brulé or Mixed offspring of the Indian and the Frenchman*, may be here awakening from the slumber of ages with carols derived from the olden France as he paddles swiftly and merrily along (emphasis is ours).

Historical evidence shows that such terms were widely used, including in Quebec, the Great Lakes area, and Illinois Country ("*Le Pays des Illinois*"). The term "*Bois-Brulé*" appears in Tocqueville's letter of 1831 to his brother Hypolythe as describing the way in which the offspring of a Canadian and an Indigenous woman self-identified in the area of Detroit (Tocqueville 1973). The term "*Bois-Brulé*" also appears in the notebook of a prospector leaving Quebec for the Saguenay region in 1830 and who describes his Métis guide Charles Verreau as a "bois brûle (Métif)." By the 1840s, Métis of the Great Plains described themselves as a "new nation," most famously under the leadership of Louis Riel, who envisioned himself as a leader for all Métis of North America, while appointing Gabriel Dumont as the specific leader to the North Western Métis.

Gabriel Franchère's writings, notably his 1820 work, *Relation d'un voyage à la côte du Nord-ouest de l'Amérique Septentrionale, dans les années 1810, 11, 12, 13, et 14*, help uncover the social processes that gave rise to the Métis community. In a footnote, he drops a reference to a François Landry, an employee killed while wintering in the mountainous back country to the south of the Walla Walla River, a man he calls "*un métif d'une humeur acariâtre, qui s'était marié à une femme du pays*" [a Métif with a sour disposition who had married a country woman] (1820, p. 216). This term predated Métis and signified somebody of mixed ancestry (or heritage). Franchère's discussion of Landry follows an incident whereby a child was heard to yell out to Franchère's party in French, "*arrêtez donc, arrêtez donc*" [Stop, please stop] while on their return trek to Canada (1820, p. 214). The child was traveling with his mother (Marie Dorion), the widow of Pierre Dorion, a voyageur who had been killed over the winter.

Louis Riel, ca. 1865

Fluent and literate in both French and English, Louis Riel had played an instrumental role in negotiating the terms for the accession of the province of Manitoba—that contained the Red River and a significant Métis population—into the Canadian federation, while trying to get the rights of the Métis enshrined in the new constitutional order. Still facing the outrage that the execution of Thomas Scott had raised in Ontario, Louis Riel fled Canada to seek refuge in the United States. In 1884, another respected Métis leader, Gabriel Dumont led a delegation to Montana to convince Louis Riel, to return to Canada to once again lead the Métis in their struggles against the expanding Canadian colonial state. The grandson of a *Canadien* Voyageur, the Métis commander Gabriel Dumont (1837-1906) was the military leader of the second resistance movement, the North-West Rebellion, that pitted Métis forces against the Canadian state. Dumont was raised as a hunter and was reputed to have spoken six indigenous languages in addition to French. Though the Métis forces were largely outnumbered in the first battle of 1885, Dumont successfully led the Métis in the Battle of Duck Lake. The Métis resistance, however, lost the four-day Battle of Batoche, the Métis forces having run out of ammunition in their battle against the North-West Mounted Police. To seek to avoid greater bloodshed, Louis Riel surrendered to the police forces and was subsequently tried for treason, found guilty and hanged in 1885. The Métis forces and resistance in disarray, Dumont could not continue the armed resistance, but managed to escape to Montana. Dumont returned in 1888, his land claim only recognized in 1902. He died four years later. Following these two episodes of resistance, many Métis were issued "scrip" a promise of land, but left destitute, many had no choice but to sell this scrip to speculators, leaving many Métis dispossessed on the margins of society, often forced to occupy lands set aside for future roads (hence the designation that was later given to the Métis as the "road allowance people") or seeking new homes farther north. Over a century later, the Métis are still seeking justice in the Canadian legal system as will be discussed.

About Gabriel Dumont, Louis Riel wrote: "Mr. Gabriel Dumont is devoted to me with such dedication, praise God, that would be a hard one to surpass. He believes that I should be recognized as the Métis leader for all Métis of British North America. He himself would be the leader of the Métis in the Northwest within and beyond the Montagnes de Roche (Rocky Mountains), *to the sea*. His position is that the Métis of Manitoba had the seventh of the land in the province: hence the Métis of British-Colombia are also entitled to their seventh land, since their title is absolutely the same" (Riel, 1985, p. 121).

Franchère's account hints at the emergence of a Métis identity, showing that the children of the voyageurs were learning French, even speaking it from a very young age. The Rocky Mountains were clearly not a barrier to culture; the entire territory from the Pacific to Fort William (i.e., Thunder Bay) and the Ottawa River had a shared culture and language that predated its nationalistic expression by the Red River Métis and stretched across the continent, a culture and a language as crucial to the voyageurs as the piles of furs in the birchbark canoes.

Conquest

The conquest of New France by the British (England and Scotland became one kingdom under the Act of Union of 1707) occasioned the restructuring of the fur trade, yet the successful French model was maintained. The British defeated the French forces on the Plains of Abraham outside the fortifications of Quebec in 1759. The French and the British signed the Treaty of Paris in 1763, bringing to an end the Seven Years' War, known significantly as "The French and Indian Wars" in the United States. Cut off from the French market and French capital, the fur trade required new markets and new sources of capital. A new Anglo-Scot merchant elite stepped into this vacuum, forming a series of partnerships that first competed and then became a consortium called the North West Company at the end of the eighteenth century. The Scots who came to work for the Montreal-based North West Company were, according to Ross Cox, young men from the junior branches of "respectable Scottish families" (1832, p. vii). If these young men proved their mettle as apprentices, they were eventually promoted to partners. Only a few partners were of French background, but the workforce would be dominated by the *Canadien* laborer, the voyageur, supplemented by Iroquois freemen and, in the Pacific Northwest, indigenous men from Hawaii.

The North West Company's structure encouraged apprentices and clerks to strive to maximize their success in the fur trade. Whereas an employee in the Hudson's Bay Company received a fixed salary and had no hope of ever becoming a proprietor, the clerks and employees of the North West Company were induced to labor wholeheartedly for the good of the Company with the prospect of better pay and eventually even becoming a company partner. Ross Cox, in describing the mindset of the clerks of the North West Company with whom he worked, claimed, "Courage was an indispensable qualification, not merely for the casual encounters with the Indians, but to intimidate any competitor in trade with whom he might happen to come in collision" (1832, p. viii). The employees of the Hudson's Bay Company had no vested interest in risking their lives for the sake of the Company, and "when challenged to single combat by a North-Wester, refused: alleging as a reason, that they were engaged to trade for furs, and not to fight with fellow-subjects" (Cox, 1832, p. viii). The drive of the North West

Company pushed them over the Rocky Mountains and down the Columbia. Even a New York-based potential competitor, John Jacob Astor's Pacific Fur Company founded in 1810, recruited partners and employees of the North West Company to try and compete against the same North West Company, which had already established a presence in the Oregon Territory when it founded Spokane House in what is now Eastern Washington State, among several other outposts in the Columbia Basin.

Though the upper echelons of the North West Company were predominantly Anglo-Scottish (and significantly more Scottish than English), the partners preferred to continue hiring French voyageurs over their own countrymen. Ross Cox, in his firsthand account of time spent working for the North West Company, stresses that the *Canadiens* were hired as canoe-men or *engagés*, as they were more submissive and easier to govern than English or Scottish employees. "These men were French Canadians, remarkable for obedience to their superiors; and whose skill in managing canoes, capability of enduring hardships and facility of adapting themselves to the habits and peculiarities of the various tribes, rendered them infinitely more popular in the eyes of Indians than the stubborn, unbending, matter-of-fact Orkney men, into whose ideas a work of supererogation never entered" (Cox, 1832, p. xii).

Carolyn Podruchny (1999, p. 47), in her analysis of the relations between the employees and the bourgeois of the fur trade, notes that a strong paternalism cut through the relations of the masters and servants of the fur trade, whereby "Masters tried to enforce obedience, loyalty, and hard work among voyageurs, while the voyageurs struggled to ensure that their working conditions were fair and comfortable, and that masters fully met their paternal obligations."

In fact, resistance did occur, both symbolically and materially. However, the main tool of resistance the employees had was desertion (Podruchny, 1999, pp. 62-63): the men could simply abandon their posts. A number of reasons might motivate desertion, be it to negotiate better terms to their contracts or simply to have some time to recover if sick. Franchère tells the story of how three men who deserted were taken prisoner by a local indigenous nation, before being freed by the company who paid their ransom on the condition that they return to work (Franchère, 1820, p. 103).

As a conquered people largely abandoned by the old French elite, the *Canadiens* understood that they could not expect the same rights as their employers, the men they called the bourgeois, but they *were* able to impose their language. Cox himself had no choice but to speak French, lamenting that he was losing his English to a mix of French and indigenous languages: "Bad French and worse Indian began to usurp the place of English." He added, "and I found my conversation gradually becoming a barbarous compound of various dialects" (Cox, 1832,

Gabriel Franchère. Hired as a clerk to serve in Astor's Pacific Fur Company, Gabriel Franchère traveled with voyageurs and clerks from Montreal to New York and boarded a ship that took them to the mouth of the Columbia River where they established Fort Astoria. He returned when the North West Company took over the Pacific Fur Company, and wrote a book based on his notes on his experiences on the Columbia River. He returned to work for Astor as chief agent of the American Fur Company in Montreal from 1828 to 1834, and then went to Sault Ste. Marie to direct the company's agency before moving to New York to serve as Pierre Chouteau, Jr.'s agent in this city.

p. 218). In his book, he freely throws out French terms and provides many examples of the partners speaking French. One example was a Mr. McDonald who, when angered, would rail in a mixture of English, Gaelic, French, and indigenous languages. As Ross Cox notes, McDonald spoke Scottish Gaelic as a child in the Highlands, learned English in Scotland, and then had to learn French when his family moved to Canada. He then was hired as an apprentice clerk with the North West Company, moving extensively over ten years and acquiring the languages of the indigenous peoples of the territory where he was working, rarely spending more than a winter in any one location. "He was subject to temporary fits of abstraction," Cox claimed, "during which the country of his auditory was forgotten, and their lingual knowledge set at defiance by the most strange and ludicrous mélange of Gaelic, English, French, and half a dozen Indian dialects" (Cox, 1832, p. 164). The same Finan McDonald had even taken a wife from the Spokane nation, fathering two children by her. The oldest of these children, a daughter named Helene, stayed in the region later having children of her own. Clearly, the partners who stayed integrated into the local population, adopting aspects of language and culture of both the fur traders and the indigenous peoples they traded and lived with, over the course of their career and new lives out West.

Life in the Fur Trade Era

The early life of the *Canadien* voyageur in the Pacific Northwest is well known in both English and French thanks to Cox and Franchère who describe attempts to establish a competing company, the New York-based Pacific Fur Company. Franchère was on the *Tonquin*, the ship that left New York in 1810 and reached the Pacific Coast in 1811. The Pacific Fur Company was a short-lived enterprise; with the outbreak of the War of 1812, the British/Canadian partners of the American firm orchestrated the sale of the company in 1813 to its rival, the North West Company. The subsequent arrival of a British ship ensured British control of the post that had been established, Astoria. Of note, however, is that the captain of the British ship the *Racoon*, Captain Black, was disappointed to learn that the Pacific Fur Company had already been sold to British interests, as he had expected to take Astoria and the trading company as a "splendid prize." Captain Black proceeded with the formalities of taking possession of Astoria for his Britannic Majesty, renaming the settlement Fort George. He thereby inadvertently re-established America's slim claim to the region by the terms of the December 1814 treaty, which required a return of territory to status "*ante bellum*."

Warring Companies

Wars between French and English colonies, then between Great Britain and the U.S. were replaced by a simmering conflict between two British companies, one that escalated into a deadly battle. The outcome was a further definition of the Métis identity in nationalistic terms in the Northwest part of the continent. The North West Company aggressively pushed westwards, disregarding the claims that the Hudson's Bay Company had on the territory draining into the bay. With operations extending across the vast continent, the North West Company needed to establish a halfway point somewhere between Montreal and the extreme West, a point where the furs moving east could intersect the trade goods being shipped west. The French had established Fort Kaministiquia (Thunder Bay), but abandoned it during the war leading up to the conquest of New France. The North West Company established a fort at Grand Portage not far from the old site, in what is now the northeastern tip of Minnesota. The Jay Treaty of 1794 negotiated between Great Britain and United States, however, placed Grand Portage on the American side of the border. And as the American traders intended to assert control of the fur trade on their side of the border, the North West Company moved its new transshipment center well inside the British territories and established Fort William in the locale of the old French Fort Kaministiquia to serve as its new midway point.

The Lard Eaters

Fort William came to define two groups of *Canadiens* working in the fur trade: the *"mangeurs de lard"* (the lard eaters), and the *"hivernants"* (the winterers). Franchère, in describing Fort William in 1814, recounts how different groups sorted themselves out within and around the fort. Inside the fort were the partners—the bourgeois—who were the elite of the fur trade. Outside the fort, the employees camped with the lard eaters on the eastern side of the fort and the winterers on the western side.

The reference to pork was an indicator of the two groups' very different lifestyles. The pork eaters were those *Canadiens* who would return to the St. Lawrence Valley, consuming pork and other produce from the farms of Lower Canada, *le Pays d'en Bas*. Salted lard played a comparable role to pemmican: it was high in energy and could be preserved for extended periods. For the winterers, eating pork (as well as beef and mutton) would have been an extremely rare event. Cox describes how the men, the voyageurs, were given eight pounds of meat every day—ten if the meat contained bones. The mainstay of their diet would have consisted of seasonal wild game such as bison, moose, and deer, as well as ducks and geese in the fall. However, in his description of life in the Columbia, Cox describes a diet that also relied on both horse and dog meat to supplement wild game and salmon. Elsewhere, pemmican would have been a mainstay, as the dried bison meat mixed with fat and berries would have been a high-energy food that could be kept for years without going rancid.

Given the voyageurs' extreme physical activity, either paddling all day or carrying ninety-pound packs of produce and furs on portages, these large quantities of meat were necessary for the men to carry out their grueling daily tasks. However, Franchère (1820, p. 123 and 126) does mention how some of the men in Astoria suffered from scurvy, noting later that the "naturals" (indigenous peoples of the Columbia) ate crabapples either to avoid coming down with scurvy, or to cure an individual already suffering from scurvy (Franchère, 1820, p. 177).

The distinction the men made between themselves also highlights their expectations in joining the fur trade. The winterers did not always expect to return to their original homelands once they had completed their contracts; it gradually dawned on many of them that they would remain in the distant territories, so they took local wives and raised children who would in turn become employees of fur trade companies. Despite this separation from their places of origin, the men maintained the language and passed on the songs, cultural practices, and folklore of their ancestors. Many knew that they would live and die in the upper country. Even when the fur trade came to an end, some descendants of the voyageurs stayed, eschewing a return to the lower country that had become foreign to them or simply because they could not afford it. This contributed further to their identity, often nurturing a disdain for the lard eaters and their often too brief passage in the *Pays d'en Haut*.

The Voyageurs Sail the Pacific

The preference given to the French-speaking *Canadien* in the fur trade is demonstrated by the Pacific Fur Company's recruitment of men from Montreal, boarding them on a ship that would travel from New York to the West Coast. The ship headed around the tip of South America, stopping in the Sandwich Islands (Hawaii) to pick up supplies and native inhabitants of the islands to work in the fur trade. Both Cox and Franchère describe their voyages to the mouth of the Columbia, and how the French voyageurs were the dominant group in the fur trade, outnumbering the Iroquois, Métis, and indigenous workers from Hawaii in the early decades of the nineteenth century. Cox emphasizes that French was the language of work on the Pacific Coast, and that he himself spoke French to the voyageurs. Other French-speaking people, who did not arrive on those company boats, also established themselves in the region.

Ross Cox recounts the story of Jacques Hoole, a French soldier who fought in Scotland at the battle of Culloden in 1745 before being exchanged as a prisoner of war. Hoole then served as a soldier in New France, fighting on the Plains of Abraham and helping to carry the dying French general, the Marquis de Montcalm, into Quebec. He became a farmer after the Conquest, and then re-enlisted to help repel the American invasion during the Revolutionary War. At the end of the war, with his wife having proven "faithless" and his children "disobedient," he went off into the interior, refusing to join the North West Company. He ended up in the Pacific Northwest as a free hunter called "Father" by the local inhabitants. Cox notes that the *Canadiens* treated him with great respect, and would greet him by saying "*Bon jour, père*" (1832, p. 172). [Good day, father.] He was later found murdered in the territory of the Flatheads, having reached a venerable age of some ninety-two years.

After terminating employment or retiring, some voyageurs chose to stay in the Northwest Territories. They were called the freemen, men who had finished their contracts, and they would continue trading with their former employer. Franchère names a number of such freemen who had settled in the West after their contracts were completed. He mentions a man by the name of Ant. [Antoine] Desjarlais, who was guide for the North West Company before becoming a freeman in 1805. He settled in the Lac la Biche territory of what is now Alberta, living there with his wife and children. He provided Franchère's expeditions with eggs, fifty pounds of meat, and twenty pounds of tallow (Franchère, 1820, p. 246). Desjarlais was clearly a *Canadien*, as he asks Franchère to read to him two letters that he had in his possession for two years, not knowing their contents. They turned out to be letters he had received from his sister living in Verchères in Quebec.

The families of such men would become the nuclei of Métis families across the West, including the Oregon Territory. At Fort William, Franchère notes that a number of retired men who had been worn down by the fur trade without accumulating any savings or credit had chosen to settle on the outskirts of the Fort with their families. They grew a bit of corn and potatoes, fishing for their subsistence and refusing to return to their villages empty-handed. Franchère identifies how, for these men, returning penniless would probably be viewed as proof to their relatives and friends back home that they had been imprudent in their conduct (Franchère, 1820, p. 271), so they prefer to live out their final years in the shadow of the fort. Again, these men's children would form the core of future Northwest Métis communities. Though it is the Métis community of the Red River Valley that is best known, other Métis communities were clearly forming on both sides of the Rocky Mountains, and both north and south of the 49th parallel.

Daily Life

The daily life of both the voyageurs and the bourgeois, the clerks and partners of the Company, was challenging. Ross Cox (1832, pp. 198-199) summarizes the miseries suffered for the sole purpose of providing Europe with the beaver pelts required for beaver hats, beaver bonnets, and beaver cloaks, demonstrating to his British audience his clear disdain for the voyageurs:

> From that moment I began to balance between the comparatively pleasing uncertainties of civilized life, and the sad realities to which the life of an Indian trader is exposed. On the one side I placed—exile starvation, Indian treachery, piercing colds, or burning heats, with the damp earth too often for a bed; no society for a great portion of the year, except stupid Canadian voyageurs, or selfish, suspicious natives: ideas semi-barbarized by a long estrangement from the civilized world; and should I even survive these accumulated evils, and amass a few thousands, to find on returning to my native country, the friends of my youth dead, and myself forgotten; with a broken-down and debilitated constitution; and Indian wife with numerous offspring, whose maternal tint, among the proud and the unthinking, too often subjects them to impertinent insult and unmerited obloquy.
>
> To a British reader it would be useless to enumerate the opposing items, or to mention on which side the scale preponderated: it is enough to say that I determined on the earliest opportunity to exchange dog for mutton, and horse for beef; icy winters and burning summers for our own more temperate climate; and copper beauties for fair ones.

Cox was literate and educated; choosing to return to his homeland, he wrote and published his memoirs of the time spent in the Columbia River region. The men that he worked with—the French *Canadien* voyageurs and their children— would remain. Theirs is the story we seek to explore.

Voyageurs at Dawn, Frances Anne Hopkins, 1871. Frances Anne Hopkins depicts the voyageurs getting ready at the crack of dawn, likely for another full day of paddling. Hopkins paid close attention to detail, notably the "cassettes" or wooden traveling boxes used to hold and transport personal belongings.

C'est l'aviron qui nous mène

Ross Cox's detailed description of the voyageurs is particularly relevant to our account as it describes the men who first came to the Oregon Territory, the ancestors to the families in this historical account. The voyageur's main task was to paddle the boats and birchbark canoes and periodically carry them and haul the cargo around rapids or from one river to another. Each canoe held six to ten men, with the most skilled paddlers (placed at the bow and stern) earning one thousand pounds per year, compared to six hundred per year for those in the middle. Each year the men received a suit of clothes and a three-pound bundle of tobacco leaves wrapped in cloth and twine called a "carrot." They were also given daily food rations consisting of the typical eight-to-ten pounds of meat, consisting of two large geese or four ducks, or an equivalent quantity of fish. The men ate almost solely meat, only occasionally consuming rarities like rice and flour—and the occasional glass of rum on special or especially exhausting days. Despite these provisions, Cox notes that few of the men had any savings. The only place to buy any extra clothes or other goods was the company store where prices were inflated. The North West Company encouraged the men to get into debt as soon as they entered the fur trade (Podruchny, 1999, p. 64), as the cost of the goods they were selling at significantly higher prices more than covered the salaries being paid to the men. Podruchny (1999, p. 65) notes that, "The French Duke de La Rochefoucauld Liancourt, traveling through North America in the late eighteenth century, commented that the NWC encouraged vice among their men by paying them in merchandise, especially luxuries and rum, so that none of them ever earned a decent wage."

They would also use the money to support their wives and children, buy horses, or even gamble. Cox (1832, p. 306) nonetheless held their work in high esteem: "I know of no people capable of enduring so much hard labour as the Canadians, or so submissive to superiors." Quite often, on trips lasting six months, the men would paddle every day from daybreak to nightfall without a single day off, even for the Sabbath. They would sing their rowing songs, the *chanson à aviron,* both to help them endure the most arduous trips and to provide a steady beat to guide them in their paddling. These songs were brought with the first French settlers to North America from France, with some dating as far back as the European Middle Ages.

Voyageur Clothing

In cold and inclement weather the voyageurs would wear a knee-length capot, a garment made of a blanket and tied with the Assomption (or arrow) Sash, a colorful belt made of worsted wool with an arrow design (*la ceinture fléchée*). The sash was named after the region of Quebec where artisanal production was concentrated. These sashes were then traded far into the interior, a commodity prized by both *voyageurs* and indigenous peoples. It was not only esthetical and with prestigious meanings, it was a practical and handy garment used to hold knives, smoking-bags filled with tobacco and a calumet pipe, and other goods the voyageurs needed. The Métis sons of the French-Canadians adopted these sashes as a colorful symbol of their identity. The men would wear leather or cloth trousers, striped cotton shirts, and a woolen or fur hat, the latter being used only in very cold weather.

Métis came also to be known for the intricate flower embroidery and beadwork they wore—artwork that originated from the St. Lawrence Valley Catholic missions—as they traveled with nuns and traders through the Great Lake Métis communities to finally reach settlements further West. On the history of Métis Flower Beadings Brasser observed: "it can be demonstrated that the correct connection is with the Roman Catholic Missions, beginning in the St. Lawrence River and moving West through the Great Lakes missions. Small and stylized semi-floral designs were used by the French Métis who came from the Great Lake missions" (Brasser, 1985, p. 225). All the men, voyageurs, and clerks alike, had adopted the indigenous people's moccasins as the footwear of choice.

Les Bois-Brulés

The children of the voyageurs (or other Europeans) by indigenous mothers were called by different names. "Half-breeds" became the predominant expression in English to describe the children of English or Scottish (often of Protestant faith) and Native American women. The French terms used, as mentioned earlier, were typically *Sang-mélé, métis, mitchif, metchis,* or *Bois-Brulés* ("Burnt Wood") to describe the descendants of French and Catholic men and indigenous women of various Nations. Cox could be quite generous in his praise of the *Bois-Brulés,* stating that "They are good canoe-men, and excellent hunters, remarkably active either on horseback or on foot; brave, daring, rather passionate, and, while they possess all the vivacity of their father, they at times manifest a slight symptom of Indian ferocity; this however is only evinced when any insulting allusion is made to their mixed origins" (Cox, 1832, p. 310).

The sons of the proprietors or partners were often sent to Canada or overseas to be educated, learning both English and French. The sons of the voyageurs, though, would have had the option of possibly being hired by the company. Cox also provides insight into the lives of the daughters of the voyageurs and other company employees, lauding their expertise in sewing as they fashioned coats, trousers, vests, gowns, shirts, shoes, and the other clothing used in the fur trade. These women were often kept as housekeepers in the employ of the lords, but Cox (1832, p. 310) notes that "they still continue the savage fashion of squatting on the ground at their meals, at which their fingers supply the place of forks."

Though subject to disdain, the children of voyageurs or clerks and indigenous women would play a vital role in the expansion of the fur trade into Washington State. In 1806, Jacques (Jaco) Raphaël Finlay, the son of a North West Company trader and a Saulteaux "country wife," crossed the continental divide and reached the source of the Columbia River. He drew a map of the region, a map later used by David Thompson to begin mapping the Columbia basin. Thompson ultimately became the first official European to travel down the entire length of the Columbia River in 1811 with his crew of voyageurs. After a falling out, Finlay was once again hired by the North West Company and charged by David Thompson with siting and building a post in the Spokane territory in 1810. Jocko, guided by the Spokane, found a location at the confluence of the Spokane and Little Spokane Rivers and built a post for the North West Company that would eventually become Spokane House.

The Iroquois

In addition to the French-Canadian voyageurs, the Iroquois were actively recruited by the North West Company to work in the fur trade following the smallpox epidemic that had decimated the indigenous populations in the North-West Territories in 1781-1782. The first reports of Iroquois in the West date to the

Canoe Manned by Voyageurs Passing a Waterfall, Frances Anne Hopkins, 1869. Depicted in the center of the canoe are the artist and her husband Edward Hopkins, a Hudson's Bay Company official. The canoe in the painting was a "bastard" (bâtard) intermediate in size between the "master" (maître) canoe used in the Great Lakes and the St. Lawrence and the northern canoe used when traveling up small rivers in distant places. A technology borrowed from Indigenous peoples, the largest birchbark canoes could carry several tons of freight and crew, while still light enough for a few people to portage.

1790s. The Iroquois who migrated west from Quebec were mostly Catholic and fluent in French, in addition to their mother tongue and often other languages or dialects. Unlike the French voyageurs, the Iroquois often moved west with their families in tow. Franchère mentions an Iroquois family that arrived by canoe with Pillet and McLennan, along with a trapper, Régis Bruguier.

Iroquois families moving west with the fur trade had reached the Pacific Coast in the 1810s. Their proficiency in French is revealed in Cox's description (Cox (1832, p. 315) of a fight he had with an Iroquois employee who called Cox *crapaud* (French for "toad"). This Iroquois man also likely spoke Mohawk or another Iroquois language as he referred to himself as Teewhattahownie instead of George.

Hauling a boat up a rapid, probably Columbia River, Henry James Warre, ca. 184. While birch bark canoes could be easily lifted out of the water and carried around rapids, boats made of solid wood had to be dragged. Henry J. Warre was a British Captain was sent to the Oregon Territory along with Lieutenant M. Vavasour on "special duty" (i.e. as a spy) to report back to the British government as to Dr. McLoughlin's attitude vis-à-vis the American settlers. Warre produced a number of sketches and paintings illustrating life in the final year of the territory, while still under HBC control. Warre, later knighted, served in the Crimean War and then was sent to New Zealand.

Conflict and Warfare

In times of conflict, the voyageurs were often called upon to serve as soldiers. Ross Cox provides many examples of individuals injured or killed in skirmishes with the local indigenous communities, but one example that stands out is a conflict that arose in the interior. An expedition was trapped on an island in the Columbia River after a tense encounter where local warriors tried to rob them of their trade goods. The expedition, expecting to be attacked, spent the night taking turns keeping watch. The voyageurs assembled the next morning and prepared for war. The commander, Mr. Keith, "reminded them of the many glorious deeds performed in Canada by their gallant French ancestors, a few hundreds of whom often defeated as many thousand Indians; and concluded by expressing a hope that they would not degenerate from the bravery of their forefathers" (Cox, 1832, p. 176).

The men replied with three cheers and affirmed they would obey his orders. Then Keith addressed the Hawaiians and asked them if they would fight. The muskets were then distributed and the men received an additional glass of rum before setting out across the river to the northern shore. Standing firm, the expedition arrived at a negotiated peace with the opposing forces, the Walla Walla and their allies. By Cox's account, the expedition was saved by the actions of the young Walla Walla chief who convinced his people not to fight and to make peace with the expedition. This being done, the expedition distributed various trade goods to cement the new alliance. As Cox notes, "We gave the man who had been wounded in the shoulder a chief's coat; and to the relations of the men who were killed we gave two blankets, two fathoms of cloth, two spears, forty bullets and powder, with a quantity of trinkets, and two small kettles for his widow. We also distributed nearly half a bale of tobacco among all present, and our youthful deliverer was presented by Mr. Keith with a handsome fowling piece, and some other valuable article" (Cox, 1832, p. 182). This particular case demonstrates that the voyageurs and other company officials could be called upon to play a number of roles, including, if necessary, bearing arms in service of the company.

Marriage and Alliance

The *Canadien* and Métis voyageurs invariably took wives in the upper country, but this was not necessarily an easy task. Ross Cox provides an intriguing example of the effort required to gain the respect of a woman's kin group and forge the necessary alliances to ensure a successful courtship and marriage. Pierre Michel, the son of a *Canadien* by an indigenous mother, was a hunter and a translator who had accompanied the Flatheads on two war campaigns, and "by his unerring aim and undaunted bravery won the affection of the entire tribe" (Cox, 1832, p. 128).

The wife that he wanted was the niece of the hereditary chief; however, in order to be married, a council was called, as another man also wanted to marry the young woman. The chief argued in Michel's favor, noting how he had fought with them and how they would be united as brothers after the marriage. The council agreed to the marriage between Michel and the niece (Cox, 1832, p. 128), and Michel proceeded to offer gifts to the uncle as well as other kin and friends of the bride. This particular example demonstrates how the voyageurs and their sons were able to develop alliances with local indigenous communities and successfully use marriage to strengthen their ties with the local nations, beyond simple or immediate sexual gratification.

Another aspect of marriage requiring attention is how the temporary wives of those not staying in the region were treated. Men who rose in the ranks in the North West Company and became partners were able to retire with sufficient funds to return east to Canada or head back to the British Isles. The men had invariably married local women, but could not simply abandon them. Although testimonies of abandoned wives and children have been heard, Cox (1832, p. 312) notes that when a partner left behind a wife, he would generally set aside an annuity or he would do his best to marry her to a voyageur, paying the voyageur a "handsome sum" so that the voyageur would happily accept to marry the *dame d'un Bourgeois,* the lady of a Lord. Clearly cultural alliances shaping the early *Canadiens* and Métis were complex affairs, often involving reciprocity and serious commitments.

The Massacre of Seven Oaks as Precursor of Change

As the early history of the Oregon Territory was closely tied to that of the fur trade, the region was shaped by events that are now woven inextricably into Canadian history. One of these events was the battle that in English came to be called the Massacre of Seven Oaks, and in French, the battle of "*la Grenouillère,*" or the battle at the frog pond. The 1816 battle itself was a consequence of the simmering conflict between the North West Company and the Hudson Bay Company.

Cox stresses the ruinous nature of the war being waged between the North West Company and the Hudson's Bay Company. The two companies were in open conflict, with each side taking the clerks and employees of the other captive and capturing one another's forts. Cox describes his stay at the fort at Île à la Crosse, a former Hudson's Bay Company fort occupied by the North West Company. The fierce rivalry between the two companies benefited on one hand the indigenous peoples, who were getting better prices for their furs, and on the other, the clerks and other employees, who could command better wages and working conditions. The overall cost was onerous, however. "The spirit of ruinous competition," writes Cox (1832, p. 269), "had at this period gained such a height, that the prices given to the Indians for their furs, after deducting the expenses of carriage and other contingent charges, far exceeded their value to the Company." The signs of the decline of the fur trade were already evident, even as the Pacific Northwest was being integrated into the fur trading networks of the North West Company.

The events in the Red River Valley would lead to both companies exhausting their capital and resources, leaving the North West Company to be subsumed by the Hudson's Bay Company in 1821. The HBC, through this merger, inherited all of the forts and trading networks that had been established in the Columbia River drainage. Thomas Douglas, 5th Earl of Selkirk, had gained control of the Hudson's Bay Company and requested a grant of land. He was granted 300,000 square kilometers in the heart of the territory that had been the home and bison-hunting ground of the descendants of the voyageurs and fur trade employees, now forming respectable sized "French-Canadian Métis" or "Half-breed" communities across the great plains. The first settlers from Scotland arrived late in 1812. Selkirk's goal was to control the fur trade while colonizing the territory with settlers from the Scottish highlands who were being cleared from their ancestral lands. This would be accomplished by pushing out the Métis and gain control of the territory.

Faced with failed harvests and a shortage of food, Lord Selkirk's appointed governor sought to outlaw the trade of pemmican in order to retain provisions and avoid a famine. The food was, however, a staple for the voyageurs of the North West Company and the local economy of the Métis and Half-breed communities.

The importance of pemmican to the voyageurs, even beyond the Rocky Mountains, should not be understated. Franchère, in his voyage from Fort George (Astoria) to Montreal, noted that once they reached the Canoe River (*Rivière au Canot*) and had exhausted their fresh supplies, they turned to a bag of pemmican found at one of David Thompson's old wintering camps. Even though the pemmican was several years old, it was a relief to find this stash (Franchère, 1820, p. 226). Pemmican could be stored for years without going rancid.

When Franchère arrived at the Red River in 1814, he described the conflict that was already brewing between the North West Company and Selkirk's colony following Governor Miles McDonnell's proclamation that no food or provisions were to be exported from the colony. Because of this, hundreds of bags of pemmican were stockpiled in a hangar in the Selkirk Colony (Franchère, 1820, p. 262). Hearing of the proclamation that robbed them of their essential food supply, the voyageurs wintering in Lesser Slave Lake, the Athabasca River, and other distant forts traveled down to the Red River Colony. Franchère (1820, p. 264) describes how armed *Canadiens* were ready to wage battle with the colony. In 1814, a compromise was reached whereby the company and the colony agreed to split the pemmican. The damage was done, however. The simmering conflict eventually led to a shootout where over twenty were killed. That battle did not only involve the Northwestern Métis directly, it also consolidated the emerging Métif/Métis identity Franchère wrote about. Already, in 1814, the Métis and Half-breeds started organizing cavalry under the leadership of Cuthbert Grant and preparing for an inevitable armed conflict.

In 1816, the new governor, Robert Semple, sought to enforce the interdiction of the pemmican trade. On June 19, Governor Semple, accompanied by a brigade of colonists, intercepted a shipment of pemmican destined for the North West Company to be sold and shipped to distant forts. A battle broke out; twenty of Selkirk's men were killed, while only one Métis fell. This battle helped cement a growing Métis identity.

Selkirk's ambitions left him largely bankrupt. After his death in 1820, the two companies were forced to merge, ending the conflict. After the battle, the United States and Great Britain would set the border at the 49th parallel up to the Rocky Mountains. In later decades, it would be extended to the Pacific.

The merger of the North West and Hudson's Bay Company companies left the Hudson's Bay Company in charge of the Oregon Territory for a generation. This changed with the American push to the Pacific and the final setting of the border, culminating in the creation of the states of Oregon, Washington, Idaho, and Montana. The Pemmican War also presaged future challenges that would face the Métis and the indigenous nations; with the arrival of settlers, both would be displaced and marginalized, their ways of life irrevocably changed.

Though the *Canadiens* and Métis did not organize an armed rebellion, one concern was whether a provisional government should be established if French was still the language of the majority of the non-Indian population in the Oregon Territory. However, the teeming masses risking their lives to cross over the Oregon Trail made this a moot question. Despite the absence of rebellion by the *Canadiens* and the Métis, Indian wars were fought as the Native Americans were being pushed out of their traditional lands and efforts were made to co-opt the *Canadiens* and Métis to facilitate establishment of American jurisdiction over the territory. The political and judicial decisions made by the British/Canadian and American governments would have profound impacts as to the identities that would be legally and politically acceptable in both countries.

The rebellions in Canada forced the state to recognize the Métis both politically and judicially, especially in Manitoba, whereas a hybridized people stemming from a European and Native American admixture had no place in the United States. Under these circumstances, a Métis identity was still possible but it faced a cultural challenge as many Métis ended up living on reservation lands either by being given title as "Indians" or by being adopted by a tribe, then allotted lands on reservations. There was little incentive in either case to openly display a Métis identity. As the *Canadien* generally did not claim to have *no* mixed-heritage, it was perhaps easier to simply keep the *Canadien* identity— understood to be Métis—as the primary descriptor of community. The next chapters will thus look at religion, culture, politics and identity in the French-speaking communities of the western United States.

Priest Meditating, Ottawa River, Frances Anne Hopkins, 1866.

CHAPTER 7

The Black Robes Return

In the history of New France, the Black Robes traveled with the explorers into uncharted territories, seeking converts in the nations to the west of the core French settlements located in the St. Lawrence Valley. They pushed into the lands of the Huron or Wyandot, and then further south and west. After the Conquest of New France, the Catholic Church faced major setbacks. Only through adept diplomacy and allegiance to the British Crown did the Catholic Church maintain its status and presence in the British conquered territories of New France, where they hunkered down in the villages along the St. Lawrence in Lower Canada. The Catholic Church was bereft of the priests and missionaries needed for the parishes of the St. Lawrence Valley, let alone the distant Indian territories through which the fur traders and voyageurs paddled and portaged while establishing themselves in the interior.

As a consequence, for over half a century, priests had been virtually absent from the country above St. Louis or northwest of Detroit, while Catholics from Canada continued to penetrate and settle ever deeper into the back country, seeking new opportunities. The Church had previously worked to limit interior settlement and trade in the seventeenth and early eighteenth centuries, in order to protect their Indian converts from the corrupting influences of the *Canadiens*.

Things took a different turn in the nineteenth century. The goal was to redeem the souls of these lapsed *Canadiens* and their Métis descendants who had proliferated in the interim all across the continent despite the efforts to contain them. This would also include the indigenous peoples from the East, especially the Iroquois. These French-speaking people of various ethnic backgrounds were now living with their Indian neighbors and kin ever deeper into the continent. Many of these nations had been indirectly exposed to the religion, through different sorts of frontiersmen, and were curious to hear more. They had to be brought back into the fold and the seeds, which they had planted with their increasingly mixed tribal relations, had to be cultivated.

In the nineteenth century, the Catholic Church and its clerics were no longer leading the way into the interior, but were now following their people, returning to the field after a long absence to re-assert their spiritual control over the lapsed Catholics. The Church needed to regain lost ground, demographically speaking. Once that was accomplished, they re-assumed a broader leadership role in the local politically disenfranchised communities of *Canadiens*, Métis, and their affiliated tribes. The Indians would sometimes label this confusing disruptive competition for their allegiance, as being one between "French" and "American" religions.

North of New Mexico, the Catholic Church only succeeded in the first half of the nineteenth century in traveling beyond the New Orleans-St. Louis axis of the Mississippi into the American West to minister to the *Canadiens*, Métis, Iroquois, and other Catholics beginning to move into these distant frontiers. Buoyed by growing numbers of French-speaking priests—many from Europe following the French Revolution as well as the growing numbers of clerics in Lower Canada (Quebec)—the Catholic Church would finally measure up to the task. The institution could now begin to recruit the numbers required to minister to the spiritual needs of lapsed Catholics, their children, and grandchildren, as well as to begin to proselytize to the indigenous nations of western North America. Here, the Church would enter into open and direct competition with the Protestant Missionaries from the American east coast, reaching the Pacific Northwest by the end of the 1830s. Aided and abetted by the Hudson's Bay Company, its influence would grow rapidly.

Within a decade, the Catholic Church would eclipse the HBC in its influence and reach. It emerged as the principal institution that included not only Métis, but an ever wider set of ethnic groups, including the Native Americans residing within the United States. The Catholic Church was instrumental in integrating the territories of Oregon, Washington, Idaho, and Montana into the expanding nation, thereby shaping the early modern history of the Pacific Northwest.

The American Catholic Church at the Dawn of the Nineteenth Century

An estimated 50,000 Catholics lived in the United States in 1800. Catholics represented a tiny fraction of the total U.S. population, which numbered 5,308,483 people in the 1800 census. The number of Catholics would double in the next decade, in large part due to the incorporation of the Louisiana territory in 1803, but would remain a small minority of the total population until mid-century. The majority of Catholics living in the U.S. to the west of the Mississippi in 1810, however, would have been largely French-speaking.

The demographic importance of French speakers in the nineteenth-century American Catholic Church is matched by the pre-eminence of French-speaking clerics and bishops in this national component of the church. In the early 1800s, the Catholic Church was a *de facto* bilingual institution. West of the Mississippi, French was a clerical *lingua franca*. The status of the language was buttressed by the prestige associated with the language in other sectors of American society; many of the founding fathers were bilingual, speaking French as the descendants of Huguenots that had immigrated to the United States, or having studied it as the international language of choice. Thousands more would permanently immigrate to the U.S. during the quarter century of turmoil following the French revolution. The prestigious West Point Military Academy required a reading knowledge of French for admission up through the Civil War, as many of the key engineering texts that the students used were in French.

Only in the late 1840s did the demographics of the American Catholic Church change with the sudden arrival of hundreds of thousands of Catholic immigrants from Ireland, adding their numbers to the growing non-Protestant, ethnic-German migrants from Central Europe. In the 1840s, the United States also annexed Mexican territory, incorporating Catholic populations with these conquests, the large majority of whom inhabited the lands of the upper Rio Grande valley. In spite of these demographic shifts, even after mid-century, the French-speaking clerics continued to maintain their hold on the church hierarchy, especially in the western part of the country. The names of Catholic institutions of higher learning across the Mid-West bear witness to this legacy: Duquesne, Notre Dame, Marquette, The College of the Clerics of St. Viator (Viateur), De la Salle, and St. Louis.

The Catholic Church's Role in the Conquest of the Old Northwest

As Americans pushed westwards, the heavily French-speaking Catholic Church found itself involved in other forms of frontier pacification. Earlier, Father Pierre Gibault of Illinois was credited with playing a major role in bringing the strategically located French-speaking *Canadien* settler population of southeastern Illinois over to the American side during the Revolutionary War. Under the command of famed frontiersman George Rogers Clark, a small detachment of Virginia militia slipped into southern Illinois country from the Kentucky settlements of the Americans. Outnumbered, Clark's force needed to co-opt the support of the local *Canadien* militia in order to eliminate the minimal, but real, British authority in the region (Bakeless, 1992).

Bearing the news of the Franco-American Alliance in 1778, Clark details in his memoirs how he surprised and subsequently won over the *Canadien* and Métis settlements: first Kaskaskia; then Cahokia, which faced the newer town of

St. Louis directly across the river; and finally the villages in between (Clark, 2001). Clark had first gained the support and trust of Father Pierre Gibault, a native of Canada who had arrived on the banks of the Mississippi ten years earlier in 1768. Father Gibault was appointed the Catholic Church's vicar-general for the region. Assured by Clark that his parishioners would be protected in their persons and property, and granted the right to continue practicing their Catholic faith, Gibault agreed to convince the *Canadiens* and Métis, and ultimately their indigenous allies, to align themselves with the American revolutionary forces.

Clark then had to win over the wealthiest merchant of the Illinois Country, Jean-Gabriel Cerré of Quebec, the future father-in-law of his wealthy counterpart on the other side of the river in St. Louis, Auguste Chouteau. After securing Cerré's house, store, and family on the east bank, Clark enticed him to return from St. Louis. Following an interview with Jean Gabriel Cerré, Clark immediately court martialed him, bringing in his accusers, who were mostly local customers heavily indebted to Cerré. Judging Cerré innocent of the charges after the hearing, Clark exonerated and released him, thereby gaining his appreciation, trust, and willingness to provide a source of financial credit. With Cerré also came a vast network of trade and diplomatic alliances.

Another local notable won over by Clark was Jean-Baptiste Laffont, originally from the French Caribbean colonies. The editor of Clark's Memoirs, Milo Milton Quaife, later commented how Laffont was another one who "proved so powerful an aid to the American cause at this juncture in Clark's affairs." Laffont spent the final decades of his life as an American citizen of Vincennes, Indiana, and later Ste. Geneviève. But first he and Father Gibault had a special mission to perform: ensure the loyalty of the indigenous peoples of the territory. Clark had worked to isolate and remove Britain's primary collaborator in the province, a loyalist Frenchman who had decided to stay on and work for the occupier after the French and Indian Wars. Philippe-François Rastel, sieur de Rocheblave, found himself left in command in Kaskaskia when the last British officer withdrew in 1776.

After this considerable achievement, George Rogers Clark then set out to gain the trust and friendship of the indigenous peoples of the region, once again with the support of his new-found allies among the French-speaking *Canadiens*. Clark summarizes his approach to the local people, and particularly the role of Father Pierre Gibault and his church:

> I was well aware of the fact that the French inhabitants of these western settlements had great influence over the Indians, by whom they were more beloved than were any other Europeans. I knew also that their commercial intercourse extended throughout the entire western and northwestern country, while the governing interest on the Great Lakes was chiefly in the hands of the English, who were not popular with the natives. These reflections, along with others of similar import, determined me to strengthen myself if possible, by adopting such a course of conduct as would tend to

attach the whole French and Indian population to our interest, and give us influence beyond the limits of the country which constituted the objective of our campaign (Clark, 2001, pp. 35-36).

...I had reason to suspect from some things I had learned, that Mr. Gibault, the priest, had been inclined to the American interest previous to our arrival in the country. I had no doubt of his fidelity to us. Knowing that he had great influence over the people, and that Vincennes was also under his jurisdiction, I sent for him and had a long conference on that subject. In response to my questions he stated that he did not think it worth my while to cause any military preparations to be made at the Falls [of the Ohio] for an attack on Vincennes although the place was strong and there were a great number of Indians in the neighborhood... He thought that when the inhabitants should be fully informed of what had happened at the Illinois and the present happiness of their friends there, and should be fully acquainted with the nature of the war, their sentiments concerning it would undergo a great change. He was certain that his appearance there would have a great weight even among the savages. If it were agreeable to me, he would take this matter upon himself, and he had no doubt of being able to bring the place over to the American interest without my being put to the trouble of marching troops against it. His business being altogether of a spiritual character, he desired that another person might be charged with the temporal part of the embassy, and named Dr. Laffont (Clark, 2001, pp. 59-60).

Clark and his deputy, Captain Helm, began a series of negotiations with several different nations and their chiefs. Clark describes discussions and summarizes the outcomes of each negotiation.

Within a short time almost all of the tribes on the Wabash as far as Ouiatenon came to Vincennes and followed the example of their head chief... The British cause lost ground daily in this section, and in a short time our influence over the Indians extended to the St. Joseph River and the lower end of Lake Michigan. The French gentlemen at the different posts in our possession engaged themselves warmly in our cause.

...I took great pains to acquaint myself with the French and Spanish methods of treating with the Indians, and with their disposition and manners in general... After the ceremonies commonly employed at the commencement of Indian treaties, they, as the petitioning party made the opening speech. They laid the entire blame for their taking up the bloody hatchet to the deception of the English, acknowledging their error and making many protestations that they would guard in future against those bad birds... (Clark, 2001, pp. 68-70).

Clark reported afterwards that he "was pleased that the great majority of those who treated with us adhered strictly to their agreement, so that before long we could send a single soldier through any part of the Wabash and Illinois Country, for in the course of this fall all the Indians of these regions came to treat with us, either at Cahokia or Vincennes" (Clark, 2001, pp. 77-78). During an encounter with the indigenous people in Cahokia, which at one point had broken out in a late night exchange of gunfire, Clark explains how he deferred to the local jurisdiction in seeking frontier justice without contributing to further violence. He delicately presided between the townspeople and the troublesome band of Native Americans, stating afterwards:

> Some of the French gentlemen, however, being better acquainted with them than the rest of us, insisted it was they that had given the alarm... I said but little to them, and as there were many Indians of other nations in town, to convince the whole of the strict union of the French and ourselves, I told them as they had disturbed the town, the people might do what they pleased with them (Clark, 2001, p. 81).

With the locals in agreement, Clark had consolidated the American position in the region. This then allowed a quick response when word arrived that the British Lieutenant Governor based in Fort Detroit, Irish-born Henry Hamilton, had reoccupied Vincennes with a small military contingent. Hamilton had become notorious to the Americans for offering bounties to the local indigenous tribes to bring in the scalps of American frontiersmen and their families. Clark's interim work in pacifying the region's inhabitants soon paid off. The Illinois country was able to rapidly absorb, isolate, and expunge the intrusion.

Clark led a difficult mid-winter march with his combined Virginia and Illinois militia to the Wabash River to attack the British stronghold at Fort Vincennes. Assembling his militia, now composed of Illinois Frenchmen and Métis from Cahokia, Kaskaskia, and the villages between, the 170 men under Clark's command crossed the Kaskaskia River on February 5, 1779, "after receiving a lecture and absolution from a priest" (Clark, 2001, p. 116). Since no other priest was in the area, he was undoubtedly referring to Father Gibault.

Much of the following week the volunteers spent wading through the region's freezing and extensive marshlands. Once they reached their destination, Clark's force laid siege to British-occupied settlement of Fort Vincennes. After a considerable exchange of gunfire, with the fort's cannon joining in, the British commander was forced to surrender. The defenders inside Fort Vincennes once again comprised mostly the local French-Canadian and Métis militia, whose willingness to fight had been severely compromised by the presence of many of their friends and relations outside the walls, now under the command of Clark. The interim visit of Father Gibault and Dr. Laffont had had its effect.

Clark would vicariously repeat the sequence performed so successfully at Vincennes a couple of years later when his representatives convinced a local Potawatomi community to remain neutral while he attacked and captured the British garrison before withdrawing (R. G. Cleland, 1992, p. 151). Clark earned the nickname "Conqueror of the Northwest" for his role in defeating the British at Vincennes. His diplomatic and military venture greatly improved the chances that the Illinois Country, along with the balance of the Old Northwest, would be ceded to the United States in the 1783 Treaty of Paris. Clark willingly spread the credit more widely by openly and repeatedly recognizing the role of Father

Gibault and other individuals from the local French-Canadian (and largely Métis) population in helping him secure the Illinois Country and thereby ensure American sovereignty over what would become the American Midwest. Much of his memoirs focus on how he built these vital relationships, which, in the end, led to his overwhelming success.

During the 1780s, the usual American frontier demographic mix, heavily seasoned with Scots-Irish "crackers," appeared. As a consequence, the peace and tranquility of the region around Vincennes deteriorated markedly. The lethal brew of posturing, bullying, violence, and alcohol inflamed indigenous-settler relations. The *Canadien* citizens of Vincennes, under the leadership of Le Gras, maintained their allegiance to the U.S. while trying to mediate on behalf of the local indigenous groups. Faced with one *fait accompli* after another, however, presented by local thugs such as Daniel Sullivan and Michael Duff, the *Canadiens* saw their leverage and their credibility with their Native American neighbors wane owing to the escalating violence.

George Rogers Clark was called upon to repeat his prior feat in the fall of 1786, but this time in confrontation with increasingly resentful indigenous groups congregating along the upper Wabash above Vincennes. His volunteer force of Virginians, Kentuckians, and *Canadiens*, joined by many of this newer crop of unruly settlers, soon disintegrated into mutiny and desertion. Forced to retreat to Vincennes, Clark abandoned the operation without ever engaging the Native Americans. With rising tensions and insecurity, many older *Canadien* settler families left Vincennes in disgust to join their Illinois countrymen in re-establishing themselves on the opposite shore of the Mississippi where some semblance of order still prevailed. Some of these families were also slave-holders, and were uncertain about the implementation of the terms of the Northwest Ordinance outlawing slavery passed by the Continental Congress in 1787. These slave owners with their Native American and black slaves headed across the river, while intertribal confederacies began to organize around the Vincennes region for self-protection against a new sort of settler (R. White, 1991b, pp. 420-435).

Through a complex stratagem, Clark had secured the support of several of the region's leading citizens. In doing so, he was able to undermine the advantages of the incumbent that the British themselves had exploited so effectively at the siege of Quebec City in 1775 and the later defense of Montreal at the Battle of Châteauguay in 1813. In short, they retained the allegiance of an occupied and resentful, but not always neutral population.

It was the standard advantage that goes to he who moves first with an initial show of strength followed by leniency. Thirty-six years after Clark's encounters in the Illinois Country and just eighteen months after the skirmish in Châteauguay, General Andrew Jackson was able to repeat Clark's feat, but south of New Orleans, rallying the local French Créoles and their militia. He accomplished this in December 1814 and January 1815, with reinforcements drawn from the militia of the Kentucky frontier, as well as Tennessee. Jackson succeeded in rallying the local citizenry and militia of the new and wavering state of Louisiana, mostly of French extraction, to drive the British out during the campaign that terminated in the Battle of New Orleans. Of course our history books only tell the story of Jackson and his boys from Kentucky and Tennessee.

The stories of the two most famous battles in the Ohio region between the War of Independence and the War of 1812 reflect the need to establish heroes of the hour and ensure that history runs in a straight line back from the present so as to provide a clear reflection of the here and now. The battles of Fallen Timbers, just upstream from Fort Miami, in 1794, and Tippecanoe in 1811 were in fact little more than skirmishes on the margins of major military demonstrations in the northern borderlands. They could have been major battles, but were not. What made them stand out was that, unlike the previous and much bloodier engagements, the U.S. troops held their ground and retained control of the battlefield while the Native Americans dispersed in a demoralized state. The context of what preceded and followed these skirmishes is what turned them into to milestones of note, not the limited military engagements that fell in between.

In both cases the indigenous groups had convinced themselves that they were about to participate in another easy victory over the American troops, following the psychological and spiritual preparation of pre-battle rituals. When events did not turn out as expected, the autonomous fighting bands—so effective in the guerrilla tactics of ambush, or quick and decisive encounters, simply dispersed in disorder. The lack of support (i.e., non-performance) of allies at a critical juncture further contributed to mutual disgust and demoralization within the Native American ranks during the first engagement. The drama really started after both "battles" when the American troops left in possession of the battlefield then proceeded to burn the local cabins, villages, and food supplies, an action that had catastrophic implications for the local residents and warriors. Combined with negotiation of the Jay Treaty, Fallen Timbers gave the Americans the upper hand in the subsequent treaty negotiations at Greenville in 1795.

The second battle was actually preceded by a treaty of sorts, or a particularly unbalanced agreement imposed by Governor Harrison through divide and conquer tactics. It subsequently outraged the balance of many Native American leaders, inciting them to fight. At Fallen Timbers, thirty American citizens and forty Native Americans were killed. Similarly, in terms of casualties, the Battle of Tippecanoe was a draw, but after they burned five thousand bushels of corn and beans, Harrison's men found thirty-six dead warriors whose bodies they scalped and mutilated. Other battles elsewhere in the Ohio Country during this period resulted in more casualties: some 270 men under General Harmar were killed in 1790, while another 630 Americans were killed serving under General St. Clair, and several hundred more were killed in 1813 at the Battle of Frenchtown on the River Raisin near the Michigan-Ohio border.

As had happened previously during Pontiac's Rebellion in the 1760s, Anglo-Americans were being killed by the warriors, but not the local French speaking people (*Canadiens* and Métis). The Americans noticed a similar occurrence in 1813. The Frenchtown disaster was marked in its aftermath by suspicions directed at the ambiguous role of the local community of frontier *Canadiens*, and a battle cry for the remaining campaigns of the war of "Remember the Raisin."

Tippecanoe led into the broader conflict that assumed the title of the War of 1812. After a horrible sequence of frontier slaughters of non-combatants on both sides of the ethnic divide, the war resulted in a draw. However, the Native Americans would henceforth be cut off from overt support from north of the border. Although the war ended with a return to *status quo antebellum*, it was to be crowned by Jackson's clear victory two weeks after signature of the indecisive Treaty of Ghent. Most importantly, one way or the other, Anthony Wayne and William Harrison became heroes to the American people. For Harrison, like Jackson, the road home eventually led to the White House. Later on, during the Indian Wars of the Pacific Northwest, there would be echoes of imposed peace treaties leading to war, followed by "victories" of sorts and heroes of the hour. This would also involve yet more French-Canadians and Métis somehow in the middle of it all, along with their equally suspect priests. But that story will come later.

The Catholic Church on the Midwestern Frontier

The people of *Canadien* origins represent only the tip of a large moving demographic block, under-served by their church. Sightings of priests were rare outside of core the region around St. Louis, including Ste. Geneviève, St. Charles, Cahokia, and Kaskaskia. Lacking human and financial resources, the Catholic Church found itself spread too thinly across the west. Struggling to hold their own for the next half century, priests like Fathers Pierre Gibault and Gabriel Richard were few and far between.

By the 1830s, however, part of a broad resurgence among the faithful in Europe, the Catholic Church once again began sending clerics in search of Catholic settlements on the frontier. In her seminal book, *Voyageurs*, first published in 1931, Grace Lee Nute (1955) tells how this movement influenced the naming of a small settlement, St. Paul, Minnesota. Founded in the the late 1830s, St. Paul illustrates how the Catholic Church was still finding its way in the lands of the Upper Mississippi in search of its lost flock. Bishop Mathias Loras initiated efforts from his base at the time in Dubuque, Iowa, a town named after Julien Dubuque, who came west from Quebec in the 1780s to develop lead mining in the area. In the late 1700s, the town of Dubuque and surrounding territories were located in what was generally known as Upper Louisiana, then under the light governance of the Spanish Bourbons. One more destination for French-Canadian migrants heading west. Dubuque was one of many settlements named and populated by French Canadians. Upriver from Dubuque, a string of settlements and cabin clusters extended along the Mississippi River and its tributaries with names like St. Pierre (St. Peter), Grand Marais (Big Marsh), and Oeil de Cochon (Pig's Eye).

Traveling upriver, Bishop Loras visited St. Pierre and enumerated the Catholics living in the area in 1839. He recorded 185 souls and the names of those he married, baptized, and confirmed into the Catholic faith. As Nute (1955, p. 193) notes, the list of names includes French names like Brunelle, Prevost, Reche, Dejarlat, Rondeau, Brisette, Papin, LeClaire, and Bouiderot. A study of the origin of these names shows that most of them were of voyageur origin. Following the Bishop's pastoral call of 1839, Father Lucien Galtier was sent to minister to the little flock of voyageurs that had been so recently discovered by the Church, a flock that included Pierre Parrant and his Oeil de Cochon distillery and tavern (Nute, 1955, p. 193).

Oeil de Cochon, located below the falls near the U.S. Army's Fort Snelling, derived its name from a one-eyed French-Canadian entrepreneur, Pierre Parrant, whose tavern was located at the mouth of Fountain Cave. Parrant had been a fur trader, working for the McKenzie and Chouteau Company before turning to an alternative but independent entrepreneurial pursuit: bootlegging. He was soon engaged in a running battle with the officers at Fort Snelling over the sale of his distilled alcohol to both soldiers and the local bands of Sioux and Chippewa (Ojibwa). Parrant had made a claim in 1838 for the land found at the mouth of Fountain Cave situated on the north bank of the Mississippi River. This cave, with a clean source of water, was ideal for Parrant's continued distilling of alcohol. Father Galtier established the rebranded St. Paul parish and built a church along the Mississippi River. St. Paul was later chosen as the name of the future city in 1848, a name considered more palatable than the original designation of Oeil de Cochon (Nute, 1955, p. 193).

St. Paul is somewhat of an exception in that the Catholic clergy arrived before the surveyors and the waves of settlers. French-speaking settlements elsewhere were overrun with Protestant American settlers before the Catholic Church could send priests. These new settlers often scorned the original settlers, the Métis descendants of the French-Canadian voyageurs that had first taken root in the territory. The settlement at Baie Verte or Baie des Puants is a case in point. In his book, *The Wisconsin Frontier*, Mark Wyman (1998) points out that Green Bay, originally *Baie Verte*, was the oldest "White" (Métis, really) settlement in what

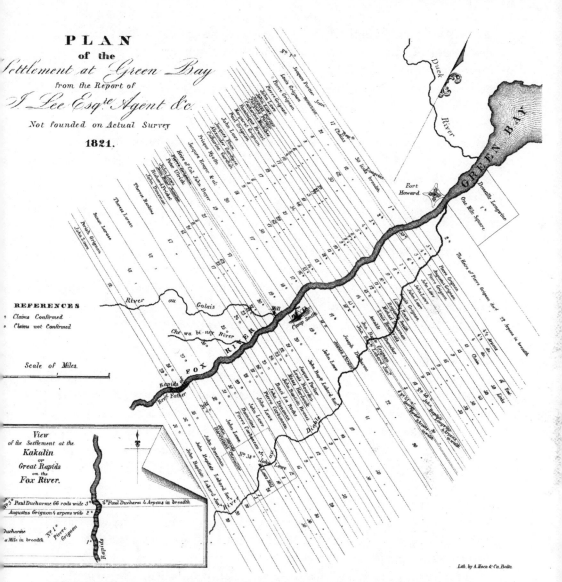

Plan of the Settlement at Green Bay from the report of J. Lee Esq., Agent, &c., 1821. The long lots were in themselves signs of a settlement founded by *Canadiens*. They brought this pattern of land tenure with them from the St. Lawrence Valley. This type of design allowed for the concentration of houses along the river, the main transportation route, while giving the inhabitants access to land stretching away from the river that supplied some of the resources they needed.

is now Wisconsin, dating back to the late seventeenth century. Along with Prairie du Chien, it was the only official permanent settlement before the British withdrew in 1815 following the War of 1812. Grafted onto older Indian settlements, both were Métis villages with lots extending back from the Fox or Mississippi Rivers. This model of settlement mirrored those in New France where farmers built their houses on the shores of the river or lake and their farm lots would extend up the valley in narrow strips of land that included a variety of eco-zones in one farmstead (Wyman, 1998, p. 132). These century-old settlements were transformed when the United States Army arrived, followed closely by the first waves of American settlers.

The first detachment of U.S. soldiers did not arrive in Green Bay until 1816, establishing Fort Howard. In 1820, Michigan Territorial Governor Lewis Cass sent a team of surveyors up to Green Bay to take inventory of the region and found sixty houses with a population numbering roughly five hundred outside Fort Howard. The surveyors reported that the inhabitants were predominantly French who had intermarried with indigenous women, and are said generally to be "indolent, gay, intemperate, and illiterate" (Wyman, 1998, p. 132).

Four years later, in 1824, the U.S. Government's Indian Agent reported that there were no more than 130 white men, seven white women, and twenty-two white children in the Green Bay vicinity. A later study put the percentage of French-speaking Métis or part-indigenous households at just under sixty percent of the total population. Given the paucity of eligible women, many of the Americans chose to marry Métis women. A visitor in 1830 observed that "it is common in this region for business men to marry those Half Blood Ladies" (Wyman, 1998, pp. 132-133). In spite of intermarriage, racial prejudices persisted.

The other settlement, Prairie du Chien, located on the upper Mississippi below the future settlement of St. Paul, was first reached by steamboat in 1823. This settlement, populated by a French-speaking Métis population, was seen as strange and unsettling by the Americans. Maj. Stephen Long viewed Prairie du Chien's French-Native American population as "degenerating" instead of improving (Wyman, 1998, p. 133). Later, Caleb Atwater called the village's inhabitants "a motley group of creatures (I can scarcely call them human beings) as the world ever beheld." He noted the mixed origins of the population, consisting of "Negro, Indian, French, English, American, Scotch, Irish and Spanish blood" (Wyman, 1998, p. 133).

Another American settler named James Lockwood who, after looking back on Prairie du Chien's origins, noted the problem as he saw it of "gentlemen selecting wives of the nut-brown natives, and raising children of mixed blood." He concluded that the old fur trading posts had gone along unchanged for years "until the Americans emigrated to them, and took hold of them with their enterprise, when they at once improved, and most of them became places of business and importance" (Wyman, 1998, p. 133).

With the arrival of the American Army in Green Bay, American laws were imposed on the territory. Judge James Duane Doty was appointed the first circuit judge of the region by President James Monroe, relocating himself to Prairie du Chien. As we will see later in the Pacific Northwest, the first order of business on the American frontier after pacifying and dispossessing the Native Americans was dealing with the legal status and suspect loyalties of the local Métis population. Doty called to session at Green Bay the first Grand Jury following the American takeover, and he directed the jury in 1824 to take up the question of persons who had not been legally wed, indicting most of the local population under the charges of fornication and adultery:

> It was a typical frontier situation, common in Wisconsin's early settlements, where whites were nominally Catholics but no clergymen had been present for years and so "marriages" took place in Indian camps located far from the justice of the peace. In this the French frontiersman had again adapted to the ways of the Indians. But the Green Bay grand jury, acting under judge Doty's instructions, wound up indicting thirty-six persons—Green Bay's principal male citizens—for fornication: two others were charged with adultery. All were informed that if they married within ten days no fines would be issued, all except two did this (Wyman, 1998, p. 134).

The fact that so many were not officially married is certainly tied to the penury of priests in the territory. The historical evidence indicates that Catholic priests had not visited the region for decades; as such, it would have been practically impossible for Catholics to marry according to the tenets of their faith. In all certainty, a Catholic identity had maintained itself in spite of the lack of priests, parishes, and sacraments. This was evident in other regions among other populations, notably the Iroquois, as well as the even more distant Métis of northern British Columbia. Jean-Baptiste Boucher, as a case in point, had certainly not seen a priest for decades in the New Caledonia district where he lived, located in the northern part of modern day British Columbia, yet when the first priests arrived in the 1840s, he had all his seventeen children baptized in 1842 and educated in their faith (Adrien Gabriel Morice, 1912, p. 38).

Faced with the hostility of the new settlers, many Métis moved farther west, others stayed behind. The large Juneau clan of Wisconsin is an example of one enterprising Métis family. This family of French-Canadian and Menominee origins rose to prominence in the Wisconsin Territory and co-founded Milwaukee; a sizable nearby town bears the name of Juneau today. In the generation that follows, another Juneau would wander the gold fields of California and the Pacific Northwest before co-founding a town that would bear the Juneau name, this time in the recently acquired territory of Alaska.

The Role of the Catholic Church in the Conquest of the Southwest

The Santa Fe Trail was established in 1821, linking Missouri with the capital of New Mexico. This trail served as a major trade route that ran through Comanche territory. The descendants of French-Canadian fur traders who had settled the Missouri opened the Santa Fe Trail to New Mexico. French-Canadians had become prominent citizens of New Mexico prior to its conquest by the United States, with many of them settling in Taos. Frustrated with the poor governance by the appointed Mexican authorities, the French-Canadian settlers sided with the United States in its conflict with Mexico. They not only played a major commercial role in the establishment of eastern terminus of the Santa Fe Trail, but the American authorities also credited them at the time with facilitating the rapid transfer of New Mexico to the American military and civil authorities in 1846.

The United States declared war on Mexico in 1846 following a skirmish in disputed territory that left sixteen American soldiers dead. French-Canadians and their clergy played an influential role in the relatively orderly occupation that followed the subsequent conquest of New Mexico in 1846. The American Army, led by American General Stephen W. Kearny, had entered Santa Fe in August 1846 without firing a shot, as the Mexican governor fled the advancing cavalry and infantry. The challenge facing the American forces was pacifying the population. Unlike in Illinois, the local Catholic priesthood encouraged their parishioners to rise up against the American forces. The priests had unleashed dire warnings that the *hereticos* were coming to pillage their homes, desecrate their churches, and debauch their women. A revolt subsequently occurred in January 1847 as rioters and armed guerrillas attacked and murdered several dozen Americans in and around the Taos area. Martinez and other local Mexican priests were generally assumed to have played at least an indirect part, and very possibly a direct role, in organizing the violence.

A year later, on February 2, 1848, American and Mexican representatives signed the Treaty of Guadalupe Hidalgo. This treaty not only extinguished all Mexican claims on Texas and territories to the north of the Rio Grande, but by signing the treaty, Mexico also ceded New Mexico, California, and the territory that now includes part of modern-day Colorado, Arizona, Nevada, Utah, and Wyoming. The United States thus came to control all the territory from Missouri to the Pacific. Just before war broke out, the Americans had secured the northern Pacific frontier flank through a demographic *fait accompli* followed by diplomatic arrangements with Britain.

Following the Mexican-American War, the American Catholic Church assumed an active role in pacifying this mostly Spanish-speaking population of the northern Mexican frontier outposts. Father Jean-Baptiste Lamy, a French missionary who had spent much of his career tending to his flock within the diocese of Vincennes covering the lower Ohio River area, was reassigned to the newly created Vicariate of New Mexico in 1850, appointed as the first American bishop of the American Southwest. Faced with a hostile population, the new bishop reorganized the Catholic Church, creating the Santa Fe diocese which covered Arizona, New Mexico, and eastern Colorado. Lamy also ended the marriage of priests and defrocked a number of clerics who were tied to some of the prominent families of the region. In spite of this opposition, Lamy remained, being later promoted to Archbishop once the Santa Fe diocese was elevated to an Archdiocese in 1875. After Lamy's death in 1888, another French-speaker, Jean-Baptiste Salpointe from Auvergne, France, succeeded him (Burns, 1977a, p. 632).

The Settling of the Pacific Northwest

In the Pacific Northwest from the 1840s until early in the twentieth century, Fathers Blanchet, Demers, and their successors faced their own set of challenges as they tried to mitigate the often arbitrary and brutal process of establishing a new American order in this corner of the land. Caught in the middle with their French-Canadian and Métis settlers while trying to protect those tribes with significant Catholic membership, the priests found themselves translating and negotiating truces, treaties, and other arrangements that fell within the political sphere. As in Canada, their countrymen might have been disenfranchised politically, but the void would be filled by the Church acting as an intermediary, providing community leadership, and reaching accommodations with the new authorities.

After the 1846 Oregon Treaty extended the 49th parallel from the Rocky Mountains to the Pacific, the negotiation and settlement of border and property disputes and the relocation of the Hudson's Bay Company north of the new border took another twenty-five years. The pending war with Mexico certainly motivated the United States to negotiate with Great Britain. President James K. Polk, a southerner, was accused of ceding lands in the Pacific Northwest in order to gain lands in the South. All the while more Canadians were arriving, and the French-Canadian-dominated Catholic Church in the American West continued the slow process of shifting away from its origins in Quebec toward becoming an integral part of the American Catholic Church.

Archbishop François Norbert Blanchet continued to work with Rome through his original channels in Quebec to obtain reinforcements and resources, reaching out to Italy as well as to the French-speaking countries or communities of Europe: France, Belgium, and Switzerland. French-speaking priests dominated the recruits, including those from Quebec and Acadia such as the Blanchet brothers, Mother Joseph (Esther Pariseau) of the Sisters of Providence, and dozens of other nuns belonging to this and other Quebec-based orders, Fathers Demers,

Rev. Father Pierre Jean De Smet (1801-1873) Catholic missionary to Indian Territory, Mathew Brady, ca. 1860-1865. Father De Smet was a tireless Belgian Jesuit missionary among the indigenous nations of the Midwestern and Western United States in the mid-nineteenth century. De Smet is said to have persuaded the Sioux war chief Sitting Bull to negotiate with the United States government for the 1868 Treaty of Fort Laramie.

Brouillet, Archambault, Préfontaine and their francophone colleagues of European extraction such as Fathers DeSmet, Pandosy, Chirouse, Hoecken, Point, Croquet, Joset, Cataldo, and Ravalli. Fathers Pierre-Jean De Smet, Alphonse Glorieux, and Adrian Croquet were Belgian; Father Joset was Swiss, while Father André Poulin was *Canadien;* and Father Rossi was a French-speaking diocesan priest of Italian-Jewish origins. One of the largest single European contingents of French-speaking clerics hailed from northern Italy, including Jesuit Fathers Ravalli, Cataldo, Rossi, Giorda, and Gazzoli. All these clerics from what is now Italy had been educated in French-language colleges and universities as Italy had yet to be united into one state and there was still no centralized Italian language. The French language was thus a language of culture and higher education. These people filled a major void in education, health care, and the painfully slow development of the Bureau of Indian Affairs and other civil authorities in the Pacific Northwest.

A Jesuit historian of the Catholic Church in the West, Robert Ignatius Burns (1977b), provided a broader perspective of the regional variation and the multicultural nature of the Church in the development of the American West. Burns summarizes the Church's development in the region:

> The Roman Catholic Church functioned on a series of frontiers that later converged to form the United States West. To some of them she imparted a distinctive flavor; in others her brief presence during an exploratory and missionary phase soon gave way to an influx of alien settlers. Sometimes the church subsisted in an underground subculture scarcely heeded by the new establishment, as among the Mexicans of the Southwest or the Canadian ex-voyageur families of the Northwest. Often she grew on several levels at a given point – as an Irish immigrant mass, a French old-settler group, a German farming community, a network of Indian missions, or an assimilated American variety scattered in professional, political, military, or other spheres (1977b, p. 1033).

The Catholic Church needed funds and missionaries, so it turned to Europe and French Canada for both. The clerics that traveled to the American West included the Spaniard Joseph Alemany for California's bishopric, the French-Canadian François Blanchet for the Pacific Northwest, the French Jean-Baptiste Lamy and his successor, Jean-Baptiste Salpointe, for the southwest, and the French Louis Dubourg and John Miège or the Italian Joseph Rosati for the church of the Great Plains (Burns, 1977b, p. 1034). The Catholic population in the United States grew exponentially over the course of the nineteenth century. From around 50,000 in 1800, the American Catholic population grew to some twelve million by 1900.

Missionary Work among Native Americans

The Catholic Church proved to be relatively effective in its missionary work with the indigenous nations in the United States. This is seen in the numbers of Catholics in the Native American communities: by 1900, up to a third of United States Indians were Roman Catholic, even though the Catholic population of the United States represented a bit more than fifteen percent of the total population in the country. This higher proportion of indigenous people of Catholic faith in the United States stems from a number of factors, including the ability of celibate priests to spend time among indigenous communities seeking converts. This difference between Catholicism and Protestantism facilitated conversion to Catholicism. Then there is the important role that indigenous believers played, such as the Catholic Iroquois and *Canadiens* of the Pacific Northwest who helped propagate the Catholic faith:

> In addition to the missionaries, there were many heroic Indian Catholic laymen and women who stand neglected in the peripheral shadow of the clerics and institutions – patriarchs such as the Flathead chiefs Happy Man (Victor) and Little Claw of Grizzly (Charlo); Christian warriors such as Pend Oreille head chief, No Horses (Alexander); strong promoters of the faith such as the head chief of the central Sioux, Man Who Strikes the Ree (Pananapapi); stubborn peacemakers such as Coeur d'Alene Seltis;

devout women leaders such as Seltis' colleague Sighouin, or Sister Mary Two Beard and her heroic band of Sioux nuns on the Cuban battlefields; and a roll call of Catholic chiefs from Seattle of the Duwamish to Pokagon of the Potawatomi to Blackbird of the Ottawa (Burns, 1977b, p. 1039).

The importance of the voyageurs must also be recognized. Though the Catholics Priests often decried the lax morals of the French-Canadian voyageurs and fur traders, the missionaries also acknowledged their work in preparing the nations with which they worked and lived for the arrival of the Catholic faith:

> A concomitant of European influence was the widespread pre-eminence of French Canada; her language and frontiersmen infiltrated the Great Plains and Far Northwest, increasing even during the early 19th century and amounting to an immigration movement of many thousand onto or near the tribal scene (Burns, 1977b, p. 1039).

In the Pacific Northwest voyageurs like Robillard were early instructors of Catholicism among the Okanagan tribes. They included Berland with the Flatbow and Pambrun with the Walla Walla and Cayuse on the lower Columbia. Moreover, the Catholic Iroquois recruited to work in the west by the fur trading companies were also active in spreading their faith, at one point forming almost a third of North West Company employees working in the region. The Iroquois La Mousse, with his twenty-four Iroquois compatriots, moved from Montreal into the territory of the Flathead in 1816, and to this day the Catholic faith is the predominant religion of the Flathead Reservation. As Burns (1977b, p. 1039) affirms: "The French-speaking American missionaries with their 'French religion' thus found many Indians prepared." If nothing else, Burns reminds us that there is more to the history of the American West than that which readily meets our eyes today.

The Catholic Church Reaches the Pacific Northwest

The first calls for Black Robes to go out from the Pacific Northwest came from deep in the interior where the multicultural mercenaries of trade, the Catholic Iroquois mostly from the Quebec reserve of Kahnawake, had been living among the Flatheads and the Nez Percé for a generation. Multiple solicitations were made over a period of several years, and some ten people from these three nations died as martyrs during this quest. The Protestant Presbyterians and Methodists in fact responded first. Additional pleas went out later from the French-Canadians and their Métis families living in the Willamette Valley during the 1830s, but here, too, Protestant missionaries were the first to arrive by several years. Nonetheless, Catholic priests finally reached the Pacific Northwest in the late 1830s.

Catholic versus Protestant Methodologies – Literacy and the Book

The Catholic and Protestant missionaries adopted decidedly different approaches toward the Native Americans, with the Catholics enjoying the assistance of an intermediary population represented by the Iroquois, *Canadiens* and Métis. The ongoing culture war along the United States' northern border, both before and after the partition of Columbia Basin along the 49th parallel in 1846, involved not only a national contest—American versus British North America— and an ethnic/racial dimension—white settler versus Native American—but also a religious component. The *Canadiens* and Métis were in the middle of all three.

In the minds of the religious contestants at the time, the Pacific Northwest represented another battleground in the wars of religion dating from the six-teenth and seventeenth centuries – Reformation and then Counter-Reformation. Thoroughly contained as a tiny marginalized minority in the early days of the republic, the Catholic Church emerged on the frontier as a competitive threat, especially in the northern borderlands. Lacking the political power to impose its faith through edict, the Catholic Church was able to present a very competitive alternative in a free market of religious ideas: a path to Christian conversion for the indigenous peoples that did not require literacy and intensive study of the scriptures. Albert Furtwangler (2005) in his work *Bringing Indians to the Book* chronicles the frustrated attempts of various American Protestant missionaries in Oregon to convert the indigenous peoples. He highlights the difference between the approaches of the American Protestant and French-Canadian Catholic missionaries who came to Oregon in 1838:

The priests, moreover, presented a challenge to the Protestants in the way they reached out to the Indians. Of all the Christian missionaries, they demanded the least in the way of formal learning and long-run discipline before they accepted Indians as Christians or likely converts. The Catholic Church had accommodated believers for centuries without requiring that they read; priests interpreted the Bible and administered sacraments appropriate for an oral society (Furtwangler, 2005, pp. 132-133).

> The first priests coming from Canada were aided and encouraged in their efforts by the Hudson's Bay Company. They began ministering to both Indians and French-Canadian settlers.

The Catholic Church was able to quickly gain converts, even though they were operating in a territory that was under the shared political control of two very Protestant states—reinforced either by legislation or by a popular predominance: Great Britain and the United States. The priests also had the advantage of trav-eling widely throughout the year, as they were unattached celibates who could devote themselves to their missionary activities. They used a variety of pictorial aids in their teachings, notably illustrations depicting hell and who was bound for that destination.

In the stories about this war of religions, the extreme poverty of the Catholic Church in its initial missionary efforts is striking as compared to the considerable resources deployed by the Eastern Protestant Churches in the Pacific Northwest. Despite this, the competition for souls in North America was fierce—at times, even bloody.

Two Protestant missionaries, Marcus and Narcissa Whitman, were murdered along with twelve male residents on November 29, 1847, at the Waiilatpu mission located in the Washington Territory. A small band of Cayuse, who believed that the missionaries were responsible for the introduction of measles and other diseases that were killing their people, murdered them. This event sparked the initial round of the Indian Wars of the Pacific Northwest that raged off and on throughout the 1850s. In periods of turmoil during the multiple Indian Wars of the 1840s and 1850s in the Pacific Northwest, three Catholic churches were looted and razed in the Ahtanum, Umatilla, and Colville Valleys. Priests were actively involved in the negotiation of truces and trying to avert a wider war. A number of Catholic priests attributed their ruined health (and premature demise) to the harassment and obstruction of their Protestant neighbors, rather than the already rigorous challenges of a frontier missionary's life.

The Flatheads, Nez Percé, and Iroquois

Early in the 1830s a heightened interest in Christianity swept the tribes of the upper Columbia following the return of Spokane Garry and Kootenay Pelly from the Anglican school at Red River. Capitalizing on this surge, early in 1831 Old Ignace, a French-speaking Iroquois, assembled the Flatheads and Nez Percé in council and proposed sending a deputation to St. Louis to request a missionary. "The proposition was enthusiastically received, and four Nez Perce offered to start at once" (Laveille, 1915, p. 99). Leaving the Bitter Root Valley of the Rocky Mountains in the spring, they all made it in October to St. Louis, where " repairing at once to a Catholic church to prostrate themselves before Him whom Ignatius had taught them to adore" (Laveille, 1915, p. 100). Three of the delegation fell ill and perished, while the surviving one returned to their mountains with Fontenelle and his trappers to tell their story. Their request was understood in general terms, but it was the Protestants who responded first by sending missionaries out in 1834, 1835, and 1836. Mutually disappointed, these missionaries continued on down river to the lower Columbia or returned east for reinforcements. Still, the Flatheads waited.

They then decided to send a second delegation to St. Louis. Ignace volunteered and left with his two sons. They reached their destination that same year in 1835,

A Nesperces Indian, Paul Kane, 1849–1856. An indicator of the strength of the French language and culture in the nineteenth century is the naming of the indigenous nations. The Nez percé (pierced noses), Coeur d'Alène (heart of an awl or heart sharp as an awl), have kept their French names. The names of others were translated into English (Têtes-Plates became Flatheads) or were rendered unrecognizable over time, such as the "Cayuse," likely derived from the French *cailloux* or small stone.

at which time a Belgian Jesuit, Father Helias d'Huddeghem, heard Ignace's confession and baptized his sons (Laveille, 1915, p. 101).

Heartened by promises that the Catholic Church would send missionaries, Ignace returned home to Flathead country with his sons. As eighteen months passed with still no indication that Black Robes were en route, a third delegation was sent to St. Louis, once again headed by Ignace, three Flatheads, and one Nez Percé. On their way, they encountered a large band of Sioux; the entire delegation was killed. Hearing the devastating news, the Flatheads decided to send a fourth group consisting of two Iroquois with some knowledge of French, Pierre Gaucher, and one of the sons of the elder Ignace, also named Ignace, though often called Young Ignatius (Laveille, 1915, p. 102). Accompanied by one Nez Percé, the party left in 1839, joining a party of trappers returning to St. Louis. Around mid-September the delegation passed by the new St. Joseph Mission to the relocated Potawatomies located at Council Bluffs. There they encountered a young Jesuit priest from Belgium named Pierre-Jean De Smet, who would come to play a central role in the efforts of the Catholic Church in the Pacific Northwest.

The delegation continued on to St. Louis where they met the Bishop Rosati, and where their efforts finally bore fruit after so many years. After a long conversation, the Bishop wrote to the General of the Society of Jesus (the Jesuits), telling him of the sterling qualities of these "Indians," recounting their efforts of the past eight years to obtain a Catholic priest. The bishop concluded his letter by stating: "For the love of God, Most Reverend Father, do not abandon these souls." The Father General agreed to send a priest; hearing of the news, Pierre Gaucher started at once to carry the good news to his tribe.

Young Ignatius remained in St. Louis to act as guide to the yet-to-be-designated missionary, who would head upriver the following spring. On their way back, they met Father De Smet, who at once offered to go to the Rocky Mountains. At last the Flatheads were to realize their long-deferred desire. Meanwhile, a parallel call for priests from the Willamette was finally answered in November 1838 when Fathers Blanchet and Demers from Quebec reached Fort Vancouver on the lower Columbia. They came by canoe with the Hudson's Bay Company express brigade via St. Boniface on the Red River, then up to Lake Manitoba, up the Saskatchewan River, and then over the Rockies and down the Columbia.

Fathers Blanchet and Demers Reach the Pacific

It had taken three months for the party accompanying Fathers François Norbert Blanchet and Modeste Demers to cross from St. Boniface and reach the continental divide and the headwaters of the Columbia. Though it was mid-October by this time and growing cold, the descent of the Columbia to the coast was swift. Unfortunately, at the Dalles des Morts near the Big Bend of the upper Columbia, one of the canoes capsized and twelve people drowned, including the Métis Chalifou children and their mother who were following their father out on a new assignment. With this disaster hanging heavy on them, the party continued on to Fort Colville, reaching it in early November. Gathered there waiting for them were five Native American nations. For four days the two priests offered Mass and taught the basics of Christianity through interpreters. The Black Robes then continued down the Columbia River with a brief stop at Fort Okanogan, arriving at Fort Walla Walla on November 18. The priests were warmly welcomed by Pierre Pambrun, a *Canadien* married to a Métisse, who had been in charge of the post since 1832. At the new Presbyterian mission located up the Walla Walla River at Waiilatpu, Dr. Whitman had gotten word of the impending arrival of the Catholic priests from Pambrun's children who were attending his school at the time. He tried to forbid the indigenous people of the area from meeting with the priests, but in spite of this, a large number of Walla Walla and Cayuse flocked to the Fort to meet the priests. Mass was celebrated before those assembled, and Blanchet reported that the Native Americans were "struck with amazement."

Pambrun had become a fervent promoter of the Catholic faith and a dedicated teacher of Catholic doctrine, not only for his own children and the Company's local servants, but also the Walla Walla and Nez Percé (Schoenberg, 1987, p. 18). Pambrun's influence would encourage the native peoples surrounding the fort to adopt the Catholic faith, much to the consternation of the Protestant missionaries. Wilfred Schoenberg, in his *A History of the Catholic Church in the Pacific Northwest: 1743-1983* cites the following example as representative of the religious cleavage that was developing:

> On a subsequent visit by Demers, a young chief brought his child to be baptized by the priest. Pambrun served as the child's godfather, which gained for him the animosity of Dr. Whitman. "Since that time," Blanchet added ominously, "the young chief and his band always preferred the priests' religion to that of the minister" (Schoenberg, 1987, pp. 37-38).

Schoenberg singled out Pierre Pambrun—along with John McLoughlin at Fort Vancouver, and the first of them all, Old Ignace—as the earliest Catholic prayer leaders in the Pacific Northwest.

In the meantime, the Willamette settlers who had signed the many petitions that prompted the Bishop in Quebec to send the priests out to the coast had gathered in anticipation of their arrival at Fort Vancouver. With multiple delays, however, after nearly a week of waiting they had given up and returned home. A committee of three of the earliest settlers among them stayed behind to welcome the priests. It was composed of community elders Joseph Gervais, Etienne Lucier, and Pierre Beleque. Leaving Fort Walla Walla after a one-day stay on November 19, the two priests reached Fort Vancouver five days later on November 24, 1838.

They received a warm welcome from James Douglas, acting Chief Factor in the absence of John McLoughlin. Now there was much work to be done. Blanchet sternly told his people, the *Canadiens* and their families, that he had come to convert them to God, and for that purpose a mission would begin that very night. There would be Mass each morning and prayers and sermons most of the day. The priests estimated the number of Catholics in the village of Fort Vancouver—*Canadien* and Iroquois—at only seventy-six, but this did not include children and wives awaiting baptism and catechism. As the fur trade marriages *à la façon du pays* were unacceptable, the priests demanded that husbands and wives be immediately separated until their marriages could be properly blessed. Blanchet's goal was to bring these lost sheep back into the fold.

Demers, who had already shown a special talent for learning indigenous languages, was assigned by Blanchet to learn the Chinook Jargon. Though Demers considered the Chinook language itself "unlearnable," he mastered the regional pidgin, the Chinook Jargon, in several weeks. Demers was then able to communicate without an interpreter up and down the river (Schoenberg, 1987, p. 41). In fact, Demers and Blanchet not only came to be proficient in this regional pidgin, they authored a dictionary of the Chinook Jargon (Blanchet, 1856; Demers, Blanchet, & Saint Onge, 1871). Both French and Chinook were used in their missions to teach their indigenous converts prayers and canticles (Blanchet, 1878, p. 85)

Blanchet and Demers forged close ties with the Iroquois Freemen, French-Canadians, and Métis. Together they were instrumental in building a Catholic mission in Washington Territory. Following a successful mission in early December to Cowlitz Prairie, a four-family Catholic settlement north of Fort Vancouver, Father Blanchet embarked on a similar mission on January 3, 1839, but this time to a larger settlement of retired *Canadiens* on the Willamette. Étienne Lucier and Pierre Beleque were in charge of the transportation to the settlement. Two large canoes paddled out with father Blanchet to the *Campement de Sable* at Champoeg. A small Hudson's Bay Company establishment there also served as landing for the French Prairie settlements. Blanchet and his escorts covered the last four miles on horseback to the log cabin that had been built several years earlier to serve as a church in anticipation of a priest's arrival in the region.

That evening, on January 5, he announced the beginning of the mission. The following day, Father Blanchet celebrated the first Catholic Mass before the French-Canadians and Métis that had gathered for the occasion. This was the first Mass celebrated in the Willamette Valley, and the small church was blessed under the patronage of St. Paul. Here too, the men agreed to be separated from their wives until the Catholic Church blessed their marriages (Schoenberg, 1987, p. 42). The Methodists, who had already been in the valley for four years and had performed Christian marriages for these same couples, considered this latter provision a provocation. Instead of cooperating in the face of enormous challenges, the two frontier religious communities were already polarizing. In Schoenberg's assessment, Blanchet was responsible for the conflict: "While it is true there had been sectarian tensions on the frontier from the very beginning, it is also true that Blanchet's rather precipitous and public denial of the validity of the freeman's marriages ticked off a new kind of friction that developed into a very real persecution of the church" (Schoenberg, 1987, p. 42). However, as shall be demonstrated, Blanchet saw his work as returning the Catholic faithful to their proper and chosen religious fold.

For his part, Blanchet saw the Protestant missionaries as "tourists" who did little to convert the indigenous peoples to Christianity. He describes the Methodist missionaries as preoccupied by profit and land speculation, referring to them as "the land-sharks and horse-jockeys" (Blanchet (1878, p. 13). Blanchet sets the Catholic missionaries symbolically above the Protestants, as the Catholics were in his view those willing to sacrifice for their faith, and the ones truly interested in converting the pagan indigenous peoples.

One thing evident in Blanchet's account is the continued existence of a *Canadien* and a (French-speaking) Iroquois identity. Blanchet (1878, p. 61), in describing the first Mass at Fort Vancouver in 1838, refers specifically to Canadians, or to be more precise French *Canadiens*: "The divine service of that day was moving, even to tears, as many of the Canadians had not heard Mass for ten, fifteen and even twenty years. That day was one for them that would never be forgotten." Blanchet then enumerates the Catholics they would serve, notably the twenty-eight forts of the fur trade, the servants being "in great majority Catholic" as well as the four families settled in Cowlitz and the twenty-six established in the "Wallamette"[1] valley, and the work to be done:

> Many of the servants and settlers had forgotten their prayers and the religious principles they had received in their youth. The women they had taken for their wives were pagans, or baptized without sufficient knowledge. Their children were raised in ignorance. One may well imagine that in many places, disorder, rudeness of morals and indecency of practices, answered to that state of ignorance (Blanchet, 1878, p. 62).

Blanchet explains that the Protestants had reached the Pacific before they did and had succeeded in converting some and marrying others. He writes, "As for the Methodist ministers we have seen before, they were visiting the French settlers, had succeeded in bringing some of them to their Sunday meetings, baptized some women and performed marriages" (Blanchet, 1878, p. 63). Of particular interest in this passage is the use of French as a means to highlight the illegitimate work of the Methodists to lead astray the *Canadien* from their national religion, and the vocabulary used to describe the work of the Methodists was that of "seduction," with the Protestants propagating "error" (Blanchet, 1878, pp. 63-64). As if to highlight the shoddy work of the Protestant missionaries, Blanchet notes that one marriage performed by Rev. D. Leslie included that of a *Canadien* who could not provide the death certificate of the wife he had left behind in Canada (Blanchet, 1878, p. 80).

Father Blanchet preached hell and damnation throughout his three-week mission. The women and children lived in tents, and the men slept elsewhere. The day began with Mass at six, followed by a sermon, general instructions, and prayers intermixed with the singing of hymns. There were short breaks at noon and again at around four in the afternoon. In the evening they picked up again. In Blanchet's own words, "At dusk, took place the evening prayer, the reading of pious books and singing of French canticles; after which some boys were taught to read in French and serve at Mass" (1878, p. 79). At the end of the three-week period, Father Blanchet had performed seventy-two baptisms, twenty-five of which involved the Native American wives of the French-Canadians along with their Métis children.

After another week at St. Paul, Father Blanchet headed back down the Willamette River to Fort Vancouver, and then back up to Cowlitz Landing where he oversaw the work being done at this first mission:

> On March 16, 1839, the vicar general arrived again at Cowlitz, this time primed and ready to give a mission. He found Augustine Rochon, "the servant of the mission," busy with his axe. He had cut six thousand fence rails and had squared the timbers

A Catholic Ladder of Heaven and Hell some two meters in length, ca. 1870-1874. This Catholic ladder was credited to Father Albert Lacombe in Alberta who developed the finely detailed pictorial map of the route to heaven. In fact, its roots trace back to the Pacific Northwest. Father François-Norbert Blanchet first developed one to use in the Cowlitz Mission in 1842. Father Lacombe developed this artistically detailed ladder that so impressed Pope Pius IX that he commissioned several thousand copies in 1874 for worldwide missionary work. In chapter 9, we propose a rhizomatic model to understand the emergence of a pancontinental Métis ethnonational community. In many ways, the Catholic Church has perfected the model. Individual clerics moved across the globe as did their ideas.

for house and barn. All that was lacking now was a team of oxen to drag these hewn logs to the building site. Blanchet moved in with Plamondon, who also provided a large room for services. There he began again with stern homilies on hell and damnation, long prayers, singing and daily Mass. The news of his presence at Cowlitz caused numerous delegations of Indians to come from even remote distances to see and hear the Black Robe (Schoenberg, 1987, p. 44).

It was at this time that Father Blanchet, confronted with the need to quickly introduce a large number of indigenous people to the teachings of Christianity, developed his visual aid, the Catholic Ladder, based upon the practice of using such aids to introduce religious teachings in a visual manner to low- or non-literate populations. Albert Furtwangler (2005), in *Bringing Indians to the Book,* considers the ladders to be the most ingenious and spectacular teaching devices used by missionaries:

> The ladder took several significantly different forms. The best known were long strips of paper or cloth, representing all of history from the creation of the world, at the bottom, to either the present year or attainment of heaven, at the top. They seem to have begun in picture teaching of some sort done by Henry and Eliza Spalding, and were followed by carved wooden towers used in catholic teaching, then painted cloth or paper ladders developed by the priests, and finally a Protestant ladder or ladders designed to rival and deride the Catholic ladders, which also circulated widely in lithographed or printed form. All of these forms involved pictorial symbols or illustrations of Bible stories and patterns (Furtwangler, 2005, p. 138).

The ladder evolved from a square rule to a "large chart containing the great epochs of the world, such as the Deluge, the Tower of Babel, the ten commandments of God, the 12 apostles, the seven sacraments and precepts of the Church" (Blanchet, 1878, p. 85).

The Catholic priests and Methodist ministers continued to crisscross the territory, seeking converts to their respective faiths. At one point Father Demers was seen passing through the Cowlitz Prairie heading north on an urgent mission. Blanchet had learned that a Methodist minister was visiting Fort Nisqually on the south end of Puget Sound, and he had dispatched Demers to that location. At the end of Demers' ten-day mission at Fort Nisqually, one of the thirteen residents to step forward to receive baptism was Mrs Hélène Kittson, the wife of the fort's Chief Trader, William Kittson. Helene was the Métis daughter of the giant Finan McDonald who had come over the Rocky Mountains in 1807 with David Thompson and Jaco Finlay.

Back in Fort Vancouver for six weeks, on June 22, Demers hitched a ride upriver with the returning fur brigade of fifty-seven men under Peter Skeen Ogden. At Fort Walla Walla, he procured horses and a Native American guide to take him back up to Fort Colville where he preached on a mission lasting thirty-three days. Returning down river by boat afterwards, Demers stopped at

Fort Okanogan where he preached for eight days. Though finding the place "forbidding and sterile," Demers was pleasantly surprised on another front. He wrote:

> For all that the population there is eager for the word of God. I had the pleasure of meeting there a Christian by the name of Robillard, who had taught the prayers to the natives. That unsuspected help spared me many difficulties (Schoenberg, 1987, p. 47).

The work of the Catholic missionaries, as mentioned, had been facilitated by the teachings of the French-Canadian, Métis, and Iroquois believers who had been living among the indigenous nations across the western United States. They not only had prepared the path for the missionaries, they also served as guides and interpreters. When Demers returned to Walla Walla, Pambrun, like Cuthbert Robillard, served as catechist and interpreter, when necessary. As Schoenberg notes, "they wanted to share the religion they themselves valued" (Schoenberg, 1987, pp. 47-48).

The Catholics and the Protestants held each other in mutual disdain, both willing to go to great lengths in proselytyzing to challenge the other's faith. Blanchet (1878, pp. 90-91) narrates the case of a Protestant missionary who, when the Hudson's Bay Governor told him that "it was none of his business" that the Catholic missionaries were aggressively competing against the "Wesleyan wolves," circulated an anti-Catholic tract titled *Maria Monk,* which "pretended to give 'awful disclosures' concerning confession and convent life, and was filled with stale slanders and exploded inventions." These efforts riled the *Canadiens* who had saved the lives of these same Methodist ministers a month before. According to Blanchet (1878, p. 91):

> It appears that an Indian had stolen some wheat and being discovered he was severely beaten at the Methodist mission: his tribe threatened to massacre the people at the mission which so alarmed Rev. David Leslie that he hastened at once to the *Canadiens* begging them to use their influence with the Indians to save them, which the *Canadiens* did most effectually.

Clearly, the *Canadiens* and their Métis offspring had established good relations with the Native Americans and could be called upon to serve as mediators. For the Americans, still numerically insignificant, they were thus essential in maintaining the peace. When American military hegemony was being imposed during the 1850s, the *Canadiens* were still useful intermediaries, though they could later be discarded when they were no longer necessary to keep the peace.

Father De Smet Answers the Call

While Blanchet and Demers were already actively engaged in their missionary work on the Pacific, in April 1840, Young Ignatius and Father Pierre-Jean De Smet joined a party of thirty men belonging to the American Fur Company as they

Meeting with Père de Smet in the Rocky Mountains, Henry J. Warre, 1846. The French-speaking and Catholic Iroquois who had settled in the Bitter Root Valley sent three delegations asking for a Black Robe to come and minister to them and the Salish with whom they shared the fundamentals of their Catholic Faith. After the fourth delegation, Father Pierre-Jean de Smet was sent west with the Iroquois delegation. He traveled countless miles in the ensuing years.

were heading to the Rocky Mountains. Twenty months after the arrival of Fathers Blanchet and Demers at Fort Vancouver by canoe, Father De Smet reached the Flatheads by horse overland from St. Louis. On his way to the Flathead lands, at the Green River rendezvous, De Smet and his party met ten warriors from the Flathead and allied tribes, who had been sent to escort the Black Robe to their camp. Pierre Gaucher had gotten through with good tidings the winter before, though exhausted, starved, half-frozen, and having lost his Nez Percé companion. De Smet recounts this joyous occasion:

> Our meeting was not that of strangers, but of friends. … I wept for joy in embracing them, and with tears in their eyes they welcomed me with tender words, with child-like simplicity. The Flatheads gave me the news of the tribe, recounting their almost miraculous preservation in a battle that lasted five days, in which they killed about fifty of the enemy without losing a single man. "We fought like braves," they told me, "by our desire to see you. The Great Spirit had pity upon us, and helped us clear of all danger the road you must follow." The Blackfeet retired weeping. It will be some time before they molest us again (Laveille, 1915, p. 106).

Though De Smet's primary goal was preaching to the indigenous peoples of the Rocky Mountains, he encountered a number of French-Canadian and Métis hunters living in the territory. "I preached in French and English (writes the missionary) to the American and Canadian hunters, and then through an interpreter addressed the Flatheads and the Snakes" (Laveille, 1915, pp. 106-107). At a gathering of French-Canadian hunters, Métis, and indigenous converts, Father De Smet, officiated a service where the French-Canadians sang their hymns in French and Latin, while the Native Americans joined in their own tongue (Laveille, 1915, pp. 106-107).

Continuing his expedition, Father De Smet headed north to a gathering of about 1600 Flatheads (Tête Platte), Nez Percé, Spokane, and Pend d'Oreille at Pierre's Hole near the foot of the Grand Tetons. Arriving there on July 12, Father De Smet presided over four Masses a day and performed over three hundred baptisms. He designated one particularly zealous chief to be his catechist. After this, the indigenous converts broke camp and headed for the continental divide, which they reached on July 22, dropping down over the other side to an area near the Three Forks of the Missouri. Here, Father De Smet encountered a French-Canadian trapper named Bruette heading to Fort Colville and dashed off a note to Father Blanchet informing him that he had begun his mission among the Flatheads, Pend d'Oreille, and Nez Percés, singling out the first two tribes as being in the "best desirable disposition." He wrote that, "The few weeks I had to pass among them, have been the happiest of my life" (Schoenberg, 1987, pp. 54-55).

The ring had been closed with Blanchet and Demers covering the lands to the west of the Rocky Mountains bordering the lower Columbia River system, and De Smet, those further to the east, along the the tributaries of the Columbia, the Clark Fork of the Columbia, the Racine Amer (Bitter Root), and the Pend d'Oreille rivers. Having accomplished his mission, De Smet returned to St. Louis in 1840. He was back as promised the following year to establish St. Mary's mission in the Bitter Root Valley, reaching the valley on September 24, 1841. In October, Father De Smet headed off across the Coeur d'Alene Mountains to visit the Kalispel on the way to the Hudson's Bay Company post of Fort Colville where he intended to obtain provisions for the mission. At Fort Colville he purchased oats, wheat and potatoes for planting, plus cows. The chief factor at the post also gave the missionary sugar, coffee, tea, chocolate, butter, crackers, flour, and poultry. The heavily laden Father De Smet was back at St. Mary's on December 8, 1841. In addition, during his forty-two-day absence he had baptized 190 people, and had preached the Gospel to over two thousand Indians. On Christmas day, back among the Flatheads at St. Mary's, De Smet, along with Fathers Mengarini and Point, administered baptism to 150 more adults and performed thirty-two marriages (Schoenberg, 1987, pp. 58-62).

Falls at Colville [Colville (Interior Salish)], Paul Kane, ca. 1849-1856. From Alaska and down the Pacific Coast, the indigenous peoples relied on the plentiful supply of food from spawning salmon. This essential component of their diet allowed for elaborate cultures, semi-sedentary villages and populations, and increasing social stratification. However, the *Canadien* voyageur generally despised the dried salmon referring to it as "bardeau" or clapboard (Tassé, 1886, 206).

West of the Cascades

Closer to the Pacific coast Fathers Blanchet and Demers contineud to labor to bring Catholicism to the Native Americans in their sector, while ministering to the on-going needs of the *Canadiens* and Métis. Head-on competition with the Protestants soon developed for the allegiance of various tribes. Brother Alvin Waller of the Methodist mission produced a Protestant Ladder to challenge the Catholic one, while father Blanchet asserted that the Clackamas preferred his Ladder to that of Waller's. One way or the other, each party started to show the other on their respective visual aids/ladders as falling into the fires of hell.

Blanchet inevitably found himself caught up in the politics and diplomacy of the Willamette Valley's increasingly mixed community. As the 1840s began, political pressure increased for sorting out the joint British and American occupancy of the Oregon Country, which had been in place since the signing of the Treaty of 1818. The North West Company, followed by the Hudson's Bay Company, had filled the void for almost a quarter of a century. However, with the wagons start-ing to roll in over the Oregon Trail, time was quickly running out.

The death of a prosperous but intestate American cattleman, Ewing Young, in February 1841 brought the problem to a head. At the meeting called to settle his estate, a motion was made to tackle the bigger issue of the lack of local gov-ernance and legislation. At a subsequent meeting held to elect officers and com-mittee members, Father Blanchet found himself appointed chairman (against his wishes). It was understood that he had been selected by the Americans to gain the support of the still larger *Canadien* and Métis community, "many of whom had been identified with the Hudson's Bay Company and were still attached to the Canadian government, which protected them" (Schoenberg, 1987, p. 64). The committee had been directed to report back on June 1, 1841, but Blanchet had never called the committee into session. His reasoning was simply that it was appropriate to consult with the highest-ranking U.S. official in the region at the time, Commodore Wilkes, who was heading up a U.S. Navy mapping expedition and fleet. Wilkes wasn't expected to reach St. Paul for another week, and Blanchet considered his input on matters of forming a provisional governing body essen-tial to the work of the committee. Some of the American settlers immediately accused him of stonewalling and acting in bad faith. Many American historians have since rejected these insinuations. Moreover, when Father Blanchet consulted Commodore Wilkes, he too was skeptical as to the feasibility of local governance, expressing in his view "that the country was too young" (Schoenberg, 1987, p. 65).

In any event, the Americans would have their own way two years later at another outdoor meeting in Champoeg in May 1843. By that time they were numerous enough that they only needed a few *Canadiens* from this ever more diverse community to cross over to give them a majority to begin the process of establishing a provisional government. There were limits to the oft-noted loyalty of the particularly independent *Canadiens* and Métis. The ambivalence toward their British overlords was beginning to show as consensus eroded. Chief Factor Jean-Baptiste (John) McLoughlin was not far behind them, as he would soon break with the Company and the British government, while increasing his ties with the *Canadien* Catholic Church. McLoughlin wasn't voting that day, yet was still adhering to the party line. The gentlemen, or renegades, that did vote included Étienne Lucier, one of the original Astorians who had arrived in the overland party in 1812 and had stayed on under the new ownership, later co-founding the French Prairie settlement; Charles McKay, who had recently arrived in the 1841 immigration organized by the Hudson's Bay Company from the Red River settlement with his Métisse wife and children, of Byrd and Montour lin-eage (Metis historian John C. Jackson is one of their numerous descendants),— McKay became disenchanted by the company's broken commitments at Fort

Nisqually; Charles Campo who was generally identified to be of French-Canadian origins but also accepted as an American due to his birth south of the border (almost certainly from the Detroit Michigan branch of the Campeau clan); and François-Xavier Mathieu, another recent arrival who had fled Quebec to the U.S. to escape British repression following the failed Rebellion of the Patriots in 1837-1838. With the arrival six months after the Champoeg meetings of the next wave of migrants coming into the Oregon Country via the Oregon Trail, in November of 1843, the Protestant Americans gained over eight hundred more adherents, and a decisive majority on the ground. They would never again need to co-opt any French-Canadians or Métis to establish a territorial government and eventually, attain the goal of statehood.

In the interim, three prominent individuals within Hudson's Bay Company officer ranks were lost to the Catholic Church in the 1841-42 timeframe. Demers lost his good friend, the chief clerk at Fort Walla Walla, in May. Pierre Pambrun, who had served the church long and well, died in the prime of life in an accident while riding a horse. Demers lost another friend, William Kittson, formerly in charge of Fort Nisqually, at Fort Vancouver after a long illness during which he requested and received baptism. The third fatality involved one of the sons of John McLoughlin, John Jr., who was killed by one of his own men at a remote coastal outpost after having returned from studying medicine in Paris. These deaths, especially that of Pambrun, impacting the lay leadership within the Catholic community would initially undermine the influence of Blanchet and Demers over the *Canadiens* and Native Americans, but would precipitate one positive development for the Church. John McLoughlin Sr., having in the interim become a soul mate of Father Blanchet, was increasingly susceptible to a return to the faith of his early years. His personal anguish was further heightened by the attitude of his superior, Governor Simpson, toward his son's culpability in the incident. This proved to be one more step in the former Nor'wester's alienation from the Anglo-Canadian authorities and their norms prevailing within the Hudson's Bay Company, contributing to his decision to accept confirmation by Blanchet in a public ceremony. Several years later he would leave the company and join his fellow *Canadiens* and his Métis children in declaring his intention to become an American, while settling on his disputed claim in Oregon City.

De Smet Sweeps through the Middle Columbia and McLoughlin Converts

After the miserable winter of 1841-42—one marked by endless snow in *les montagnes* (Montana) and endless rain in the lower Columbia—Father De Smet readied himself for a journey to a conclave with Fathers Blanchet and Demers at St. Paul's in French Prairie. It would take almost two months to get there due to a busy agenda along the way for the missionary. He turned his trip into a wide

The American Village, Oregon City, ca. 1848 by Henry J. Warre. In 1829, the Chief Factor of the Hudson's Bay Company claimed the land between the Willmette Falls and the Clackamas River and built three log houses. In 1832, he built a sawmill and later a gristmill. With the arrival of increasing numbers of American settlers, McLoughlin had the land surveyed and renamed the settlement Oregon City, which was the territorial capital until it was moved to Salem in 1853.

sweep, spending days with many of the interior tribes that had shown the highest level of interest in Christianity.

Father De Smet's itinerary during this journey to the coast and back corresponds to the location of Catholic missions which were later built, resulting ultimately in the consolidation of much of the indigenous population into heavily Catholic reservations with sizable Métis populations. The St. Ignatius, Sacred Heart, and St. Francis Regis missions, after the forced relocation of indigenous populations, would be the *loci* of the Flathead, Coeur d'Alene and Colville reserves. Most of the Spokanes, principally the Catholic bands, would eventually be relocated to one of these three reserves. In the end several smaller bands of Catholics joined the Protestant Indians on the Lower Spokane River who did get a reservation of their own in their homeland. This would be next to the Protestant Tshimakain Mission of the Walkers and the Eells.

Jean-Baptiste (John) McLoughlin. Born in Rivière-du-Loup and baptized Jean-Baptiste, John McLoughlin was raised in Lower Canada and trained as a physician. He signed up with the North West Company to serve as a physician and apprentice clerk and rose through the ranks to become the chief factor of the Columbia district. When the lands south of the 49th parallel became American, McLoughlin left the Hudson's Bay Company and sought American citizenship. He spent his final years in Oregon City as a merchant and mill owner. He was later credited as the "father of Oregon."

When De Smet arrived at Fort Vancouver on June 8, Father Modeste Demers greeted him. Together they traveled up the Willamette to St. Paul where they met Blanchet, and the three French-speaking priests spent eight days in informal discussions over the needs of the church in the Pacific Northwest. On Sunday, De Smet sang a high Mass and preached in the church at St. Paul. One enthusiastic comment of De Smet's during this conclave was noted as worthy of translation into English for purposes of posterity. Blanchet showed De Smet the Catholic ladder. "That plan, De Smet exclaimed with characteristic magnanimity, will be adopted by the missions of the whole world" (Schoenberg, 1987, p. 67). Feeling renewed, the three priests returned to Fort Vancouver where as guests of Chief Factor John McLoughlin, they held the first Oregon Council. It was agreed that they would establish a base of operations at St. Paul for the Jesuits in *les montagnes* (Montana), the Jesuits assuming the lead with missions east of the Cascades, while those to the west side in the coastal regions would continue to be under the responsibility of the missionaries from Quebec (Schoenberg, 1987, p. 68). This was good business for the Hudson's Bay Company as well. Both Catholic orders would be reliant on the HBC for provisioning and credit as they expanded operations throughout the northwest. But then, perhaps there was more involved for McLoughlin than mercantile considerations.

After the Council, De Smet and Demers departed for Fort Walla Walla with an HBC fur brigade heading upriver. At Fort Walla Walla they separated. Demers continued on to the upper Columbia in New Caledonia with the HBC brigade, while De Smet traveled on by horseback, a journey which turned into a cattle drive, bringing thirty-one head over the mountains to St. Mary's. Arriving back at St. Mary's on July 27, 1842, he found Father Nicolas Point had left to accompany most of the Flatheads of the Bitterroot Valley on their summer buffalo hunting expedition across the Rockies and out onto the Great Plains. De Smet appointed Mengarini as acting superior of the Rocky Mountain Mission, then sought out the Flatheads and Father Point, finding them on the Madison River, above Three Forks. After they had returned with the Flatheads to the Bitterroot Valley, DeSmet directed Father Point to accompany Brother Huet to establish a mission for the Coeur d'Alenes. De Smet then headed down the Missouri to St. Louis with an escort of ten Native Americans. Once in St. Louis, De Smet prepared to set off for Europe to raise funds and recruit more priests and nuns, soon to be followed by Father Blanchet.

The plan devised by the three priests in charge of the Catholic Church in the Pacific Northwest was coming to fruition. In September 1842, two more priests arrived from Canada, Fathers Antoine Langlois and Jean Baptiste Zacharie Bolduc. Langlois was sent south to St. Paul, Oregon, and Bolduc north to the Cowlitz. Another major event, which occurred in December at Fort Vancouver was the formal return of Dr. John McLoughlin to the church of his parents and maternal grandmother. Schoenberg describes this event with dramatic flourish:

> Dr. John McLoughlin, practically speaking the lord and master of all of Oregon, formally returned to the Catholic Church. At the hands of the vicar general the White Headed Eagle made his profession of Faith and had his marriage blessed. Following this, during the four weeks of Advent, he lived on his claim at Willamette Falls, fasting every day to prepare for his first Communion. …
>
> For the Christmas Midnight Mass, the little chapel at the fort was crowded with whites, and Indians. It had been decorated lavishly, and numerous lamps had been placed "for brilliant illumination"—enough for a pope with weak eyes. "Christmas hymns sung in French and Chinook Jargon stirred the souls of all, as well as the holy functions around the Altar." At the proper time, McLoughlin made his First Communion "at the head of 38 communicants." For the Native Americans of Oregon, this was the conversion of their king; for the Methodists, this was the crack of doom (Schoenberg, 1987, p. 70).

Around this same time, McLoughlin had also been supervising a team of surveyors who were measuring lots and blocks to be sold in what would become Oregon City. He was preparing for retirement and life after the Hudson's Bay Company, a life on the side of the Columbia expected to fall to the Americans, and he was finalizing his legacy. There were others, however, who were making different plans altogether.

De Smet Returns: 1843-45

In the 1840s, Blanchet and De Smet received more reinforcements and opened additional missions throughout the interior. After the 1846 partition, Father Demers would be redeployed north of the 49th parallel to become the first Bishop of Vancouver Island, and eventually British Columbia. Father De Smet continued to work tirelessly for the Catholic cause in the Pacific Northwest. By early 1843, he had prepared his first book for publication and had toured most of the major cities of the U.S., raising five thousand dollars that he would use to outfit three more Jesuits for the mountain missions. In April, De Smet escorted three priests to Westport, Missouri where they were to join a wagon train for the crossing. Shortly thereafter, De Smet headed to New York, and from there back to Europe for some time, while even even more Jesuits and Oblates were arriving in places like New Orleans.

While the Jesuits' call for volunteers was being answered from Europe, Protestant missionaries in the United States were becoming extremely concerned by the perceived foreign threat. The intensity and drama of the heightened competition for saving the souls of the indigenous peoples can be felt in a poignant letter written by Dr. Whitman's wife, Narcissa, who had remained behind in the Northwest while her husband was back east trying to save the mission from threatened closure:

> "Romanism," Mrs. Whitman had written a few months earlier, "stalks abroad on our right hand and on our left, and with daring effrontery, boasts that she is to prevail and possess the land. I ask, must it be so? The zeal and energy of her priests are without parallel, and many, both white men and Indians, wander after the beasts. Two are in the country below us and two are above in the mountains" (Schoenberg, 1987, p. 73).

In August of 1844, Father DeSmet returned from Europe with five more Jesuits and six nuns. On their ship, the *Indefatigable*, which they had boarded in Belgium on December 12, 1843, they cleared the Schelde estuary on January 9, 1844, rounded Cape Horn on March 20, and came perilously close to being shipwrecked crossing over the Columbia bar on July 31. The primary task of the new priests during the crossing had been studying a foreign language: English. They would tackle the Native American languages once they were ashore and had been farmed out into the interior. Upon arriving, however, the nuns were quickly disillusioned in the Willamette Valley and soon left for warmer climes. The notables assembled to meet the Jesuits and sisters at Fort Vancouver included Dr. John McLoughlin and his wife Marguerite Wadin, along with the Hudson's Bay

Company doctor, Dr. Forbes Barclay. Dr. Barclay was the son-in-law of the late Pierre Pambrun of Fort Walla Walla, having married his older daughter, Marie Pambrun. Once notified of their arrival, Father Blanchet descended the river from St. Paul to join them several days later.

De Smet summoned Father De Vos from the Coeur d'Alene mission in the mountains, called St. Joseph's mission at that time, to direct the new mother-house of the Jesuits to be established in the Willamette Valley. De Vos had been in the country longer and had a better command of English than the other Jesuits. His ease in the use of the language allowed him to establish his influence over the growing English-speaking Catholic community now arriving in larger numbers, beginning with Oregon City. Two of the newly arrived Jesuits, Father Vercruysse and Father Nobli, were given respective assignments to the *Canadiens* in the Willamette Valley and to the village of Fort Vancouver—the latter to work with the Métis and indigenous populations.

In 1844, De Smet, with the help of the sturdy Dutchman, Father Hoecken, traveled to St Michael's located on the Pend d'Oreille River in order to re-establish the flood-damaged mission over on the other side of the river, renaming it St. Ignatius. The new name was chosen due to the site reminding them of descriptions of the surroundings of the cave where St. Ignatius Loyola had composed his famous *Spiritual Exercise*. The following year, De Smet established a mission in the Colville Valley to serve the area's growing Métis population gathering to the south of the Hudson's Bay Company's Fort Colville, which was located just above *les Chaudières*, translated to Kettle Falls. The HBC had a farm and ranching operation in the valley, and an increasing number of Cree and Métis Freemen, along with Company retirees, were establishing their own farms and ranches in the Colville Valley. Amongst these settlers were many Métis of French-Canadian and Cree extraction. In De Smet's own words:

> "I left Kettle Falls August 4th," he wrote, giving an account of his activities in late 1845, "accompanied by several of the nation of the Crees to examine the lands they have selected for the site of a village. The ground is rich and well situated for all agricultural purposes. Several buildings were commercial; I gave the name of St Francis Regis to this new station, where a great number of mixed race and beaver hunters have resolved to settle, with their families" (Schoenberg, 1987, p. 97).

The settlement, centered on a village named Chewelah, is still present on the map today. This community became one of the major Frenchtown settlements of Washington Territory, though it kept an earlier name of indigenous origin.

In 1845, Father De Smet undertook his final missionary expedition in the American West, though he would return with a U.S. Army commission thirteen years later, serving as an Army chaplain on a peace mission to pacify the Indians following the Indian War of 1858. This final exploration phase of church history in the region pushed him as far north as Fort Edmonton. He had even explored southern Alberta, reaching the Bow River. He met with the Crees, Chippewas, and Blackfeet of the area. He proceeded on from Rocky Mountain House to Fort Edmonton, where he wintered. He then left for Jasper House in the spring and worked his way across the mountains, descended the Columbia River and worked his way back to Fort Vancouver in 1846. From here, De Smet would leave for St. Louis, Missouri, where he would spend most of his remaining years, only traveling to Europe on a number of occasions to continue raising funds for the Catholic missions of the West. One of his final achievements was his open discussion with Sitting Bull, who came to accept the Treaty of Fort Laramie.

Father Blanchet

In the interim, on November 4, 1844 Father Blanchet had received word that he was to become bishop of a new northwest diocese, as per a brief from Rome dated December 1, 1843. He needed first to return to Quebec to receive his Episcopal consecration. Before departing, Blanchet compiled a report on his vicariate. According to his best calculation, the indigenous population of the region still numbered about 110,000, of which 6,000 could be classified as Christians. The numbers were split roughly in two, with half in the valleys of the Columbia headwaters in the Rocky Mountains and half in the lower Columbia and Fraser valleys. His estimate of the Catholic white and Métis population was around 1000: 600 in the Willamette Valley, 100 at Vancouver, 100 at Cowlitz Prairie, and the balance of 200 scattered around various trading posts elsewhere in the interior along the Columbia and Fraser Rivers, or along the coast up to Alaska.

On a small ship named the *Columbia*, it took almost half of a year for Blanchet to reach Europe. Doubling Cape Horn on March 5, 1845, they reached England on May 22. Before embarking on a ship returning him to Quebec via Boston, Blanchet penned a letter to the general of the Jesuit Order in Rome, J. Roothaan, pleading for more Jesuits to staff his vicariate. Blanchet wrote a request for twelve priests, preferably having some knowledge of English. In his missive, Blanchet indicated he needed these recruits "before Protestant missionaries come and sow error" (Schoenberg, 1987, p. 91).

On July 25, 1845 at the St. Jacques Cathedral in Montreal, François-Norbert Blanchet was consecrated Bishop of Drasa (the Pacific Northwest) by the Bishop of Montreal, Ignatius Bourget. This achievement was a stunning victory. As Schoenberg relates, "In one of the most amazing decisions in the history of the church, Gregory XVI created an archdiocese in the Oregon wilderness and for a brief time Titular bishop of Drasa, as the archbishop of Oregon City, a mere village, the second only archbishop in the entire United States—Baltimore being first and Kenrick's St. Louis, the third" (Schoenberg, 1987, p. 92). After a month and a half in Quebec, Blanchet headed for Paris via Boston, Liverpool, and London.

Blanchet was in Paris to raise funds and troops for another round in the battle for men's souls in the Pacific Northwest. While there, he received a letter from Father Demers summarizing the activities and developments in the rapidly growing region. Things were changing fast in this ill-defined borderland. The letter noted that Dr. McLoughlin was preparing to leave the Hudson's Bay Company and retire to Oregon, indicating that "a provisory government" had been established with George Abernathy as governor. The Hudson's Bay Company joined the provisory government, with Vancouver, Cowlitz, and Nisqually forming a district with Chief Factor Douglas as the appointed chief judge (Schoenberg, 1987, p. 93). A new church had been built in Vancouver (Washington) called the St. James Church, named in honor of Chief Factor James Douglas—who had helped in the erection of a Catholic Church, even providing the land, despite being himself a member of the Church of England.

Touring the capitals of Europe and circulating with Catholic monarchs, Blanchet received considerable attention and generosity. Money was flowing in, but it was time to proceed to Rome to deal with other matters. While in Rome, word came that the British had settled with the Americans on a definitive border at the 49th parallel. Six weeks later, on July 26, Gregory XVI created the Archepiscopal See of Oregon City, with the two dioceses of Walla Walla and Vancouver Island. Francois-Norbert Blanchet became Archbishop, Demers was to become bishop of Vancouver Island with all districts remaining under British jurisdiction, and Blanchet's younger brother, Augustin Magloire Alexandre Blanchet, would become the Bishop of Walla Walla.

During the winter of 1847, the new Archbishop chartered a small ship (which he blessed, naming it *L'Etoile du Matin*) in the French port of Brest. On board, in addition to the Archbishop, were seven sisters of Notre Dame de Namur; three Jesuit Fathers, Goetz, Gazzoli, and Menetrey, with three Jesuit lay brothers; five secular priests, Lebas, McCormick, Deleneau, Pretot, and Veyret; two deacons, B. Delorme and J. F. Jayol; and a cleric, T. Mesplie. Two years and seven months after Blanchet's departure, the ship arrived at the mouth of the Willamette on August 26, 1847.

Ten days later, on September 5, the Archbishop's younger brother, Augustin Blanchet, arrived overland from Westport, Missouri, reaching the Columbia at Fort Walla Walla. Appointed the first and only Bishop of Walla Walla, Blanchet had left Montreal on March 23, 1847 accompanied by an Acadian priest named Jean-Baptiste Abraham Brouillet and two students destined for the priesthood. They traveled by stagecoach and railroad to Pittsburgh, then down the Ohio by riverboat to St. Louis, arriving in mid-April. In St. Louis they joined up with five

Oblates that had arrived from Marseille, France. The Oblate Superior was father Pascal Ricard. The three priests were Eugene Casimir Chirouse, Charles Pandosy, and Georges Blanchet. There was also a lay brother named Celestin Verney.

At Fort Walla Walla, William McBean—Pierre Pambrun's successor as the post's chief trader—greeted the bishop. McBean, a Catholic of Métis origin, provided the group with temporary housing at the fort. The Bishop of Walla Walla and Father Ricard proceeded to tour the area, meeting with the local indigenous groups while seeking sites for new missions. After eighteen days at the fort, the Bishop met Dr. Marcus Whitman, who was returning to his Waiilatpu mission after having been downriver. Reportedly Dr. Whitman initially expressed himself in abusive language, shouting that he would like to take his own blood and smear it on the Catholic ladder to show the persecution of Protestants by Catholics (Schoenberg, 1987, pp. 106-107).

The doctor was overwrought. Though his mission was prospering financially after an investment of over a decade of his life, measles and dysentery had devastated the Cayuse and Walla Walla populations, and Dr. Whitman could do very little for them. Reports of threats on his life also increased, including those transmitted by Dr. McLoughlin and the Canadian artist Paul Kane. As was widely known, local Native American custom entailed the right of family and friends to take matters into their own hands to settle accounts with medicine men that had failed to cure their ailing patients. A growing number of American settlers also fell sick, but seemed to the indigenous people to have a much better recovery rate while under the doctor's care; suspicions and pent up anger were mounting.

After discussions with Walla Walla Chief Peopeo Moxmox and other tribes, the Oblates opted to establish themselves on the right bank of the Columbia in the Yakima Valley, leaving the left bank with the Walla Walla and Cayuse to the care of Bishop Blanchet and Father Brouillet. The Oblates dedicated their mission to St. Rose on the Yakima. Finally, on November 27, Father Brouillet opened St. Anne's Mission near the Umatilla River, about 35 miles southeast of the Whitman Mission. The diocese of Walla Walla had already reached its pinnacle.

The Sequel

During the 1840s and 1850s, the priests and nuns in the territories of Oregon and Washington had their share of challenges. Members of the various religious orders—the Jesuits, the Oblates, the Sisters of Notre Dame, the Sisters of Providence (later on and north of the river), as well as the secular priests attached to the Diocese or Archdiocese—worked under desperate conditions. Though all attempted to do some good, their work was primarily damage control. With virtually no resources other than personal suasion, around two dozen of them, labored to set up and operate missions to the indigenous peoples. They also established schools, farms, and flour mills. They even provided what medical care they could to the communities. Despite treaties and promises, Congress was tragically slow to fund the commitments made to the Native Americans in return for surrendering their lands. The Office of Indian Affairs was more often than not late to the scene and slow to get started.

Times were also turbulent; the battle of words between the Catholics and Prebytarian Congregationalists like the Whitmans and the Spaldings fueled the flames of the bloody final rounds of the 'Indian-white' wars. Both parties were no doubt guilty of excess in their theological and partisan tirades and insinuations. Catholic priests did stay on with the Native Americans east of the Cascades, providing valuable services to mitigate the damage following the Whitman Massacre. The requirement for their services followed the slew of killings starting in late 1847, and later in 1855-56, and then again in 1858 after the battles with Colonels Steptoe and Wright southwest and west of Spokane. The Catholic-Protestant dimension to this ill will included the mostly French-speaking priests trying to be peacemakers with the new authorities, while protecting the French-Canadians, Métis and Native Americans to whom they ministered.

More importantly, considering the location and configuration of several of the major reservations of the Pacific Northwest and the resident tribes, these priests played a role in mediating and helping coalesce the disparate peoples competing for sovereignty in the region. Robert Ruby's and John Brown's *Indians of the Pacific Northwest* tells us much about the process itself, and the final destination of a significant portion of the regional Métis caught in the middle of it all. "As the fur-trade and missionary eras overlapped, it was quite common for natives to cluster around the far-flung company posts to conduct their devotionals. They were often found speaking and singing prayers beneath the frowning bastions of Fort Walla Walla, at Flathead Post, and at Fort Colvile" (Ruby & Brown, 1981, p. 70).

CHAPTER 8

The March to Statehood

The Oregon Trail consists of a brutal two thousand miles traversing the continent. Thousands of colonists followed it, across the mountains to get to the Oregon Country during the 1840s and 1850s. Because of it, the Americans ensured that the entire Oregon and Washington territories would become part of the United States, leaving the indigenous peoples and the original settlers to be minorities in their homeland. The trail was blazed by a group of eighteen men who left Peoria, Illinois on May 1, 1839. Peoria was a former Illini and later Potawatomi settlement established during the French Regime of the Old Northwest, home to a significant *Canadien* and Métis population before American frontier militia razed it during the War of 1812.

Though the Oregon territory already sported a number of thriving *Canadien* and Métis settlements, and though the migrants followed routes that had been well traveled by hundreds of French, Métis, and American trappers and traders, the main narrative of Americans marching into the wilderness carrying the torch of "civilization" has remained. They called themselves the "Oregon Dragoons," carrying a flag bearing the motto "Oregon or the Grave." Only half of the original eighteen reached Oregon and Fort Walla Walla in 1840. Once the trail had been thoroughly mapped, larger contingents of colonists traveling by wagon left for the Oregon Country each succeeding year. By 1843, up to a thousand migrants were leaving for Oregon annually, with thousands more to follow. In total, over 400,000 settlers traveled westwards on the Oregon Trail, including those that opted for the California, Bozeman, and Mormon branch trails. Wave after wave of settlers pushed forward, altering the political and social landscape of the Pacific Northwest. In the span of one generation, wars were fought and reservations established as the territories were reorganized and Americanized. The State of Oregon was admitted to the American Union in 1859, the first state to be carved out of the former Oregon Territory. The others followed thirty years later.

Born in the Baie Verte—Green Bay—Wisconsin, Alexandre Guérette dit Dumont moved west. He and his trapping partner Joseph Laverdure were among the first settlers in Oregon's Umpqua Region. Alexandre and his wife Josephte Finlay eventually claimed 483 acres in the Walla Walla region in 1854. In his claim form, he noted that he was an "American half-breed Indian" born in Green Bay (Barman, 2015, p. 241).

In Search of a Place to Settle Down; Oregon, Canada or Somewhere In Between

The earliest independent settlement in the Pacific Northwest was located in Willamette Valley, above the falls. The first settlers' farms lay within about a three-and-a-half-mile radius of the modern day village of St. Paul. The valley was ideally suited for agriculture, as the open plains could be readily plowed; moreover, a variety of ecosystems of wetlands and forests provided a diversity of plants and environmental niches that could be exploited by settlers. At the time the first Euro-American hunters entered this valley in the early 1800s, it was still the territory of the Ahantchuyuk Kalapuyans. Having trapped and camped all over the Pacific Northwest since arriving in 1811, these trappers and their wives knew the best spot for locating their small farms when the time came to retire. As Melinda Jetté (2004, p. 125) writes, "In selecting Ahantchuyuk territory for settlement, the 'French-Indian' families chose an environment that was highly desirable in terms of the regional subsistence practices of native women and the agrarian culture of the French Canadians." The Willamette Valley permitted the French-Canadian and Métis settlers to shape the territory, modeling it after settlements in the St. Lawrence and Red River valleys: narrow farm lots were located on the rivers, stretching back to the forest providing all families timber, fields, and water (Jetté, 2004, p. 127).

The trio of retiring Hudson's Bay Company employees generally credited with establishing the French Prairie settlement—Étienne Lucier, Louis Labonté, and Joseph Gervais—had arrived with the Astor Party in 1811 and 1812. Though Astor

Louis Labonte II, 1909. Louis Labonté's father, who was born in Montreal, accompanied William Hunt across the continent to join the other Pacific Fur Company employees at Fort Astoria. Louis the son was born in 1818. His mother was a daughter of Chief Kobayway of the Clatsop nation. Louis would be one of the first retired Hudson's Bay Company employees to settle in French Prairie in the Willamette Valley. The HBC, however, had him travel to Montreal to be discharged, even though he had been first hired in the Oregon Territory.

was a German immigrant of French Huguenot ancestry who had become one of the leading naturalized American entrepreneurs headquarted in New York, he chose to rely heavily on *Canadiens* and Scots from Canada experienced in the fur trade. A fourth *Canadien* who arrived around 1818 in the employ of the North West Company, Pierre Beleque, joined the other three as one of the community's leaders. One co-founder, William Cannon, was American, The oldest member of the group, Cannon was born in Virginia in 1755. Like the *Canadiens* and Scots, Cannon had signed on with the Astorians at Mackinaw Island at the confluence of lakes Michigan and Huron, where he had been in the employ of the North West Company. When Astor's local Pacific Fur Company partners sold out to the North West Company under duress in 1813, a certain number of the employees continued working for the new owners. Others such as the American Crooks and Gabriel Franchère of Montreal returned east of the Rockies, continuing their employment with Astor's American Fur Company in Michigan Territory and the broader Missouri basin.

Amongst the elders of the settler community, Gervais, Labonté, and Cannon each married daughters of Lewis and Clark's associate, Chief Coboway (or Kobayway) of the Clatsops. Gervais married Yaimust, and Labonté, Kilakotah.

Étienne Lucier married Josephite of the Nouete tribe, and Pierre Beleque married the Métisse Geneviève St. Martin, daughter of an early fur trader named Joseph St. Martin and a Chinook Indian woman. Further Métis family clans were therefore added to what was already a growing Métis population well-underway in the French Prairie settlements. Although independent in origins from the more famous Red River Métis "ethnogenesis" and its associated nationalistic narrative, these Métis clearly exhibited similar cultural, social, and organizational patterns to those of Red River stock, suggesting the emergence of a Métis culture prior to its nationalist expression in the Assiniboia region at its apex around 1850.

As of 1833, the number of *Canadien* and French-speaking families living in French Prairie had grown to ten. Nine were headed by *Canadiens*, and one by a Métis of French-Algonquin origin, Jean-Baptiste Desportes McKay. Jean-Baptiste was also the only one to have had a Kalapuyan wife, Marguerite. He simultaneously had a second wife, a Chehalis woman named Marie. Though Jean-Baptiste was apparently among the initial settler group, perhaps even the first settler, he was often omitted from the inner circle in later documentation. This was possibly due to his status as both a bigamist and Métis, according to historian Melinda Marie Jetté.

Then there was the ubiquitous independent trapper, Nicolas Montour, from the powerful Métis Montour clan, originating itself from the Couc dit Lafleur Métis clan from Trois-Rivières, Quebec. Montour, like many of the others, spent a considerable number of years practicing his trade in the region, traveling in and out of the valley over many years. He had long-established relations with the local peoples before definitively retiring there later in the 1830s. Under the heading of the "Ahantchuyuk (Kalapuyan)," Ruby and Brown (1992, p. 3) refer to Nicolas Montour in their book, *A Guide to the Indian Tribes of the Pacific Northwest,* when describing the origins of the first white settlement on French Prairie, Chemaway (now Chemawa), named by former Hudson's Bay Company employees who had followed Joseph Gervais in 1828. They specify that, "Tradition has it that a free trapper, named George Montour, had settled on the Prairie about fifteen years earlier." Meanwhile, one of Nicolas's future sons-in-law, the Métis Thomas McKay, was farming on the Scappoose Plains near the mouth of the Willamette during the 1830s. Ruby and Brown also note one of the more sordid elements of the history of the French-speaking settlers of the Pacific Northwest: the Ahantchuyuks and other Kalapuyan speakers sold slaves to a number of *Canadien* settlers, who then put these slaves to work on their farms.

Quebec's Lasting Footprint

Interestingly, the balance of five among this core group of ten families were all from Quebec, or Lower Canada as it was known until 1840: Joseph Delard of

Sorel, Quebec, married to a Shushuwap woman whose Christian name was Lisette; Jean-Baptiste Perrault from St. Antoine, Quebec, married to a Chehalis woman named Angelique; Amable Arquette from St Laurent, Quebec, married a Chinook woman named Marguerite; Pierre Depot of St. Roch, Quebec, married to another Marguerite, but this one of the Clackamas tribe; and André Picard of St. Thomas, Quebec, married an Okanogan named Marie. These unions between *Canadien* men and indigenous women—yet from different nations—is at the core of one of the most important facets of the common denominator of Métis identity across North America. It best exemplifies how the nexus of new indigenized identities distinctively *"Métis"* were being shaped through the reunion of inherently mobile French-Canadian-indigenous families, which often include different indigenous kinships and cultural traditions shaped by generations of fur trade and trapping activities. The "mixing" not only of "bloods" but of various indigenous traditions with French-Canadian and Catholic heritage helps to explain how these individuals have been able to form French-indigenous communities (Métis) irreducible to the common binary assumption of them being easily assimilated either by their indigenous groups or European counterpart.

Yet another daughter of Coboway, Celiast, took a different route to upward mobility within the fur trapper *cum* settler community. Celiast had originally married a French-Canadian laborer named Basil Poirier, but left him in the early 1830s while living in the village outside Fort Vancouver. According to Jetté (2004, p. 122), "She then entered a life-long relationship with a more socially desirable man, Solomon Smith." At that time, Smith was teaching the Métis children of company employees at a school located at Fort Vancouver. Smith had come west with the fur trade expedition of New Englander Nathaniel Wyeth in 1832. By 1834, she notes that the couple was living with Celiast's sister, Yiamust, and brother-in-law, Joseph Gervais, in French Prairie (Jetté, 2004, p. 122). The Lower Chinook through the progeny of Clatsop chieftain Caboway would be well represented in the new Willamette community of French Prairie.

One might wonder what motivated the local Kalapuyans to allow these early French-Native American families to settle in their territory. Though it is not possible to answer this question with certainty, Melinda Jetté (2004, pp. 130-131) offers us the following explanation: "From a Kalapuyan perspective, permitting these few families to settle in the Ahantchuyuk territory was seen as a way to further incorporate the newcomers into aboriginal systems of trade and kinship, ties that had developed with the newcomers over the previous fifteen years." This practice was surely not limited to the Columbia River region, being evident in numerous locations throughout the Americas. On the receptivity of neighbouring indigenous communities to Métis settlers, it can be suggested that the composition of Métis communities, with their various kinship connections to multiple indigenous

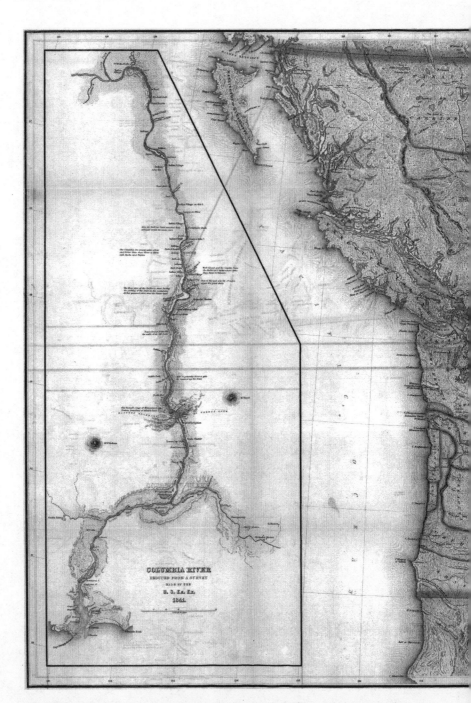

Map of the Oregon Territory, by the U.S. Ex. Ex. Charles Wilkes, Esqr. Commander, 1841. The Wilkes Expedition, seeking lands and potential ports for the United States, produced a detailed map of the Pacific Northwest that guided American politicians in their border negotiations with the British. Some American politicians were pushing for the border to be

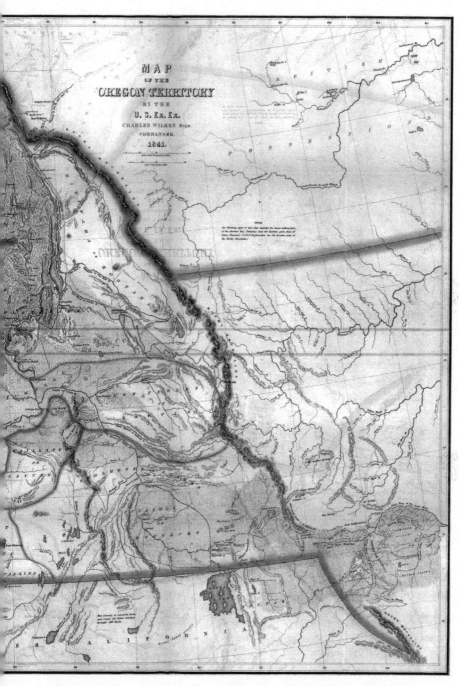

drawn at the 54th parallel, in what is now central British Columbia, while the Hudson's Bay Company would have preferred the Columbia River as the boundary. The 49th parallel was agreed upon, with the exception of Vancouver Island that remained British. The smaller islands between it and the mainland were divided between the British and Americans.

nations in addition to French-Canadian connections often criss-crossing many regions throughout North America, came as great opportunities for these Indigenous communities to form tantalizing and far-reaching alliances. Already on the basis of the history of the many rapprochements between indigenous peoples and French-Canadians, it can also be suggested that these Native American communities didn't see the *Canadiens* and their Métis families as any typical European settler, but rather as indigenized—if not indigenous—settlers or even, on occasions, as refugees moving away from the encroaching influences of American and/or British colonialism and impending statehood.

One member of the second generation of the core settler families, Louis Labonté (junior), provides the only recorded first-hand account of relations between the settlers and the Ahantchuyuk Kalapuyans during the transition years of the early 1830s. His father Louis had left Montreal and traveled to St. Louis as a young man of eighteen where he was hired by the American Fur Trade Company. Louis had worked for the company for four years before being relocated to the Pacific Coast. When the North West Company took over Fort Astoria, Louis signed on with it and later became an employee of the Hudson's Bay Company (Lyman, 1900, p. 170). Born in Astoria in 1818, his son, Louis Labonté II, spent his entire life in the Pacific Northwest until his death in 1911. Lyman (1900, p. 169) stresses his fluency in a number of indigenous languages, including his mother's: "the Clatsop or Chinook, the Tillamook, Tualatin and Calapooya, of which he says he knew a few words, and the Spokane which he understood almost perfectly. Besides these, he talked fluently in the Indian jargon and in French and English." His memoirs "speak of lively social relations between the indigenous peoples and the newcomers" and "French-Indian families also appear to have been privileged to attend weddings of the Ahantchuyuk," affirms Jetté. "Labonte's memoirs describe in detail the wedding ceremony of the local Kalapuyans, including the exchange of gifts that solemnized the marriage between two families, and between two tribal groups" (Jetté, 2004, pp. 131-132). Unfortunately, shortly thereafter, the situation for the Kalapuyans began to deteriorate dramatically as epidemics decimated their communities.

In describing the first *Canadien* settlers who chose to stay in the Willamette Valley, Louis Labonté II explains that the Hudson's Bay Company did not want its men to either get married or stay once their contracts ended. The men signed contracts for three years, then had to go to Montreal to receive the salary owed to them (minus any items charged to their account and bought from the Company). Their contracts could be renewed, but as Father De Smet noted, many of the men at the end of twenty or thirty years finished their terms as engagés as poor as the day they were hired (P. J. De Smet & Vercruysse, 1844, p. 45). Louis Labonté, when recounting the story of his father, affirms that his father's contract ended in 1828;

the elder Louis tried to argue that he had been hired in Oregon and could there-fore be discharged in Oregon, as men were to be discharged where they were hired. However, he argued in vain and was obliged to return to Montreal in March. But with his contract officially terminated, he returned to Oregon independently to settle in the Willamette Valley (Lyman, 1900, pp. 170-171).

In July 1831 an outbreak of an intermittent fever, "fever and ague" in the his-torical documents or "*la fièvre tremblante*" as the *Canadiens* called it, swept through the Pacific Northwest. One widely accepted story as to its origins is that an infected crew member of a visiting American ship, the *Owyhee*, under Captian John Dominis, was generally considered to have been the source of the epidemic (which was almost certainly malaria). Though it was present in other parts of North America, the Northwest had previously been spared this tropical disease. The intermittent fever first appeared throughout the Lower Columbia over the summer and fall of 1830, then reappeared after a winter respite, spreading quickly up the Willamette Valley. The local population was very vulnerable, having had no genetic or acquired immunity. Once bitten by the local mosquitoes that had picked up the disease from the convalescing *Owyhee* crewmember, fever and death often followed. The first three years of the epidemic, 1830 to 1833, were probably the most deadly, and "probably constitute the single most important epidemiological event in the recorded history of what would eventually become the state of Oregon," also ravaging what is now western Washington State (Jetté, 2004, p. 141). Upwards of 90 per cent of the indigenous population were killed by these epidem-ics (Jetté, 2004, p. 153). Facing an almost unimaginable sequence of devastation, "the surviving Kalpuyans, carried on, regrouping into reformulated families and smaller communities" (Jetté, 2004, p. 157). Despite the demographic shift follow-ing the outbreak in 1831, "the settlers maintained their connections to the local Ahantchuyuk Kalapuyan band at Champoeg and provided assistance to the group in times of distress. This practice of offering assistance to the Kalapuyans con-tinued through the 1840s as demonstrated by the number of natives who were cared for in French-Native American or Métis homes (Jetté, 2004, p. 293).

With the Kalapuyan numbers reduced from thousands to hundreds, they became vulnerable on other fronts as well. On the spiritual side, the Methodists arrived, followed by the Roman Catholics four years later, with both parties con-testing for Kalapuyan souls. In this weakened demoralized state, those left alive were vulnerable. By the 1840s their lands had been overrun, and they offered little resistance when Oregon's Superintendent of Indian Affairs, Joel Palmer, offered them the opportunity of signing their lands away completely in 1855 with removal to a nearby reservation. The survivors ended up shortly thereafter at the Grand Ronde Reservation, just to the west of Salem in the eastern foothills of the Coast Range in the Yamhill River watershed.

Portrait of Rear Admiral Charles Wilkes, CA. 1866. Wilkes, an American naval officer, was appointed by the American Congress to lead the United States Exploring Expedition, 1838-1842. The Wilkes Expedition, sent six naval ships around South America into the South Pacific before sailing to the Hawaiian Islands and then to the Pacific Coast. This massive expedition included navy personnel as well as scientists and other scholars. Wilkes also disembarked in Puget Sound and went overland to Fort Vancouver. He provides a detailed account of life in the Oregon Territory a few years before the border would be established between the United States and British North America.

In addition to St. Paul, French Prairie was eventually composed of four other villages: St. Louis, Gervais, Champoeg, and La Butte now called Butteville. The settlement's starting date is variously listed as 1828, 1829, or 1830. French Prairie now encompasses an area enclosed within the loop of the Willamette between the River itself and Pudding River as far south as Lake La Biche. The Pudding River itself is a translation from an earlier French-Canadian name, *Boudin,* for blood pudding.

By the time Fathers Blanchet and Demers arrived in 1838, twenty-six farms were operating in the area, mostly run by former *Canadien* employees of the HBC, their indigenous wives, and their Métis families. Petitions for a priest sent

Valley of the Willamette River, Henry J. Warre, ca. 1848. The Willamette Valley was the primary destination for the waves of American migrants crossing the mountains on the Oregon trail. Unlike other territories, it features rich and arable lands that could be farmed without irrigation. Its mild climate reminiscent of Pennsylvania and fertile soils, lured thousands of settlers to push westwards across desert and mountains. However, *Canadien* and Métis who had been employees of the Hudson's Bay Company established the first farms.

repeatedly to Monsignor Provencher in St. Boniface (Winnipeg) in the Red River valley between 1831 and 1837 were finally answered. The place where the log cabin church that had been built two years earlier in anticipation of their arrival was named after the mission church, St. Paul (McKay 1980: 5-6). The petitions sent from the region in 1836 and 1837 contain a list of the early settlers. The names of the petitioners on the last petition of March 8, 1837, are provided below. Each signature was marked with an X on the original document. An earlier petition sent in 1836 also listed the number of children each signatory had in order to reinforce the necessity of sending priests to minister to their western flock:

- Pierre Beleque (3)
- Charles Rondeau (3)
- Joseph Desportes (3)
- Joseph Delard (5)
- Charles Charpentier

- Louis Labonté
- André Longtain (4)
- Louis Forcier (3)
- Jean Baptiste Desportes McKay (8)
- Pierre Depot (1)
- Antoine Laferte
- Amable Arquette (3)
- F. Xavier Laderoute (1)
- Étienne Lucier (6)
- Joseph Gervais (7)
- Charles Plante (4)

This list by no means represents the entire population of the settlement, but is representative of sixteen families who had fifty-one children. The number of children of Louis Labonté and Antoine Laferte was not provided in this particular petition, and the 1836 petition listed four additional families not represented on the 1837 signatory listing: Charles Rondeau (3); André Picard (4); Jean-Baptiste Perrault (2); and William Johnson (2). In 1838 there were twenty-six families; within four years, by 1842, the number of families reached a total of eighty-three. Harvey McKay's (1980) book, *St. Paul Oregon: 1830-1890*, provides a sampling of other early farmers clustered around St. Paul comprising mostly French-Canadians originating from Lower Canada (Quebec) and their wives from Métis/Indian ancestry:

- Jacques Servant - a native of Montreal who came west in the 1812-1815 timeframe and married a woman of the Okanogan tribe whose Christian name was Josephte.
- Augustin Raymond – also a native of Montreal who came west in the early 1830s and married one of Jacques and Josephte Servant's métisse daughters, Marie in 1843.
- Louis Pichet - an early fur trader form Montreal came west about 1820 married one of the Bercier girls whose mother was métisse Emilie Finlay who was either part Cree, Pend d'Oreille or Spokane Indian.
- David Mongrain – a native of Canada who came west in 1830 and retired to a farm near St. Paul around 1840, married a métisse daughter of Jacques Lafantaisie who arrived on the Tonquin with the Astorians in 1811, Catherine Lafantaisie.

In the early 1840s, as more Americans flowed in, the *Canadiens* and their Métis families continued to settle in the valley. However, the Americans were rapidly gaining on the *Canadiens* in number. These are some of the people who arrived from Canada in the early 1840s.

- Jean-Baptiste Deguire was another early fur trapper who settled in St. Paul, marrying Métisse Marie Anne Perrault, the daughter of an old trapper, Jean Perrault, and a Chinook woman. In addition to his farm, he operated a ferry about two miles northwest of St. Paul.
- Louis Bergevin was a *Canadien* who came west and married another métisse daughter of the Servants, Madeleine, shortly after her first husband, Charles Jeaudoin, died in 1848.
- Thomas Laird arrived from Canada and married Métisse Céleste Rocbrune, a daughter of Joseph Rocbrune and Lissette of the Walla Walla tribe.
- François Bernier was a native of Canada who relocated to St. Paul, working as a miller as well as having his own farm. He married Etienne Lucier's métisse daughter, Pelagie. (McKay, 1980, pp. 7-8)

These families grew wheat, oats, legumes, vegetables, and fruit on their farms. Their domesticated animals included horses, cattle, pigs, and sheep, and they brought with them an array of practices and traditions that can be traced back to Lower Canada, including the usage of French, Catholic rituals, kinship structures, agricultural patterns, hybrid style of clothing, and folkloric songs and music by which French-Canadian and Métis recognized one another.

In this early period, the Métis economy relied on a combination of Lower Canadian agricultural and husbandry practices, fur trapping, hunting, trading, and the productive work of native women engaged in traditional subsistence activities. The process of agrarian settlement by the freemen and their families hastened a process that began with the introduction of horses to the Willamette Valley in the 1810s. These Métis families introduced livestock, cropping, deforestation, and an agricultural system that began a major transformation of the landscape (Jetté, 2004, p. 139).

Surplus farm products from French Prairie were sold to the Hudson's Bay Company. Given the increasing volume of the business, the HBC decided in 1841 to establish a warehouse at a river landing located at Champoeg. This was the community's third landing on the river, the first two being the St. Paul Mission landing, and Jean-Baptiste Deguire's landing and ferry operation. The community had come a long way by the time a representative of the French government showed up in the area that same year, 1841. In his official report, Duflot de Mofras noted that about 600 French-Canadians attended Mass at St. Paul and that there were 30,000 bushels of wheat and 10,000 bushels of other grains stored in the Champoeg warehouse (McKay, 1980, pp. 8-12). This agricultural surplus was sold at an expanding local market. By the early 1840s the settlers were no longer as dependent as in earlier years upon the HBC for procuring and exporting produce to Russian America with its fur trading outposts sprinkled along the southern perimeter of the territory claimed by the Russian Empire and now encompassed by the modern state of

Alaska, purchased in 1867 by the U.S. The wagon trains brought in increasing numbers of exhausted and famished immigrants who needed to obtain provisions on credit to cover their first winter in the new land. The HBC was the principal source of credit to see those Americans through the winter. However, disintermediation was setting in, and arrangements could be negotiated with local farmers, Canadian or American, to provide food for later reimbursement.

On The Eve of Partition

Eugène Duflot de Mofras, a French diplomat who reconnoitred the Pacific Coast between 1840 and 1842, provides a fascinating account of life in the Pacific Northwest before the U.S. annexed the Oregon Territory in 1846. His account provides a rough census of the inhabitants of the territory, the language spoken, and their cultural allegiance; American historians have unfortunately largely ignored his work. His description of the *Canadien* inhabitants of the Pacific Northwest provides useful hints as to the forces that would shape the French settlements of the region following their integration into the United States. His writing presents a population that was fervently French-speaking and proud of its language, culture, and faith.

When Duflot de Mofras traveled to Oregon, he described the preparations that were being made for the eventual integration into the United States, even though the United States and Great Britain were both still claiming the territory. He also narrated life in a territory where the fur trade was increasingly becoming of secondary economic importance, and where the Hudson's Bay Company and the French-Canadian settlers were developing a rich agricultural economy. The *Canadiens* were a growing population; in Oregon, according to Duflot, there were 100 Englishman, employees of the Hudson's Bay Company; 2,000 Americans that had settled on the left bank of the Willamette River; and 3,000 *Canadiens*, former employees of the fur trade or migrants who had come to the territory directly from Quebec (de Mofras, 1846, p. 13). Fort Astoria (Fort George) had become a mere shadow of its former glory, with only one Hudson's Bay Company employee remaining in the vicinity of the old fort. The economic heart of Oregon was Fort Vancouver, a fort with no palisades and only two old cannons in the middle of the settlement. Seven hundred inhabitants were at the Fort, of which 25 were Englishmen and 100 were French-speaking *Canadien* employees or engagés of Métis or *Bois-Brulé* heritage and their families (de Mofras, 1846, p. 20). He describes the engagés thus:

> *Le nom d'engagés s'applique indistinctement à tous les travailleurs de la Compagnie, aux ouvriers forgerons, charpentiers, tonneliers, aux trappeurs de castors, chasseurs, bateliers, et même aux fermiers. Seuls, les matelots anglais des navires ne sont pas compris dans cette catégorie. Les engagés sont des Canadiens parmi lesquels on trouve quelques hommes de sang mêlé appelés bois brûlés, et des Iroquois métis. La langue*

française est la seule qu'ils parlent; ils professent la religion catholique et nourrissent pour les Anglais une antipathie très-marquée. Ceux d'entre eux chargés de parcourir le pays en canots pour le transport des marchandises sont désignés sous la dénomination de voyageurs. (de Mofras, 1846, p. 17)

The name of *"engagé"* [literally a hire or employee] is applied without distinction to all the personnel of the Company, to the working blacksmiths, to the coopers, to the trappers of beaver, to the hunters, to the ferrymen and even to the farmers. Only the sailors on the ships are not included in that category. The *"engagés"* are *Canadiens* [French-Canadians] among whom we find a few men of mixed blood called bois brûlés [Burnt Wood] and some Iroquois Métis. The French language is the only one they speak; they profess their Catholic Faith and they nourish an antipathy for the English that is quite marked. Those among them who are tasked with covering the country in canoes for the transportation of merchandise are designated under the denomination of being voyageurs.

In this passage, we see that the term *engagé* is applied to a variety of professions including not only voyageurs, but also carpenters, coopers, trappers, hunters, and even farmers. Only the sailors on the ships are not called engagés. Interestingly, Duflot uses the term *bois brûlés* to identify individuals who are French-descent *Sang-Mêlés* (or mixed-blood). He then uses the term "Métis" in association with the Iroquois to denote another form of collective Métis identification associated with the Iroquois identity. Despite these differences within the realm of Métis identities, Duflot underlines that the French language is the only language that they speak, and that even the Iroquois, among others, appear to harbor a strong antipathy to the English, while at the same time professing their Catholic Faith.

The language skills of the children of the *Canadiens* are also emphasized by the Catholic missionaries, with the daughters certainly as adept and fluent in the language of their fathers, as the sons. In a report entitled *Mission de la Colombie*, the unspecified author notes how Hélène Kittson, daughter of the giant Finan McDonald, speaks a number of the local indigenous languages as well as French and English:

Mde. Kitson [sic], baptisée dans la mission précédente par Mr. Demers, s'exprime avec facilité dans ces diverses langues, ainsi que dans l'anglais et le français. Cette dame, dont le père, M.T. McDonald, est catholique, et réside au Canada, et dont la mère est de la tribu des Têtes plates, douée d'une intelligence remarquable, d'une foi vive et d'une piété éclairée, servait d'interprète avec une patience admirable. (L'association de la propagation de la foi, 1841, p. 61)

Mrs. Kitson baptized in the preceding mission by Mr. Demers expressed herself with ease in these various languages as well as English and French. This woman, whose father M.T. McDonald was Catholic, and resided in Canada, and whose mother was from the Flathead tribe, was gifted with a remarkable intelligence, a vivacious faith and insightful piety, [she] served as an interpreter with an admirable patience.

Fort Vancouver, Henry J. Warre, ca. 1848. Though at the outset Fort Vancouver had been a fur trading post, by the 1840s, it had developed into an agricultural and commercial center. The Hudson's Bay Company had expanded its operations to include dairy production, sheep farming, orchards, and a host of other industries that could then be integrated into the ledgers of the company, and eventually the affiliated company it spun off to be registered in the United States.

This is a vivid example of the transmission of language across generations. Kittson spoke her mother's Salishan language (variuosly identifed as either Tête Plate or Pend Oreille), plus French as well as English, and would play an important role in helping the first Catholic missionaries establish a foothold in the Pacific Northwest. After her husband's death *circa* 1841, Hélène McDonald re-married Richard Grant, the HBC officer in charge of Fort Boisé. Richard was the father of the famous Métis rancher, Johnny (Jean-François) Grant, who returned to the Pacific Northwest after going east to Quebec to be schooled with his siblings in Trois-Rivières under the care of his French-Canadian paternal grandmother.

Eugène Duflot de Mofras evinces a number of occasions where French is the *lingua franca*. In his description of Fort Vancouver, he notes that the white men are married to Native American women, but that they generally speak French. As he had enumerated these men to include both Englishmen and *Canadiens*, this indicates that even the former used French at Fort Vancouver (de Mofras,

1846, p. 20). Duflot also states that French is the sole language used in the *Canadien* settlement in the Willamette Valley, even if the wives are Native American: *"Bien que la plupart d'entre eux aient épousé des femmes indienne, la langue française est restée la seule usitée dans la colonie"* (de Mofras, 1846, p. 24). [Though most of them had married an Indian woman, the French language remained the only language used in the colony.] Not only do they speak French, the farmers of the Willamette also steadfastly refuse to speak English. Duflot reports that when Governor George Simpson visited the colony and spoke to the gathered crowd in English, he was told to speak French: *"Lors de la visite que nous fîmes au Ouallamet avec le gouverneur Simpson, nous ne pûmes nous empêcher de remarquer la pénible impression qu'éprouvaient les Canadiens en se voyant gouvernés par une personne d'une race et d'une religion différente de la leur, et qui ne se servait pas même de leur langue. Plusieurs fermiers, en effet, répondaient à sir George, qui leur demandait en anglais des nouvelles de leurs affaires et de leur santé: 'Nous ne parlons pas anglais, nous autres; nous sommes tous Français ici'"* (de Mofras, 1846, p. 24). [During a visit that we made to Willamette with Governor Simpson, we could not help but to remark the pained impression that the *Canadiens* felt seeing themselves governed by a person of a different race and religion who did not even make use of their language. Many farmers, indeed, answering Sir George who asked them in English news as to their business and their health: "We do not speak English us; we are all French here."] Duflot also underlines the primary identity of the French-speaking inhabitants of Oregon, who are "Canadians of the French race" or *"Canadiens de race française"* (de Mofras, 1846, p. 43).

Though the engagés, according to Duflot, have a deep disdain for the English, the Catholic Church enforced a strict obedience to the British Crown. Duflot identifies how a Catholic Mass he attended along with six hundred other French-speaking parishioners in the Willamette Valley featured a prayer in French dedicated to Queen Victoria:

> *Cependant, si nous avons éprouvé une joie bien vive en retrouvant sur ces rivages éloignés, dans une contrée sur laquelle la France s'est laissé enlever tous ses droits, un presbytère et des villages qui rappelaient ceux de nos provinces, nous n'avons pas ressenti moins de surprise ni de tristesse lorsque le dimanche, dans l'église où six cents Canadiens étaient rassemblés, nous entendîmes un prêtre français dire en français à une population toute française 'Prions Dieu pour notre saint-père le Pape et pour notre bien-aimée reine Victoria!' Il est enjoint aux prêtres de faire une fois par mois et publiquement cette étrange prière, sous peine de destitution* (de Mofras, 1846, p. 27).

> If, however, we experienced a great joy in finding on these distant shores, in a country where France let herself be stripped of all her rights, a rectory and villages that reminded us of those in our own provinces, we did not feel any less surprise or sadness when on Sunday, in the church where six hundred *Canadiens* were gathered, we

heard a French priest say in French to a wholly French population "Let us pray for our holy father the Pope and to our beloved Queen Victoria!" The priests are required to do once a month in public this strange prayer on pain of dismissal.

Duflot even suggests that the *Canadiens* were not simply connived by the Americans to sign the 1838 call for the United States to oversee Oregon. He writes that the Hudson's Bay Company feared that they may lose control over the free men, the *Canadiens*, and thus ensure their loss of Oregon: "*La Compagnie d'Hudson pressent que la population libre qui s'y est établie doit lui échapper un jour, et cette prévision, il faut le reconnaître, est parfaitement motivée par la démarche faite ouvertement en mars 1838 par les principaux colons américains et français-canadiens, lesquels, en réclamant la protection du gouvernement des Etats-Unis, l'ont invité à prendre possession du territoire de l'Orégon*" (de Mofras, 1846, p. 27). [The Hudson's Bay Company foresaw that the free population which has established itself must escape it one day, and with this expectation, admittedly, is entirely motivated by the request openly made in March 1838 by the leading American settlers and French-Canadians, which, in calling for the protection of the United States government, invited it to take possession of the Oregon territory"].

Duflot also gives an inventory of the agricultural production of the Willamette Valley, providing a detailed accounting of both livestock and grain holdings. He noted that some had even built mills and sawmills, using the numerous sources of flowing water to power these installations. The farmers of the Willamette would sell (or rather trade) much of what they produced to the Hudson's Bay Company, but Duflot tells us that many *Canadiens* would travel down to San Francisco to trade in cattle and horses (de Mofras, 1846, p. 24). In short, Duflot describes a population that is thriving and proudly French, with noticeable Métis families and distinguishable cultural traditions similar to those in Lower Canada, Illinois Country, and the Red River colony. Even the Iroquois take pride in France in Duflot's account, and it is perhaps these qualities that would infuriate the later American settlers. The Americans who were living at this time in the Willamette Valley were in some ways closer in spirit to the French-Métis than later Americans who would follow. Duflot comments that the Americans who had settled in the valley were "backsettlers," as he referred to the backcountry settlers, who had arrived without families, had traveled overland, and—once settled in the Willamette Valley–had taken wives from the local Native American communities (de Mofras, 1846, p. 32).

Finally, Duflot explains how the leading agents of the Hudson's Bay Company in Oregon, even though they had once again been granted a continued monopoly by the British Crown, created their own company completely independent (and with differing interests) from the Hudson's Bay Company: "*Cependant, ses agents*

résidant en Amérique, voyant la race des animaux à fourrure s'éteindre, et craig-
nant que le gouvernement anglais n'abandonne la rive gauche de la Colombie, ont
formé entre eux, il y a six ans, une société entièrement indépendante de la
Compagnie d'Hudson, sous le titre de Compagnie d'Agriculture de la baie de Puget
(Puget's Sound Agricultural Company)" (de Mofras, 1846, p. 22). ["However, its
agents residing in America, seeing the race of fur bearing animals becoming
extinct, and fearing that the British government would abandon the left bank
of the Columbia River, founded, six years ago, a company fully independent of
the Hudson's Bay Company, under the title of Agriculture Company of Puget's
Bay (Puget's Sound Agricultural Company)"]. This company owned 7,000 head
of cattle and 12,000 sheep. Seeking to establish the Puget Sound as a major center
for the production of wool, the company had brought eight thousand sheep from
California as well as some from Scotland for cross-breeding to produce what
they hoped would be high quality wool capable of competing with the best of
European wool (de Mofras, 1846, p. 23). Everybody understood that the fur trade
was a dying industry, and both the Hudson's Bay Company and the *Canadien*
farmers were developing markets for their growing agricultural production.

The later Americans who crossed the mountains following the Oregon Trail
certainly did not enter into a "wilderness." Quite the contrary, they arrived in
an area that had established the foundations of agriculture, the lumber industry,
and the manufacturing of tools. They also had competitors, the *Canadiens*, who
were as proud and as nationalistic as the Americans themselves, but who entertained very good relations with the indigenous nations. The eventual cultural
supremacy of the American settlers was not due to their cultural superiority, but
rather the sheer numbers of migrants that would eventually come to settle in the
Oregon Territory as part of the U.S. nation-building already well underway. This
made the French speakers (*Canadien* and Métis) a small minority in the region
where they had once imposed their language and culture.

Snowshoe mail carriers in Sault Ste. Marie, Michigan, ca. 1900, top, photographer unknown; bottom, William J. Bell. Owing to the long winters, Sault Ste. Marie was cut off from the world when ships could not come to port. The largely Métis and Native American mail carriers, like John Boucher (right) and Antoine Piquette (left) in the photo below, kept communications open, traveling all day and camping in the snow at night with their dogs.

CHAPTER 9

The Politics of Becoming

"A renowned Canadian historian once asked me, 'When is a Metis no longer a Metis?'
I had answered, 'When he/she no longer considers himself/herself as such'."

Antoine S. Lussier
Quoted in *The Identities of Marie Rose Delorme Smith*

The Western genre—novels and movies—defined for generations of Americans the history of the West and shaped the national narrative. The previous chapters have demonstrated how the French and their descendants—*Canadien*, Métis, Créole—along with French-speaking Native Americans—Iroquois among others—were there at every step of American expansion. Before the ink was dry on the Declaration of Independence, the Americans fighting the British were calling upon the *Canadien* of the Illinois Country to provide supplies to their troops to fight the British. When the Anglo-Americans pushed farther to the west, they invariably came across French-speakers, whether in the Ohio country, Michigan Territory, Saint-Louis, and Missouri as well as the Pacific Northwest. When revered pathfinders pushed west—be it Lewis and Clark or Frémont—they did so with the essential help of *Canadien* and Métis guides and interpreters and along the way encountered French-speaking traders and trappers. American history, both popular and academic, has largely erased their contribution from the national narrative. Traces remain, but they are orphaned collections in local museums or footnotes in academic texts, artifacts devoid of their larger historical context, one that can only be understood at a continental scale. Instead, the narrative was fixed by movies such as "How the West Was Won," a movie that completely evacuates any reference to any French-speaking people at all stages of the history being recounted. The only fleeting hint of the buried past was a "Pierre," the name of one of the men at the River pirate clan, thrown out, yet never explained. Yet, it hints at the disparaged other, the "Frenchman" that could not be truly trusted, nor could be truly honorable. Even when the film is set in locales such as St. Louis at a period when the French-speakers would have been predominant in the elites and the population, which inspired men such as Jim Bridger who had to learn to speak French in order to survive, the movie is peopled with Anglo-Americans. Academic works are not much better in addressing the missing Métis and *Canadiens* of the American Western.

Michael Coyne (1998) provides a scathing critique of the ideological inferences of the film "How the West Was Won." He writes: "Spencer Tracy's opening narration marks the film as a saga of essentially benevolent conquest, which might more cynically be subtitled the *'The Whiting of America'*" (Coyne, 1998, p. 117). Coyne stresses that the film "avoids either depiction or mention of Blacks" (1998, p. 118), and never alludes to slavery by name, yet he himself also ignored the prominent group that is also elided in the film: the *Canadien*, Métis and Créole as well as the French-speaking slaves and blacks who spoke French and were freed slaves. While Coyne provides an important critique of the film and how it shapes a very "White Anglosaxon Protestant" or WASPish vision of the past, he himself ignores the buried history of the American West that also goes unmentioned in this movie and countless other films of the Western genre. The goal of this book has been precisely to challenge this mythic history and to provide a balanced account whereby the role of the *Canadien* and Métis in the American West—from Detroit and New Orleans and Saint-Louis to Seattle—would be given their due credit.

With the relevant historical artifacts excavated and the assumptions that have shaped the analysis of the history and identity of the French-speaking populations of the western United States challenged, it is important now to show how this revamped historical account obliges a rethinking of the history of Métis culture. Much as Americans have a distorted vision of their history, Canadians also have a mythologized past. (It should be noted that in Quebec in French some of these myths have been challenged.) Moreover, even when national narratives are challenged, these challenges to the past often overlook the larger continental forces that have shaped it. While the history of the Métis is known in Canada—or at least snippets of it—the Métis in Canada are rarely examined from a continental perspective. Instead, they are often understood as strictly a Red River or Pariries phenomenon that overflowed a bit into some lands in the Dakotas bordering on the Canadian Red River Valley lands. Canadian analysis of the Métis past and ethnogenesis rarely ventures south, even though, as indicated above, the populations of French-speaking *Canadien*-Métis were significantly larger in the United States than in Canada.

A bridge between the history of the Métis in Canada and the United States is thus required to enable a new analysis and theoretical model of Métis ethnogenesis, a model to understand Métis nationhood in all its facets.

Binary Politics. The Historical Hardships of American Métis

As Jennifer S. H. Brown stated in 1993: "Métis is not an ethnic term well known in American history." Much of her statement still resonates as true in 2016. Brown suggested then that the persisting "blind spot" on the contributions of Métis south of the 49th parallel can be explained by the heritage of an ethnology framed by "cultural categories" that tend to offer no distinctive voice to "mixed" indigenous-European cultures in the U.S.—such as the Lumbee, the Mashpee and the Métis (Brown, 1993). As a result, Brown reminds us that "Indian" identities were often created or adopted by the Métis living in the United States in order to survive a politico-legal setting that gave no credence to their distinct identities (Brown, 1993, p. 21). Attempts to assimilate the Métis in the United States have been framed by racist and often dichotomist social, political, and juridical categories. As Brenda Macdougall (2012, p. 450) puts it: "although Metis people have clearly existed and asserted their rights in that country, there has been no recognition for them as a people under American law." Martha Harroun Foster summarizes our perspective when suggesting (2006, p. 224):

> In much of the northern plains, the Great Lakes area, and the Mississippi River drainage Métis were central to the story of early settlement. Nevertheless, their role in the history of the United States has been and continues to be overlooked and misunderstood.

As the previous chapters have emphasized, this "blind spot" is not only true of the early *Canadiens* and the Métis, but all the French-speakers who shaped the history of the American West. Both popular and academic historians have largely overlooked the role and importance of the French-speakers—Acadians, French-Canadians, Métis and Créoles—in both the historical American narrative and popular culture. Kit Carson was lionized even though he was in effect quite secondary in importance to men such as Basil Lajeunesse in John Charles Frémont's (1845) expedition. History thus amplified the importance of Anglo-Americans and largely wrote out of history the contributions of French-speakers who were the dominant force in the American fur trade, the largest demographic component of the "mountain men." It is thus more than a "blind spot," rather a collective wilful blindness to the historical contribution of French-speakers regardless of their origins—often suspiciously regarded has half-indigenized and of shady loyalty. This historical amnesia is consequential. History is often used to either give or deny rights, and in the United States, the devaluing of the contribution of these actively forgotten French-speakers and often indigenous communities has enduring consequences. A careful rereading of the primary documents provides, it is hoped, a more complex understanding of various *Canadien*-Métis historical communities, while providing community members a better understanding of their past, too often belittled.

Ethnogenesis and Primordialism: The Case of the Métis-*Canadiens*

By examining the history of American Métis from Detroit to the Pacific Northwest, we came to describe a broader and more complex picture about Métis-*Canadien* identity: one that challenges the cultural, ethnological and political criteria by which some scholars evaluated the "genuineness" of this recently revamped notion of ethnogenesis. In the case of the Métis, the notion of "genuineness" of the emergence of the Métis as a distinct "people," or their ethnogenesis, is usually supported by an array of criteria, including the demonstration of a sufficient number of individuals linked by endogamic unions, which would then give rise to the contours of a distinct ethnicity and culture emerging within the boundaries of a discrete geographical location marked by a history of conflicts with significant "Others" that would act as the condition of possibility for sparking a "separate ethnic group consciousness" (Peterson, 2012, p. 43). The focus proposed by Peterson (2012) to warrant a "true" ethnogenesis thus emphasizes binary notions of separateness, through homogenizing and often primordialist narratives insisting on a single and self-countained point of origin for a people, while depicting the necessity of belligerent acts and conflict as well as the need for geographical limits and borders.

In addition to the problem of historical amnesia, we have also challenged in earlier chapters the usage of discrete notions of "separateness" and "collective consciousness" currently evoked by a number of scholars to legitimate what would be a "true" or "mature" Métis or the early *Canadien* peoplehood. The case of the French-Canadian Métis, we suggest, illustrates a complex, mobile and diverse set of relationships by which emerges nevertheless a "cultural consciousness" hardly containable in the dualist and binary assumptions that attempt to box it in. The French-Canadian Métis displayed a degree of cultural adaptability and syncretism or fusion between indigenous and French culture (predominantly) that made them who they were (and still are). As illustrated in chapter 8, French-Canadian Métis were a people whose relations blossomed in contiguity with indigenous pragmatic notions of identities/worldviews based on the horizontal notions of kinship and adoption, held together by what was often a semi-nomadic indigenized lifestyle (voyageurs, trappers, fur traders, etc.). They were not just a transient cultural phenomenon that missed somehow the mark of "mature peoplehood" because they didn't acquire the culture homogeneity/territorial discreteness by which some now rank such maturity.

Here it is interesting to highlight the contribution of scholar Anne Waters on notions such as "nondiscrete nonbinary dualism" by which she describes as central to many indigenous worldviews the valuing of thinking two constructs together in such a way that each would remain itself, and also be part of the other. Consequently, Waters suggests, "an hierarchical valuing of one being better, superior or more valued than another cannot be, or rather is, excluded by a non-binary logic" (Waters, 2004, p. 99). It is this way of understanding the world and one's relation to it, we suggest, that can be found in the construction of the French-Indian or Métis identity shaped under various indigenizing influences; a worldview in which dualism is not viewed as division but rather as complementarity, a relational quality at the core of Métis identities (Waters, 2004, p. 103).[1]

The critiques arguing the possible distorted effect of "relabeling" fur trades communities as "Métis" to fit current political interests are only to be expected. This criticism can however be turned on its head, especially when we consider the composition of the Métis families and communities in St. Louis, Gervais, Champoeg, and La Butte. Is the "distorted effect" not even more perilous to postulate that the term "Métis" should now be reserved only for the Métis that have existed only in the Assiniboia region (Red River, Manitoba) or their descendants? We submit that this is the "distorted effect" in favor of neo-nationalistic interpretations of Métis identity that has first and foremost created such definitional tension. The critique of historical revisionism can in fact be redirected toward those adjusting and even restricting the historical meanings of "Métis" identity according to binary and artificially dualistic theories that make it only "mature" or meaningful when amenable to narrow nationalist representations of Métis people in line with Classic Western or Prairie Métis nationalist historiography. Likewise, the Métis story has been buried in the Canadian national narrative, with the Frasers and Mackenzies lionized, while the contribution of the French-speaking *Canadien* and Métis buried as there is little interest to acknowledge that they were essential to Canadian history across western and northern Canada. Such exclusive, abstract, and essentialist depiction of Métis identity is at odds with the values and cultural characteristics identified above as pertaining to what we described as people born of horizontal, co-substantial, and concrete relations, namely of Euro-Indigenous relationality.

Throughout this book, we have presented historical and documentary evidence pointing toward a wider usage of the term "Métis" that warrants its usage beyond the scope of contemporary expression of Métis Prairies-centric nationalism. Indeed, to battle neo-nationalist narratives and their revisionist theories on Métis identity, we have examined *in fine* the composition of Métis families described as such (*bois-brulés*) in Oregon, which reveals cultural patterns (agricultural, religious, linguistic, arts) that transcend the straitjacket required by a single nationalist expression for a people to legitimately exist. Our analysis suggests that the criteria put forward by a number of Métis scholars that insist on cultural homogeneity—this based on abstract and often too rigid notion of separateness—is not well-suited to the study of the *Canadien*-Métis as part of a nomadic, decentered and indigenous culture born out of the interconnected pathways sprouted mainly from the fur trade routes. This is especially true when we examine the Métis and French-Indian communities that have existed in the United States. These communities "[d]espite restrictions on possible formal or legal ethnic identities," have continued to be the bearers of a "flexible, multilayered, multifaceted and permeable" Métis identity certainly *distinct*, yet resisting a classification committed to rigid binary cultural/ethnic *separateness* and evolutionary assumptions working along strict linear progression (Foster, 2006, p. 222). This point is crucial to understanding the salient aspects of the French-Canadian Métis culture all across North America. It is also important if we wish to better understand why we have used the term "Métis" to describe independent French-Indian American communities found in Oregon and elsewhere, rejecting *en passant* some recent revisionist definitions that makes "true" Métis a phenomenon one can only find after the historical events associated with Red River historiography and the courageous resistances of Métis leader Louis Riel.

Métis Ethnonyms

Only when the disparate historical accounts that remain are pieced together does it become evident that a shared sense of broad and de-territorialized collective culture akin to nationhood existed, as evidenced mostly in the names given by the Métis/*Bois-Brulé*/*Canadiens* to themselves. Benedict Anderson (1983, p. 6) posited that the nation was an "imagined political" community as "the members of even the smallest nation will never know most of their fellow-members, meet them, or even hear of them, yet in the minds of each lives the image of their com-munion." Anderson's work, however, does have its limitations as it is founded on the concept of "print-capitalism" and argues for the modernity of nations. The "imagined nation" is a "modern" nation—with modern usually meaning post-French Revolution, and religion is largely evacuated out of the discussion (M. Bouchard, 2004; M. Bouchard & Bogdan, 2014). As we have seen in the pre-vious chapters, the idea of nation existed in the French narrative in the seven-teenth century—certainly not modern, as Anderson would define it—and a strong popular Catholicism informed the populations descending from the first French settlers. Likewise, the often inter-connected identities that emerged—Acadian, Créoles, *Canadiens* and Métis—were founded on cultural distinctions (folk songs, folklore and ways of life). Quickly, the children of French settlers came to see themselves as new peoples—new nations—and this would later be the case for the Métis of the Assiniboia region—a nationalism that Louis Riel hoped inclusive to all Métis and "Halfbreed" descendants of North America, irrspective of their location or dissimination. (See box on Louis Riel, page 275.)

In the case of the Métis, what is evident is that a triad of ethnonyms—*Mitif* (derived from "Métif" an older French spelling of Métis), *Bois-Brulé,* and

The Red River Expedition at Kakabeka Falls, Frances Anne Hopkins, 1877. The Red River Expedition was a military force under the leadership of Colonel Garnet Wolseley that was dispatched by the newly created Canadian state to confront the Métis in 1870 and to put down the Red River Rebellion. The expedition was also sent to ensure that these territories, Rupert's Land acquired from the Hudson's Bay Company in 1869, would remain under Canadian control. The expedition arrived at Upper Fort Garry and ended Louis Riel's Provisional Government. In 1870, the province of Manitoba was created and added to the Canadian Federation. Though they had been pivotal in the creation of this province, the Métis would be promised land, but given scrip, and most would be driven from their ancestral territories in the Red River Valley. Kakabeka Falls is just northwest of Fort William (now Thunder Bay, Ontario).

Canadien—were being used across the continent by individuals, who certainly never met, yet shared this collective and cultural awareness of themselves. Thus, Alexis de Tocqueville (Tocqueville & Vallée, 1973, p. 36), while traveling in the forests of the Great Lakes in 1831, describes an encounter with a man who by all appearances was indigenous, yet spoke French with a Normand accent (in modern parlance he would certainly have been close to the current French-Canadian accent spoken today) and defined himself as Métis and *Bois[-]Brulé* when explaining why in spite of his appearances he spoke French.

Ross Cox (1832, pp. 309-316), who was working in the Oregon Territory in the 1810s, likewise devotes a section of his autobiographical work discussing the "half-breeds" who refer to themselves as *Bois[-]Brulés*. His contemporary, Gabriel Franchère in turn describes a man he met as *mitif* in his handwritten manuscript though this was corrected in the 1820 publication as "Métif" (Franchère, 1820, p. 216) and the contemporary version as "Métis" (Aubin & Franchère, 2002). Clearly both Franchère and Cox were relaying the ethnonyms in use in the Pacific Northwest in the 1810s. George Simpson in his account of his time spent in the Northwest (what would now be Northwestern Alberta) describes the children of the *Canadien* and French-speaking Iroquois as "Meitiff" in a letter dating to 1821 (Simpson, 1938, p. 381). De Mofras also refers to the *Bois-Brulés* in Oregon country, referring to families that we know are directly from Quebec, hence independent from the Red River-only theory, yet sharing with the Métis found in Red River or Cahokia or Saguenay an astonishing degree of cultural similarities—including a number of Patriots in exile from Lower Canada after the repression of 1837-1838 such as Francois-Xavier Mathieu who took refuge in Oregon and in Red River. Indeed, Charles Verreau, for anyone doubting the existence of the *Bois-Brulé* in Eastern Canada, is also described as a local "*Bois Brûlé* (Métif)" by Nicholas Andrews in a Report made to the legislative assembly of Lower Canada in 1831 describing the exploration of the Saguenay River in Quebec.[2] Finally, on his 1886 death certificate from l'Ile Bizard in Quebec, Louis Boileau is identified as "*Métis autrement dit sauvage*," as many others were in the 1839 and 1851 historical census in the Saguenay region and elsewhere in Quebec (R. Bouchard, 2008a).

A careful scrutiny of the historical lived accounts shows clearly that before 1830, both the terms Mitif/Métis and *Bois-Brulé* were being used across the continent. This usage predated the political organization of the Métis in the Red River colony under the political influence of Louis Riel. If it is agreed that the driving force behind the Métis/*Bois-Brulé* ethnogenesis cannot be reduced to the imagined "pinnacle" of nationalist expressions of Métis identity found in Red River, then surely other factors have to be called upon to explain the emergence of "independent" Métis communities. One factor largely overlooked is the role played by what John Armstrong (1982) referred to as the *mythomoteur*. Anthony D. Smith (1986, 1991, 1999, 2000, 2003, 2008) took this up in his discussion of the ethnosymbolism that girded nations and nationalism and the role of religion as a catalyst for the emergence of nations. The historical accounts of the *Canadien*/Métis Voyageurs and *les gens libres* of the American and Canadian West abound with examples of the Métis *mythomoteur*. There is of course the presence of an already and widely shared language (French), religiosity, identity-initiate rituals, songs, even of a unified and shared sense of culture emerging with what can be seen as the "backbone" of so many Métis communities, namely the voyageur-Métis culture (Podruchny, 2006, p. 200). Practically each and every reference to the voyageurs includes a mention of the songs, those songs that would

Louis Riel, Chef Métis, ca. 1885. A leaflet circulated in Québec following the hanging of Louis Riel. His execution on November 16, 1885 was met with outrage among the Quebec people and political leaders. This poster describes him as a political martyr killed to satiate "Orange [Order] fanaticism." The Orange Order was a prominent organization throughout Ontario and the English in Quebec, virulently anti-Catholic and anti-French. The Métis in the West were seen as oppressed compatriots.

be sung as the voyageurs were paddling the canoes across a continent. These songs were largely derived from the French folk songs that were carried by the first French settlers who became *Canadien* or "Country Born" in North America. There were not only songs, but the folklore, indigenized clothing including flower embroideries (the evolution of a syncretic practice traced back to the St. Lawrence Valley in Quebec) and other markers of identity that were shared from the Pacific to the Mississippi and up to the Arctic Ocean, and then back into Lower Canada/ Quebec.[3] There is also the shared nostalgic memory of ancestry and the ancestral homeland forming the backbone of *Canadien* French voyageurs, from which sprouted the *Bois-Brulé* which identified the *Canadiens* with "Indian blood into their veins," as Johann Georg Kohl reported, while emphasizing *Canadien* and *Bois-Brulé* overlapping identities:

"Où je reste? Je ne peux pas te le dire. Je suis Voyageur—je suis Chicot, monsieur. Je reste partout. Mon grand-père était Voyageur: il est mort en voyage. Mon pere était Voyageur: il est mort en voyage. Je mourrai aussi en voyage, et un autre Chicot pren- dra ma place. Such is our course of life." I must remark here, in explanation, that my Canadian had some Indian blood in his veins, either on the father or the mother's side, and hence, jestingly, called himself "Chicot." That is the name given in Canada to the half-burnt stumps, and has become a nickname for the half-breeds. They also called themselves, at times, "Bois-Brulés," or "Bois grilles," in reference to the shades of colour that bronze the face of a mixed. Frequently, too, pure-blooded French Voyageurs, if they lived entirely among the Indians, and intermarry with them, are counted among the Chicots. How much these French Voyageurs identify themselves with the Indians against the Anglo-Saxons, I had often opportunity of seeing (J.G. Kohl, 1860, pp. 260-261).

The formation of early voyageur-*Canadien* identity—and even the later French-Canadian proto-nationalism blossoming in Quebec triggered to signifi- cant proportion by the execution of the most famous Métis leader, Louis Riel, by the Canadian government (anecdotally then an American citizen)—often blurs the lines ethnologists draw between collective identities as necessarily *separate* in order to gain status of "maturity." At a huge demonstration in Montreal's Champs de Mars following the hanging of Riel, Quebec Premier Honoré Mercier addressed demonstrators saying, *"Louis Riel, notre frère est mort."* (Louis Riel, our brother is dead). The reality of ethnic and cultural identities are often more complex than is assumed.

Being Métis, Embracing the Capital M

It can be argued that distinguishing Métis from métis (in lower case) takes the prod- uct of a recent political modulation associated with the revival of Western Métis nationalism to discriminate against the historical heritage of entire "métis" communities, with the dividing assumption being that these latter communities were only biologically mixed. That assumption has no basis in the historical record, but rather in a revisionist interpretation of Métis identity that rewrites historical identities at the expense "other Métis" whose voices have nonetheless been heard publicy in Canada (Dyck & White, 2013; Royal Commission on Aboriginal Peoples, 1996). The theoretical division between "Métis" and "métis" comes across as attemps by researchers to be politically correct, but often at the expense of the more vulnerable descendants of independent Métis communities who deserve equal consideration. We have capitalized "Métis," since both métis/Métis were used historically without any of the discrimination currently taking place but also as a sign of respect for the descendants of these independent Métis communities who still identify themselves as such. When people choose to cherish their ethno-cultural French-Indian heritage as "Métis," they deserve the upper case M.

The Voyageur Worldview

The evidence gathered thus far does not support this notion of neat identities that inform linear trajectories wished by ethnologists checking-boxes that would confirm "pure" or self-contained forms of identity. Instead, various and overlapping circles of identities inter-penetrating one another can be interpreted, starting with the voyageurs who were the bearers of a *distinct* yet *porous* culture with social codes, rituals, solidarity beyond their working functions, and even worldviews. As Carolyn Podruchny (2006, p. 200 and 308) points out:

> [...] voyageurs tried to form a unified and somewhat collective culture in the face of centrifugal forces caused by their transience and mobility of their job [...] voyageurs do not fit the regular pattern of contact. Their impact on Aboriginal environment was light. They adopted many aspects of Aboriginal cultures, and some formed hybridized connections with them. Voyageurs represent a time of possibility, when the pattern of colonization was not inevitable or inexorable.

If we apply the non-binary dualism as articulated by Waters, we can see how *distinct* yet overlapping collective identities, have existed by cross-fertilizing one another, beyond what are now regarded as "national" identities that must be separated in mutually excluding ways. The emergence of *Canadien/Bois-Brulé/*Métis, we suggest, is a perfect example. The emergence and development of these overlapping identities cannot be adequately represented by theories filled by linear, homogenizing, and monological assumptions about the notion of a Métis peoplehood. Yet, many scholars, including Carolyn Podruchny (2006, p. 306), appear to adopt hierarchical distinctions ranking between "métis" (people of mixed and Aboriginal and European Ancestry) and Métis ("an explicit assertion of ethnic identity"), crafting an analytics of Métis peoplehood that arbitrarily favors the latter at the expense of the former. Such a distinction is problematic because it often assumes that "Métis" ought to correspond to only one ethnic identity (or only one nationalist identity) in order to deserve the capitalization of the term as signifying somewhat a more "mature" Indigenous identity. By the same token, it downplays as assimilated or not fully coalesced the other "half-breeds" (see for example Andersen, 2011; Murphy, 2014, p. 293; Petersen, 2009).*

---

* The most revelatory example of this linear and quasi Darwinian view of Métis identity that waited for supposedly ripe sociological conditions to fully mature only out West can be seen in the chapter *Prelude to Red River* by Jacqueline Petersen. After detailing the many cultural markers that made the Métis in the Great Lake area precisely the bearers of a "Métis" identity, Petersen arbitrarily and abruptly concludes: "What separate identity remained, rightfully belongs to the Canadian prairies where it continues to nourish itself"(Petersen, 2009, p. 554). Here she clearly underestimates the resilient power of "Métis" identity, which has survived the transformation of its sociological conditions of emergence, as equally demonstrated by the Western 1960 Métis nationalist resurgence, followed now by its eastern, northern and United States counterparts.

Historical evidence, however, points to the complexities of the *Canadien*-Métis identity that cannot be so easily swept aside using undiscriminating distinctions. As discussed previously, authors such as the French General Georges Collot (1826, pp. 318-319), who traveled through the territories of Louisiana that would be sold a few years later to the United States, remarked that the *Canadiens* who remained took the great pride in their French ancestry. In the case of *Canadien*-Métis or *Bois-Brulé*, that sense of collective awareness further challenges from the onset current ethnological criteria that insist on cultural oneness and homogeneity to assess "mature" versus "immature" cultures and identities (Royal Commission on Aboriginal Peoples, 1996). Examples of the valuation by "half-breeds" of their dual heritage can be found in reports by Kohl (1860), on the usage of both French and "Indian" personal names by *Canadien* "half-breeds," or the story of a well-off *Canadien* "half-breed" who had engraved both his French coat of arms and his Indian totem (an otter) on his seal-ring (Johann Georg Kohl, 2008, p. 314 and 298).

These behaviors cannot simply be reduced to "immature" identities, depicted too often as facing the only prospect of being assimilated by either their French or "Indian" parentage. They are the result of choices and valuations by individuals of "half-breed" descent honoring their distinct, because hybrid, indigenous culture. On this topic, Jennifer S.H. Brown gives further indications of Métis consciousness and distinct identity, showcasing fur trader Pierre Pambrun declaring that some of the *Bois-Brulés* have been sent to Lower Canada to receive their education, mentioning that "they do not consider themselves as white men, nor do they consider themselves as only on a footing with the Indians" (Brown, 2009, p. 524). As we can see, the *Bois-Brulé* identity is not defined on the basis of strict or rigid notion of territoriality or Red River nationalist expressions, but rather on the valuation by individuals of what constitutes their irreducible Euro-indigenous identity, making them culturally and ethnically distinct.

Contemporary Forms of Exclusions: Academic "Truth-Telling"

The problem now faced is not solely tied to historical amnesia or even Eurocentric forms of chauvinism. Rather it is the emergence of a Métis scholarship that incorporates the complex ramifications by which a neo-nationalist and Red-River-centric reinterpretation of all Métis cultures has developed. In short, we now find scholars suggesting that many American descendants of "French-Indian" communities would not be "real" Métis, a term that ought to be reserved to the bearers of the Red River nationalist events and their descendants only (Andersen, 2014). A glance at recent scholarship exposes the effect of a growing malaise among scholars over these politically charged questions: they either avoid the "Métis" terminology altogether, favoring instead creative combination of "French-Canadian and Indigenous" (Barman, 2014, p. 290) or adopt names such as "Créole." The latter clearly doesn't fit the historical French terminology and historical records where "Métis" identified people of French-Indian ancestry, especially in the context of the fur-trade societies (Murphy, 2014). One of the main arguments we now find would be that the "not-real métis" ancestors lacked a "collective consciousness" similar to the one they associate with the Red River Métis. An example of such exclusionary interpretation can be found in the latest work of historian Jacqueline Petersen. After years of keen insights on the "preludes" of the Red River Métis, Peterson recently authored a chapter in which she unequivocally concludes that no "Métis" ever existed in the Great Lakes area, a region that also includes historical Métis communities below the 49th parallel such as Peoria, Green Bay, Drummond Island, etc. (Peterson, 2012). According to Peterson, our error would be to conflate merely "mixed-blood" populations with the only real "Métis," those of the historical Red River colony. In short, the "mixed-blood" populations historically found in the Great Lakes area (and possibly beyond) would be only that: loose aggregations of "Halfbreeds" that may have presented visible similarities in term of ethnic and cultural compositions, but ultimately confused with the Red River Métis she describes as constituting the only "true" Métis People due to their distinct nationalistic culture (Murphy, 2014). As Peterson (2012, p. 40) puts it:

> Actually, there is no evidence that prior to, or even subsequent to 1815, mixed-descent residents of Great Lakes fur-trading communities had developed a *separate ethnic group identity* or *political consciousness* even though many of the cultural characteristics of Great Lakes fur trade communities were similar to these seen among the Red River Métis.

Peterson's negation of the historical existence of the Great Lakes Métis may seem trivial. But in the Canadian legal context, her dismissal of the Great Lakes Métis can potentially affect the Aboriginal rights of descendants of the Métis historical community of Sault-St-Marie (and more largely Ontario), to mention only one example. In the American context, Peterson's position can be interpreted as challenging our views about the existence of *Canadien*-Métis communities found in the Pacific Northwest as part of a nomadic Métis-*Canadien* people due to their alleged lack of "collective self-consciousness" as "Métis." In short, they would lack nationalistic expression and cases where they ascribe to themselves the national identity. In other words, Métis of the Pacific Northwest are facing the prospect of being labeled as not "real" Métis, if Peterson's line of reasoning is applied as she did in denying the existence of Great Lakes Métis. Exploring this sensitive topic brings us to the crossroads of anthropological, historical, legal, and political treatments of Métis identity in Canada, a subject matter arguably important to the descendants of American Métis who might wish to better understand the current debates involving "Métis" to the north of the 49th parallel.

At such a crossroads, it is important to note that a number of Métis organizations are working hard to influence the legal perception of Métis identity—either in restrictive or more inclusive manners (Sawchuk, 1995). Actors who articulate a narrower interpretation, for instance, provide primordialist accounts of Métis identity that establish the "genuineness" of Métis identity as a Prairie-centric articulation of Métis neo-nationalism, often cast in attempts to sway the opinion of Canadian courts. This much is clear when we read documentation prepared by Jean Teillet, the lawyer associated with the Metis Nation of Ontario.

Teillet (2013) insists on the cultural homogeneity of the "Métis Nation" by evoking some alleged cultural ties to Métis Prairie settlements which would confer a unique nationalistic "collective consciousness" upon their descendants, who are then held as truly "Métis" by comparison to other peoples of merely mixed heritage.[4] It is interesting to note that Teillet *strategically* criticizes the notion of "Indianness" as too broad a category, allegedly guilty of allowing ethnic considerations to trump cultural and political ones in describing who are the Métis. We emphasize "strategically" here because Jean Teillet clearly exaggerates the homogenous and monological attributes she associates with the historiography of the Red River Métis Nation. For example, she exaggerates when she insists on linguistic homogeneity of the North-Western Métis and on the historical portrayal of the "Michif" language as having singly unified all Métis across the Plains, an exaggerating tendency also denounced by Métis scholar Paul L.A.H. Chartrand when he discussed the Daniels case.[5]

Robert Papen (1984, p. 117) highlights the difference between the French dialect spoken by the Métis, which many but not all call "Michif," and the language that has come to be known as "Michif" which is a veritable bilingual mixed language, formed by combining French and Cree. The former was simply French. In the French spoken by the Métis, unlike Michif, there were few terms borrowed from Cree (Papen, 1984, pp. 136-137). The linguist Robert Papen notes that the promotion of Michif, the French-Cree bilingual mixed language—or the French-Cree intertwined language, a term used by Bakker (1997)—is based more on political choices than linguistic evidence regarding the actual historical languages spoken. Papen suggests that the influence of indigenous languages on the French spoken by the Michifs was relatively weak (Papen, 2009). He adds that the problem with referring to the French spoken by the Métis is that it leads one to deny that it was indeed French. Furthermore, differences are often exaggerated in writing the oral language as it is spoken by the Métis since the transcription can be deftly used to make the language sound much more exotic, and thus somehow not French.[6] Papen (2009) notes somewhat ironically that a great deal of effort is invested in creating a written form of Métis for words that would have been largely pronounced the same way by the Métis and French-speakers elsewhere in Canada—and surely in some regions in France. Thus, *quarante* (40) is spelled out as *karánt* and *soixante* (60) becomes *swesáñt* even though the pronunciation would have been certainly identical (2009). Here Papen suggests that either due to a simple ignorance of French or because of a mistrust of this language, French words that are taught as Michif are more than often written as to completely mask their Euro-French origins and identity.

Although representations of Michif as this national language of the Métis is perhaps politically convenient, it does not fit the extant linguistic evidence. Instead, as Papen notes, a study of Métis French would say much about the French spoken in the earliest years of New France, and would certainly have shared elements with the French spoken in Louisiana and the now almost extinct French spoken in the intermediate region lying along the Mississippi River, such as the "pawpaw" French, which is still spoken in places close to St. Louis (Papen, 2004). Métis French, if only one form of such language can be isolated, would thus have been a continental language tied to the spread of the first *coureurs de bois* followed by the voyageurs and the various Métis communities across North America.

Métis, Cultural Essentialism, and Names

Another exaggeration we find in Jean Teillet's depiction of Métis culture is the alleged cultural homogeneity of Métis identity, and the single political agency that would be associated with such an ethnonym. In fact, it is interresting to note that at least thirty-five ethnonyms have been reported within the population of the Red River Colony alone. This makes it quite difficult to build, after the fact, an exclusionary criterion on the basis of the term "Métis," as if it were inherently loaded by a political meaning that would necessarily exclude or include "Halfbreeds," or any people qualified by other close synonyms, as fundamentally Métis or non-Métis (Jean, 2011). Policing ethnonyms in the context of "French-Indian" communities during the fur trade era as a measuring stick of Métis authenticity is therefore a bad idea. Claims attributing a divisive and definitive meaning to the word "Métis" on a nationalist/nominalist basis are challenged by a number of important facts. These include historical evidence of numerous ethnonyms used by French-Indian populations, the existence of many different and independent "Métis" communities often at great distance from one another, as well as the relative ease by which individuals of mixed Indigenous-European heritage often shifted identities in strategic ways. See for example the life of Marie Rose Delorme Smith (MacKinnon, 2012).[7]

Evidence shows that interchangeable ethnonyms were used when it came to Métis. Examples include Bonnycastle's (1846) work *Canada and the Canadians,* where synonymic usages between French-Canadians of mixed-indigenous heritage and the *Bois-Brulés* are found; Taché's (1863) *Forestier et Voyageurs* describing the voyageurs who married "*sauvagesse*" as "*gens libres*," "*mitis*" or "*Bois-Brulé*" (Taché, 1884, pp. 199-200); the 1885 reports of Bryce (1885, p. 9) in the *Old Settler* where the composite term of "French *Halfbreed*" is used interchangeably with "Metis" and "*Bois-Brulé*"; as well as the definitions in the 1894 *Dictionnaire Canadien-Francais*, in which "*Sang-Mélé*" (a noun here, not an adjective) is considered a synonym of "Métis," "*Bois-Brulé*" and "*Homme-libre*" (Clapin, 1894). Not only were there multiple often equivocal ethnonyms in the Red River Colony, but it has also been reported that "the French half-breeds" were generally called "the French," a designation indifferently "applied to [French] Canadians, métis of all grades [of French blood] and even pure Indians who associate with métis and speak their *patois*" (MacBeth, 1898, p. 314; O'Toole, 2010, p. 157).

This is not to suggest that distinct groups didn't exist or were impossible to identify because of multiple and often overriding names. Evidence presented herein demonstrates, for example, that the "Métis" in the Red River area and across North America spoke mostly French and were Catholics, while the "Halfbreeds" formed other communities, predominantly English-speaking and Protestant. Brenda Macdougall (2012, p. 423) affirms that the term "Half-breed" and occasionally "country-born" had been applied to the Scottish English-speaking communities, those who had been much more closely associated with the Hudson's Bay Company, as opposed to the North-West Company that harbored a greater concentration of French-Métis. In other words, the presence of many different ethnonyms does not make it impossible to distinguish between the different Métis communities. Yet, from a strictly historical perspective, it is an exaggeration to portray what is now perceived as the "Metis Nation" as this unified or homogenous cultural phenomenon perennially driven by a single and continuous agency, acting as this one organic body. It is even worse to retroactively suggest that the Métis whose ancestors happened to experience the turmoils associated with the Red River colony are the only "true" Métis. Historically speaking, especially considering the wide culture shared by the *Bois-Brulés* across North America (including in Oregon), it simply doesn't hold. Attesting to such diversity even within the confines of the Red River colony, Macdougall (2012, p. 434) discusses the work of Frits Pannekoek (1977) who concluded that differences between the Métis and the "country-born" were so great that the French-speaking Métis and English-speaking self-designated "Half-breeds" were "unable to unite in common self-interest against the Canadian state in 1869-1870." (MacDougall, 2012, p. 434). Though such conclusions might be exaggerated, they highlight the dangers of retroactively imposing a neo-nationalist homogenizing Métis blanket across the historical Prairies corridor between 1816 and 1885.

It remains therefore difficult—if not bizarre—to substantiate an exclusionary analysis by which the descendants of "other Métis" across North America would be deprived of their Métis identity or heritage. In academia, such exclusion is now articulated on the basis of sociological theories that merge the expressions of past Métis nationalism as a necessary condition for the expression of Métis "collective consciousness." This leads some to believe that only nineteenth-century Métis nationalist revisionism would ensure a "true" or "mature" Métis ethnogenesis.

As a result, we find at least one scholar calling unapologetically other French-Indian descendants who self-identify as Métis "soup kitchen," leaving little doubt as to the derogatory undertones of such an expression (Andersen, 2014: 24). Surely to highlight the racial tensions we find at the roots of Métis identities is both helpful and commendable. But to elevate nineteenth-century Métis nationalism from the prairies above all other expressions of Métis identities—because anything but Red River Métis nationalism would be inherently flawed as "racist"—is misguided. Clearly not all expression of "collective consciousness" ought to be nationalist in tone to be authentic or "mature." Moreover, to scale Métis cultures along new "evolutionary" charts on the basis of recent ethno-nationalist assessments, by which some Métis would deserve proper capitalization and others not (or worse derogatory terms), puts one on a very slippery slope. These points become even more salient when we realize that the Pan-American nationalist project proposed by Louis Riel remains largely under construction; a project which Riel himself never shied away from articulating in reference to both ethnic and cultural considerations, insisting, for example, on the Indian "blood" connection of the Métis (not the amount, let us be clear) when he argued for the political rights of the Métis peoples to Aboriginal title. Riel argued that the justification for the "Indian title" of the Métis was due to the presence of "Indian Blood" in their veins, or their part-Indigenous ethnicity. Riel did not geographically limit this inherent right to "Indian title" only to the Métis of the Northwest, as he explicitly recognizes the same right to the Eastern Métis of Canada. Moreover, Riel did not subscribe to any notion of blood quantum required to be Métis (Martel, G., 1984 p. 238; Riel, L., 1985, pp. 171, 273).

"Truth-Telling" in Canadian Courts: Telling the Métis Who They Are

At this point, many readers may be puzzled by the agressivity caracterizing the current struggles over Métis identities in Canada. While the examples presented certainly show the dangers of producing simplified imageries of the Métis peoples, we have also illustrated that another problem lies in adopting a primordialist or "blood-based" interpretation of "peoplehood"—primordialism being the definitions of nations as natural, unchanging entites usually with blood ties that can be traced back to one point in place and time, usually a mythical or heroic event—which would combine the legal requirements for establishing a Métis identity with a romanticized vision of Métis nationhood. Competing to influence Canadian Court on its "truth-telling" about Métis identity and its bind-ing consequences give rise to numerous conflicts between the Métis involved and other stakeholders. The question of Métis identity is therefore not only a historical or academic topic; it is a subject penetrated by relationships of power and even political feuds between Métis organizations. Paradoxically, it can be suggested that the 1982 Constitutional recognition of the Métis as Aboriginal have fueled these feuds.[8] Not only are probing questions about who can qualify *legally* as Métis being inceasingly asked, but fratricidal conflicts between Métis organizations have emerged ever since the Constitutional recognition of the Métis as Aboriginal peoples, fueling an ongoing competition for political influ-ence and the access to resources and services linked to that recognition.[9]

To better understand these tensions, it should be noted that Canadian author-ities are under mounting pressure to amend the racist language that has histor-ically framed the *Indian Act* and other legislation pertaining to the Aboriginal peoples of Canada, including the Métis. Legislation openly grounded in racial segregation would be regarded as morally reprehensible in Canada today, even possibly challengeable under the Canadian Charter of Rights and Freedoms.

This shift in both moral and legal culture has pressured Canadian authorities to articulate new rationales to justify the inclusions and exclusions that underpin Aboriginal membership from a legal standpoint, and at the same time to sup-press any racist undertones. Examples of such reworked rationales are visible in the creation of a *two*-generational cut-off applied to Status Indians following the readjustments of Bill C-31,[10] and the juridical creation of a cultural cut-off for the Métis based on a community acceptance criterion following the 2003 *Powley* decision. Interestingly enough, none of these cut-offs designed to evaluate and limit the legal status of Aboriginal peoples in Canada refers to blood quantum measurement—a rationale now widely condemned for its racism and its equiva-lency to termination policies toward the indigenous peoples. These new rationales rather insist respectively on the status held by the parents to determine who is able to pass Indian status, and community criteria based on the existence of this notion of "Historical Métis communities." Termination tendencies are however still palpable despite the moral readjustments that inform these new cut-offs, especially for any future Métis in Canada (Fiske & George, 2006; Keung, 2009; Lawrence, 2004).

The "two-generational cut-off" for Status Indians was designed after a dispar-ity between Indian men and women in Canadian laws was addressed. Interestingly, the problem arose from... *métissage*. Before the *Indian Act* was amended in 1985,

Status Indian men could pass their status to their wives, and, as a result, their children are considered of Indian status. Conversely, if women had "married out," the women lost their Indian status, and their children were not considered Indian. These measures have been challenged based on sexual discrimination by indigenous women of Canada. At first, the discriminative principle was struck down in its entirety by the Canadian court, which made it possible to rehabilitate anyone who could show that a woman in their lineage was deprived of their Indian title due to "marry-out" as an Indian. Deemed too "broad" in application by the Court of Appeal, and most likely out of fear of the countless inflow of new "Indians," the correction to the *Indian Act* essentially kept a two-generation cut-off, but rescinded any preferential treatment for an Indian man marrying a non-Indian person. Ever since, the child of a "pure" Indian from an administrative standpoint (6.1) is identified as a 6.2, if born out of a union in which the partner is either an unidentified or non-indigenous person. Then, if a child is born from a 6.2 Indian and an unidentified or non-indigenous person, that child loses his or her Indian status. This policy effectively places all status Indians of Canada two generations away from legal extinction, if two consecutive unions with Non-Indians people are contracted. The sheer weight of current demographics makes this prospect very likely (Cannon, 2014). More disturbing, this cut-off redirects focus for possible blame arising from this termination policy by placing responsibility for disenfranchisement on an "Indian" person's choice of partner instead of the government as a rule-maker. Assimilation appears therefore imputable to "bad" or even "treacherous" personal decisions involving moreover the stigma of marrying non-Aboriginal persons.

In comparaison, the cultural cut-off affecting Métis peoples in Canada may seem inoffensive, and perhaps even fair. The insistence on cultural criteria to circumscribe constitutionally-protected Métis rights is mainly the product of the 2003 *Powley* decision by the Supreme Court of Canada that first recognized Métis harvesting rights. (It is the case of the *Powley* brothers charged for hunting a moose for food outside the hunting season and without permit in the area of Sault St. Marie, Ontario, Canada). One of the main difficulties faced by the Canadian Court is that, although the Métis are recognized as "Aboriginals" under the Canadian Constitution of 1982, they do not fall under the arbitrariness or legal positivism of the *Indian Act*. Moreover, there is no generational cut-off for assessing the Aboriginality of the Métis, which would amount to reintroducing infamous blood quantum policy. In addition, no clear definition of Métis identity has been offered in the Canadian Constitution—arguably in line with international legislation underlining the fundamental rights for Métis to self-define their identity. Hence, the Canadian authorities, in addition to dealing with a diversity of conflicting interpretations on what constitutes Métis identity, must operate from a moral standpoint increasingly sensitive to decolonizing rationales that condemn undue governmental interference in Indigenous "internal" affairs, especially on membership issues.

This helps to explain why the *Powley* test did not attempt to define who are the Métis *per se* in Canada. Yet the effects towards terminating Métis rights associated with the *Powley* decision are no less subtle. In short, to define Métis rights as "Aboriginal rights" the Court had to make Métis harvesting claims amenable to the precedents informing Canadian Aboriginal Law. These precedents insist on proving the cultural relevance of a practice in regard to the Aboriginality of the claimant while also testing for possible legal infringement. Tensions at the heart of this process remain however tangible, oscillating between affirmations that only the Métis should be empowered to determine their identity and the need to develop membership systems to make it possible to determine, "consistent with that definition set out in *Powley*, who the Metis are in an objectively verifiable way" (Dyck & White, 2013).

The effects of these tensions can be detected in the various strategies used by both Métis and governmental actors who use the *Powley* decision to either formulate their demands for recognition or to police Métis identity. The *Powley* test, once again, is carefully devised to avoid any reference to a blood quantum requirement or provisions that would be based explicitly on race.[11] Tests applied to Métis claimants focus instead on cultural checkpoints and community-based criteria where claimants are asked to prove their acceptance by a contemporary Métis community. This community, in turn, must exhibit a sufficient degree of continuity in regard to a historical Métis community. Most importantly, the recognition of a "historical Métis community" is further contingent upon three criteria: it had to exist "post-contact" due to the obvious mixed European-indigenous ancestry of the Métis peoples; it should be culturally distinct from both European and indigenous predecessor societies; and it had to exist before the colonial authorities assumed effective control over the historical community in question. Assessed under these criteria, many descendants from historical communities in Oregon could potentially secure Métis rights, if they were under Canadian jurisdiction.

When we look at possible legal interpretations of the *Powley* test in Canada, we can however still see terminating tendencies of Métis rights in action. When interpreted narrowly, the *Powley* test could imply that only the actual descendants of members from historical Métis communities who still live on their geographical location can be recognized as the bearers of constitutionally protected Aboriginal harvesting rights in Canada. This has the effect of dramatically reducing the possible numbers of right-bearing Métis by making the emergence of any future Métis ethnic identity legally impossible. It also effectively circumscribes the geographical scope of any rights that Métis may successfully claim, this without any form of explicit consent as to the geographical limitation of their rights.[12]

Taken together, these two "cut-offs" frame the legal outcomes associated with the question of *métissage* in Canada. On the one hand, *métissage* with non-indigenous people can be perceived as threatening for the legal recognition of the descendants of a status Indian. This is the case when *métissage* occurs in two generations in a row. A policy of assimilation is simultaneously created for any new Métis that could have been absorbed by Métis cultures (as it was often historically the case). They would now be deemed too diluted culturally to join formally recognized Aboriginal group. On the other hand, under the *Powley* test, the emergence of a Métis ethnic identity is now frozen in the past and held to strict geographical and genealogical conditions. Métis identity is thus framed by a political and legal system that associates them with the past and owns the rule of their future in terms of identity and attribution of privilege.

Despite constitutional recognition, the Métis in Canada now find themselves under an intense process of legal scrutiny that still tends towards termination of rights of many Métis. Aside from mixed aboriginal and non-aboriginal ancestry, a Métis claimant under section 35 of the 1982 Constitution has minimally to prove some ancestral family connection (not necessarily genetic); identifies himself or herself as Métis; and shows acceptance by a Métis community or a locally organized community branch, chapter or council of a Métis association or organization with which that person wishes to be associated.[13] On the personal level, the *Powley* decision pressures Métis individuals to adopt and even assert publically their identity to match the criteria enforced by Canadian legal system.[14] The outcome of amalgamating ethnological and legal considerations on the emergence of a "Métis" ethnic identity has clearly had mixed results. One example is that it has been legally subordinated to historical estimates determining when the European authorities gained "effective control," which leaves many Métis powerless. Moreover, this subordination is central to the justification of freezing the ongoing emergence of a Métis ethnic identity in the past. It also justifies the confinement of Métis rights to geographical boundaries arbitrarily associated with a particular historical Métis community.[15] Harvesting rights are thus limited to practices of the past in which the expression of Métis culture is frozen in stereotypical images.[16] We can thus begin to appreciate how slippery is the process of experiencing or reclaiming one's Métis identity in Canada, even under more favorable legal conditions.

"Half-Breeds" Dispossessed in the United States

Though the legal frameworks are quite different in the United States—aboriginal rights were never granted to "half-breeds" *per se*—there were a few cases of lands being set aside for "half-breeds." These "half-breed tracts" included the Half-Breed Tract established in Iowa in 1824 when a treaty was signed between the Sacs, Foxes and the United States. Under the original treaty, the land could be occupied, but individuals could not buy or sell the land. The United States Congress repealed this rule in 1834, and claim-jumpers immediately occupied the land. What's more, the process whereby the "Half-breeds," who would certainly have been French-speaking *Canadien*-Métis, lost their lands parallels the dispossession of the Métis in Canada. In the Manitoban and Canadian case, the Métis were given scrip, a voucher to be redeemed for land at a later date, as opposed to being given land communally. Largely impoverished and facing a great deal of hatred following the resistances of 1870 and 1885, most Métis sold their scrip to speculators and were left landless. In the case of the Half-Breed Tract in what had been the Ohio Territory, the territorial legislature did everything to ensure that the lands would end up in the hands of white settlers.

In 1838, the Ohio territorial legislature enacted a requirement that all claimants file with the clerk of the District Court of Lee county within one year: "Lands not thus disposed of were to be sold and the proceeds to be divided among such half-breeds as could properly establish their claims and had not otherwise been fully paid in lands" (Wick, 1905, p. 21). Two commissioners were appointed and the work being conducted over two years clearly did not gain the favor of the territorial legislature. The lands, 119,000 acres, were finally sold to an attorney, Hugh T. Reid, for $5,778.32 (Wick, 1905, p. 22). Wary of alienating the white squatter, the territorial legislature then passed legislation in 1839 providing for any person who had settled and improved the land to be paid in full value for their improvements (Wick, 1905, pp. 22-23). In 1840, more legislation was passed allowing for any settler to select not more than one section and hold such land until title was settled. As Wick (1905, p. 23) explains: "The Legislature, by its various acts, had tried to protect the actual white settlers against the claims of the speculators, who were seeking to get possession of these lands, which had become the most valuable in the territory." In 1846, however, the Iowa Supreme Court ruled in favor of Reid, affirming that he was the owner of the 119,000 acres. The United States Supreme Court struck down this ruling in 1850, upholding the 1841 partition (Flanders, 1965, p. 29). The 1841 partition had given 101 individuals the right to a share with lots being drawn giving each shareholder the option of selection of a tract of land (Union Historical Company, 1880, p. 136). Lucy Murphy (2014, p. 260) notes that few of the shareholders were the "half-breeds": "About twelve of them were held by the original 'half-breed' grantees and the rest went

Métis Prisoners, North-West Rebellion, 1885, Charles William Jefferys, ca. 1920. This drawing was based on a photo of Métis prisoners taken after the battles of 1885 pitting the Métis led by Louis Riel and Gabriel Dumont against the North-West Mounted Police and other volunteer soldiers sent by the Canadian Government. The handcuffed men were pressured to plead guilty to treason-felony. The charge would have been high treason, a capital offense leading to a potential death sentence. The prisoners received various prison terms.

to the people who had purchased, cajoled, or cheated the métis Sauk or Fox people out of their rights to the land."

A few other "half-breed" tracts were set aside in the western United States, but the outcome was similar: scrip was issued, but rarely did the Métis benefit. The same held true when scrip was instituted in Canada and given to the Métis of the Red River Valley. Wick's (1905, p. 28) description of the fate of the "half-breeds" of the Iowa territory would also be familiar to the Canadian Métis case in Manitoba after 1870 and the North-West Territories after 1885, which included the future provinces of Saskatchewan and Alberta, when scrip was issued to extinguish aboriginal land title: "Although many of the descendants of the half-breeds can still be found in various walks of life, scattered over the State, most of them gradually wandered to the west to be with their own people, with whom they had much in common, and where perhaps they could more easily obtain a scanty living." As for the Half-Breed Tract: "The lands were largely in the hands of speculators, and so this ideal home, which had been in the possession of their ancestors for centuries, slipped away for a mere song" (Wick, 1905, p. 28). If the treaty had been respected and the "half-breeds" had been able to keep their tract of land, this might have become an American Métis homeland where the emergence of a Métis identity as political identity in the United States would have been facilitated. Unfortunately, it was not to be. No ruling comparable to the *Powley* decision exists in the United States and neither the American Constitution nor the Supreme Court have granted any recognition to their Métis or "half-breeds" as Aboriginal peoples. The challenge for mixed indigenous populations in the United States has been and remains to gain recognition as indigenous peoples, and thus go from unrecognized tribes to federal recognition. The Cowlitz, for example, were only recognized in 2002 and obtained a 152-acre reservation in 2015. Of interest, many of the contemporary Cowlitz are descendants of Simon Plamondon, a nineteenth-century migrant originally from Quebec.

Not only were the Métis dispossessed of lands granted in treaties in the nineteenth century, but they also risked deportation in the early decades of the twentieth century. In 1907, as part of a broader effort to severely limit non-European immigration into the U.S., the Bureau of Immigration and Naturalization made a number of rulings involving the Métis. The Bureau confirmed the ineligibility of "half-breed Canadian Indians" for U.S. citizenship. This ruling in turn was followed by a district court ruling in 1909 that found that the Métis or "half-breeds" were legally neither white nor Indian and as a consequence they feared deportation.

"French Breeds" Face Deportation

Martha Foster writes: "And since, in Montana French breeds were associated with Canada (and possible deportation), the Chippewa-Crees were unlikely to identify themselves as Metis, Michif, or Mitsif as did many Turtle Mountain enrollees. For mixed-descent people in Montana, even more than those of North Dakota, a mixed-blood designation risked not only losing rights as Indians but also as U.S. residents" (Foster, 2006, p. 219). Under such conditions, the politics of identity become ever more complex. In the case of the Montana Métis, some came to identify themselves as "French Canadian" as a way of escaping some of the stigma associated with being Métis, without necessarily rejecting their mixed or Métis ancestry entirely. Foster emphasizes that the term French Canadian "while deemphasizing an Indian ancestry (yet not necessarily excluding it), emphasized a French/Catholic heritage that could and often did include Métis culture and lifestyle" (2006, p. 207). This certainly corresponds to the evidence presented in the preceding chapters that the Métis were *Canadien* first and that being *Canadien* did not preclude them from being Métis or vice versa. Montana Métis identification as French Canadian is a logical extension of past practice, and did not represent an outright rejection of Métis identity or Métis kinship ties as Foster discovered (2006, p. 207).

Relational and Roots-based Schema of Métis Identities

Illustrating the complexities associated with Métis identities should not be construed to mean that the Red River "Métis Nation" in Canada never existed as a political reality, nor that the descendants of the Prairies Métis don't have the legitimacy to perceive themselves as a "Métis Nation." On the basis of reciprocity, however, it is hoped that the exposure of the diversity and historical difficulties faced by the descendants of other "French-Indian" historical communities, who often cherish oral testimonies of their Métis identity passed down by families, triggers the same respect about their decision to identify as "Métis." Otherwise, a series of painful questions that some must endure could be as easily redirected. For example, what could possibly allow the descendant of the "English-Halfbreed" of the Red River Colony to now call themselves "Métis," while the descendants of the Great Lakes or Oregon "Halfbreeds" cannot do the same? How can we prove beyond reasonable doubt that the "Halfbreeds" from Red River had the very same collective or national awareness as the Red River French-Métis? Or how can we empirically prove, generation by generation, the transmission of this collective and homogenized Métis collective consciousness for every single self-identifying Métis in Manitoba? The difficulty of answering these questions should cast serious doubt on the project of using revisionist and nationalist interpretations fetishizing the historiography of the Red River Métis to restrict the scope and study of other Métis identities across North America.

It should be clear here that a search for reciprocity and relations guides our quest for alternative ways to conceptualize Métis identities. Evidence presented above suggests that, from the beginning, Métis communities have all generated an environment in which their members bear multiple group identities, while maintaining a sufficient degree of cultural coherency stemming from their unique yet distinctively similar fusion of indigenous and mainly *Canadien* voyageur culture. In-depth genealogical examinations of the Prairie Métis have revealed that the fur trade routes were home to already nomadic Métis families and individuals who constitute *ad hoc* Métis-*Canadien* communities. More precisely, they bear the heritage of a pre-existing cultural societal pattern stemming from the voyageur society, where a predominantly French *Canadien* culture primed the blending of various indigenous elements together. Study of the Métis kinship connections across the Pacific Northwest thus reveals a malleable—yet recognizable—sociocultural pattern structured by marriages both within and outside the community shaping the contours of a predominantly French-*Canadien*-Métis identity across North America. Simply put, the Métis identity did not emerge solely in the Red River area.

This pattern could be imagined as "rhizomatic," a term referring to a model for envisioning cultures as suggested by Gilles Deleuze and Felix Guattari (1987).

The rhizomatic model uses the metaphor of a plant extending itself through an underground and horizontal tuber-like root system to develop new plants (Stagoll, 2010). The prime example of this is the Honey fungus that grows in the Blue Mountains of Oregon. Though at first sight the small clumps of yellow-brown mushrooms that are visible to the uninitiated are innocuous enough, they grow out of one genetically identical rhizomatic mass that runs far and wide in the topsoil, following the roots of plants, covering over two-thousand acres making it the largest biological organism. The small visible clumps of mushrooms are connected by shoestring-like tubes that together can run miles in length and together this one organism has potentially been alive for thousands of years (Fleming, 2014).

This organism ironically is located in the Malheur National Forest (Schmitt & Tatum, 2008), *malheur* being French for misfortune, and the name is certainly yet another trace of the buried and forgotten *Canadien* and Métis past. This image is opposed to a tree-like structure evolving from a unique source of origin, thus enforcing a dualist metaphysical conception of identity. A tree-like schema enforces an imagery that is strictly hierarchical, viewed from one core as superior to subordinate. The result is a perception of superiority or supremacy from the core, here arguably the Red River Métis, and the burying or planned disappearance of the others Métis. Simply put, the Métis would share more in common with the Honey fungus than a tree, as each Métis settlement, much like the isolated patches of mushrooms, was connected by language, culture, and kinship to other such communities often separated by hundreds or thousands of miles. Rather than seeing each "Frenchtown" as an individual tree, we propose that it is much like the Honey fungus rhizomatic mass connected to other such communities. The stringy rhizomes that tied together the larger organism were in this case the rivers of the fur-trade and the shared memories that continue to shape the lives of the descendants of the *Canadien* and Métis across the continent, but also among the French-speaking populations in Quebec and elsewhere. These are precisely the transitory and as yet undetermined routes described by Deleuze and Guattari, who also suggested, "rather than narrativize history and culture, the rhizome presents history and culture as a map or wide array of attractions and influences with no specific origin or genesis, for a 'rhizome has no beginning or end; it is always in the middle, between things, interbeing, intermezzo'" (1987, pp. 10, 25). Thus, using this "rhizomatic model" each Métis community is connected to another and each is equally important as there is no true center to the rhizomatic mass, rather connected communities whereby each is tied to the other by a barely visible mass of threads which would be culture and memory (Parr, 2010, p. 234).

Described as such, the rhizomatic model is a powerful alternative to the contemporary models of nation and nationalism as applied to the Métis, at fault for their abstract and homogenizing tendencies. This rhizomatic model also describes quite well the nomadic activities of the *Canadien*-Métis following the fur trade routes establishing small settlements that were invariably related to the inhabitants of other communities whether in the Canadian Arctic, the Great Lakes, the Missouri and all points in between. The underground lateral movement of the rhizome, a biological model used as our primary metaphor, does not require a founding myth and is inherently better suited to the historically scattered, yet connected, *Canadien*-Métis. As Deleuze and Guattari put it: this model "resists the organizational structure of the root-tree system which charts causality along chronological lines and looks for the originary source of 'things' and looks towards the pinnacle or conclusion of those 'things'" (1987, p. 7).

In contrast, the dominant narrative of Métis nationalism tends to produce an overly simplistic, linear and evolutionary model of Métis nationhood. By negating the collective existence of all Métis beyond the scope of what amounts to Red River Métis nationalism, we risk negating the importance of other political expressions through which Métis have shared collective sentiments and group identities. More disturbingly, by excluding other French-Indian communities as "merely mixed" and allegedly unaware of themselves on a collective basis as "Métis," we risk adhering to a scaling civilizational paradigm that ranks some "Métis" as "more evolved" or "genuine" than others based on the location of the political history of their ancestry or ramification to an imagined core of cultural importance.

The Gift of the Interconnected

To focus on the intersecting ramifications of the various *Canadien*-Métis communities might reveal the porous contour of intersecting micro political cultures that had multiple centers of dissemination. In that respect, the Red River Colony was certainly not the first "French-Indian" community to contest colonial powers or restrictions on trade. The rhizomatic points of emergence of the Métis culture as *Gens libres* were numerous, fluid, and horizontal in their manifestations. For instance, Métis or "French-Indian" communities were monitored for their inclination toward claiming political "autonomy" as early as 1687. This suggests a degree of political cohesion in distinct French-indigenized groups similar to the Métis of Manitoba. In the case of St. Louis, Denonville reports this phenomenon as early as 1687:

> Mr. de la Salle gave concessions at Fort St. Louis has several François [French] staying there for several years, and they no longer wish to come back [descend to the colony], which gave rise to endless disorders and abominations. Those people are boys who have done nothing to cultivate the land. Every week they marry the savages according to Indian custom, they pay off parents at the expense of our merchants. These people claim to be independents and [master] on their own concessions.[17]

The Fight at Seven Oaks, 1816, Charles William Jefferys, 1914. The Battle of Seven Oaks or "La Grenouillère" on June 19, 1816 pitted the Métis, largely working for the North West Company, against the rival Hudson's Bay Company. At stake was the pemmican trade which was essential to the fur trade. Hudson's Bay Company officers and employees had seized the North West Company's Fort Gibraltar, effectively cutting off supply of pemmican. This set off a string of violent clashes that led to the forced merger of the two companies in London in 1821. It is seen as a pivotal moment in the genesis of Métis political activism in the Red River.

Karen L. Marrero (2012) also suggests the existence of French-Indian communities in the Windsor-Detroit area, a population curiously identified as "Metchis" in other documents, who Marrero describes as culturally distinct and politically active.[18] Louise Seymour Houghton moreover confirms the activities of the "Middle West" Métis coalescing around what is certainly a collective identity, when she reports that three hundred Metis, "who were the only male inhabitants of Mailletstown, learning from their founder, Paulette Maillet, of the defeat and capture by the British of 'Mr. Tom' Brady of Kaskaskia, at La Salle's old fort St. Joseph on Lake Michigan, uprose 'as one man,' marched swiftly and secretly across the prairie, captured the fort, though defended by British regulars and cannon, took all the stores, and brought them with the wounded of Brady's party to Cahokia" (Houghton, 1918, p. 81). If that is not a victory akin and as glorious as the Battle of Seven Oaks, but in the "Middle West," then we can only wonder what will it take to unsettle the Red River neo-nationalist Métis scholars. Finally, we can also state the example of the "Half Breeds" around the north shore of Lake Huron, who appeared sufficiently organized to formulate political demands of their own, as this letter sent to the Honourable John Macauley, dated September 19, 1838, confirms:

> During the past summer I have been engaged in a tour around the North Shores of Lake Huron, and amongst the Islands scattered along that coast. In the course of my journey I had repeated and earnest solicitations from the Half Breeds as the progeny of European and Indian parents are commonly called to use my best endeavours to obtain for them and their families the same privileges and advantages, as the pure Indians have inquired by their arrangements with Sir Francis Bond Head. The principal benefit the spiritual wants of the hundreds of children of the forest.

To better understand the descendants of the "children of the forest" it is necessary to develop new conceptual tools to grasp the resurgence of Métis identity both north and south of the 49th parallel and as far away as the Pacific Northwest.

Conclusion

Whether it is in Hollywood movies or academic works, the tendency has been to present the *Canadien* and other French-speakers as curious oddities never central to the main narrative. Yet it is evident when the historical record is analyzed holistically that people who spoke French were central to the history of the American West and Pacific Northwest as they were in Canada. Already in the 1600s, French *coureurs de bois* or free traders were pushing deep inland and were becoming *Canadien*, the native-born children of the continent. They not only adopted many elements of First Nations culture, but they also eagerly sought marriage alliances with First Nations women, much as Samuel de Champlain had wished. These alliances occurred in spite of the best efforts of either priests or colonial officials to censure the men. The threat of excommunication was not sufficient to deter the men seeking furs and developing kinship ties in the forests and plains of the continent. Their numbers are too often underestimated and even if they paled in comparison to the swelling population on the eastern seaboard, they nonetheless were the pathfinders who established the trade routes and posts and acquired the knowledge that would prove essential to the later migrants. This contribution is too often glossed over in the national historical narratives.

Until the Conquest of Canada and the Treaty of Paris in 1763, the *Canadiens* were also part of an empire that had the ambition to control much of North America. That changed irrevocably after 1763. From being native-born people of North America under the French Crown, they became successively subjects of the British Crown, the Spanish Crown, the French empire (under Napoleon), before becoming citizens of the United States. All this occurred in a single life for people such as Pierre-Louis de Lorimier, founder of Cape Girardeau, Missouri. Their statelessness after 1763 explains partially why they have been written out of the history of the West, both in Canada and the United States. Added to that is the fact that as descendants of former enemies of both the Americans and the British—"France, our most inveterate enemy," wrote Benjamin Franklin in 1747

(Bigelow, 1904, p. 167)—they were not to be trusted and their importance had to be played down in the interest of new national narratives. There was no way they could be credited with history-making feats.

The process of writing the French out of the historical narrative began even while the *Canadien*, Créole, and Métis populations were still more numerous than the Anglo-Americans heading West. As the work of Janet LeCompte (1997) clearly demonstrates, the ratio of "Frenchmen" to Americans was four to one and not one to four. These "Frenchmen" were not only the boatmen or voyageurs, but also the clerks and quite often partners and founders of fur trade companies. It is also too easy to forget how the fur trade helped to found the wealth of the United States. A case in point is the metropolis of New York. It was merely a small center when John Jacob Astor sent a ship filled overwhelmingly with *Canadien* employees around South America to the mouth of the Columbia. Though this first venture failed, he would nonetheless partner with a prominent Créole family in Saint-Louis, the Chouteaus, to establish his American Fur Trade Company as they acted as his western agents. The profit generated from the fur trade, largely produced by the labor of French-speakers, provided Astor with the wealth to buy up much of the real estate of Manhattan. This would ensure that the Astor family would be the city's wealthiest clan for generations. Astor's story, authored by Washington Irving, in his 1836 book *Astoria: Or, Enterprise Beyond the Rocky Mountains*, would denigrate the very men that gave Astor his wealth. He essentially presented the *Canadien* voyageurs as somewhat childish, largely savage souls whose culture was destined to quickly disappear:

> In the course of years they will gradually disappear; their songs will die away like the echoes they once awakened, and the Canadian voyageurs will become a forgotten race, or remembered, like their associates, the Indians, among the poetical images of past times, and as themes for local and romantic associations.
>
> An instance of the buoyant temperament and the professional pride of these people was furnished in the gay and braggart style in which they arrived at New York to join the enterprise. They were determined to regale and astonish the people of the "States" with the sight of a Canadian boat and a Canadian crew. They accordingly fitted up a large but light bark canoe, such as is used in the fur trade; transported it in a waggon from the banks of the St. Lawrence to the shores of lake Champlain: traversed the lake in it, from end to end; hoisted it again in a waggon and wheeled it off to Lansingburgh, and there launched it upon the waters of the Hudson. Down this river they plied their course merrily on a fine summer's day, making its banks resound for the first time with their old French boat songs; passing by the villages with whoop and halloo, so as to make the honest Dutch farmers mistake them for a crew of savages. In this way they swept, in full song, and with regular flourish of the paddle, round New York, in a still summer evening, to the wonder and admiration of its inhabitants, who had never before witnessed on their waters, a nautical apparition of the kind (Irving, 1836, pp. 31-32).

In his historical account of Astoria Irving already sets the fate of the *Canadien* as insignificant and destined to disappear even before the first ship sets sail. Throughout Irving's account, the *Canadien* are depicted as mongrel and culturally inferior. However, Irving (Irving, 1836, p. 107) does distinguish between Creoles and *Canadien* and defines the inhabitants of Saint-Louis in these terms: "a population at St. Louis even still more motley than that at Mackinaw. Here were to be seen about the river banks, the hectoring, extravagant, bragging boatmen of the Mississippi [i.e. Créoles], with the gay, grimacing, singing, good-humoured Canadian voyageurs." Irving certainly sets the tone, one that will be imitated by generations of authors.

While Irving does mention the *Canadien* quite frequently, often it is to highlight their inferiority. Irving is much more generous in his description of the few Kentucky men featured in his work. For example, describing John Day, the Kentucky hunter, he writes, "in general he [Day] was remarked for his cheerful, manly deportment" (Irving, 1836, p. 308). This is a narrative feature in the accounts of the men of the fur trade: the Americans are described as being masculine, manly, true men, whereas the *Canadien* is invariably portrayed as childish and vain.

Other authors such as James Hall[1] (1825), who incidentally wrote the first account of trapper Hugh Glass, the hero of the 2015 film *The Revenant,* trip over French names, topography, and cultural references, refer to *engagés* or voyageurs, yet are mute as to who these men were. Hall's account is full of French names of places, vegetation, and topography that had no English equivalent yet. For example, he wrote about *grains de bœuf* (later buffalo berries) and *Les côtes noires* (The Black Hills). Hall was obviously traveling in an American West where French was the lingua franca (Hall, 1825, p. 217 and 218).

Seeking to find real American heroes, the journalists and writers scouring the plains and forest of the western frontier had to find a way to write the French out of their accounts, even though they were still the dominant force in trade and settled communities. This was done by choosing a very narrow literary depth of field that focused on only one persona leaving all others on the periphery. Hall focused on Hugh Glass, while others chose Jim Bridger and Kit Carson. Hall (1825, p. 217) did not even mention by name any of the five *engagés* Glass joined when they left Fort Kiowa "bound, in a *piroque* (sic), to Yellow Stone River." In Hall's account, Glass had crawled to Fort Kiowa, before continuing on to seek the two men who had abandoned him to his fate. Similarly, the accounts of Bridger and Carson rarely mention that Frémont (1845) did not hold them in high regard in his own account of that expedition, whereas he expressed appreciation particularly for the *Canadiens* and Créoles who formed the backbone of the expedition.

Writing the French-speaking *Canadiens,* Métis and Creoles out of the history meant excluding them from being "white men" or among the "civilized." Whereas Meriwether Lewis prided himself on being the "first civilized man" to go up the Missouri, he was probably some one hundred years behind the first Europeans, which is probably what he meant by civilized. More recently, Frederick Feikima Manfred, who published *Lord Grizzly* in 1954 about the same Hugh Glass, recounted in an interview why he chose to write the novel.

> I ran across a reference to Hugh Glass in the *South Dakota Guide Book* and it instantly caught my eye—this man fighting the bear alone—**it struck me that here was the first real contact of the white man with the raw West**. When I saw what Hugh Glass did—he did a greater thing than Achilles did. Achilles killed Hector and then dragged him around Troy. So I thought we've got heroes bigger than the Greeks had (Manfred, 2011, pp. ix-x). (our emphasis)

Even historian Michael Punke (2015, p. 256), author of *The Revenant,* falls into the trap, making Jim Bridger "the first white man to touch the waters of the Great Salt Lake," and having Fitzgerald trapped in St. Louis in 1822, "the northernmost outpost of civilization on the Mississippi."

Later historians and authors would in turn focus on the Anglo-American heroes, while omitting entirely the French-speakers. This process culminated with the film *How the West was Won* featuring the All-(Anglo)-American actor James Stewart as the mountain man in his birch bark canoe. By the 1960s, the last of the traces of any meaningful understanding of the French substrate of the history of the American West had been buried in popular culture and history.

Much like an archaeological excavation where disparate artifacts are pieced together, the documents left behind when the historical record is exhumed testify to a common continental story of the French-speakers who shaped the history of both the United States and Canada. Until now, most of these documents have only served to understand local community history. Whereas American authors have presented these communities as having no true sense of national identity, the evidence unearthed and reanalyzed highlights the ties that linked communities from Détroit to Saint-Louis, passing through Kaskaskia and onwards to the Pacific Coast. Commercial and kinship ties linked these distant communities as well as a shared language and culture. The *Canadien* moved into the Great Lakes Region and then down the Illinois River to the Mississippi, while the Créole moved up the Mississippi, and both groups converged in Saint-Louis. From there, they pushed westward to reach places that La Vérendrye had first visited in the 1730s. It is these men that Lewis and Clark relied upon as guides, hunters and interpreters to get their expedition to the Rocky Mountains and to the Pacific. Whereas Sacagawea was largely sanctified in American mythology, her husband

Toussaint Charbonneau was either ridiculed, forgotten or made into a rapist, as in the film *The Revenant*.

A careful rereading of the documentary evidence not only highlights the depth and scope of the *Canadien* and other French-speakers in the larger continental history, it also suggests the emergence of a continental and multilayered Métis ethnic identity. The evidence presented highlights how the *Canadien* national identity emerged in the mid-to-late seventeenth century and how a *Canadien* could be of mixed heritage and still be considered *Canadien*. The evidence points towards an identity that can best be described as "Canadien Métis" whereby the Métis component is defining a particular *Canadien*. The two identities were inter-twined and one did not negate the other, provoking interesting questions per-taining to the emergence of complex French-indigenous identities defined in relationship to indigenous kin. Rather than claiming that a Métis identity is tied to a unique political process that occurred solely in the Red River area, we sug-gest that this Métis identity should be recognized as being pancontinental and spanning at least two hundred years. The terms "Métis" and "Bois-Brûlé" are even paired with other ethnonational terms such as the "Acadian Métis" or the "Métis of Pasbebiac" in 1886 ("Nouvelles de Paspébiac," 1886). As early as 1760, the term "Mitchif" is in fact used by Bazagier to describe sixteen families with one hun-dred individuals in Acadia. Rameau also speaks of "Métis" and "Bois-Brulés" in 1899, as forming this "small People" born out of unions between the first Acadians and Mi'kmaq peoples (Know, 1914, p. 394). The very same ethnonyms are used in 1830 to describe Charles Verreau in his guiding capacities at La Malbaie, Quebec as a "Métif" and "Bois-Brulé" (Stuart, Stuart, & Andrews, 1831, p. 4).

In the Great Lakes area, we know that at this same time Alexis de Tocqueville encounters a "savage" who speaks fluent French, identified as *Canadien* by our touring Frenchman shocked to see a man he thought to be native speak fluently his language. This *Canadien* in turn explains to our wanderer in the "*désert*" (wildnerness) that he is Métis and a "*Bois-Brûlé*." A decade earlier, George Simpson (1938, p. 381) in what is now northern Alberta refers to the children of the *Canadien* and French-speaking Iroquois as "*Meitiff*," while Gabriel Franchère describes one cantankerous man encountered in the Pacific Northwest in the early 1800s as "*mitif*" (Aubin, 2002). and the Irishman Ross Cox devotes an entire section of his book on his adventures in the Columbia to the "Bois-Brûlé."

A shared ethnicity thus seems to have emerged from the St. Lawrence Valley through the Great Lakes region, the American Midwest, the Pacific Northwest, and even to the far North. The evidence counters the current orthodoxy that the scattered communities could not possibly share a common identity, especially when we consider the common struggles and political resistance against British colonial officials.

The *Acadiens*, including any "*Acadien* Métis" were displaced, with all those who did not succeed in fleeing and finding refuge being boarded on ships in 1755 and deported to the four winds. Then there was the resistance of the voyageurs to the establishment of the Selkirk Colony and the desire of the governor to lay claim to the pemmican that was essential to the fur trade and the *hivernants* spending their winters in distant forts. Likewise, the *Canadiens* and some self-identified "Bois-Brulés" took part in the 1837-1838 Rebellion in Lower Canada, some of whom relocated to the Oregon Territory after this rebellion was crushed by the British. Finally, there is the Métis resistance of the Red River Valley and more distant locales of 1869 and 1885 where the combatants were largely the "French-Canadian Métis" led by the charismatic Louis Riel. Most, if not all, of these actors shared a common language (French), a common fur trade culture and ethos, popular folk Catholicism transmitted and maintained for decades before the arrival of priests, and finally the presence of a dual indigenous-French heritage visible enough to be noticed by historians and officials at that time, while not fully integrating into Indigenous communities. It is through the web of these intersecting cultural experiences that the terms "Bois-Brulé" and "Métis" came to mean something distinctive enough to be used trans-continentally, yet not sufficiently distinct to bar its combination with other ethnonyms such as Canadian and Acadien. In short, the term "Métis" was used historically to identify peoples of French-Indigenous heritage, a definition that Louis Riel attempted to expand through his political project to include all who were shaped by the fur trade (i.e. the English-speaking "country born" in addition to the French-speaking Métis), by virtue of having any European and Indigenous heritage to whatever degree. It is by pursuing a fine cultural analysis that it is possible to posit the emergence of a multi-sited, decentered model of national identity formation that best fits the complexity of French-indigenous peoples that were found from the Atlantic, to the Pacific and practically to the Arctic Oceans.

We have therefore argued that such national identity can best be described by a rhizomatic model. Essentially, distant communities and individuals are tied together by a shared culture, including language and history—rhizomes of belonging. These communities stretched across the continent in the same way that clumps of mushroom in Malheur National Forest are connected over miles of forest to countless other such clumps to form a massive single living organism. We submit that the Métis identity is not limited to just one region of Canada. We moreover suggest that other communities can legitimately claim a Métis identity of their own, in line with Louis Riel's inclusive political vision. A careful reading of the evidence presented invites us to a renewed awareness of the deep cultural ties that link all these communities. To fully understand the Métis history, we believe it is necessary to broaden our search and to look south of the 49th parallel, which included the *Pays d'en Haut*, the old American Northwest.

What's more, to understand the history of the Pacific Northwest, it is necessary to understand how it is tied to this much larger continental history. By tying together the history of the Saint Lawrence Valley and the Iroquois re-settlement during the French Regime, the history of the *Canadiens* in the entire Great Lakes Region, both to the north and the south, and onwards to the Mississippi and the Missouri, one can better understand the larger historical tides that pushed the descendants of Champlain westwards and over the mountains as well as down the Hudson to embark on the Tonquin. Analyzing and grasping the scope of the presence of French-speaking people throughout the western half of North America is crucial to understanding the history of the continent, be it Canada or the United States. That has been the goal of this book.

Notes

Chapter 1
Writing History, Burying the Past
1. See in particular his letter at J.-V Grandin (84/0905), p. 23: […] "*Si vous le voulez, bénissez-nous, particulièrement, nous les Métis Canadiens Français. Bénissez-nous avec les Métis de toutes autres origines.*" Trad: "If you will, bless us in particular, us the *Métis French Canadien*. Bless us with all the other Métis from all origin" (emphasis added). For the usage of the "*Métis Canadien Français*," see also the letter 3-028, p. 75 [St-Laurent, 85/02/17], the letter 3-050, p. 81 [Batoche, 85/04/10], the letter 3-052, p. 83 [Batoche, 85/05/01], the letter 3-076, p. 137 [Regina, 85/07/24]; for the term "Representatives of the French Half-breeds," see the letter 3-046 [Duck Lake, 85/03/27] (Riel, 1985).

Chapter 7
The Black Robes Return
1. Father Blanchet (1878, p. 81) discusses the correct spelling of the name of the river. He notes that Wallamette was the "true Indian name" rather than Wallamet or Willamette. He notes that between 1812 and 1842 all—American, British, Scotchmen, and French Canadian—spelled the name of the river with an "a" instead of an "i" and ended the name with "-ette." He notes that the terminal sound would have rhymed with the French word *gazette*. He refers to the other spellings of the name as "corrupted and fabricated ones of modern date."

Chapter 8
The March to Statehood
1. See the fascinating life of Madame Montour and her Métis tantatalizing kinship system in Simone Vincens (1979) *Madame Montour et son temps* and Jon Parmenter's (1999) "Isabel Montour: Cultural Broker on the Frontiers of New York and Pennsylvania."
2. This estimate is higher, however, than others, notably Blanchet's more solid estimate of 1,000 Catholic individuals in early 1844.

Chapter 9
The Politics of Becoming
1. Inspired by Anne Waters description of an Indigenous ontology, we can suggest that the social ontology pertaining to the emergence of Métis cultures can be described as animated (continuously alterable), inclusive (nonbinary) rather than exclusive (discretely binary), and have nondiscrete (unbounded) rather than discrete entities (discretely bounded) entities. These ontological qualities could be seen as characterizing the very matrix of Métis identities, recognizable by the manifestation of cultural features of European and Indigenous heritages merging together under conditions that allowed the blossoming of new kinship relations, the bedrock of Métis ethnicity and its various political expressions (Waters, 2004, p. 107).
2. The original passage, in French, as cited previously in footnote 2, chapter 6: "*Mercredi, 17 Juin 1830.-Je m'embarquai à 6 heures à bord de la goëlette Héloïse, Capitaine April,- destinée à la Malbaie, qui devait me mettre à terre à la Baie Saint-Paul. Je me suis occupé depuis le 6 du courant à préparer mes provisions et tout ce qui était nécessaire pour mon expédition. Le 12, j'engageai*

deux hommes pour m'accompagner, savoir:-Charles Verreau, bois brûlé, (métif,) en qualité de voyageur et de guide dans les bois, et D, Paulin, le premier à raison de quinze piastres et le dernier de dix piastres par mois" (Stuart, Stuart, & Andrews, 1831, p. 4). [Wednesday, June 17, 1830. I embarked at 6 o'clock aboard the boat Héllï, Capitan April, sailing for the Malbaie, that was to bring me to land at the Baie Saint-Paul. I kept myself busy since six preparing my provisions and all that would be necessary for my expedition. At noon, I hired two men to accompany me, that is, Charles Verreau, bois brûlé [burnt wood], (métif) for his skills as voyageur and guide in the forest, and D. Paulin, the first for fifteen bucks and the latter for ten bucks per month.]

3. Ted J. Brasser demonstrates that "the correct connection is with the Roman Catholic Missions, beginning in the St. Lawrence River and moving West through the Great Lakes mission. Small and stylized semi-floral designs were used by the French métis who came from the Great Lake missions»" (Brasser, 1985, p. 225).

4. See the Memorandum of fact and Law of the intervener Metis Nation of Ontario, in particular para 11, 12, 13, at: http://www.metisnation.org/media/457807/daniels%20-%20intervention%20 factum%20-%20mno.pdf"[...](11) *In the absence of an historic Métis collective, the simple fact that an individual has aboriginal ancestry does not make that person 'Métis'.* Historical references to 'half-breeds' or to the fact that Indians are not "pure-bloods" should not be taken to mean that these individuals are 'Métis.' *A Métis is not an individual who does a genealogy, discovers an 'Indian' or 'sauvage' ancestor and joins a society.* These uses of the term 'Métis' diminish the distinctive culture of the Métis people. This type of analysis confuses the courts and the public and reduces Métis to a search for a racial connection to Indians. This we submit is wrong."

5. When discussing the paragraph 96 of the Federal Court of Appeal in the Daniels Case, which states that "The Métis have their own language, culture, kinship connections and territory. It is these factors that make the Métis one of the Aboriginal peoples of Canada," Chartrand suggests that none of this is correct. "Métis people speak a variety of languages, including Cree and Ojibwe, French and English. A very small group speaks a language that linguists have labelled Michif for their own scholarly purposes. The concept of "culture" is so vague that anthropologists do not agree on its meaning, so that statement cannot be taken as having any intelligible content." In Chartrand, P. LAH (2014). "Understanding the Daniels Case on s.91(24) Constitution Act 1867." In Aboriginal Policy Studies, Vol. 3, no. 3, pp. 115-131, p. 128.

6. The linguistic evidence collected by Guy Lavallée (1988) from the predominantly Métis community of Saint-Laurent in Manitoba showed that none of the Métis spoke the bilingual mixed language, and likely would never have spoken it; instead most spoke French (Papen, 2004). Likewise, Papen states that virtually all would have spoken French in the Red River Valley, even the English-speaking "country-born" or "Half-breeds" as the French-language was the koiné language (Papen, 2004). Even those who spoke the bilingual mixed language would also have also spoken French. Interestingly, even an obscure French broadcast highlights this linguistic predominance of the French language. In the summer of 1987, a French television crew traveled to Belcourt, the main settlement of the Chippewa Turtle Mountain Reservation in North Dakota (Abouchar, 1987). There they interviewed a number of elders, one in her eighties, in French. Thus, more than 100 years after the 1885 Rebellion, some of the descendants of the French Métis, most of whom indubitably spoke Michif, the mixed language, still also spoke French and spoke it well enough to be interviewed for French television to be broadcast in France without requiring translation or subtitles (Abouchar, 1987).

7. The 1894 *Dictionnaire Canadien-Francais (Clapin, 1894)* defines *"Bois-Brulé"* as follows: "*s. m., Métis de sauvage et de blanc, dans le Nord-Ouest, et surtout issu du mélange de sang français et indien. Le bois-brûlé fait remonter son origine à quelques-unes des familles appartenant à la plus pure noblesse de France. À l'époque où le drapeau fleurdelisé régnait ici en maître, beaucoup de cadets de noblesse, poussés par un insatiable besoin d'aventures, étaient accourus*

dans le Nord-Ouest grossir les rangs des coureurs-des-bois, des voyageurs, des trappeurs, etc. Plus tard, des établissements florissants commencèrent à surgir. Ces établissements étaient sous la conduite de chefs comme M. le baron de Saint-Castin, celui-là même que Longfellow cite dans l'un de ses poèmes, MM. le Camarade de Mandeville, de Saint-Georges, de Laporte, de Saint-Luc, de Lépinais, de Chaumont-Racette, de Charlais, etc. Tous ces noms se rencontrent encore, plus ou moins altérés, dans le Nord-Ouest." ["S. m., mixture of white and savage, in the [Old] North West, especially from the mixture of French and Indian blood. The bois-brulé [burnt wood] traces their origin to some of the families of the purest nobility of France. At the time when the fleur-de-lys ruled supreme here, many noble cadets, driven by an insatiable craving for adventure, had assembled in the Northwest swelling the ranks of the coureurs des bois [runners of the woods], voyageurs, trappers, etc. Later, flourishing settlements began to arise. These institutions were led by leaders such as the Baron de Saint-Castin, the very one that Longfellow quoted in one of his poems, Misters Comrade Mandeville, St. George, Laporte, Saint-Luc de Lépinais, Chaumont-Racette de Charlais, etc. All these names are still found more or less altered in the Northwest."]

8. The Constitution Act, 1982, Schedule B to the Canada Act 1982 (UK), 1982, c 11, <http://canlii.ca/t/ldsx> retrieved on 2014-11-24

9. In line with the arguments previously explored, some Métis organizations argue that Métis identity should only belong narrowly to the Métis *Nation* as per represented in Canada by the Métis National Council, an organization emerging in 1983 following an internal schism with the Native Council of Canada (now the Congress of Aboriginal Peoples). Others, including Métis leader Harry Daniels who negotiated the entry of Métis in section 35 (2) of the *Constitution Act, 1982*, understood that the constitutional recognition of the Métis was a victory for all Métis across Canada, irrespective of their connection to the Red River historical communities. Métis identity would go beyond regionalism, or even restrictive expressions of Métis nationalism (Daniels, 1979; Dyck & White, 2013).

10. In their Report for Status Women of Canada, Jo-Anne Fiske and Evelyn George describe the matter as following: "Section 6(2) of the current Indian Act results in the termination of Indian status after two successive generations of intermarriage between status and non-status persons as defined by the Act. Descendants of out-marrying women do not have the same access to status as the descendants of men who married non-Indians. Women who have been reinstated are registered under section 6(1)(c) of the Act. Because their non-Indian male spouses have never acquired status, their children are registered as 6(2) and are prohibited from transferring status to the third generation unless they partner with someone who is also registered." (Fiske & George, 2006, p. 6).

11. As per the *Powley* decision: "[32] Second, the claimant must present evidence of an ancestral connection to a historic Métis community. This objective requirement ensures that beneficiaries of s. 35 rights have a real link to the historic community whose practices ground the right being claimed. We would not require a minimum "blood quantum," but we would require some proof that the claimant's ancestors belonged to the historic Métis community by birth, adoption, or other means. Like the trial judge, we would abstain from further defining this requirement in the absence of more extensive argument by the parties in a case where this issue is determinative. In this case, the Powleys' Métis ancestry is not disputed" (Emphasis added). R. v. Powley, [2003] 2 SCR 207, 2003 SCC 43 (CanLII), <http://canlii.ca/t/51pd> retrieved on 2014-12-05

12. For an example of a narrow interpretation of the *Powley* test, which imposes the need on the defendant to trace his or her ancestry to a local historical community before "effective control," see the paragraph 9 of the *Paquette* decision (R. v. Paquette, 2012 ONCJ 606): "The defendant must also trace his **own** ancestry to a local historic Métis community in the area where he was hunting. The evidence provided by the defendant (namely the family trees located in composite exhibit 2) show that the defendant traces his aboriginal roots back to Quebec. His evidence supports the fact that his ancestors did not arrive in the Sturgeon Falls area until sometime

between 1856 and 1902. This is after the date of effective European control and therefore would not meet the Powley test."

13. *Daniels v. Canada*, 2013 FC 6, para 127.

14. For harvesting demands, 10 additional criteria apply as per *Powley*. They can be summarized as follow: (1) The characterization of the right claimed (eg: was it hunting for food?); (2) Whether the claimant is a member of a contemporary Métis community; (3) Identification of the historic Métis community; (4) Identification of the contemporary Métis community; (5) The historical time-frame of the practice; (6) Whether the practice is integral to the culture of the claimant; (7) Whether the proposed practice is continued by the Métis community; (8) Whether the right was extinguished; (9) whether the right was infringed upon; (10) If the right was infringed, can that infringement can be justified. See R. v. Powley, [2003] 2 SCR 207, 2003 SCC 43 (CanLII), <http://canlii.ca/t/51pd> retrieved on 2014-12-07

15. Examples of these shortcomings can be seen in *R v Hirsekorn*, where the Aboriginal right for Métis to hunt in central and southern Alberta (in the Cypress Hills and Blackfoot territory of Treaty 7) was denied on the basis that Métis were only able to access Blackfoot territory after the effective control of the region by the Northwest Mounted Police in 1874, and that no historic Métis community—in addition of being insufficient in numbers—existed in southern Alberta or in the Cypress Hills at the time of effective control. *R v Hirsekorn*, 2013 ABCA 242 (CanLII), <http://canlii.ca/t/fzhvd> retrieved on 2014-11-24

16. Another example of termination can be seen in *R. v. Paquette* in which aboriginal harvesting rights have been denied to a Métis claimant residing in Ontario on the basis that he actually had Métis ancestry from Quebec, thus invalidating the on-site historical continuity required, on top of failing to prove the existence of a historic Métis community in the area of Sturgeon Fall, Ontario (Teillet, 2013, p. xviii). See *R. v. Paquette*, 2012 ONCJ 606 (CanLII), <http://canlii. ca/t/ft4ok> retrieved on 2014-11-24

17. "Denonville au Ministre, 25 août 1687," AC, C 11 A, vol. 9, folios-61-78. Cited in Bouchard (2008a). The original in French: *"Mr. de la Salle a donné des concessions au fort St. Louis a plusieurs françois qui y sejournent depuis plusieurs années sans vouloir dessendre, ce qui a donné lieu a des desordres et abominations infinies. Ces gens a qui Mr. de la Salle a concedé sont tous garçons qui n'ont rien fait pour cultiver la terre. Tous les 8 jours ils epousent des Sauvagesses à la mode des Sauvages de ce pays là, qu'ils achetent des parens aux depens des marchands. Ces gens se pretendent independans et [maîtres] sur leurs concessions."*

18. "[I]t was obvious that the Quakers hailing from New Jersey and Philadelphia considered Chene and other metis at Detroit as a culturally distinct and an almost entirely inscrutable collective following their own political agendas, and who therefore could not be trusted." Quoted from unpublished paper from Karen Marrrero: "What the Indians desired them to say.The complex role of French-Native intermediaries in the later eighteenth centuries." Original source: Joseph Moore (Moore, 1892, p. 645), Journal of a Tour to Detroit to attend a Treaty proposed to be held by the Indian at Saundusky.

Conclusion

1. Though the original publication was anonymous, historians later discovered James Hall's authorship in reviewing the Hall family papers where it was discovered that Harrison Hall, one of the publishers of *The Port Folio*, had noted James' authorship of the article in his set of bound copies of the magazine. James was the younger brother of the two publishers of *The Port Folio*, John Elihu and Harrison (Myers, 1976, p. 9).

Acknowledgements

Much work has been dedicated to this project and much like the canoe on the rivers of yore, the paddling is easier when we are pushed along by strong currents of support.

The people we must thank include our wives and children, who inspired us, but also tolerated many hours away as we toiled. A big *merci* to Sheila O'Hara Foxcurran, Ekaterina Bouchard and Natacha Godbout as well as Jake and Ry Foxcurran; Isabelle, Gabriel, Sophie and Louis-Philippe Bouchard; and Kali and Mederik Malette-Godbout.

A notable word of thanks must be extended to Dean Louder and Denis Vaugeois who acted as catalysts to bring together the team that would produce this book.

Without mentors and guides, family, colleagues and community members, we would be fighting rapids without a paddle. Many thanks to those who still guide us, and those who have left us: Georges Guay, Bill Bennett, Gilbert Bouchard, Jim McDonald, Dolores Gosselin and Marcel Labelle.

Finally, as we enter this historical conversation, it is necessary to recognize the work of historians and anthropologists who have shaped our understanding of the continental Métis: John Findlay, John Jackson, Mike Evans, Denis Vaugeois, Denis Gagnon, Serge Bouchard, Junius Rochester, Jean Barman, Bruce Watson, Steve Lehman, Sarah Hurlburt, Christine Elsey, and Maurice Guibord.

The history is certainly not ours, and we are grateful to the community members on both sides of the border who have helped us in our efforts to excavate and rethink a buried past. These include notably Sam Pambrun as well as Judith Fortney and many others: Russel Bergevin, Joey Lavadour, Chalk Courchane, Rejean Beaulieu, Joanne Plourde, Ron Pelletier, Arnie Queener, Michael Hubbs, Eugene Felsman, Wade Thomson, Dan Clark, Melissa Minthorne-Winks and Luana Gendron.

Our gratitude as well to the Maria Pasqualy and Christina Dubois at the Washington State Historical Society as well as David Steele who provided critical copy editing in the early stages and suggested the title of the book and Kathy Plett for her proofreading and indexing of the book.

A word of gratitude is owed to Robin Philpot and his wonderful team at Baraka Books. Publishing this book certainly came at great risk as it seeks to challenge many orthodoxies including the main narrative of American history. Robin demonstrated patience in dealing with three neophyte authors and we owe him greatly for this *beau risque*. Josée Lalancette, Baraka Books' graphic designer and production manager, in turn produced an exquisite book that places the *Canadien* and Métis back into the pages of the history of the United States and Canada in stunning visual detail.

We would also like to acknowledge the financial support of the University of Northern British Columbia.

To all we are grateful. *Milles mercis*, a thousand thanks!

Sources Cited * **

Abouchar, Jacques. 1987. *Francophonie : les Indiens. Le journal de 20 Heures.* Paris: France 2.

Adams, Henry, and Earl N. Harbert. 1986. *History of the United States of America During the Administrations of James Madison, Literary Classics of the United States.* New York: The Library of America.

Albright, Harry. 1991. *New Orleans: Battle of the Bayous.* New York: Hippocrene Books.

Andersen, Chris. 2014. *Métis: Race, Recognition, and the Struggle for Indigenous Peoplehood.* Vancouver: UBC Press.

Anderson, Benedict. 1983. *Imagined communities : reflections on the origin and spread of nationalism.* London: Verso.

Armstrong, John Alexander. 1982. *Nations before nationalism*: University of North Carolina Press Chapel Hill.

Arsenault, Bona. 2004. *Histoire des Acadiens.* Anjou QC: Fides.

Au, Dennis. 2007. "The Mushrat French: The Survival of French Canadian Folklife on the American Side of Le Détroit." *Humanities Research Group Working Papers* 11.

Aubin, Georges, and Gabriel Franchère. 2002. *Voyage à la côte du Nord-Ouest de l'Amérique et fondation d'Astoria, 1810-1814*: Montréal: Lux.

Audubon, John James. 1990[1897]. *Journal du Missouri.* Paris: La table ronde.

Bagley, Clarence. 1916. *The History of Seattle from the earliest settlement to the present time.* Vol. 3. Chicago: J. Clark Publishing Company.

Bakeless, John. 1992. *Background to glory: the life of George Rogers Clark. Introduction by James P. Ronda.* Lincoln: University of Nebraska Press.

Bakker, Peter. 1989. "Relexification in Canada: the case of Métif (french-cree)." *The Canadian journal of linguistics* 34 (3):339-350.

Bakker, Peter. 1997. *A language of our own: The genesis of Michif, the mixed Cree-French language of the Canadian Métis.* Vol. 10, *Oxford Studies in Anthropological Linguistics.* New York and Oxford: Oxford University Press.

---

* The authors would like the acknowledge that the primary historical sources were obtained using publicly available scanned copies of primary texts from a number of online databases and archives inlcuding Google Books and Archive.org among others.
** See Barakabooks.com for a complete bibliography.

Bakker, Peter. 2003. "Mixed languages as autonomous systems." In *The mixed language debate: Theoretical and empirical advances*, edited by Yaron Matras and Peter Bakker, 107-150. Berln and New York: Walter de Gruyter.

Bakker, Peter. 2012. "Ethnogenesis, Language and Identity: The Genesis of Michif and Other Mixed Languages." In *Contours of a People: Metis Family, Mobility, and History*, edited by B. MacDougall, M. Campbell, N. St-Onge and C. Podruchny, 169-193. Norman: University of Oklahoma Press.

Barman, Jean. 2014. *French Canadians, Furs, and Indigenous Women in the Making of the Pacific Northwest*. Vancouver: UBC Press.

Barman, Jean, and Bruce McIntyre Watson. 2006. *Leaving Paradise: Indigenous Hawaiians in the Pacific Northwest, 1787-1898*. Honolulu: University of Hawaii Press.

Beals, Frank L. 1943. *Kit Carson, The American Adventure Series*. Chicago: Wheeler Publishing Company.

Beld, Gordon. 2012. *Grand Times in Grand Rapids: Pieces of Furniture City History*. Charleston and London: The History Press.

Berry, Don. 1961. *A majority of scoundrels: an informal history of the Rocky Mountain Fur Company*. New York: Harper.

Blanchet, Francis Norbert. 1856. *A Complete Dictionary of the Chinook Jargon: To which is Added Numerous Conversations, Thereby Enabling Any Person to Speak the Chinook Correctly*: S.J. McCormick, Franklin Book Store, Front St.

Blanchet, Francis Norbert. 1878. *Historical Sketches of the Catholic Church in Oregon, During the Past Forty Years*. Portland OR.

Bonnycastle, (Sir) Richard Henry 1846. *Canada and the Canadians in 1846*. II vols. London: Henry Colburn.

Bonnycastle, Richard Henry. 1849. *Canada and the Canadians*. Vol. 1. London: Henry Colburn Publisher.

Borrows, John. 1998. "Wampum at Niagara: The Royal Proclamation, Canadian Legal History, and Self-Government." In *Aboriginal Treaty Rights in Canada*, edited by Michael Asch, 155-172. Vancouver: University of British Columbia Press.

Bouchard, Michel. 2004. "A Critical Reappraisal of the Concept of the Imagined Community and the Presumed Sacred Languages of the Medieval Period." *National Identities* 6 (1):3-24.

Bouchard, Michel. 2008a. "De l'Acadie à l'Alberta en passant par le Kansas : sur les traces de la famille Comeau." In *Franco-Amérique*, edited by Dean Louder and Éric Waddell, 235-250. Sillery: Septentrion.

Bouchard, Michel, and Gheorghe Bogdan. 2014. "From barbarian other to chosen people: the etymology, ideology and evolution of 'nation' at the shifting edge of medieval Western Christendom." *National Identities*:1-23. doi: 10.1080/14608944.2014.920805.

Bouchard, Russel. 2005. *La communauté métisse de Chicoutimi: fondements historiques et culturels*. Chicoutimi: Chik8timitch.

Bouchard, Russel. 2008b. *Communauté métisse de Chicoutimi: fondements historiques et culturels*. Chicoutimi: J.-M. Tremblay.

Bouchard, Russel. 2008c. *Le Peuple Métis de la Boréalie*. Québec: Cornac.

Bouchard, Serge. 2009. "Isabelle Montour." In *Rencontrer Trois-Rivières: 375 ans d'histoire et de culture*, edited by René Beaudoin, 25-30. Trois-Rivières: Éditions d'art Le Sabord.

Brasser, Ted J. 1985. "In search of métis art." In *The New Peoples: Being and Becoming Métis in North America*, edited by Jacqueline Peterson and Jennifer S. H. Brown, 221-230.

Brock, Isaac, and Ferdinand Brock Tupper. 1847. *The Life and Correspondence of Major-General Sir Isaac Brock, K. B.* Second ed. London: Simpkin, Marshall & Company.

Brown, Jennifer SH. 1993. "Métis, Halfbreeds, and Other Real People: Challenging Cultures and Categories." *History Teacher* 27 (1):19-26.

Bryce, G. 1885. "The Old Settlers of Red River." *Manitoba Daily Free Press*.

Burns, Robert Ignatius. 1977a. Lamy, Jean Baptiste. In *Readers' Encyclopedia of the American West*, edited by Howard Roberts Lamar. New York: Thomas Y. Crowell.

Burns, Robert Ignatius. 1977b. "Roman Catholic Church." In *The Reader's Encyclopedia of the American West*, edited by Howard Roberts Lamar, 1033-1044. New York: Thomas Y. Crowell.

Cable, George W. 1885. *The Creoles of Louisiana*. New York: Charles Scribner's Sons.

Caesar, Gene. 1961. *King of the Mountain Men The Life of Jim Bridger*. New York: E.P. Dutton Co., Inc.

Cannon, Martin J. 2014. "Race Matters: Sexism, Indigenous Sovereignty, and McIvor." *Canadian Journal of Women and the Law/Revue Femmes et Droit* 26 (1):23-50. doi: doi:10.3138/cjwl.26.1.23.

Catton, Bruce. 1976. *Michigan: A Bicentennial History (States and the Nation)*. New York: W. W. Norton.

Chandler, Alfred D., and Richard S. Tedlow. 1985. *The Coming of Managerial Capitalism: A Casebook on the History of American Economic Institutions*: R.D. Irwin.

Chartrand, Paul L.A. H. 2014. "Understanding the Daniels Case on s.91(24) Constitution Act 1867." *aboriginal policy studies* 3 (3):115-131.

Clapin, Sylva. 1894. *Dictionnaire canadien-français ou Lexique-glossaire des mots, expressions et locutions ne se trouvant pas dans les dictionnaires courants et dont l'usage appartient surtout aux Canadiens-Français*. Montréal and Boston: Beauchemin & Fils and Sylva Clapin.

Clark, George Rogers. 2001. *The Conquest of the Illinois*. Edited by Milo Milton Quaife. Carbondale and Edwardsville IL: Southern Illinois University Press.

Clarke, Charles G. 1970. *The Men of the Lewis and Clark Expedition: A Biographical Roster of the Fifty-one Members and a Composite Diary of Their Activities from All Known Sources*. Lincoln: University of Nebraska Press.

Cleland, Charles E. 1992a. *Rites of conquest: the history and culture of Michigan's Native Americans*. Ann Arbor: University of Michigan Press.

Cleland, Robert Glass. 1992b. *This reckless breed of men: The trappers and fur traders of the Southwest*. Lincoln: University of Nebraska Press.

Collot, Georges Henri Victor. 1826. *Voyage dans l'Amérique septentrionale, ou Description des pays arrosés par le Mississipi, l'Ohio, le Missouri, et autres rivières affluentes; observations exactes sur les cours et les sondes de ces rivières; sur les villes, villages, hameaux et fermes de cette partie du nouveau-monde; suivi de remarques philosophiques, politiques, militaires et commerciales ; et d'un projet de lignes frontières et de limites générales. Plans, vues et figures par feu le général Collot, ex-gouverneur de la Guadeloupe.* Paris: Chez Arthus Bertrand.

Cox, Ross. 1832. *Adventures on the Columbia River: Including the Narrative of a Residence of Six Years on the Western Side of the Rocky Mountains, Among Various Tribes of Indians Hitherto Unknown: Together with a Journey Across the American Continent*: J. & J. Harper.

Coyne, Michael. 1998. *The Crowded Prairie: American National Identity in the Hollywood Western.* London and New York: I. B. Tauris.

Davis, James Edward. 2000. *Frontier Illinois.* Bloomington: Indiana University Press.

Dawson, Nelson M. 2008. *Fourrure et forets métissèrent les Montagnais. Regard sur les sang-mélés au Royaume du saguenay.* Sillery: Septentrion.

de Bacqueville, Claude-Charles Le Roy. 1753. *Histoire de l'Amérique septentrionale* Paris: Brocas.

de Catalogne, Gédéon. 1871. *Recueil De ce qui s'est passé en Canada au sujet de la guerre, tant des Anglais que des Iroquois, depuis l'année 1682.* Edited by Société littéraire et historique de Québec. Québec: Middleton & Dawson.

de Catalogne, Gédéon. 1948. "Recueil de ce qui s'est passé en Canada au sujet de la guerre tant des Anglais que des Iroquois depuis l'année 1682." In *Histoire de la Nouvelle-France : les sources narratives du début du XVIIIe siècle,* edited by Robert Le Blant. Dax: Éditions P. Pradeu.

de Charlevoix, Pierre-François-Xavier. 1744a. *Histoire et description générale de la nouvelle France, avec le journal historique d'un voyage fait par ordre du roi dans l'Amérique septentrionale.* Vol. I. Paris: Chez Nyon Fils.

de Charlevoix, Pierre-François-Xavier. 1744b. *Histoire et description générale de la Nouvelle France, avec le journal historique d'un voyage fait par ordre du roi dans l'Amérique septentrionale.* Vol. III. Paris: Chez Nyon Fils.

de Charlevoix, Pierre-François-Xavier. 1744c. *Journal d'un voyage fait par ordre du roi dans Amérique septentrionale.* Vol. III. Paris: Chez Nyon Fils.

de Lom d'Arce baron de Lahontan, Louis Armand. 1703. *Nouveaux voyages de mr. le baron de Lahontan dans l'Amérique septentrionale. (Mémoires de l'Amérique septentrionale).*

de Lom d'Arce de Lahontan, L.A. 1703. *Nouveaux voyages de Mr. le baron de Lahontan dans l'Amérique septentrionale*: chez les frères L'Honoré.

de Mofras, Eugène Duflot. 1846. *L'Orégon.* Paris: Imprimé par Plon frères.

de Saint-Père, Edme Rameau. 1861. *Notes historiques sur la colonie canadienne de Détroit: lecture prononcée*: Montréal: JB Rolland.

de Smet, Pierre-Jean. 1848. *Missions de l'orégon et Voyages aux montagnes Rochouses aux sources de la Colombie, de l'Athabasca et du Sascatshawin.* Gand: Ve A. I. Vander Schelden.

de Smet, Pierre-Jean. 1853. *Voyage au grand désert en 1851, par le R.P. Pierre de Smet.* Bruxelles: impr. de J. Vandereydt.

de Smet, Pierre-Jean. 1875. *Voyages aux Montagnes Rocheuses, chez les tribus indiennes du vaste territoire de l'Orégon, dépendant des États-Unis d'Amérique.* 6 ed. Lille and Paris: L. Lefort.

de Smet, Pierre-Jean, and André van Iseghem. 1844. *Voyages aux Montagnes Rocheuses: et une année de séjour chez les tribus Indiennes du vaste territoire de l'Orégon, dépendant des États-Unis d'Amérique.* Bruxelles: P. J. Hanico, imprimeur du Saint Siége, de la Sacrée Congrégation de la Propagande et de l'Archevêché de Malines.

de Smet, Pierre-Jean, and Aloïs Vercruysse. 1844. *Lettres des RR. PP. P. De Smet et A. Vercruysse, missionnaires belges aux Montagnes Rocheuses.* Bruxelles: Ve A. I. Van der Schelden.

de Trobriand, Philippe Régis. 1951. *Military Life in Dakota: The Journal of Philippe Regis de Trobriand, ed. and trans. by Lucile M.* Translated by Lucille M. Kane. St. Paul: Alvord Memorial Commission.

De Voto, Bernard. 1975. *Across the Wide Missouri, The American Heritage Library.* Boston: Houghton Mifflin Company.

Dearborn, Henry, Howard H. Peckham, and Lloyd A. Brown. 2009. *Revolutionary War Journals of Henry Dearborn, 1775-1783.* Westminster MD: Heritage Books.

Delâge, Denys. 2011. "La peur de 'passer pour des Sauvages'." *Les Cahiers des dix* 65:1-45.

Deleuze, Gilles, and Félix Guattari. 1987. *A Thousand Plateaus: Capitalism and Schizophrenia.* Duluth: University of Minnesota Press.

Demers, Modeste, Francis Norbert Blanchet, and Louis-Napoléon Saint Onge. 1871. *Chinook Dictionary, Catechism, Prayers and Hymns.*

Denig, Edwin Thompson. 1961. *Five Indian Tribes of the Upper Missouri: Sioux, Arickaras, Assiniboines, Crees, Crows, The Civilization of the American Indian.* Norman: University of Oklahoma Press.

Dickason, Olive Patricia. 1985. "From "One Nation" in the Northeast to "New Nation" in the Northwest: A look at the emergence of the métis." In *The New Peoples: Being and Becoming Métis in North America*, edited by Jacqueline Peterson and Jennifer S. H. Brown, 19-36. Winnipeg: University of Manitoba Press.

Dorge, Lionel. 1974. "The Metis and Canadien Councillors of Assiniboia. Part I." *The Beaver* 1:12-19.

Dusenberry, Verne. 1985. "Waiting for a day that never comes: The dispossessed métis of Montana." In *The new peoples: being and becoming Métis in North America. The University of Manitoba Press, Canada*, edited by Jacqueline Peterson and Jennifer S. H. Brown, 119-136.

Dyck, Lillian Eva, and Vernon White. 2013. The people who own themselves: Recognition of Métis identity in Canada. Ottawa: Parliament. Senate.Standing Committee on Aboriginal Peoples.

Eccles, William J. 1983. *The Canadian Frontier: 1534-1760.* Albuquerque: University of New Mexico Press.

Edmunds, Russell David. 1978. *The Potawatomis: Keepers of the Fire*. Norman: University of Oklahoma Press.

Edmunds, Russell David. 1985. "Unacquainted with the laws of the civilized world: american attitudes toward the Métis communities in the old northwest." In *The new peoples: being and becoming Métis in North America. The University of Manitoba Press, Canada*, edited by Jacqueline Peterson and Jennifer S. H. Brown, 185-193.

Edmunds, Russell David. 1993. *The Fox Wars: The Mesquakie Challenge to New France*. Norman: University of Oklahoma Press.

Englebert, Robert. 2014. "Gabriel Cerré marchand canadien." In *Vivre la Conquête à travers plus de 25 parcours individuels*, edited by Gaston Deschênes and Denis Vaugeois, 48-57. Québec: Septentrion.

Etulain, Richard W. 1996. *Re-Imagining the Modern American West: A Century of Fiction, History and Art*. Tuscson: University of Arizona Press.

Ewers, John C. 1961. "Introduction." In *Five Indian Tribes of the Upper Missouri: Sioux, Arickaras, Assiniboines, Crees, Crows*, edited by John C. Ewers, xiii-xxxvii. University of Oklahoma Press.

Ficken, Robert E, and Charles P LeWarne. 1988. *Washington: a centennial history*: University of Washington Press.

Fischer, David Hackett. 2009. *Champlain's Dream*. New York, Toronto, London and Sydney: Simon & Schuster.

Fiske, Jo-Anne, and Evelyn George. 2006. *Seeking alternatives to Bill C-31: from cultural trauma to cultural revitalization through customary law*: Status of Women Canada Ottawa.

Flanders, Robert B. 1965. *Nauvoo: Kingdom on the Mississippi*: University of Illinois Press.

Fleming, Nic. 2014. "The largest living thing on Earth is a humongous fungus." BBC, Last Modified November 19, 2014 Accessed November 28, 2015. http://www.bbc.com/earth/story/20141114-the-biggest-organism-in-the-world.

Flores, Richard R. 2010. *Remembering the Alamo: Memory, Modernity, and the Master Symbol*. Austin: University of Texas Press.

Foster, Martha H. 2006. *We Know Who We Are: Metis Identity in a Montana Community*. Norman: University of Oklahoma Press.

Foxcurran, Robert. 1986. "NATO: A Business History." Masters in Business Economics and (Business) History Master's thesis, School of Business, University of Washington.

Foxcurran, Robert. 2012. "Les Canadiens: Resettlement of the Metis into the Backcountry of the Pacific Northwest," *Columbia, The Magazine of Northwest History*, Fall 2012.

Franchère, Gabriel. 1820. *Relation d'un voyage à la côte du Nord-ouest de l'Amérique Septentrionale, dans les années 1810, 11, 12, 13, et 14*. Montréal: L'Imprimerie de C.B. Pasteur.

Frégault, Guy. 1944. *La civilisation de la Nouvelle-France, 1713-1744*. Vol. 33: Fides.

Frémont, John Charles. 1845. *Report of the exploring expedition to the Rocky Mountains in the year 1842 and to Oregon and North California in the years 1843-44: Printed by order of the Senate of the United States*. Vol. 174. Washington DC: Gales & Seaton.

Frémont, John Charles, and Samuel Mosheim Smucker. 1856. *The life of Col. John Charles Fremont: and his narrative of explorations and adventures, in Kansas, Nebraska, Oregon and California.* New York: Miller, Orton & Mulligan.

Furtwangler, Albert. 2005. *Bringing Indians to the Book.* Seattle and London: University of Washington Press.

Garst, Shannon. 1952. *Jim Bridger: Greatest of the Mountain Men.* Cambridge, Massachusetts: The Riverside Press.

Gilpin, Alec R. 1970. *The Territory of Michigan (1805-1837).* East Lansing, MI: Michigan State University Press.

Gitlin, Jay. 2009. *The bourgeois frontier: French towns, French traders, and American expansion.* New Haven and London: Yale University Press.

Gougeon, Gilles. 1993. *Histoire du nationalisme québécois. Entrevues avec sept spécilistes.* Montréal: VLB Éditeur et Société Radio-Canada.

Gravier, Jacques. 1857. *Relation de ce qui s' est passé dans la mission de l'Immaculée Conception au pays des Ilinois, depuis le mois mars 1693, jusqu'en février 1694*: Jean-Marie Shea.

Green, Joyce. 2011. "Don't Tell Us Who We Are (Not): Reflections on Métis Identity." *Aboriginal Policy Studies* 1 (2):166-170.

Hafen, LeRoy R. 1965. "Etienne Provost." In *Trappers of the Far West: Sixteen Biographical Sketches*, edited by LeRoy R. Hafen, 1-15. Lincoln and London: University of Nebraska Press.

Hall, James. 1825. "Letters from the West. No. XIV. The Missouri Trapper." In *The Port Folio*, edited by John E. Hall, 214-219. Philadelphia: Harrison Hall.

Harrison, Lowell H. 2014. *George Rogers Clark and the War in the West.* Lexington: University Press of Kentucky.

Harroun Foster, Martha. 2006. *We Know Who We Are: Metis Identity in a Montana Community.* Norman, OK: University of Oklahoma Press.

Havard, Gilles. 2003. *Empire et métissages: Indiens et Français dans le Pays d'en Haut, 1660-1715.* Sillery: Les éditions du Septentrion.

Historic Fort Wayne Coalition. 2015. "PETER AUDRAIN, ESQ.: Clerk of everything from time immemorial." Last Modified April 1, 2011 Accessed July 19, 2015. http://www.historicfortwaynecoalition.com/AudrainConway.html.

Houghton, Louise Seymour. 1918. *Our Debt to the Red Man: The French-Indians in the Development of the United States. With an introduction by the Hon. Francis E. Leupp.* Boston: Stratford Company.

Howard, Joseph Kinsey. 1952. Strange Empire: A Narrative of the Northwest New York: William Morrow & Co.

Howay, Frederick William. 1943. "Origin of the Chinook Jargon on the North West Coast." *Oregon Historical Quarterly* 44 (1):27-55.

Hunter, John. 1996. *Scottish Highlanders, Indian Peoples: Thirty Generations of a Montana Family.* Helena: Montana Historical Society Press.

Hutchison, Craig E., and Kimberly Hutchison. 2004. *Monroe: The Early Years*. Charleston SC, Chicago IL, Portsmouth NH and San Francisco CA: Arcadia Publishing.

Hyde, Anne F. 2011. *Empires, Nations, and Families: A History of the North American West, 1800-1860*. Lincoln and London: University of Nebraska Press.

Ingersoll, Thomas N. 2005. *To Intermix with Our White Brothers: Indian Mixed Bloods in the United States from the Earliest Times to the Indian Removals*. Albuquerque: University of New Mexico Press.

Ioway Cultural Institute. 2013. "Overview of Iowa and Otoe Genealogy." Accessed November 27, 2013. http://ioway.nativeweb.org/genealogy/overview.htm.

Irving, Washington. 1836. *Astoria: Or, Enterprise Beyond the Rocky Mountains*. Paris: Galignani & Company.

Irving, Washington. 1850. *Adventures of Captain Bonnville or Scenes Beyond the Rocky Mountains of the Far West*. London: George Routledge and Co.

Irving, Washington. 1857. *The Works of Washington Irving: The adventures of Captain Bonneville, U.S.A.* New York: G. P. Putnam & Company.

Irving, Washington. 1886a. *The Adventures of Captain Bonneville*. New York: John B. Alden.

Irving, Washington. 1886b. *Astoria or Anecdotes of an enterprise beyond the Rocky Mountains*. New York: John B. Alden.

Jackson, John C. [an unpublished two volume manuscript on the transcontinental history of seven generations of the Montour family]: Volume 1, *An Age of Half-Kings: Tracing the impact of dispossession upon the native peoples of North America; Volume 2, Skin Games, Montours in the North American Fur Trade, 1755-1877*.

Jardin, André. 1984. *Alexis de Tocqueville: 1805-1859*. Paris: Hachette.

Jean, Denis. 2011. *Ethnogenèse des premiers métis canadiens (1603-1763)*: Département d'histoire-géographie, Faculté des arts et des sciences sociales, Université de Moncton.

Jetté, Melinda Marie. 2004. ""At the hearth of the crossed races": intercultural relations and social change in French Prairie, Oregon, 1812-1843." PhD, History, University of British Columbia.

Josephy, Alvin M. 1965. *The Nez Perce Indians and the Opening of the Northwest*. New Haven CT: Yale University Press.

Kane, Paul. 1859. *Wanderings of an Artist Among the Indians of North America: From Canada to Vancouver's Island and Oregon, Through the Hudson's Bay Company's Territory and Back Again*: Longman, Brown, Green, Longmans, and Roberts.

Karahasan, Devrim. 2006. "Métissage in New France and Canada 1508 to 1886." Doctor of History and Civilization, Department of History and Civilization, European University Institute.

Karel, David. 1992. *Dictionnaire des artistes de langue française en Amérique du Nord: peintres, sculpteurs, dessinateurs, graveurs, photographes, et orfèvres*. Québec: Presses de l'Université Laval.

Keating, William H. 1825. *Narrative of an Expedition to the Source of St. Peter's River, Lake Winnepeek, Lake of the Woods, & C., Performed in the Year 1823*. Vol. I. London: Geo. B. Whittaker.

Keung, Nicholas. 2009. "Many First Nations communities will die out within a few generations, in terms of registered Indians. Because of intermarriage, some communities will see their last status Indian born as soon as 2012." *The Toronto Star*. http://www.thestar.com/news/canada/2009/05/10/status_indians_face_threat_of_extinction.html.

Knox, John. 1914. *An historical journal of the campaigns in North America for the years 1757, 1758, 1759, and 1760 (Includes reproduction of t.-p. of original edition, London, 1769)*. Toronto: Champlain Society.

Kohl, Johann Georg. 1860. *Kitchi-Gami: wanderings round Lake Superior*. Translated by Lascelles Wraxall. London: Chapman and Hall.

Kohl, Johann Georg. 2008[1860]. *Kitchi-Gami: Life Among the Lake Superior Ojibway*. Translated by Lascelles Wraxall. St. Paul: Minnesota Historical Society Press.

L'association de la propogation de la foi. 1841. "Mission de la Colombie." In *Rapport sur les missions du diocèse de Québec*, 35-80. Fréchette & Cie.

Laforte, Conrad. 1981. *Survivances médiévales dans la chanson folklorique: poétique de la chanson en laisse*. Québec: Presses de l'Université Laval.

Lamarre, Jean. 2003. *The French Canadians of Michigan: Their Contribution to the Development of the Saginaw Valley and the Keweenaw Peninsula, 1840-1914*. Detroit: Wayne State University Press.

Lang, George. 1991. "Voyageur discourse and the absence of fur trade pidgin." *Canadian Literature* 131:51-63.

Lang, George. 2009. *Making wawa: The genesis of Chinook jargon*. Vancouver: UBC Press.

Larpenteur, Charles. 1898. *Forty years a fur trader on the upper Missouri: the personal narrative of Charles Larpenteur, 1833-1872*. Vol. 1. New York: FP Harper.

Lavallée, Guy. 1988. "The Métis People of Saint-Laurent, Manitoba: an Introductory Ethnography." UBC.

Laveille, Eugène. 1915. *The Life of Father De Smet, SJ (1801-1873)*. Translated by Marian Lindsay. New York: PJ Kenedy & Sons.

Lawrence, Bonita. 2004. *" Real" Indians and Others: Mixed-Blood Urban Native Peoples and Indigenous Nationhood*: U of Nebraska Press.

Le Blant, Robert. 1948. *Histoire de la Nouvelle-France : les sources narratives du début du XVIIIe siècle*. Edited by Robert Le Blant, *Histoire de la Nouvelle-France : les sources narratives du début du XVIIIe siècle*. Dax: Éditions P. Pradeu.

Le Canadien. 1886. "Nouvelles de Paspébiac." *Le Canadien*, February 19, 1886, 3.

LeCompte, Janet. 1982. "Pierre Chouteau." In *Mountain Men and Fur Traders of the Far West: Eighteen Biographical Sketches*, edited by Leroy Reuben Hafen, 24-56. Lincoln: University of Nebraska Press.

LeCompte, Janet. 1997. "Introduction." In *French Fur Traders and Voyageurs in the American West*, edited by LeRoy R. Hafen. Lincoln and London: University of Nebraska Press.

Ledoux, Étienne, ed. 1835. *L'Amérique Septentrionale et Méridionale: ou Description de cette grande partie du monde… un extrait des voyages au Pôle boréal; et enfin l'Islande, Groenland, le Spitzberg, etc. Avec un précis de la découverte, de la conquête et de l'origine des anciens peuples; de leurs mœurs, usages, coutumes et religions. Les arts, sciences, commerce, manufactures et gouvernemens divers dans leur état actuel; les productions naturelles, les curiosités, etc., etc*: É. Ledoux.

Levasseur, Auguste. 1829. *Lafayette en Amérique en 1824 et 1825 ou journal d'un voyage aux États-Unis*. Vol. 2. Paris: Librairie Baudoin.

LeWarne, Charles P. 1986. *Washington State*. Third Edition ed. Seattle & London: University of Washington Press.

Lewis, Meriwether, and William Clark. 2002. *The Journals of Lewis and Clark*: National Geographic Society.

Lyman, H. S. 1900. "Reminiscences of Louis Labonte." *The Quarterly of the Oregon Historical Society* 1 (2):169-188. doi: 10.2307/20609456.

MacBeth, RG. 1898. *The making of the Canadian West, being the reminiscences of an eye-witness. With portraits and illustrations, William Briggs*. Toronto: William Briggs.

MacDougall, Brenda. 2012. The Myth of Metis Cultural Ambivalence. In *Contours of a People: Metis Family, Mobility, and History*, edited by Brenda MacDougall, Maria Campbell, Nicole St-Onge and Carolyn Podruchny. Norman: University of Oklahoma Press.

Mackie, Richard. 1997. *Trading Beyond the Mountains: The British Fur Trade on the Pacific, 1793-1843*. Vancouver: UBC Press.

MacKinnon, Doris J. 2012. *The Identities of Marie Rose Delorme Smith: Portrait of a Metis Woman, 1861-1960*. Vol. 60, *Canadian Plains Studies*. Regina: University of Regina.

MacLeod, Katie K. . 2013. "Displaced Mixed-Blood: An Ethnographic Exploration of Métis Identities in Nova Scotia." MA, Anthropology, Carleton University.

Magazine, The Outing. 1905. "John Boucher, Rapids Pilot." *The Outing Magazine: The Outdoor Magazine of Human Interest* 46:478-481.

Manfred, Frederick. 1954. *Lord Grizzly*. New York: McGraw-Hill.

Manfred, Frederick. 1959. "West of the Mississippi: An Interview with Frederick Manfred." *Critique: Studies in Contemporary Fiction* 2 (3):35-56.

Manfred, Freya. 2011. "Introduction." In *Lord Grizzly*. Lincoln and London: University of Nebraska Press.

Mann, Charles C. 2011. *1493: Uncovering the new world Columbus created*. New York: Alfred a Knopf Incorporated.

Margry, Pierre. 1887. *Découvertes et établissements des français dans l'ouest et dans le sud de l'Amérique Septentrionale (1683-1724)*. Vol. 5, *Découvertes et établissements des français dans l'ouest et dans le sud de l'Amérique Septentrionale (1614-1754)*. Paris: Maisonneuve Frère et Ch. Leclerc

Marrero, Karen. 2011. "Founding Families: Power and Authority of Mixed French and Native Lineages In Eighteenth Century Detroit." PhD, Department of History, Yale University.

Marrero, Karen. 2012. "Families, clans and kins." The Long Struggle for the Ohio Valley, 1752-1815 Louisville, KY.

Martel, Gilles. 1984. *Le messianisme de Louis Riel*. Waterloo: Wilfrid Laurier University Press.

Mattes, Merrill J. 1949. "Robidoux's Trading Post at "Scott's Bluffs," and the California Gold Rush." *Nebraska History* 30 (2):95-138.

Mattes, Merrill J. 1965-1972. "Joseph Robidoux." In *The Mountain Men and the Fur Trade of the Far West*, edited by LeRoy R. Hafen, 287-314. Lincoln: University of Nebraska Press.

Mattes, Merrill J. 1966. "Fur Trade Sites: The Plains and the Rockies." *Minnesota History*:192-197.

Mattes, Merrill J. 1988. "Joseph Robidoux's Family: Fur Traders and Trail Blazers." *Overland Journal* 6 (3):2-9.

Maximilian, Prince of Wied. 1843. *Travels in the interior of North America*. Translated by Hannibal Evans Lloyd. London: Ackermann and Co.

McKay, Harvey J. 1980. *St. Paul, Oregon, 1830-1890*. Hillsboro OR: Binford & Mort Publishing.

McLaughlin, Andrew C. 1891. *Lewis Cass*. Boston and New York: Houghton, Mifflin, and Company.

Morice, Adrien G. 1897. *Au pays de l'ours noir: chez les sauvages de la Colombie britannique*. Paris and Lyon: Delhomme et Briguet.

Morice, Adrien Gabriel. 1912. *Dictionnaire historique des Canadiens et des Métis français de l'Ouest*. 2 ed: J.-P. Garneau.

Murphy, Lucy Eldersveld. 2012. "Women, Networks, and Colonization in Nineteenth-Century Wisconsin." In *Contours of a People: Metis Family, Mobility, and History*, edited by B. MacDougall, M. Campbell, N. St-Onge and C. Podruchny, 230-264. Norman: University of Oklahoma Press.

Murphy, Lucy Eldersveld. 2014. *Great Lakes Creoles: A French-Indian Community on the Northern Borderlands, Prairie du Chien, 1750–1860*: Cambridge University Press.

Myers, John M. 1976. *The Saga of Hugh Glass: Pirate, Pawnee, and Mountain Man*. Lincoln and London: University of Nebraska Press.

Nash, Linda Clark, ed. 2012. *The Journals of Pierre-Louis de Lorimier* Montréal: Baraka Books.

Nester, William. 2012. *George Rogers Clark: "I Glory in War."* Norman: University of Oklahoma Press.

Nevins, Allan. 1992. *Fremont, Pathmarker of the West*. Lincoln and London: University of Nebraska Press.

Nicolay, Charles Grenfell. 1846. *The Oregon Territory: A Geographical and Physical Account of that Country and Its Inhabitants, with Outlines of Its History and Discovery*. London: Charles Knight & Co.

Nisbet, Jack. 2005. *The Mapmaker's Eye: David Thompson on the Columbia Plateau*: Pullman: Washington State University Press.

Nute, Grace Lee. 1955. *The Voyageur*. St. Paul: Minnesota Historical Society. Reprint, Reprint Edition.

O'Brien, Steven, Paula McGuire, James M. McPherson, and Gary Gerstle. 1991. *American Political Leaders: From Colonial Times to the Present*: ABC-CLIO.

O'Toole, Darren. 2010. "The Red River Resistance of 1869-1870: The Machiavellian Moment of the Métis of Manitoba." PhD, Political Science, University of Ottawa.

O'Toole, Darren. 2010. "Thomas Flanagan on the Stand: Revisiting Métis Land Claims and the Lists of Rights in Manitoba." *International Journal of Canadian Studies/Revue internationale d'études canadiennes* 41 (1):137-147.

Pannekoek, Frits. 1977. "Some Comments on the Social Origins of the Riel Protest of 1869." *Transactions of the Historical and Scientific Society of Manitoba* 3 (34):39-48.

Pannekoek, Frits. 1991. *A snug little flock: the social origins of the Riel Resistance, 1869-70*. Winnipeg: Watson and Dwyer.

Papen, Robert A. 1984. "Quelques remarques sur un parler français méconnu de l'Ouest canadien: le métis." *Revue québécoise de linguistique* 14 (1):113-139.

Papen, Robert A. 2004. "Sur quelques aspects structuraux du français des Métis de l'Ouest canadien." *Variation et francophonie. Paris, L'Harmattan*:105-129.

Papen, Robert A. 2009. "La question des langues des Mitchifs: un dédale sans issue?" *Histoires et identités métisses: hommage à Gabriel Dumont= Métis Histories and Identities: A Tribute to Gabriel Dumont, Winnipeg, Presses universitaires de Saint-Boniface*:253-276.

Parkins, Almon Ernest. 1918. *The Historical Geography of Detroit*. Chicago: University of Chicago.

Parkman, Francis. 1983. *France and England in North America*. Vol. 2: Library of America.

Parmenter, Jon. 1999. "Isabel Montour: Cultural Broker on the Frontiers of New York and Pennsylvania." In *The Human Tradition in Colonial America*, edited by Ian K. Steele and Nancy L. Rhoden. Wilmington, DE: Scholarly Resources.

Parr, Adrian. 2010. *The Deleuze Dictionary*: Edinburgh University Press.

Peterson, Jacqueline. 1985. "Many roads to Red River: Métis genesis in the Great Lakes region, 1680-1815." In *The New Peoples: Being and Becoming Métis in North America*, edited by Jacqueline Peterson and Jennifer S. H. Brown, 41-67. Winnipeg: University of Manitoba Press.

Peterson, Jacqueline. 2012. "Red River Redux: Métis Ethnogenesis and the Great Lakes Region." In *Contours of a People: Metis Family, Mobility and History*, edited by Nicole St-Onge, Carolyn Podruchny and Brenda Macdougall, 22-58S. Norman: University of Oklahoma.

Pierson, George Wilson. 1938. *Tocqueville and Beaumont in America*. New York: Oxford University Press.

Pike, Zebulon Montgomery. 1812. *Voyage au Nouveau-Mexique, à la suite d'une expédition ordonnée par le gouvernement des États-Unis, pour reconnoître les sources des rivières Arkansas, Kansés, La Plate, et Pierre-Jaune, dans l'intérieur de la Louisiane occidentale: Précédé d'une excursion aux sources du Mississippi, pendant les années 1805, 1806, et 1807*. Vol. 1. Paris: Chez D'Hautel.

Pike, Zebulon Montgomery, and William M Maguire. 1889. *Exploratory travels through the western territories of North America: comprising a voyage from St. Louis, on the Mississippi, to the source of that river, and a journey through the interior of Louisiana,* and the north-eastern provinces of New Spain. Performed in the years 1805, 1806, 1807, by order of the government of the United States. Denver: WH Lawrence & Co.

Pinkerton, John. 1812. *A General Collection of the Best and Most Interesting Voyages and Travels in All Parts of the World; Many of which are Now First Translated Into English. Digested on a New Plan.* Vol. 13. London: Longman, Hurst, Rees, and Orme and Brown, Paternoster Row and Cadell and Davies.

Pioneer and Democrat. 1854. "Washington Legislature--First Sesson." *Pioneer and Democrat*, March 11, 1854, 1-2. http://www.sos.wa.gov/history/images/newspapers/ SL_dir_olympiapiondemo/pdf/SL_dir_olympiapiondemo_03111854.pdf.

Podruchny, Carolyn. 1999. "Unfair Masters and Rascally Servants? Labour Relations Among Bourgeois, Clerks and Voyageurs in the Montréal Fur Trade, 1780-1821." *Labour/Le Travail*:43-70.

Poore, Benjamin Perley. 1883. *Collection de manuscrits contenant lettres, mémoires, et autres documents historiques relatifs à la Nouvelle-France: 1492-1712.* Québec: Impr. A. Coté et cie.

Pouchot, Pierre. 1781. *Mémoires sur la derniere Guerre de l'Amérique septentrionale entre la France et l'Angleterre.* Vol. Tome Premier. Yverdon-les-Bains: Yverdon.

Prévost, Antoine-François. 1777. *Histoire générale des voyages ou Nouvelle collection de toutes les relations de voyages par mer et par terre, qui ont été publiées jusqu'à présent dans les differentes langues de toutes les nations connues.* La Haye: Chez Pierre de Hondt.

Punke, Michael. 2015. *The Revenant: A Novel of Revenge* New York: Picador.

Quaife, Milo M., ed. 1916. *The Journals of Captain Meriwether Lewis and Sargeant John Ordway.* Madison: The State Historical Society of Wisconsin.

Reid, Robie L. 1942. "The Chinook Jargon." *British Columbia Historical Quarterly*, VI:1-11.

Richards, Kent D. 1993. *Isaac I. Stevens: Young man in a hurry.* Pullman WA: Washington State University Press.

Riel, Louis. 1985. *The Collected Writings of Louis Riel / Les ecrits complets de Louis Riel.* Edited by George F. G. Stanley. 5 vols. Vol. 3. Edmonton: The University of Alberta Press.

Rolle, Andrew F. 1999. *John Charles Fremont: Character As Destiny.* Norman: University of Oklahoma Press.

Ronda, James P. 1984. *Lewis and Clark among the Indians.* Lincoln and London: University of Nebraska Press.

Rosenberg, Ruth. 2014. *Music, Travel, and Imperial Encounter in 19th-Century France: Musical Apprehensions.* Vol. 5, *Routledge Studies in Ethnomusicology.* New York: Taylor and Francis.

Ross, Alexander. 1957 [1856]. *The Red River Settlement. Its Rise, Progress and Present State.* Minneapolic: Ross and Haines, Inc.

Royal Commission on Aboriginal Peoples. 1996. Report of the Royal Commission on Aboriginal Peoples. Ottawa: Indian and Northern Affairs Canada.

Ruby, Robert H, and John A Brown. 1981. Indians of the Pacific Northwest: A history. Norman: University of Oklahoma Press

Ruby, Robert H, and John A Brown. 1992. *Guide to the Indian Tribes of the Pacific Northwest*. Norman: University of Oklahoma Press.

Saint-Pierre, Télesphore. 1895. *Histoire des Canadiens du Michigan et du comté d'Essex, Ontario* Montréal: Typographie de la "Gazette."

Sawchuk, Joe. 1995. "Fragmentation and Realignment: The Continuing Cycle of Metis and Non-Status Indian Political Organizations in Canada." *Native Studies Review* 10 (2):77-95.

Schmitt, Craig, and Michael Tatum. 2008. "The Malheur National Forest Location of the World's Largest Living Organism [The Humoungous Fungus]." http://www.fs.usda.gov/Internet/FSE_DOCUMENTS/fsbdev3_033146.pdf.

Schoenberg, Wilfred P. 1987. *A history of the Catholic Church in the Pacific Northwest, 1743-1983*. Washington DC: Pastoral Press.

Schwantes, Carlos A. 1989. *The Pacific Northwest: An Interpretive History*. Lincoln and London: University of Nebraska Press.

Siddali, Silvana R. 2005. *From Property to Person: Slavery and the Confiscation Acts, 1861-1862*: Louisiana State University Press.

Simpson, George. 1938. *Journal of occurrences in the Athabasca department*: The Champlain society.

Sleeper-Smith, Susan. 2001. *Indian women and French men: rethinking cultural encounter in the Western Great Lakes*. Amherst MA: University of Massachusetts Press.

Smith, Anthony D. 1986. *The ethnic origins of nations*. Oxford: Blackwell.

Smith, Anthony D. 1991. *National Identity*. Reno, Las Vegas and London: University of Nevada Press.

Smith, Anthony D. 1999. "The Problem of National Identity: Ancient, Medieval and Modern?" In *Myths and Memories of the Nation*, 97-124. Oxford: Oxford University Press.

Smith, Anthony D. 2000. *The Nation in History: Historiographical Debates about Ethnicity and Nationalism*. Hanover: University Press of New England.

Smith, Anthony D. 2003. *Chosen peoples*. Oxford ; New York: Oxford University Press.

Smith, Anthony D. 2008. *The cultural foundations of nations : hierarchy, covenant and republic*. Malden, MA, USA: Blackwell Pub.

Sommerville, Suzanne. 2004. "Marie-Anne Magnan dite Lespérance, called Hope: A Cautionary "Tale"." *Michigan's Habitant Heritage* 25 (1).

Spry, Irene M. 1985. "The métis and mixed-bloods of Rupert's Land before 1870." In *The New Peoples: Being and Becoming Métis in North America*, edited by Jacqueline Peterson and Jennifer S. H. Brown, 95-118. Winnipeg: University of Manitoba Press.

Stagoll, Cliff. 2010. "Arborescent Schema." In *The Deleuze Dictionary*, edited by Adrian Parr, 14-15. Edinburgh: Edinburgh University Press.

Stoddard, Amos. 1812. *Sketches, Historical and Descriptive, of Louisiana*. Philadelphia: Mathew Carey.

Stuart, A., D. Stuart, and N. Andrews. 1831. *Rapport des commissaires nomme pour l'exploration du pays, borne par les rivieres Saguenay, Saint-maurice et Saint-laurent*. Québec: Chambre d'Assemblée.

Sturken, Marita. 1997. *Tangled memories: The Vietnam War, the AIDS epidemic, and the politics of remembering*: Univ of California Press.

Sulte, Benjamin. 1894. "Les Tonty." In *Mémoires Et Comptes Rendus de la Société Royale Du Canada pour l'année 1893/Proceedings and Transactions of the Royal Society of Canada For the Year 1893*, 3-32. Ottawa, Montréal and London: John Dubie & Fils, W. Foster Brown & Co. and Bernard Quaritch.

Taché, Joseph-Charles. 1863. "Forestiers et voyageurs." In *Les Soirées canadiennes*, 13-260. Québec: Brousseau & Frères.

Taché, Joseph-Charles. 1884. *Forestiers et voyageurs: moeurs et légendes canadiennes*. Montréal: Librairie Saint-Joseph, Cadieux et Derome.

Teillet, Jean. 2013. *Métis Law in Canada*. Vancouver: Pape Salter Teillet.

Teillet, Jean. 2014. "L'interprétation de la Loi constitutionnelle de 1867 à la lumière de la 'race' exclut les Métis des peuples autochtones du Canada." In *From Pierre-Esprit Radisson to Louis Riel: Voyageurs and Métis* edited by Denis Combet, Luc Côté and Gilles Lesage. Winniped: Presses universitaires de Saint-Boniface.

Thorne, Tanis C. 1996. *The Many Hands of My Relations: French and Indians on the Lower Missouri*. Columbia and London: University of MIssouri Press.

Thorpe, F.J. 1969. Catalogne, Gédéon. In *Dictionnaire biographique du Canada, vol. 2*. Université Laval/University of Toronto.

Tocqueville, Alexis de. 1860. "Quinze jours au désert: Souvenirs d'un voyage en Amérique *"Revue des deux mondes: recueil de la politique, de l'administration et des moeurs* 30:565-606.

Tocqueville, Alexis de. 1865. *Oeuvres complètes de Alexis de Tocqueville. Mélanges, fragments historiques et notes sur l'ancien régime, la révolution et l'empire: voyages, pensées entièrement inédits*. Vol. 8. Paris: Michel Lévy Frères.

Tocqueville, Alexis de. 1998. *Quinze jours dans le désert américain*. Paris: Mille Et Une Nuits.

Tocqueville, Alexis de, and Jacques Vallée. 1973. *Tocqueville au Bas-Canada*: Éditions du Jour.

Todd, Edgeley W. 1982. "Benjamin L. E. Bonneville." In *Mountain Men and Fur Traders of the Far West: Eighteen Biographical Sketches*, edited by Leroy Reuben Hafen, 272-290. Lincoln: University of Nebraska Press.

Trigger, Bruce G., ed. 1979. *Northeast*. Edited by W.C. Sturtevant. Vol. 15, *Handbook of North American Indians*. Washington DC: Smithsonian Institution Press.

Trouillot, Michel-Rolph. 1995. *Silencing the past: Power and the production of history*. Boston: Beacon Press.

Twain, Mark. 1892. *The Adventures of Tom Sawyer*. Watson Gill Syracuse, New York: American Publishing Company.

Union Historical Company. 1880. *The History of Boone County, Iowa: Containing ... Biographical Sketches ... War Records of Its Volunteers in the Late Rebellion, General and Local Statistics, Portraits of Early Settlers and Prominent Men, History of the Northwest, History of Iowa, Map of Boone County ... Etc*: Union historical Company.

Vaugeois, Denis. 2009. "Lieu de rencontres, d'échanges et de métissage." In *Rencontrer Trois-Rivières: 375 ans d'histoire et de culture*, edited by René Beaudoin, 44-45. Trois-Rivières: Éditions d'art Le Sabord.

Villemure, Gilles. 2005. "Un retour tant attendu!: Il y a 150 ans... La Capricieuse entrait dans le port de Québec." *Cap-aux-Diamants: La revue d'histoire du Québec* (81):44-49.

Vincens, Simone. 1979. *Madame Montour et son temps*. Montréal: Québec/Amérique.

Warnes, Kathy C. 2009. *Ecorse Michigan: A Brief History*. Mount Pleasant, SC: The History Press.

Waters, Anne. 2004. *Language Matters: Nondiscrete Nonbinary Dualism*. Malden, MA: Blackwell.

White, Richard. 1991a. *"It's Your Misfortune and None of My Own": A New History of the American West*. Norman: University of Oklahoma Press.

White, Richard. 1991b. *The middle ground: Indians, empires, and republics in the Great Lakes region, 1650-1815*: Cambridge University Press.

White, Sid, and Sammy Edward Solberg, eds. 1989. *Peoples of Washington: perspectives of cultural diversity*. Pullman WA: Washington State University Press.

White, Sophie. 2013. *Wild Frenchmen and Frenchified Indians: Material Culture and Race in Colonial Louisiana*: Univ of Pennsylvania Press.

Wick, B.L. 1905. "The Struggle for the Half-Breed Tract." *The Annals of Iowa* 7 (1):16-29.

Wilkes, Charles. 1856. *Narrative of the United States Exploring Expedition During the Years 1838, 1839, 1840, 1841, 1842*. Vol. 4. New York: G. P. Putnam.

Wolf, Eric R. 1982. *Europe and the people without history*. Berkeley, Los Angeles and London: University of California Press.

Wyman, Mark. 1998. *The Wisconsin Frontier*. Bloomington: Indiana University Press.

Index

Sources of Illustrations

P. 12 Courtesy of Sam Pambrun **p. 15** Normal Rainville fonds, Tamastslikt Cultural Institute; **p. 18** Courtesy of Sam Pambrun **p. 21** ROM, 921.76.10; **p. 23** LAC, C-113193; **p. 27** ROM, The Honourable George William Allan Collection, 912.1.48; **p. 29** LAC, 1970-188-2244 and C-019041; **p. 31** ROM, The Honourable George William Allan Collection, 912.1.26; **p. 34** Architect of the Capitol; **p. 35** BAnQ, 0002663694; **p. 37** ROM, The Honourable George William Allan Collection, 912.1.60; **p. 39** Cover of The fighting trapper: or, Kit Carson to the rescue. A Tale of Wild Life on the Plains, Issue 139 of Frank Starr's American Novels. Edward Sylvester Ellis, New York: Frank Starr and Company, 1874; **p. 42** LAC, 1989-401 and C-002771 and e011153912; **p. 46** Courtesy of Washington State Historical Society; **p. 48** Burton Historical Collection. Detroit Public Library : 977.4 D45 c39 1752; **p. 54** Barclay Gibson; **p. 56** LAC, C-021112; **p. 59** Gilder Lehrman Collection, GLC04222; **p. 61** LAC, e010966035; **p. 69** LoC https://lccn.loc. gov/2011647869; **p. 83** *Voyage dans l'intérieur de l'Amérique du Nord, exécuté pendant les années 1832, 1833 et 1834, par le prince Maximilien de Wied-Neuwied* LoC, online http://hdl.loc.gov/loc. rbc/gen.0002, plate 43; **p. 89 (left)** François Pierre Guillaume Guizot's *A Popular History of France from the Earliest Times*, Vol. 6, Chapter 53, p. 190, Boston: Dana Estes & Charles E. Lauriat. **(right)** Henry Dwight Sedgwick's *Samuel de Champlain*, 1902, Boston And New York: Houghton, Mifflin And Company; **pp. 90-91** W. K. Morrison Special Collection of the J.B. Hall Library at the NSCC Centre of Geographic Sciences (http://nscc.cairnrepo.org/islandora/object/ nscc%3A168); **p. 93** Robin Philpot; **p. 98** Edward E. Ayer Manuscript Map Collection, Newberry Library, Vault drawer Ayer MS map 30 sheet 109, http://publications.newberry.org/frontierto-heartland/archive/fullsize/nl000519_d382d13303.jpg; **p. 101** LAC, C-013580; **p. 105** ROM, The Honourable George William Allan Collection, 912.1.2; **p. 116** Julie Benoît; **p. 128** LAC, C-013573; **pp. 130-131** W. K. Morrison Special Collection of the J.B. Hall Library at the NSCC Centre of Geographic Sciences (http://nscc.cairnrepo.org/islandora/object/nscc%3A594); **p. 132** LAC, C-010645k; **p. 144** *Voyage dans l'Amérique Septentrionale*. Paris, A. Bertrand, 1826. LoC. https:// lccn.loc.gov/01021531; **p. 154** Burton Historical Collection, Detroit Public Library, resource ID bh006562, http://digitalcollections.detroitpubliclibrary.org/islandora/object/islandora%3A 142305; **p. 170** Image provided by the Monroe County Museum; **p. 172** River Raisin National Battlefield Park; **p. 173 (Left)** Central Michigan University's Clarke History Library **(Right)** *The pictorial field-book of the war of 1812; or, Illustrations, by pen and pencil, of the history, biography, scenery, relics, and traditions of the last war for American independence* by Benson John Lossing, 1896, New York, Harper & Brothers, p. 358; **p. 176** Wiki Commons original housed at the Musée de l'Histoire de France, Château de Versailles; **p. 195** Gordon Daun Collection, Bayliss Public Library in Sault Sainte Marie (Michigan); **p. 196** LoC, LC-USZC4-10207, http://www.loc. gov/pictures/item/det1994000210/PP/; **p. 200** Gordon Daun Collection, Bayliss Public Library in Sault Sainte Marie (Michigan); **p. 219** LAC, C-002772k; **p. 224** *Voyage dans l'Amérique*

Septentrionale. Paris, A. Bertrand. LoC, https://lccn.loc.gov/01021531; **p. 226** *Voyage dans l'Amérique Septentrionale*. Paris, A. Bertrand, 1826 LoC. https://lccn.loc.gov/01021531; **p. 233** LoC, 2004662336; **p. 237** *Voyage dans l'intérieur de l'Amérique du Nord, exécuté pendant les années 1832, 1833 et 1834, par le prince Maximilien de Wied-Neuwied* LoC, online http://hdl.loc.gov/loc.rbc/gen.0002, plate 29; **p. 238** *Voyage dans l'intérieur de l'Amérique du Nord, exécuté pendant les années 1832, 1833 et 1834, par le prince Maximilien de Wied-Neuwied* LoC, online http://hdl.loc.gov/loc.rbc/gen.0002, plate 29, plate 30); **p. 241** *Voyage dans l'intérieur de l'Amérique du Nord, exécuté pendant les années 1832, 1833 et 1834, par le prince Maximilien de Wied-Neuwied* LoC, online http://hdl.loc.gov/loc.rbc/gen.0002, plate 23); **p. 243** St. Louis Mercantile Library, U. of Missouri-St. Louis; **p. 245** *Voyage dans l'intérieur de l'Amérique du Nord, exécuté pendant les années 1832, 1833 et 1834, par le prince Maximilien de Wied-Neuwied* LoC, online http://hdl.loc.gov/loc.rbc/gen.0002, plate 26); **p. 250** LAC, 1970-188-1064 and C-041273k; **p. 251** Sir Henry James Warre fonds, LAC, C-030777; **p. 257** Missouri History Museum identifier N24238; **p. 266** LAC, R9266-346 and e011161353; **pp. 268-269** W. K. Morrison Special Collection of the J.B. Hall Library at the NSCC Centre of Geographic Sciences (http://nscc.cairnrepo.org/islandora/object/nscc%3A607); **p. 272** LAC, 1968-115-1 and c035952; **p. 275** LAC, C-006688d; **p. 278** BAnQ, 0002743990, http://collections.banq.qc.ca/ark:/52327/2070780; **p. 283** LAC, 1989-401-3 and C-002773k; **p. 286** LAC, 1989-401-1 and e011153912; **p. 287** LAC, C-055331k; **p. 292** LAC, C-013569; **p. 303** Wisconsin Historical Society, TP126000, http://www.wisconsinhistory.org/turningpoints/search.asp?id=126; **p. 308** LoC, https://www.loc.gov/item/brh2003000194/PP; **p. 313** ROM, The Honourable George William Allan Collection, Gift of Sir Edmund Osler, 912.1.72; **p. 318** Glenbow Museum image number M-1154; **p. 321** Sir Henry James Warre fonds, LAC, C-058154; **p. 323** ROM, The Honourable George William Allan Collection, 912.1.64; **p. 326** Sir Henry James Warre fonds, LAC, 1969-4-29 and C-001620; **p. 327** Oregon Historical Society, bb002957, OrHi 67763; **p. 336** Umpqua Valley Museums, N2791; **p. 337** St. Paul Mission Historic Society Archives, Oregon State University, Catalog Number 2005.2.0611; **pp. 340-341** LoC, (https://www.loc.gov/item/2004627252); **p. 344** LoC, (https://www.loc.gov/item/cwp2003000419/PP/); **p. 345** Sir Henry James Warre fonds, LAC, 1969-4-39 and C-001612; **p. 350** Sir Henry James Warre fonds, LAC, 1969-4-31 and C-001628; **p. 354 (top and bottom)** Gordon Daun Collection, Bayliss Public Library in Sault Sainte Marie (Michigan); **p. 361** LAC, 1989-400-1 and e011154374; **p. 363** LAC, C-018084; **p. 377** Imperial Oil Collection series, LAC, 1972-26-214 and e010835247; **p. 382** Imperial Oil Collection series, LAC, 1972-26-779 and e007914369.

BAnQ – Bibliothèque and Archives nationales du Québec
LAC – Library and Archives Canada
LoC – Library of Congress
ROM – Royal Ontario Museum

Printed by Imprimerie Gauvin
Gatineau, Québec